THE MEDIA AND FINANCIAL CRISES

Comparative and historical perspectives

Edited by
Steve Schifferes and Richard Roberts

Routledge
Taylor & Francis Group

LONDON AND NEW YORK

First published 2015
by Routledge
2 Park Square, Milton Park, Abingdon, Oxon, OX14 4RN

and by Routledge
711 Third Avenue, New York, NY 10017

Routledge is an imprint of the Taylor & Francis Group, an informa business

British Library Cataloguing in Publication Data
A catalogue record for this book is available from the British Library

Library of Congress Cataloging in Publication Data
The media and financial crises : comparative and historical perspectives / edited by Steve Schifferes, Richard Roberts.
Includes bibliographical references and index.
1. Financial crises--Press coverage. 2. Global Financial Crisis, 2008-2009--In mass media. I. Schifferes, Steve. II. Roberts, Richard, 1952-
HB3722.M442 2014
070.4'49338542--dc23
2014011540

ISBN: 978-1-13-802278-2 (hbk)
ISBN: 978-1-13-802279-9 (pbk)
ISBN: 978-1-31-575457-4 (ebk)

Typeset in Bembo
by Taylor & Francis Books

Printed and bound by CPI Group (UK) Ltd, Croydon, CR0 4YY

THE MEDIA AND FINANCIAL CRISES

The Media and Financial Crises provides unique insights into the debate on the role of the media in the global financial crisis. Coverage is interdisciplinary, with contributions from media studies, political economy, and journalists themselves. It features a wide range of countries, including the USA, UK, Ireland, Greece, Spain, and Australia, and a completely new history of financial crises in the British press over 200 years.

Editors Steve Schifferes and Richard Roberts have assembled an expert set of contributors, including Joseph E. Stiglitz and Lionel Barber, editor of the *Financial Times*. The role of the media has been central in shaping our response to the financial crisis. Examining its performance in comparative and historical perspectives is crucial to ensuring that the media does a better job next time.

The book has five distinct parts:

- The Banking Crisis and the Media
- The Euro-Crisis and the Media
- Challenges for the Media
- The Lessons of History
- Media Messengers Under Interrogation

The Media and Financial Crises offers broad and coherent coverage, making it ideal for both students and scholars of financial journalism, journalism studies, media studies, and media and economic history.

Steve Schifferes is Marjorie Deane Professor of Financial Journalism at City University London. He covered the financial crisis for BBC News.

Richard Roberts is professor at the Institute of Contemporary British History, King's College London. Publications include studies of HSBC, Schroders, the City, Wall Street, Bank of England, Equitable Life and financial crises.

CONTENTS

FIGURES AND TABLES

Figures

Tables

CONTRIBUTORS

Ángel Arrese is Professor of Economic Journalism, and Director of the PhD Programme on Communication at the School of Communication (University of Navarra, Spain). He is author of *La identidad de The Economist* (1994), *Economic and Financial Press* (2001), and *Fundamentos de Periodismo Económico* (2011).

Gerben Bakker is Associate Professor in Economic History and Accounting at the London School of Economics. He has published widely on the economic history of media industries, and has acted as Specialist Adviser for the House of Lords and consultant for the UK Department of Business.

Lionel Barber has edited the *Financial Times* since 2005. Previously, he was responsible for the US edition and all US news on FT.com. He joined the *FT* in 1985. He has also been editor of the continental European edition, news editor, and Brussels bureau chief.

Michael Bromley is Professor of International Journalism in the Department of Journalism at City University London. A former journalist, he has taught at universities in Australia, the US, and the UK, and has published seven books and more than 50 journal articles and book chapters.

Jeff Hulbert is a media historian and an honorary research fellow in the Department of Journalism at City University London. Previously, he managed projects at ITN and the British Film Institute. He is co-author of *When Reporters Cross the Line* (with Stewart Purvis, Biteback Publishing, 2013), and several academic articles.

Sophie Knowles has completed a PhD on a comparative study of three financial crises, including the global financial crisis, and the media in the US, the UK, and

Australia, at Murdoch University, Australia. The study analysed changes in financial news quality and practices over the past three decades.

Duncan Needham is a Research Fellow at Darwin College, Cambridge and Associate Director of the Centre for Financial History, Cambridge. Previously he was a credit trader at JP Morgan and a portfolio manager at Cairn Capital. He is author of *UK Monetary Policy from Devaluation to Thatcher, 1967–82* (Palgrave Macmillan, 2014).

James Nye followed a career in finance and commerce, and is now a Visiting Fellow at the ICBH at King's College London. An award-winning historian of technology, and council member of the AHS, he founded The Clockworks in 2011, which is dedicated to the history of electric timekeeping. He is author of *A Long Time in Making: The History of Smith's* (Oxford University Press, 2014).

Mark O'Brien teaches in the School of Communications, Dublin City University and chairs the Newspaper and Periodical History Forum of Ireland. He is the author of *The Irish Times: a History* (Four Courts Press, 2008) and *De Valera, Fianna Fáil and the Irish Press: the Truth in the News?* (Irish Academic Press, 2001).

Stylianos Papathanassopoulos is Professor at the Department of Communication and Media Studies at the National and Kapodistrian University of Athens. He edits the Greek communication journal *Zitimata Epikoinonias/Communication Issues* and has published 19 books about the media (as author or editor).

Richard Roberts (*joint editor*) is Professor at the Institute of Contemporary British History, King's College London. Publications include studies of HSBC, Schroders, the City, Wall Street, the Bank of England, Equitable Life, and financial crises. He advises the Gulbenkian Foundation and the Official Monetary and Financial Institutions Forum. He is author of *Saving the City: The Great Financial Crisis of 1914* (Oxford University Press, 2013).

Chris Roush is the Walter E. Hussman Sr. Distinguished Scholar in business journalism at the University of North Carolina, Chapel Hill School of Journalism and Mass Communication and senior associate dean of undergraduate studies. He is author of three books about business journalism.

Steve Schifferes (*joint editor*) is Marjorie Deane Professor of Financial Journalism at City University London where he directs the MA course in Financial Journalism and is Principal Investigator on the EU Social Sensor project. He has held fellowships at Columbia and Oxford. As a BBC economics correspondent he covered the global financial crisis.

Anya Schiffrin is the director of the media and communications program at Columbia University's School of International and Public Affairs. She is on the advisory board of the Open Society Foundation's Program on Independent Journalism. Her forthcoming book is *Global Muckraking: 100 Years of Investigative Reporting from Around the World* (The New Press, 2014).

Dean Starkman is an editor at the *Columbia Journalism Review*, author of *The Watchdog That Didn't Bark: The Financial Crisis and the Disappearance of Investigative Journalism* (Columbia University Press, 2014); and a fellow at the Nation Institute, and Central European University's Center for Media and Communications Studies.

Joseph E. Stiglitz is University Professor at Columbia University and has taught at Stanford, Princeton, MIT and Yale. He was a member of the Council of Economic Advisers from 1993 to 1995, during the Clinton administration, and served as CEA chairman from 1995 to 1997. He then became Chief Economist and Senior Vice-President of the World Bank from 1997 to 2000. In 2001, he was awarded the Nobel Prize in economics for his analyses of markets with asymmetric information, and he was a lead author of the 1995 Report of the Intergovernmental Panel on Climate Change, which shared the 2007 Nobel Peace Prize.

Damian Tambini is Research Director of the LSE's Media and Communications Department. He is director of the LSE Media Policy Project, and author of numerous publications on citizenship, media and regulation. He has researched and taught previously at IPPR, at Oxford University and at Humboldt University Berlin.

James Taylor has written widely on the development of the corporate economy in Britain since 1720. His articles have appeared in leading historical journals, and his books have received prizes from the Economic History Society and the Business History Conference. He teaches history at Lancaster University.

Peter A. Thompson is a political economist in the media studies programme at Victoria University of Wellington. His research interests include information/communication processes in global financial markets and media policy in New Zealand. He is a founding co-editor of the IAMCR's *Political Economy of Communication Journal*.

ACKNOWLEDGEMENTS

Many people contributed to this project. First of all, we would like to thank our contributors for their hard work and dedication in producing such excellent chapters while meeting our deadlines and responding to numerous requests. In the final proofreading and editing process, we were greatly assisted by the meticulous work of John Hobart as proofreader and Jeff Hulbert who organized the editorial process. Jeff was also responsible for the final section of the book, and selectively edited the testimony of leading financial journalists before the House of Commons Treasury Committee. Steve Schifferes would also like to thank his research assistant and collaborator Sophie Knowles for her comprehensive work on improving his two chapters. Richard Roberts is grateful to Anders Mikkelsen for his painstaking and resourceful research at the British Library Newspaper Library in Colindale.

We would like to thank our editors at Routledge, Natalie Foster and Sheni Kruger, for their unstinting support for this project. We are also grateful to the British Academy, which sponsored the Soothsayers of Doom conference at City University London that inspired this volume. The discussions among academics, journalists, and policy makers at this conference and numerous other settings helped inform our understanding of the issues we address in the book.

Steve Schifferes would also like to thank his colleagues in the Department of Journalism at City University London, and in particular Professor George Brock, the head of the department, and Professor Howard Tumber, the research director, for their support for this project, and to City University's research office for funding the opinion poll that forms the basis of Chapter 11. He is particularly grateful for the generous support of the Marjorie Deane Foundation whose funding of his post has allowed him to pursue the interests explored in this book. Richard Roberts would like to thank colleagues at the Institute of Contemporary British History, King's College London, for their interest and backing, especially Robert Blackburn, director of the ICBH at the time of writing.

We would like to thank the *Columbia Journalism Review* for permission to reprint Dean Starkman's article, to New Press for permission to reprint the chapter by Joseph E. Stiglitz, and Taylor and Francis for permission to reprint Damian Tambini's article, which originally appeared in *Journalism Studies*.

Finally, last but not least, we would like to thank our families, and particularly our wives, Caroline and Sarah, for their love and support during the period of writing this book.

Steve Schifferes and Richard Roberts

EDITORS' INTRODUCTION

Steve Schifferes and Richard Roberts

The global financial crisis that struck the world economy with devastating force from 2008 put the role of the media under the spotlight. The complex nature of the crisis, its global reach, and its effects on government finance challenged policymakers, regulators, and the media alike. Journalists themselves engaged in much soul-searching, while facing a storm of criticism from politicians, bankers, and the public.

This volume explores the many dimensions of the crisis, and the media's role, through a variety of perspectives. Our objective is to bring fresh insights to discussions about the media's role in the crisis, and situate the coverage in historical and comparative perspectives. The book is divided into five parts. Parts I and II examine the role of the media in an array of countries during and after the banking crisis of 2007–8 and the Euro-crisis from 2010. Part III looks at key dilemmas faced by the media from a range of interdisciplinary perspectives. Part IV situates crisis coverage in the context of the 200-year evolution of the British financial press. In Part V, and in the Overview by Lionel Barber, editor of the *Financial Times*, journalists themselves reflect on their role in the crisis.

The coverage of financial crises raises a number of key questions that recur throughout the chapters of this book:

Did the financial press see the crisis coming?
Did the press act as a cheerleader for the preceding boom?
Does the press have a duty to report what it knows about the crisis, or should it exercise self-restraint to prevent panic?
How did the financial press of the day get the story? Was it compromised by getting too close to bankers and policymakers as sources?
Who did the media blame for the crisis – and how much was it blamed?

Did the press seriously consider alternative policies for dealing with the effects of
the crisis, and did it question government responses?

Did the press give enough coverage to the effects of the crisis on ordinary people,
or was it too focused on the debates among the political and policy elites?

Throughout history, the media has been the lens through which the public – and
the players – have understood financial crises. By framing the crisis in certain ways,
journalists have not only reflected what was going on, but also influenced the
course of events and the policy response. It is noteworthy that the most powerful
frame for interpreting a contemporary crisis is the collective memory of the previous
one. The image of the Great Depression of the 1930s, as portrayed in the media,
coloured the policy response to the current crisis. Right from the earliest financial
crisis, panics have been reinterpreted in light of previous crises. It was no accident
that the collapse of the South Sea Bubble in 1720 led to a renewed focus on Dutch
Tulipmania of the 1630s as a parable of human folly, most notably by the publication of *The Great Mirror of Folly*, a contemporary volume of prints. The salutary
significance of the South Sea Bubble was given new resonance by excesses of stock
market speculation in the nineteenth century, playing a prominent role in Scottish
journalist Charles Mackay's influential book *Extraordinary Popular Delusions and the
Madness of Crowds* (1841).

One common theme running through these early perspectives was the idea that
financial crises were a sign of moral failure, a breakdown of society's norms, or a
collective madness where normal logic was replaced by unalloyed greed. In this
view, there was little the media and policymakers could do to affect the powerful
but irrational public mood – if indeed they did not get swept up in the madness
themselves.

There is another, and equally powerful, historical frame that has shaped much of
the debate about the role of the media. This portrays journalists as crusaders against
the perceived excesses of financiers and big business. This way of framing the
media's role has its origins in the 'muckraking' journalists of the US Progressive
Era. Investigative journalists such as Ida Tarbell, Upton Sinclair, and Lincoln Stef-
fens attacked the power of large corporations and corrupt local governments,
leading to significant changes in public policy, such as regulation of food and drug
safety, tougher enforcement of antitrust laws, and reforms to local government.

Part I: The banking crisis and the media

The first two chapters interpret the US media's role in the crisis in light of these
two contrasting narratives. They also demonstrate the passionate and highly contested
nature of the initial debate. Dean Starkman (Chapter 1) vigorously argues that the
business press abandoned its investigative role and therefore failed to spot the crisis
and warn the public. Using a large group of articles selected by nine influential
newspapers and magazines, who were asked to submit examples of their best coverage from 2000 to 2007, he shows that only a small proportion of their reporting

was critical or questioning, and that the proportion actually declined over time. Starkman blames changes in the business press, including the lack of leadership, the reduction in resources put into investigative stories, and the rise of 'access journalism', characterized by exclusive interviews with leading businessmen, for the failure.

Chris Roush (Chapter 2) also focuses on the press coverage of key issues in the run-up to the crisis, but comes to the opposite conclusion. In his view there was ample warning of the dubious practices of the mortgage industry and the excesses of the banking sector. The problem was that the public, policymakers, and politicians, swept up in the illusion that the boom would last forever, were not receptive to these messages. In his view, the irrational logic of the crowd overrode any rational discussion in the press.

The power of the press to shape the policy debate is also the subject of Anya Schiffrin's piece (Chapter 3), the third piece to examine the US media and the crisis. She scrutinizes the coverage of the Obama administration's stimulus package in 2009, which was aimed at boosting the economy. She finds that much of the debate was focused on politics, not policy, and that there was little critical exam-ination of the effectiveness of the stimulus plan and whether it should have been increased or extended. Her piece paints a picture of the press as, with a few exceptions, having limited capacity for analytic debate or willingness to challenge the conventional wisdom.

Much of the discussion of the role of the media in the crisis has been shaped by this American debate, which puts the failure of investigative journalism at the heart of the problem. But looking at the coverage of the crisis in a comparative perspective suggests that a different set of questions about the media's role might also be impor-tant. Any critique of the media role also has to take account of the different timing of the crisis in different countries, as well as the different media and political systems.

The UK was the other epicentre of the global financial crisis, with a large and active financial press. Steve Schifferes and Sophie Knowles (Chapter 4) suggest there was far less soul-searching in the UK about the investigative role of the media, but much more concern about the role of the coverage in causing financial panic – perhaps reflecting the power of television images, especially during the run on the Northern Rock bank, to influence the public mood. The British press is distinguished by a strong analytic tradition, and engaged in an earlier policy debate than elsewhere – although eventually coalescing around an acceptance of austerity that contrasted with the Keynesian approach still being discussed in the US. Meanwhile, the large and vibrant UK popular press provided a parallel narrative of moral decay, with bankers briefly replacing celebrities and sports personalities as the focus of scandal.

The Australian media's role in the global financial crisis shows some parallels with other Anglo-Saxon countries. In recent years it had also expanded its business coverage and focused more on personal finance. But the Australian case illustrates the difficulties of independent reporting in the era of global media corporations. In the account by Michael Bromley (Chapter 5), business coverage in the Australian media is dominated by Rupert Murdoch, who controls 60–70 per cent of newspaper circulation. The influence of his flagship publication the *Wall Street Journal* was felt in the tone of coverage in Australia, particularly in the strident critique of the Rudd government's post-crisis stimulus package. As in the UK and the post-crisis US, politics ultimately trumped economics as the frame of media analysis.

Part II: The Euro-crisis and the media

The Anglo-Saxon countries, despite some differences, all had a long history of a well-developed business press with the primary focus on markets and companies (the 'City pages'). In contrast, business coverage in much of Europe was less well developed, and this was a particularly important factor in the case of those southern European countries engulfed by the Euro-crisis from 2010.

In Ireland, according to research by Mark O'Brien (Chapter 6), the small circle of business journalists were very much caught up in the property boom, which was strongly promoted by prominent developers with the connivance of politicians. The journalists relied heavily on the property developers and other insiders as sources, and risked being excluded from off-the-record briefings if they questioned the boom. (The Irish Taoiseach, or Prime Minister, Bertie Ahern, even wondered why journalists who criticized the economy 'didn't commit suicide'.) In this climate of intimidation, journalists were ill-equipped to anticipate the almost complete collapse of the banking system, and to question the hasty decision of the government to assume all its bad debts, leading to a doubling of Ireland's national debt and an IMF bailout package.

A free press in Spain only emerged after the end of the Franco regime and the emergence of democracy in 1978, but according to Ángel Arrese (Chapter 7) it was not until 1986, when Spain joined the EU, that a real business press was created. EU membership sparked a remarkable boom in the Spanish economy, which dampened media criticism in the early stages of the crisis. But he argues that as Spain became engulfed in the crisis, the press did adopt an increasingly sceptical view of over-optimistic government pronouncements. Like Steve Schifferes, he focuses on the different media responses at key points in the crisis. He suggests that in Spain, unlike Ireland, the press was sceptical of the sustainability of the real-estate bubble before the crisis; but it took much longer to recognize the weakness in the banking system. For Arrese, as the economic crisis deepened, the press became more critical of the politicians' denial that the crisis would affect Spain. He also notes a growing strain of economic nationalism, which was expressed in opposition to an external bailout and encapsulated in the phrase 'Spain is not Greece'.

There was an even stronger growth of economic nationalism in Greece, where a series of bailouts with increasingly harsh conditions created hostility to the EU and, in particular, to Germany, seen as the architect of the rescue plans. Stylianos Papathanassopoulos (Chapter 8) raises the interesting question of whether this hostility was reciprocal, by looking at the coverage of the Greek crisis in the European media. He finds it was surprisingly sympathetic, at least in the early stages of the crisis, and shows that there was a lively debate about the appropriateness of the bailout plan. Not surprisingly, there was more coverage in the German media than anywhere else, focusing on the role of Angela Merkel. His contribution raises the question as to whether the nation state is the right unit of analysis when considering the media coverage of a pan-European crisis, and what role the media played in the emergence of Greece rather than Ireland, Portugal, or Spain as the poster child of the Euro-crisis.

Part III: Challenges for the media

What role should journalists have played in the crisis, and what are the constraints they face? Picking up on many of the themes that run throughout the individual country accounts, Damian Tambini (Chapter 9) directly addresses one of our fundamental themes: how business journalists understand their role. Focusing mainly on the UK and the US, he finds that there is no consensus among journalists about whether they should be playing a watchdog role in relation to markets and corporate behaviour. Their ability to play such a role was also affected by increasing pressures on their work, including the dependence on a limited number of sources and the rise of PR agencies, the need to write more quickly to meet productivity targets, and the increasing complexity of the stories they covered. He suggests that a clearer definition of their legal, regulatory, and institutional roles will be needed to strengthen business journalism in the future.

Joseph E. Stiglitz (Chapter 10) applies his theory of information asymmetry – for which he won the Nobel Prize in Economics – to the situation of financial journalists trying to cover the crisis. He argues that reporters face an inherent problem in that those they are covering have more information than they do, and little incentive to share it. Stiglitz's work points to a deeper explanation of the problems economic journalists face in regard to sources, and warns that the result can be 'cognitive capture'. He points to some of the ways journalists can reduce that asymmetry – for example, by improved training in economics and by independent funding of investigative stories.

While much of the debate is focused on the norms of journalists themselves, Steve Schifferes (Chapter 11) explores the views of the UK public towards the media during the crisis. He finds a remarkable lack of trust in the idea that journalists will offer fair and balanced coverage of the crisis, along with concerns that they are too close to their sources. The public is also critical of their inability to explain the crisis clearly, and to cover its effects on the lives of ordinary people – but less critical of their failure to play a watchdog role. He also suggests that there are two very different audiences for crisis news: a well-informed specialist audience that journalists have been used to writing for, and a much bigger, and new, generalist audience with much more limited understanding of economic and financial issues.

The different audiences who view business news are also the focus of Peter A. Thompson's work (Chapter 12). His piece looks at a very specialized audience – the traders whose decisions, based on media information, are actually moving markets. He shows that market professionals use the media in a very different way from the general public, relying on it mainly for key data and short news announcements rather than interpretation – which is much more likely to be carried out through informal networks of other traders or company analysts. He also points out that the kind of market information viewed by traders is very self-reflective; the price data is itself created each day by their decisions and is always at the mercy of market sentiment. Thus the instantaneous transmission of market data can itself contribute to the collapse of sentiment and market meltdowns.

But how can the media afford to pay for crisis coverage? This fundamental question lies beneath much of the concern about the pressures on today's financial journalists. Gerben Bakker (Chapter 13) shows that news organizations, especially wire services, have had to adopt a number of strategies to overcome the paradox that once we know what is in the news, it no longer has any value. They have bundled news into subscriptions, gained exclusive rights to cover certain areas, and invested heavily in technology to gain the advantage of speed and volume. Subscribers are willing to accept large amounts of less valuable news if they can be sure of receiving the latest news of a crisis. News organizations, however, are rarely able to recover the extra costs of covering crises. His analysis shows that these dilemmas stretch right back to the origins of the financial press itself.

Part IV: The lessons of history

The five chapters in this section provide a unique account of the evolution of the British financial press, and its reporting of financial crises from the crash of 1825 to the IMF crisis of 1976. A number of themes recur among these historical studies. Overall, the expansion and development of the financial press was notably a feature of upswing phases of the business cycle that often, though not invariably, culminated in a crisis. Crises saw heightened demand for information, but reporting them posed a perennial dilemma for financial journalists: should they tell all they knew and risk fuelling the panic, or should they exercise self-censorship? Getting the story requires close relations between the financial press and market players, and latterly also with the financial authorities. But this held the hazards of getting drawn into a compromising commercial process or becoming a mouthpiece for government, instead of providing independent reporting. Down the years the aftermaths of financial crises in their various forms have seen recurring reactions – revulsion, recrimination, and reform.

The financial press was born, relates James Taylor (Chapter 14), in the securities market boom from 1821 that ended with a major crisis in late 1825. It advanced significantly during the boom and bust in railway shares of the 1840s and finance companies of the 1860s, which culminated, respectively, in the crises of 1847 and 1866. The 1880s saw the advent of the 'new financial journalism', which was 'snappier' and more opinionated than the traditional factual style. But this lent itself to 'tipping' and, as James Nye recounts (Chapter 15), a 'significant symbiotic, incestuous, and Machiavellian relationship' between company promoters and financial journalists, featuring bribery and blackmail with investors footing the bill. This was not entirely new, but it expanded significantly in the heyday of the company promoter from 1880 to 1914. Naturally, it was most flagrant in market upswings and go-go sectors, notably the speculative bubble in gold shares in the second half of the 1890s. In reaction, a set of Edwardian City editors who wrote for leading daily and weekly newspapers sought to draw a line between themselves and the practices of the tipsters. As the foremost financial and economic commentators of the day, they endeavoured through their financial journalism, books, and public lectures to serve the needs of the growing ranks of private investors for honest information and guidance and to raise the general level of financial literacy.

The financial crisis of 1914, the subject of Richard Roberts's study (Chapter 16), was not the culmination of a business cycle but a scramble for liquidity prompted by fear of a European war. Financial journalists were caught off guard, but so were bankers, officials, and politicians. As during the Barings crisis of 1890, the press exercised self-censorship in reporting the unfolding financial crisis for fear of exacerbating market anxieties and triggering bank runs. When a leading financial journalist spotted a newsboy outside the Bank of England crying 'Run on the Bank', he promptly had him arrested.

In the pre-war period, financial journalists relied for information on contacts in the markets, especially the Stock Exchange. During the war and afterwards they also developed ties with the 'authorities' – the Bank of England and the Treasury – as these institutions assumed more significant roles in financial matters and endeavoured to communicate with the public. This marked the beginning of a much larger role for government in the economy, which became an increasingly vital dimension for the financial press. Journalists' dependence on official sources, plus their own sense of patriotic duty in times of national emergency, repeatedly presented problems regarding the reporting of sterling crises from the 1930s to the 1970s, as analysed by Richard Roberts (Chapter 17). Again, the dilemma was how to inform readers without fuelling market or public panic. In the devaluation crises of 1931, 1949, and 1967, financial journalists mostly lent support to governments' defence of the established exchange rate and reported the pronouncements of ministers uncritically. The aftermath of the devaluation of 1967 marked a turning point in the deference of financial journalists, notably the new genus of 'economic journalist' who was more reluctant to toe the official line.

The sterling and sovereign debt crises of 1975–6 raised profound questions about the future of the British economy and governments' economic competence. This perception, and the greater economic sophistication and independence of mind of the financial press, and, on occasion, the broadcast media, made the IMF crisis of 1976 'different', writes Duncan Needham (Chapter 18). 'To an unprecedented degree, it played out in and through the British press', which helped achieve a successful negotiation with the IMF 'by providing the outlet for extensive high-level leaking and briefing', he relates. The press was even more sceptical during the ERM crisis of 1992 when the government tried to defend the pound's pegged parity to the Deutschmark. This time the pound's travails were a prime time television event, the prominent exposure raising the stakes for ministers intent on defying the markets. The outcome of the showdown, on which they spent billions of reserves, was a humiliating defeat and derision in the media. All in all, the sterling crises and their prominent media coverage contributed to the discrediting of the economic management of the incumbent administration and each was followed by the defeat of the party in power at the subsequent election, a pattern repeated in the 2007–8 crisis.

The dot.com boom of the late 1990s saw elements of the financial media acting as cheerleaders for investment bank promoters of speculative technology issues, many of which ultimately proved worthless. The media's role had distinct echoes of the financial press's collusion in the company promotion excesses a century earlier. The bursting of the bubble in 2000 was followed by widespread recriminations and accusations of media myopia or worse. Meanwhile the Asian financial crisis of 1997–8, which rapidly spread to emerging markets in Latin America and Russia, showed how interconnected the global financial system had become. These faraway crises, which were largely overlooked by US and UK financial journalists, reinforced the misperception that financial crises were now confined to emerging markets – a notion that was dramatically overturned by the global financial crisis that began in 2007.

Part V: Media messengers under interrogation

The final chapter of the book (Chapter 19) comprises the key elements in the testimony of the leading UK financial journalists to the House of Commons Treasury Committee shortly after the global financial crisis began. Under questioning by MPs, they gave a robust account of their reporting of the financial crisis and the dilemmas they faced, notably whether to warn the public in advance of the impending collapse of parts of the banking system. This unique document captures in detail the challenges and stresses of those in the front line of the crisis.

This has been the biggest financial crisis faced by this generation of journalists, but it will not be the last. Learning the lessons of the coverage of this global financial crisis will be crucial for understanding and reporting the next one.

OVERVIEW

Soothsayers of doom?

Lionel Barber

Since its launch in 1888, the *Financial Times* has always aspired to set the gold standard. That is a declaration of journalistic principle, not a statement of economic theory. Today, the good news for a troubled news industry is that we are in the middle of the biggest financial story since the Great Crash of 1929. Around the world, people who make or influence decisions in business, finance, and public affairs are turning to the *FT* and *ft.com* for trusted news, analysis, and commentary. Indeed, they are not only turning to our website and newspaper: they are paying. There are 440,000 digital subscribers at the latest count (as at December 2013).

When I delivered the keynote speech to the 'Soothsayers of Doom' conference in December 2011 about how the media – the so-called soothsayers of doom – have covered the global financial crisis, I said that it was an alluring subject, almost worthy of a Leveson Inquiry. But before naming the guilty men and women, I issued two warnings.

The first was that the crisis was far from over. It was then four years in, and we had watched the crisis metamorphose from the private sector to the public sector and back again, from stricken banks to stricken sovereigns, from sub-prime mortgages in the US to the heart of the eurozone. It has been one long vicious cycle.

My second health warning was that journalism is no more than the first draft of history. There are inherent flaws in the craft, even as we strive to provide accurate accounts and explanations of current affairs and events.

Of course, our reactions and our analysis have at times been deeply flawed. Two years before the Wall Street crash, in April 1927, *Barron's*, the investment weekly, predicted 'a new era without depressions'.

On New Year's Day, 1929, the usually sober *New York Times* delivered the following verdict: 'It has been twelve months of unprecedented advance, of wonderful prosperity. If there is any way of judging the future by the past, this new year will be one of felicitation and hopefulness.'

I will return later to the media's dual role of cheerleader and doom-monger, but let us first tackle the substantive charge against the media: that we took our eye off the ball in the run-up to the spring/summer of 2007 when the global financial crisis entered its first phase with the tightening and later freezing of credit markets.

As a general observation, I would say that financial journalists focused on the 'good news', the credit boom, at the expense of the bigger, more worrying picture. In no particular order, they ignored flashing warning signs: excess leverage in the banking sector, which posed a systemic threat to the world's financial system; global imbalances, notably between the US and China, which were fuelling the growth of credit, specifically to fund mortgages in the US sub-prime market; the exponential growth of sophisticated financial products such as derivatives that were supposedly hedging risk in the system; and crucial regulatory weaknesses, including the conflicted role of the credit ratings agencies employed by the banks to assess the value of their debt exposure.

First, by way of mitigation, it must be said that journalists were not the only ones to fall down on the job. Political leaders were happy to break open the champagne at the credit party; many lingered long after it had gone flat. Regulators in the US, UK, and continental Europe (with the notable exception of the Bank of Spain) all failed to identify, manage, and contain the risks building up within the financial system. Central bank governors paid too much attention to inflation rather than financial stability, put too much focus on budget rather than current account deficits (an affliction which persists today regarding the eurozone crisis).

Many economists, too, fell short. Only a gallant few identified pieces of the puzzle, even if, crucially, they failed to fit them together. Nouriel Roubini, now celebrated as the thinking man's prophet of doom, warned as early as 2004 that the world's current account imbalances were unsustainable, and he was quicker than most to link problems in the financial sector with the real economy.

William White, former chief economist of the Bank for International Settlements, the central bankers' bank in Basel, Switzerland, was a persistent critic of lax monetary policy and the failure to stem credit expansion. Warren Buffett, boss of Berkshire Hathaway conglomerate, warned in 2003 that derivatives were 'financial weapons of mass destruction', and that some contracts had been devised by 'madmen'. (This did not discourage Berkshire and Mr Buffett from using derivatives, but that is another story.)

Why did financial journalists not pay more attention to these warnings and give them more prominence? This is a tricky question that deserves several answers. First, the financial crisis started as a highly technical story that took months to go mainstream.

The crisis's origins lie in the credit markets, the coverage of which in most news organizations counted as little more than a backwater. Most reporters working in the so-called shadow banking system found it hard to interest their superiors who controlled space on the front page or the airtime on the nightly news bulletin. Most were far more interested in broadcasting the 'good news' story of rising property prices and economic growth – and the associated stories such as the excessive rewards for those working in private equity at that particular time.

The *Financial Times* was and is an exception to the rule. Back in 2004, we appointed a remarkably talented journalist named Gillian Tett to head our capital markets coverage. A trained anthropologist who earned her PhD after studying goat herders in Tajikistan – I am told this helped her to get to grips with exotic financial instruments – Gillian had covered the banking crisis in Japan for the *FT* in the late 1990s. Her appointment as capital markets editor, which was accompanied by a significant strengthening of our markets team in London and New York, proved to be inspired.

As late as 2004, few journalists wrote regularly about credit derivatives. Markets reporting was tilted in favour of equities rather than debt. Moreover, exotic derivatives such as credit default swaps and collateralized debt obligations were extremely opaque. They demanded a sophisticated grasp of risk management, preferably supported by an understanding of advanced mathematical models.

More fundamentally, the prevalent view among banking executives and regulators – the regular sources for financial reporters – was that the more risk was dispersed and hedged, the fewer risks to the system. This view was espoused by, among others, Alan Greenspan, when he served as chairman of the Federal Reserve.

For virtually his whole tenure in office, what Mr Greenspan said was treated in the markets as akin to receiving guidance from the oracle at Delphi – as shown by the deferential treatment of the Fed chairman by no less a journalist than Bob Woodward, of Watergate fame, in his biography *Maestro*.

It is no surprise that markets were lulled into complacency; and even less surprising that journalists were unwilling to challenge the conventional wisdom about risk modelling. Gillian Tett's warning in early 2006 that the more risk was dispersed, the greater the risk to the system, was very much a lone voice in the wilderness.

However, I would also single out University of Chicago professor and former IMF economist Raghuram Rajan, now installed as governor of the Reserve Bank of India, who in 2005 pooped at Mr Greenspan's celebration party in Jackson Hole by warning specifically about the accumulation of risk in the financial system.

The second, broader criticism is that the financial media were more interested in building up a good news story than in knocking it down. Jon Stewart's on-air demolition of the booster-turned-doomster Jim Cramer demonstrates there is a case to answer. Indeed, Stewart goes so far as to suggest that CNBC, which hosts Cramer's *Mad Money* show, overlooked market shenanigans because it was too close to its core community: the Wall Street traders and investment bankers.

Danny Schechter, writing in the *British Journalism Review*, is equally critical if less persuasive, alleging newspapers had no interest in pursuing scandals in mortgage lending for fear of alienating property advertisers.

Journalists routinely face tensions between relying on their sources and 'burning' them with critical coverage. Think of the White House press corps or the British 'lobby' press that covers Number 10 Downing Street and Parliament. The incentive to 'go along' to 'get along' is always present, in perpetual competition with the basic journalistic instinct, which is to speak truth to power.

Two years ago, I found myself, along with four other senior journalists from the press and television, obliged to answer before the House of Commons Treasury select committee at Westminster. Among the more improbable accusations was that the financial press in Britain had deliberately buried the bad news because bad news did not sell newspapers.

This charge from a Scottish Labour MP aptly named Mudie (pronounced Moody) conveniently overlooked a decade of Labour government claims that it had abolished 'boom and bust', and that the British economy and the City of London were in far better shape than the rest of Europe – claims that were frequently reported on the front page of the British press, including the *FT*. Indeed, if anything, the British press might be accused of not questioning more closely the foundation of prosperity in the City.

Over in the US, some of my journalistic colleagues have been more forthcoming in acknowledging failures of omission, if not commission. Charlie Gasparino, a much-feared former investigative reporter for the *Wall Street Journal* and now of the Fox Business Network, is uncharacteristically contrite. 'We all failed', he told Howard Kurtz, then of the *Washington Post*. 'What we didn't understand was that this was building up. We all bear responsibility to a certain extent.'

Kurtz himself goes further: 'The shaky house of financial cards that has come tumbling down was erected largely in public view: overextended investment banks, risky practices by Fannie Mae and Freddie Mac, exotic mortgage instruments that became part of a shadow banking system. But while these were conveyed in incremental stories – and a few whistle-blowing columns – the business press never conveyed a real sense of alarm until institutions began to collapse.'

Marcus Brauchli, formerly *Wall Street Journal* news editor and also formerly executive editor of the *Washington Post*, admits that the press may have fallen down on the job, but offers a partial alibi: 'These are really difficult issues to convey to a popular audience ... You do have an obligation as a journalist to push important issues into the public consciousness. We also have to remember you're pushing against a powerful force, which is greed.'

Yet there were plenty of examples of journalists who did push the other way. Think of Gretchen Morgenson of the *New York Times*, a constant thorn in the side of Wall Street, who has written powerfully and authoritatively about perverse incentives, excessive remuneration, and other dubious aspects of the credit boom and bust. Think of Jeff Randall, the Sky News anchor who both on air and in print warned about the risks inherent in the debt binge in the West. Think of the *FT*'s own columnists, John Plender and Martin Wolf.

For better or worse, journalism holds a mirror up to society. When the good times are rolling, journalists are sorely tempted to join the party, not least because they have no power to take away the punchbowl. Those in charge must strike the right balance between reporting on the here-and-now and carving out enough time (and, crucially, resources) to cover those subjects that are 'over the horizon'. That's a struggle I face every day of the week.

In the final analysis, the financial media could have done a better job, just as it could have done a better job ahead of the dot.com crash in the early part of this decade. Then as now, many in the profession have taken the solemn vow: never again. In this spirit of self-criticism, I would single out five specific weaknesses in the financial media's coverage of the events leading up to the financial crisis and its aftermath, and offer some prescriptions for the future.

First, financial journalists failed to grasp the significance of the failure to regulate over-the-counter derivatives that formed the bulk of counterparty risk in the explosion of credit in the middle of this decade, following the dot.com bubble. Alan Greenspan was opposed to such regulation, but how many commentators took the Fed chairman to task and warned of the risks to the financial sector? For the most part, journalists were a little too enamoured with the prevailing tide of deregulation, a tide that stretched back well beyond the passage of the 1999 Gramm–Leach–Bliley Act (which formally scrapped the Glass–Steagall Act) to the Thatcher–Reagan era.

Second, journalists, with a few notable exceptions, failed to understand the risks posed by the implicit state guarantees enjoyed by Fannie Mae and Freddie Mac, the mortgage finance giants. Here, we should tip our hats to the now much-maligned Mr Greenspan. He raised alarms early and often about the risks involved in government-sponsored entities such as Fannie and Freddie. Overall, however, Fannie and Freddie's political clout, especially on Capitol Hill, meant that there was far too little media scrutiny of their activities or, indeed, their overwhelmingly generous remuneration for executives.

Third, journalists failed to grasp the significance of off-balance-sheet financing by the banks and its relationship with the pro-cyclical Basel II rules on capital ratios. The explosive growth of structured investment vehicles at the height of the credit boom was under-reported. This was part of a broader failure to understand leverage and the ensuing weaknesses in risk management in the financial sector. At the same time, many journalists accepted at face value the continental European argument that hedge funds posed the most serious systemic threat to the financial system, rather than highly leveraged investment banks, an assertion that proved dead wrong.

Fourth, financial journalists were too slow to grasp that a crash in the banking system would have a profoundly damaging impact on the real economy. The same applies to regulators and economists. For too long, too many self-styled experts treated the financial sector and the wider economy as parallel universes. Thus, banking journalists failed to understand the significance of global imbalances, while economists failed to grant sufficient weight to credit risk. In the same vein, many financial and economic journalists were too gullible in swallowing claims that the rest of the world had decoupled from the US, and that therefore the risks to world economic growth were limited. As we now see, this was fundamentally wrong.

Fifth, financial journalists followed the natural tendency to seek rationales for events as they unfold, rather than question whether they are sustainable. Again, they were in good company, alongside bankers, regulators, and politicians. While it is true that it is difficult to make a living as a 'perma-bear', it is also fair to say that there was an alarming suspension of critical faculties among financial and business journalists during the credit bubble. Hard questions were left unasked; markets sceptics were dismissed as party poopers. The inconvenient truth about the credit bubble was ignored.

Here I would like to say a word about the current sovereign debt crisis and the European monetary union. In this country, views are passionately held about the viability of the single currency and Britain's membership of the European Union.

For the record, the *FT* remains of the unequivocal view that membership of the euro is not in Britain's interest because the economic case against it is overwhelming.

However, we are not against monetary union per se. While it is clear that the original design of monetary union was flawed, we believe member states, led by France and Germany, are entitled to make the necessary adjustments to allow it to work. While the new tighter rules on budgetary discipline are welcome, they still do not address the fundamental weakness in the system: the lack of competitiveness of certain countries and the ensuing balance of payments crisis. Unless these weaknesses are addressed, the medium-term prospects for the euro are bleak. And even if they are addressed, the period of adjustment for euro member states must be measured in years rather than months.

So how to do better? Our own experience at the *Financial Times* suggests that training is critical. After the Enron debacle, we introduced regular and deeper lessons in areas such as reading balance sheets. We also made a handful of hires in the financial sector to improve our specialist knowledge of markets. And, finally, in the finest spirit of the 122-year-old *FT*, we studiously avoided what the French call 'la pensée unique'. Being a broad independent church, we were – and are – happy to host a variety of views both on the op-ed page and in the analysis spots on our news pages, which causes all of us to challenge our assumptions.

Journalists, in this respect, have a crucial role to play. Flawed they may be, but they are more than soothsayers of doom. They still have the capacity to be the canaries in the mine. Long may it be so.

PART I

The banking crisis and the media

1

WILLFUL BLINDNESS

The media's power problem

Dean Starkman

The business press did everything but take on the institutions that brought down the financial system.

> "The government, the financial industry and the American consumer—if they had only paid attention—would have gotten ample warning about this crisis from us, years in advance, when there was still time to evacuate and seek shelter from this storm."
>
> Diana Henriques, *New York Times* business reporter, speech at
> The George Washington University, November 8, 2008

> "But anybody who's been paying attention has seen business journalists waving the red flag for several years."
>
> Chris Roush, "Unheeded Warnings," *American Journalism Review*,
> December/January, 2009

> "I'm kind of curious as to … why is it that people were shocked, given the volume of coverage."
>
> Nikhil Deogun, deputy managing editor, *The Wall Street Journal*,
> quoted in "Unheeded Warnings"

> "For in an exact sense the present crisis in western democracy is a crisis of journalism."
>
> Walter Lippmann, *Liberty and the News*, 1920

These are grim times for the nation's financial media.[1] Not only must they witness the unraveling of their own business, they must at the same time fend off charges that they failed to cover adequately their central beat—finance—during the years prior to an implosion that is forcing millions of low-income strivers into undeserved poverty and the entire world into an economic winter. The quotes above give a fair summary of the institutional response of the mainstream business press to the charge that it slept on the job while lenders and Wall Street ran amok. And while the record will show this response is not entirely wrong, one can see how casual business-press readers might have a problem with the idea that final responsibility for failing to stop escalating dangers in the financial system has somehow shifted to them.

Dang, Margaret, we blew it again.

It is understandable that the business press would want to defend its record. But it is equally understandable, I hope, that some readers might want to see some support for these claims. You know the old journalism saying, "If your mother says she loves you," etc.

For if the institutional response is correct, and all was done that could be done, then journalism has even bigger problems than Google and Craigslist. In the best case, if this response is to be believed, the financial press faces the problem of irrelevance—all that newsprint and coated paper, those millions of words, the bar graphs, stipple portraits, glossy photos of white guys, the printing presses, delivery trucks, and Yale degrees, is worth about as much as a New Century share.

Lippmann, I think, would understand the problem. Without facts, the public is powerless. With them, well, it can lick Countrywide and Goldman Sachs put together. In his book, *Liberty and the News*, Lippmann wrote: "Everywhere today men are conscious that somehow they must deal with questions more intricate than any church or school had prepared them to understand. Increasingly, they know they cannot understand them if facts are not quickly and steadily available." Without them, he says, there can be no liberty.

He was talking about a crude and corrupt press that manipulated public opinion around World War I. We're dealing with a financial press that is neither of those things, but is nonetheless a battered and buffeted institution that in the last decade saw its fortunes and status plummet as the institutions it covered ruled the earth and bent the government. The press, I believe, began to suffer from a form of Stockholm Syndrome. Now, it is in the awkward position of telling its readers they were insufficiently attentive to what it wrote.

I can think of several reasons why this is a bad approach, optics-wise. For one thing, it sounds a bit like telling customers they didn't read the documents carefully enough, just what Ameriquest used to say about its Pay-Option ARMs. Don't go there, press friends.

For another thing, readers could answer that while it is true that they may have missed warnings, they do recall hearing messages that didn't sound like warnings at all. Anyone "paying attention" might have thought that the most important thing about Washington Mutual on a given day was that its "Creative Retail Approach" had turned "the Banking World Upside Down" (*Fortune*, 3/31/03); that Lehman Brothers was "Trading Up" (*The Wall Street Journal*, 10/13/04); that Ken Lewis had become the "Banker of America" by "Ignoring His Critics" (*Fortune*, 9/5/05); that Angelo Mozilo was merely pugnacious ("The Mortgage Maker vs. The World," *The New York Times*, 10/16/05); that Citigroup was "Cleaned Up" (!) though "Falling Behind" (*Businessweek*, 10/05/06); and, additionally, that Goldman (drum roll) had "Sachs Appeal" (honk) (*Forbes*, 1/29/07).

Nothing about mortgage boiler rooms and CDO factories there, no matter how carefully you read.

Finally, if reader inattention is really the problem, then what's an appropriate policy response—mandatory exams on "Personal Journal" stories? But would the jump be included on the final? My pet idea is to pipe *Squawk Box* into people's homes 24/7, with no turning it off, à la North Korea. If we're nationalizing everything, we might as well go all the way, right?

I'd say a better approach in the wake of this disaster is to reflect on why all these "warnings" went "unheeded" and failed to penetrate the thick skulls of Pick-a-Pay Nation. Alas, the business press does not appear to be in a reflective mood. But, business press, as Jimmy Cayne might say, it's not about you. It's all about us. We citizens, like it or not, rely on journalists to provide word of rampant wrongdoing, and now we find ourselves well beyond the worst of all worst-case scenarios, caused, by general consensus, to an overwhelming degree by this most central of business-press beats: finance. We need to learn the lessons of the past eight years or so, even if the press doesn't want to go along, and re-examine, from top to bottom, all the firewalls that were supposedly designed to protect us from precisely the financial catastrophe that has just occurred. These firewalls start with risk managers, officers, directors, etc., within the financial institutions, then extend outward to accounting firms, rating agencies, regulators, and yes, journalists.

The press's role is, as always, ambiguous. On the one hand, no one at *Forbes* sold a single collateralized debt obligation to any German pension fund, so the press certainly can't be blamed for causing the crisis. On the other hand, Bloomberg News employs 2,300 business journalists, *The Wall Street Journal*, 700-plus, *The New York Times*, 110, etc., and all business-news organizations purport to cover the financial system and imply, if not claim outright, mastery over a particular beat—the one that just melted down to China to the shock of one and all. So the press isn't exactly an innocent bystander, either. It's not 100 percent responsible, and it's not zero percent. It's somewhere in the middle, closer to zero than fifty, I'd say, but it had *something* to do with it.

Right now, the business press, which firmly believes it did all it could do, is in something of a standoff with those who believe that cannot be true. The discussion so far has been conducted largely at a schoolyard level: "You missed it!" "Did not." We also see a lot of defensiveness among business journalists, as though somehow individual reporters are to blame. This is preposterous. These are institutional questions. Senior editorial leaders and news executives are in the dock here, as is an entire media subculture. Leaders had the power; they set the tone; they set the frames, not this reporter or that one.

Major news outlets so far have not trained their resources on the question, a drive-by or two by Howard Kurtz notwithstanding. The *American Journalism Review*, quoted above, did take a look and found in the business press's favor. With all due respect to our cousins in Maryland, I find *AJR*'s approach—in effect, sticking a thumb into several years of coverage and pulling out some plums—inadequate. Of course *somebody* did *something*. And a few did a lot of things. But did the coverage even come close to reflecting the radical transformation of the mortgage industry and Wall Street in 2004, 2005, and 2006? Tellingly, "Unheeded Warnings" contains a disturbing number of examples from 2007, when warnings were about as useful as a garden hose during the Tokyo fire bombings. It also dwelled on coverage of Fannie Mae and Freddie Mac, which, odious as they were, *followed* the private sector into subprime.

In this debate, the business press has the advantage because the public cannot be sure whether in fact it did miss something. Being sure would require reading the entire record of what was printed on the topics of lending and Wall Street in several outlets over many years—hundreds and hundreds of stories. Who in their right mind would do such a thing?

Well, somebody had to.

It struck us that it is impossible to avoid trying to assess the business press's performance in the run-up to the meltdown. The business press is the sole means by which normal citizens would know of goings-on in the lending industry and on Wall Street. It is the vital connection between the public on one side and regulators and financial institutions on the other. It is the only instrument capable of catalyzing the virtuous cycle of reform that emerges when dangers and abuses come under the public gaze. If readers screwed up, so be it. But if it is the business press, readers are going to have to insist on identifying weak points, cultural problems, skewed priorities, and areas in which the business press's institutional interests might be out of alignment with those of the broader public. If members of the public must go elsewhere for warnings, they need to know that, too.

It is true that few sectors of journalism, with the possible exception of the Washington press corps, are as infected with the extreme form of know-it-all-ism as the business press, which wields the complexities of its subject area like a cudgel against *non-cognoscenti*. But readers should not shrink from asking relevant questions merely because they don't know the precise mechanics of a credit default swap and don't read *Fortune* as closely as they might, say, the Torah.

The fact is, you don't need to be a media critic or a quant to assess whether proper warnings were provided. What's more, I suspect most rank-and-file reporters would welcome scrutiny, as long as it's fair. And so we undertook a project with a simple goal: to assess whether the business press, as it claims, provided the public with fair warning of looming dangers during the years when it could have made a difference.

I'm going to provide a sneak preview of our findings: the answer is no. The record shows that the press published its hardest-hitting investigations of lenders and Wall Street between 2000–2003, for reasons I will attempt to explain below, then lapsed into useful-but-not-sufficient consumer- and investor-oriented stories during the critical years of 2004–2006. Missing are investigative stories that confront directly powerful institutions about basic business practices while those institutions were still powerful. This is not a detail. This is the watchdog that didn't bark.

To the contrary, the record is clogged with feature stories about banks ("Countrywide Writes Mortgages for the Masses," *WSJ*, 12/21/04) and Wall Street firms ("Distinct Culture at Bear Stearns Helps It Surmount a Grim Market," *The New*

York Times, 3/28/03) that covered the central players in this drama but wrote about anything but abusive lending and how it was funded. Far from warnings, the message here was: "All clear."

Finally, the press scrambled in late 2006 and especially early 2007 as the consequences of the institutionalized corruption of the financial system became apparent to one and all.

So the idea that the press did all it could, and the public just missed it, is not just untenable. It is also untrue.

We went into the project with the working hunch that something was wrong. This stems from our belief in journalism itself. As journalists, we have to believe that what we do is not entirely ineffectual and that it has some impact on the outcome of events. Otherwise, why bother? Given that the system failure here is absolute, whatever journalism did do, as a matter of logic, was insufficient.

But a second idea going in was that this "debate" about business press performance is not really a matter of opinion at all. Either the work is there, or it isn't. Facts have a way of obliterating assumptions.

Our approach was fairly straightforward. We picked a date range of January 1, 2000 through June 30, 2007, with the idea that the early date would capture the entire housing bubble and the later date marked the period right after two Bear Stearns hedge funds collapsed very publicly and all warnings were moot.

We then came up with a common-sense list of the nine most influential business press outlets: *The Wall Street Journal*, *The New York Times*, the *Los Angeles Times*, *The Washington Post*, Bloomberg News, *Financial Times*, *Fortune*, *Businessweek*, and *Forbes*. CNBC and other television outlets were excluded both for practical and substantive reasons. With the help of some colleagues, we searched the Factiva database for the names of important institutions—Bear Stearns, Countrywide, etc.—and matched them with search terms that seemed appropriate, such as "predatory lending," "mortgage lending," "securitization," "collateralized debt obligations," and the like.

We then asked the news outlets themselves to volunteer their best work during this period. Some institutions were more diligent than others, so, on that score, *The New York Times* might tend to be overrepresented, while *The Washington Post*, which declined to participate, might get shorted. Similarly, Bloomberg, the *FT*, and the *Los Angeles Times* posed technical challenges. But, while we won't hesitate to differentiate between the relative performance of different outlets (and reporters, for that matter), the goal was to assess institutional performance, not who "won." Nobody won.

The articles are in a spreadsheet. I was a staff writer at the *Journal* from 1996 through 2004, covering commercial real estate during the relevant period, and on contract at *The Washington Post* for 2005, covering white-collar crime; nothing of mine is on the list or deserves to be there. When compiled in 2008, the sheet contained 730 entries, but it remains open and we plan to add stories indefinitely as we come across them. Feel free to send your entry to editors@cjr.org. The database is meant to be used as a companion to this story. I hope it will be a reference for further research and that readers will use it to argue for or against CJR's conclusions.

The list, then, was designed to capture all significant warning stories, not just some of them. And while 730 may seem like a lot of relevant stories, keep in mind the *Journal* alone published 220,000 stories during this period, so in a sense these were corks bobbing on a news Niagara. The list also includes as guideposts bits of context that we felt would give readers some sense of what was happening on the finance beat at the time (e.g. "Fed Assesses Citigroup Unit $70 Million in Loan Abuse," *NYT*, 5/28/04). Sprinkled throughout are some of those rah-rah stories ("Mortgage Slump? Bring It On; Countrywide plans to grab more of the market as the industry consolidates," *BW*, 12/15/03), and a tiny fraction of the run-of-the-mill stories about important, and guilty, institutions that in retrospect were so far from the salient point that one wishes we could have the space and the reporters' time back ("Power Banking: Morgan Stanley Trades Energy Old-Fashioned Way: In Barrels ... " *WSJ*, 3/2/05).

Let's get to it.

The most striking thing about the list for me is that the best work during the entire period—stories that hit hard at abusive practices and established the critical link between bucket shops and their Wall Street funders and bundlers—was done early, from 2000 to 2003. *Businessweek*'s Dean Foust, et al., explored Wall Street's foray into the hard-money lending business, including subprime mortgages and payday lending ("Easy Money: Subprime lenders make a killing catering to poorer Americans. Now Wall Street is getting in on the act," 4/24/00). A handy chart at the bottom of the story ranks subprime securitization leaders: Lehman was number one. Citigroup's 2000 acquisition of Associates First Capital, a notoriously corrupt outfit (it employed a "designated forger," ABC's *Prime Time Live* reported in 1997), spurred *The New York Times* to publish "Along With a Lender, Is Citigroup Buying Trouble?" in October of that year. This fine 3,258-word story documented Associates' execrable practices fairly well (though it couldn't beat the anecdote from a 4/23/97 *Journal* story that described how an illiterate quarry worker who owed $1,250 for—get this—*meat* discovered that this loan had been sold to Associates, which convinced the quarry worker to refinance ten times in four years until he owed $45,000, more than half of it in fees, with payments that took more than 70 percent of his income. He had signed each note with an "X"). The *Times* duly noted Citi's promise to clean up its new acquisition by, among other things, holding upfront fees to a mere nine (!) points.

Business journalism during this period came close to reaching the holy grail—the critical Wall Street/subprime connection—when *The New York Times*'s Diana Henriques, in a joint project with Lowell Bergman and ABC News (including, though he doesn't have a byline, the underappreciated Brian Ross), published "Mortgaged Lives: Profiting From Fine Print With Wall Street's Help" (3/15/00), linking another now forgotten but once powerful and rapacious subprime lender, First Alliance Corp., with Lehman Brothers and other Wall Street firms engaging in precisely the kind of practices that brought down the financial system. The story captures the boiler-room culture that was then overrunning traditional mortgage underwriting, here with a quote from a twenty-seven-page sales manual:

"Establish a common bond," the loan officers were taught. "Find this early in the conversation to make the customer lower his guard." The script listed good bond-building topics (family, jobs, children, and pets) and emphasized, "It's really important to get them laughing."

The piece goes on to describe the Wall Street connection in some detail: "No Wall Street investment bank had a bigger share of that reviving 1999 [subprime] market than Lehman Brothers, Wall Street's fourth-largest brokerage house."

This story and others were based on groundbreaking litigation in California that, importantly, would hold a Wall Street firm responsible for the practices of its lender-clients. Had that principle stood up (an Orange County jury found for the borrowers in 2003 but the award against Lehman, $5 million, was small), there would have been no mortgage crisis. The *Los Angeles Times*, led by E. Scott Reckard, also dogged the litigation, recognizing the journalism opportunity for what it was.

John Hechinger of *The Wall Street Journal* also wrote fine warning stories, including one about how brand-name lenders were convincing the poor to refinance zero-percent loans from the government and Habitat for Humanity (!?) with rates that reset to the mid-teens and higher ("Best Interests: How Big Lenders Sell a Pricier Refinancing to Poor Homeowners—People Give Up Low Rates to Pay Off Other Debts … " 12/7/01). The dishonor roll is here:

> Some of the nation's biggest subprime lenders have refinanced zero-interest and low-interest loans from Habitat, including Countrywide, units of Citigroup Inc., Household International Inc., Ameriquest Mortgage Co. and a unit of tax giant H&R Block Inc.

Meanwhile, the *Journal*'s Jess Bravin and Paul Beckett painted a devastating portrait of a compromised Comptroller of the Currency ("Friendly Watchdog: Federal Regulator Often Helps Banks Fighting Consumers—Dependent on Lenders' Fees, OCC Takes Their Side Against Local, State Laws," 1/28/02). And *Forbes* did a beat-down on Household ("Home Wrecker," 9/2/02).

What is important to remember about the period around the turn of the decade—and this is not a knock on the press—is that predatory lending was high on the public's agenda, mostly in response to marauding behavior of old-line subprime lenders like Associates, First Alliance, Conseco Finance, Household, etc., who at the time were being joined by the new generation of subprimates—Ameriquest, New Century, et al. From the mid-nineties to the early '00s, foreclosures began to jump in urban areas around the country, rising half again in Chicago's Cook County, doubling in Detroit's Wayne County, Newark's Essex County, and Pittsburgh's Allegheny County, tripling in Cleveland's Cuyahoga County, according to *American Nightmare: Predatory Lending and the Foreclosure of the American Dream*, a muckraking book by Richard Lord published in 2005, based on his reporting in the *Pittsburgh City Paper* on this early subprime boomlet.

Between 1999 and 2004, more than half the states, both red (North Carolina, 1999; South Carolina, 2004) and blue (California, 2001; New York, 2003), passed anti-predatory-lending laws. Georgia touched off a firestorm in 2002 when it sought to hold Wall Street bundlers and holders of mortgage-backed securities responsible for mortgages that were fraudulently conceived. Would that such a measure had survived. We forget now, but beginning in 2004 Michigan and forty-nine other states battled the U.S. Comptroller of the Currency and the banking industry (and *The Wall Street Journal*'s editorial page) for the right to examine the books of Wachovia's mortgage unit, a fight the Supreme Court decided in Wachovia's favor in 2007—about a year before it cratered. Iowa Attorney General Tom Miller and Roy Cooper, his counterpart in North Carolina, made predatory lending the centerpiece of their tenures (see: "They Warned Us About the Mort-gage Crisis," *BW*, 10/9/08), while in New York Eliot Spitzer gave grandstanding a good name in trying to bring attention to the issue ("Spitzer's Ghost," CJR.org, 10/14/08).

This isn't about identifying which journalist or economist was "prescient," the business-press parlor game du jour. What's important is that forthright press coverage and uncompromised regulation combined to create a virtuous cycle of reform.

Citigroup, remember, was forced to sign a $240 million settlement with the Federal Trade Commission covering two million customers. This is marketing deception on a mass scale, revealed and policed. A coalition of states forced an even bigger settlement, for $484 million, on Household. This was in 2002. It wasn't perfect, but it was working.

Alas, any fair reading of the record will show the business press subsequently lost its taste for predatory-lending investigations and developed a case of collective amnesia about Wall Street's connection to subprime, rediscovering it only after the fact.

There are a number of explanations (though no excuses) for this. First and foremost was the abdication of regulatory responsibility at the federal level. Uncompromised regulation and great journalism go hand-in-hand. But when such regulation disappears, journalistic responsibilities only increase. What is important to understand first is that this press failure did occur. Readers needn't be bullied into believing they missed relevant independent press investigations of Country-wide, New Century, IndyMac, Citigroup, Bear Stearns, Lehman Brothers, or Merrill Lynch. Check the sheet; they aren't there.

What makes this development especially maddening is that subprime lending and Wall Street's CDO production at this point were only just getting started. Sub-prime mortgages in 2002 were $200 billion, 6.9 percent of all mortgages. By 2006 they were $600 billion and 20 percent of the market. Add poorly documented "Alt-A" mortgages and the 2006 figures rise to $958 billion and 32 percent. CDO production went from next to nothing in 2000 to half a trillion in 2006.

Behind those numbers were the boiler rooms, underwritten by the Wall Street masters of the universe depicted on business magazine covers. Yes, we must beware of hindsight-ism. But let us acknowledge that today, at least, we know that the lending industry from 2004 through 2006 was not just pushing it. It had become unhinged—institutionally corrupt, rotten, like a fish, from the head. I argued last fall ("Boiler Room," *Columbia Journalism Review*, September/October 2008) that post-crash reporting has given short shrift to the breathtaking corruption that overran the mortgage business—document tampering, forgery, verbal and written misrepresentations, changing of terms at closing, nondisclosure of fees, rates, and penalties, and a boiler-room culture reminiscent of the notorious small-stock swindles of the nineties.

Now the muck is finally bubbling to the surface as the Justice Department and several states gear up to prosecute "dozens" of leaders ("Financial Fraud is Focus of Attack by Prosecutors," *NYT*, 3/12/09) and journalists latch onto the story in all its lurid glory. *Businessweek*'s excellent Mara Der Hovanesian reports, for instance, that Wall Street demand for mortgages became so frenzied that female wholesale buyers were "expected" to trade sex for them with male retail brokers, according to "dozens" of brokers and wholesale buyers ("Sex, Lies, and Mortgage Deals," 11/13/08). But:

> The abuses went far beyond sexual dalliances. Court documents and interviews with scores of industry players suggest that wholesalers also offered bribes to fellow employees, fabricated documents, and coached brokers on how to break the rules. And they weren't alone. Brokers, who work directly with borrowers, altered and shredded documents. Underwriters, the bank employees who actually approve mortgage loans, also skirted boundaries, demanding secret payments from wholesalers to green-light loans they knew to be fraudulent. Some employees who reported misdeeds were harassed or fired. Federal and state prosecutors are picking through the industry's wreckage in search of criminal activity.

There's a Coen brothers movie in this. Yet sadly, as corruption heated up, business-news coverage generally downshifted into what I call service and consumer pieces: warning about the bubble and pointing to patently defective types of mortgage products. Indeed, business-news outlets, to their credit, seemed to fall over themselves to be first (bubble talk appears, surprisingly, as early as the fall of 2001) and/or loudest about calling the end of the bubble: "Is a Housing Bubble About to Burst … ?" (*BW*, 7/14/04), for example, or "Boom vs. Bust: The housing-price run-up can't last … " (*WSJ*, 6/14/04).

I don't mean to disparage bubble stories: these were real warnings. *Fortune* might well win the prize, if there were one, for bubble-bursting with "Is the Housing Boom Over?"—4,539 words by Shawn Tully, in September 2004; a year later, in October 2005, Tully answered himself with another five-thousand-plus words, "I'm Tom Barrack and I'm getting out," about a real-estate investor. Meanwhile, the press was also warning consumers not to agree to a mortgage product containing terms that no well-regulated system would allow. "The Ever More Graspable, And Risky, American Dream" (*NYT*, 6/24/04). "Armed and Dangerous? Adjustable-rate mortgages are pulling in new home buyers—but the risks are high" (*BW*, 4/12/04).

Indeed, the *Journal* kept after the issue and essentially called these mortgages bad on their face: "For These Mortgages, Downside Comes Later" (10/5/04); "The Prepayment Trap: Lenders Put Penalties On Popular Mortgages" (3/10/05); "Mortgage Lenders Loosen Standards" (7/27/05).

It should be said these usually ran on D1, not A1, and so gave the impression of low-priority bleats from the back of the paper. Even so, there they were, and, so, yes, regulators and lawmakers did have information they could have used had they wanted to. So shame on them. These are valuable stories. But to get the public involved you need more. You need stories of institutionalized corruption. There's no way around it.

I would suggest that in approaching the mortgage story as a consumer or investment story, the business press was trying to fight the Battle of Tarawa with a Swiss Army Knife. What was missing—and needed—were more stories like the one that ran on February 4, 2005 in the *Los Angeles Times* by Mike Hudson and Scott Reckard: "Workers Say Lender Ran 'Boiler Rooms.'"

This, CJR reader, was the real thing, a 3,220-word investigation that kicks in the door. It uses court documents and interviews with ex-employees and customers, nothing fancy, to expose Ameriquest, which at the time was one of the nation's leading lenders, "Proud Sponsor of the American Dream" and the 2005 Super Bowl halftime show, and owned by the politically well-connected Roland Arnall, soon to be named U.S. ambassador to the Netherlands:

> Slugging down Red Bull caffeine drinks, sales agents would work the phones hour after hour, he said, trying to turn cold calls into lucrative "sub-prime" mortgages—high-cost loans made to people with spotty credit. The demands were relentless: One manager prowled the aisles between desks like "a little Hitler," Bomchill said, hounding agents to make more calls and push more loans, bragging that he hired and fired people so fast that one worker would be cleaning out his desk as his replacement came through the door.

The *Los Angeles Times*, it's worth pointing out, also probed Ameriquest's attempts to co-opt critics ("Ameriquest's Ties to Watchdog Group Are Tested," 5/22/05), chronicled possible forgery at the lender ("Doubt is Cast on Loan Papers," 3/28/05), and, crucially, explained how at least 20 percent of all subprime loans were going to prime borrowers, what I call the boiler-room effect ("More Homeowners With Good Credit Getting Stuck With Higher-Rate Loans," 10/24/05). It turns out that the number actually reached more than 50 percent, *The Wall Street Journal* found in December 2007. These all ran at over two thousand words on A1 and helped catalyze a multistate investigation that forced Ameriquest into an embarrassing $325 million settlement the next year.

Clearly, then, such reporting was gettable.

Two years later, the *Journal* published an Ameriquest story ("Lender Lobbying Blitz Abetted Mortgage Mess," 12/31/07), but by then, the lender was closed.

So let's be clear: stories like the *Los Angeles Times*'s Ameriquest probes are the exceptions that prove the rule. And while handwringing about the bubble and pointing out defective mortgage products is hard, muckraking about specific, powerful institutions is harder, more useful, and more fun to read:

> Lisa Taylor, a former loan agent at Ameriquest's customer-retention office in Sacramento, said she witnessed documents being altered when she walked in on co-workers using a brightly lighted Coke machine as a tracing board, copying borrowers' signatures on an unsigned piece of paper.

Great, right? If the muckraking story—a straight investigation aimed at the heart of the business model of an industry leader—was scarce in mortgage lending, it was rarer still on Wall Street's end of the mortgage machine. As far as I can tell it was the unicorn of business coverage.

One looks in vain for stories about Wall Street's ties to the subprime industry, even though the Lehman–First Alliance case had outlined it in detail and nearly all the major investment banks would, by the middle of the decade, go on actually to buy their own retail subprime operations (who remembers Bear Stearns Residential?). What was happening was a vast change, a paradigm shift. Citizens did not see it coming. Now we know why.

And a word about head-on investigations of powerful institutions: they're not optional. There is no substitute. The public needed warnings that the Wall Street-backed lending industry was running amok. It didn't get them. Remember Lippmann: no facts, no democracy.

It is disingenuous, I believe, to suggest, as many financial journalists do, that they are unfairly expected to have been soothsayers in the economic crisis (e.g. "Financial Journalism and Its Critics," Robert Teitelman, TheDeal.com, 3/6/09: "Why, among all other journalists, are financial reporters expected to accurately predict the future?"). Rather, the expectation is merely that financial outlets do their best to report on *what is happening now*, including, one would hope, confronting powerful institutions directly about basic business practices. This is not complicated.

Of course, anyone would applaud the astute and highly skilled journalists who looked at brewing systemic problems, as did Bloomberg's David Evans ("Credit Swaps, Some 'Toxic,' May Soar to $4.8 Trillion," 6/26/03); *Businessweek*'s Der Hovanesian ("Taking Risk To Extremes; Will derivatives cause a major blowup in the world's credit markets?" 5/23/05); the *Journal*'s Mark Whitehouse ("Slices of Risk: How a Formula Ignited Market That Burned Some Big Investors," 9/12/05; "Risk Management: As Home Owners Face Strains, Market Bets on Loan Defaults," 10/31/06); and Gillian Tett, John Plender, and others at the *Financial Times* (numerous stories). But even these virtuoso efforts are still not the same as confronting a Wall Street firm head-on for its role in underwriting mortgage boiler rooms across the country.

A good place to start would have been Citigroup, apparently, since Hudson—he of the Ameriquest stories—did it in his spare time. Freelancing while working full time for *The Roanoke Times*, he pulled the cover back on Citigroup's huge subprime operation in 2003 (!?) and won a Polk Award in the process ("Banking on

Misery: Citigroup, Wall Street and the Fleecing of the South," *Southern Exposure*, summer 2003). He mentions the mortgage aftermarket only in passing, but that's where the national press can take over for ground-level reporting. If only.

No reader, not even one really applying herself, would have found adequate warnings about the Wall Street/subprime nexus. She would instead have found plenty of coverage focused on the earnings horserace ("Putting the Muscle Back in the Bull; Stan O'Neal may be the toughest—some say the most ruthless—ceo in America. Merrill Lynch couldn't be luckier to have him," *Fortune*, 4/5/04), personalities ("Rewiring Chuck Prince; Citi's chief hasn't just stepped out of Sandy Weill's shadow—he's stepped out of his own as he strives to make himself into a leader with vision," *BW*, 2/20/06), and situated comfortably within frames set by the industry itself ("Joining the Club—Inside Goldman's Secret Rite: The Race to Become Partner," *WSJ*, 10/13/06). I find Lehman and Citi coverage to have been especially poor, again, given what was known by 2003 ("Lehman's New Street Smarts; Under CEO Fuld, the bond house has become a dealmaking power," *BW*, 1/19/04; "The Unlikely Revolutionary: Critics are sniping and the stock is lagging, but Citigroup's Chuck Prince keeps charging ahead, blowing up business practices put in place by his famed mentor, Sandy Weill," *Fortune*, 3/6/06).

Only after the crackup had already begun is Wall Street's role in subprime again laid bare ("Debt Bomb—Lending a Hand: How Wall Street Stoked The Mortgage Meltdown ..." *WSJ*, 6/27/07):

> Lehman's deep involvement in the business has also made the firm a target of criticism. In more than 15 lawsuits and in interviews, borrowers and former employees have claimed that the investment bank's in-house lending outlets used improper tactics during the recent mortgage boom to put borrowers into loans they couldn't afford. Twenty-five former employees said in interviews that front-line workers and managers exaggerated borrowers' creditworthiness by falsifying tax forms, pay stubs and other information, or by ignoring inaccurate data submitted by independent mortgage brokers. In some instances, several ex-employees said, brokers or in-house employees altered documents with the help of scissors, tape and Wite-Out.

Suddenly, the story—the one that counts—was gettable again. It referred, after all, to documents available for years. There really is no excuse.

The author of this *Journal* piece, by the way, was Hudson. He left the paper later that year and is writing a book about subprime.

It is true that Bush-era deregulation and the media's financial travails hampered investigative journalism (of course, the *Pittsburgh City Paper* could manage it, but never mind). But the business press also disarmed unilaterally. CJR's study, I believe, provides strong support for the idea that sometime after 2003, as federal regulation folded like a cheap suitcase, the business press institutionally lost whatever taste it had for head-on investigations of core practices of powerful institutions.

Too bad that's precisely what was needed.

In light of this general system failure, what are the lessons for the general reader and the business press itself?

First, the public should be aware—warned, so to speak—that its interests and those of the business press may not be in perfect alignment. The business press exists within the Wall Street and corporate subculture and understandably must adopt its idioms and customs, the better to translate them for the rest of us. Still, it relies on those institutions for its stories. Burning a bridge is hard. It is far easier for news bureaucracies to accept ever-narrowing frames of discourse, frames forcefully pushed by industry, even if those frames marginalize and eventually exclude the business press's own great investigative traditions.

Second, there's a difference between reporting from an investor's perspective and from a citizen's. The business press is better at the former than the latter, and the gap has only been growing. I would only caution that what's good for investors in the short and medium terms may not be good for anyone over the long haul.

Third, remember the nexus between uncompromised regulation and great journalism.

Fourth, lament the decline of the great business sections of general-circulation dailies, specifically those of the *Los Angeles Times* and *The Washington Post*.

Fifth, seek alternatives. Read *Mother Jones*, or something, once in a while.

Sixth, never, ever, underestimate the importance of editorial leadership and news ownership, for in them rests the power to push back against structural conflicts and cultural taboos fostered by industry, to clear a space for business journalism to do the job it is clearly capable of, the one job that really needed doing.

Note

1 From Starkman, Dean (2009), 'Power Problem', *Columbia Journalism Review*, May/June 2009, pp. 24–30; reprinted with kind permission of the *Columbia Journalism Review*.

2

WHY THE MEDIA GOT IT RIGHT

Chris Roush

At the end of 2008, I examined the business journalism coverage in America of the economic crisis and concluded that, 'The business media have done yeoman's work during the past decade-plus to expose wrongdoing in corporate America.'

What's more, I added this: 'In fact, a review of the top business publications in the country shows that they blanketed the major issues – from subprime loans to adjustable-rate mortgages to credit derivatives – that caused so much economic pain.'[1]

That opinion was controversial. Virtually all of the media critics in the United States – and overseas for that matter – believed that the financial media had not done their job. *Columbia Journalism Review* compiled an exhaustive review of the coverage and concluded that it wasn't enough.[2] Even Swedish fiction writer Stieg Larsson wrote in *The Girl With the Dragon Tattoo* that business reporters 'were thus either naive and gullible that they ought to be packed off to other assignments, or they were people who quite consciously betrayed their journalism function'.[3]

Five years later, I have yet to hear any argument that would persuade me to change my opinion. Those who believe that financial journalism could have prevented the economic crisis by being more vigilant in its reporting are living with Alice in Wonderland.

Here's where they fall down:

1. They make it sound as if reporters and editors have the ability to thwart corporate wrongdoing with one article and a couple of well-placed phone calls to regulators;
2. Their argument suggests that government agencies take their cues from the media in terms of regulatory enforcement at a time when society's trust of the media is at a record low;
3. Their argument also requires that business reporters be able to predict the cause and extent of future economic calamities.

I'm not here to be an apologist for the financial media. Could they have done a better job? The answer to that is an obvious yes. No one is perfect. But to blame business journalists for failing to do their job in protecting society from the ills of big business is to set up an argument that turns reporters and editors into all-powerful government officials with unlimited abilities in terms of issuing sub-poenas and seizing documents, and blames the messenger without addressing what really went wrong. In January 2010, Federal Reserve Board Chairman Ben Bernanke blamed federal regulation, not lax business reporting, for the problems that led to the two-year-old recession.[4]

And the argument is also wrong in one key area. Business journalism did warn its readers. In fact, the twenty-first century has produced more top-notch business journalism than any other decade since the creation of mass communication. In the years 2001 to 2010, there have been at least three business journalists who have won Pulitzer Prizes, and countless other stories – in print, online, and broadcast – that have given consumers enough information about what was going on. Only those who turned a blind eye to the situation were surprised when housing prices started to fall and companies that invested in mortgage-backed securities began going under.

I have two problems with those who have criticized recent business journalism coverage. The first is that they have not looked closely enough at the coverage themselves to make such a determination. The second is that they are falling back on a convenient scapegoat of the messenger without considering the role of the receiver of the message.

Let's dissect a few of these arguments

'Of course, just as we're getting more self-pity than humility from Wall Street these days, we're not exactly getting much in the way of mea culpas from the financial press,' *Advertising Age* media critic Simon Dumenco wrote on 29 September 2008. 'Nobody's really been stepping up to the plate to say, "With our woefully incom-plete and often shamefully gullible reporting on the murky financial underpinnings of the real-estate bubble, we let our readers and/or viewers down."'[5]

My reply to Dumenco is that the reason the financial media weren't writing mea culpas is that they didn't do anything wrong, and I will show in the second half of this chapter the great examples of how they did get into the murky underpinnings.

In a 6 October 2008 story titled 'Press May Own a Share in Financial Mess', *Washington Post* media writer Howard Kurtz added, 'As in the savings-and-loan scandal of the late 1980s, the press was a day late and several dollars short.'[6]

Like Dumenco, Kurtz is not a nuanced journalist who understands how business journalism works or who took the time to understand that a major shift in financial reporting took place after the tech bubble burst in 2000.

The problem isn't that the business media were dazzled by soaring real-estate prices and Wall Street profits and failed to see rot beneath the surface. Rather, it was that government regulators and the general public weren't paying attention.

And the warning signs were plentiful:

As far back as 1994, *Fortune* magazine's Carol Loomis predicted that derivatives could be 'a villain, or even the villain, in some financial crisis that sweeps the world'.[7] The complicated investments she mentioned are those we saw unravel in 2008 and 2009.

The *Wall Street Journal*'s aggressive coverage of government-based lenders Fannie Mae and Freddie Mac dates back nearly a decade. In 2004, one piece in the *Journal* compared Fannie Mae to Enron and WorldCom, two companies that crashed and burned the last time business journalists were blamed for an economic downturn.[8]

Back in 2007, under the headline 'Mortgages May Be Messier Than You Think', Gretchen Morgenson of the *New York Times* wrote, 'As is often the case, only after fiery markets burn out do we see the risks that buyers ignore and sellers play down.'[9] Her colleagues Diana Henriques and Floyd Norris exposed shady lending to military personnel and shaky accounting practices, respectively, in the past five years.

Washington Post columnist Steven Pearlstein has been warning of financial trouble for years. On 1 August 2007, in a column titled 'Credit Market's Weight Puts Economy on Shaky Ground', Pearlstein wrote, 'This financial engineering has encouraged debt to be piled on debt, making the system more susceptible to a meltdown if credit suddenly becomes more expensive or unavailable.'[10]

Investigative business journalist Gary Weiss exposed nefarious behavior on Wall Street in his 2007 book, *Wall Street Versus America: A Muckraking Look at the Thieves, Fakers, and Charlatans Who Are Ripping You Off*. The title pretty much sums it up.

Although business news coverage often struggles to explain the complexities of the field to average citizens, writers such as Morgenson and Pearlstein avoid the jargon found elsewhere. They made it clear that serious trouble was brewing in the economy and on Wall Street.

Anybody who's been paying attention has seen business journalists waving the red flag for several years. 'The fact that housing was a bubble was printed millions of times,' says Allan Sloan, a *Fortune* columnist and arguably the country's pre-eminent business journalist. 'This is one time that we did what we were supposed to do.'[11]

Please, don't take my word for it, or the word of Sloan, whom I consider the top business journalist of the past 30 years. Their effectiveness in naming the recent scoundrels is supported by academic research. In 2003, then-Harvard Business School Professor Greg Miller studied more than 260 cases of accounting fraud. He determined that nearly a third of them were identified by the business media before the Securities and Exchange Commission or the companies involved said they were targets of investigations. 'In each of these articles, it is the reporter making the case for accounting impropriety based on analysis of public and private information,' wrote Miller, who now teaches at the University of Michigan. 'No other information intermediaries (i.e. analysts, auditors, or the legal system) are cited.'[12]

In other words, business journalists, who again have no regulatory power over the companies and the economy, have been proactive in their coverage.

'It's not we who are charged with taking away the punchbowl,' said Marcus Brauchli, the former executive editor of the *Washington Post* and a top editor at the *Wall Street Journal* for much of the first decade of the millennium, in a phone conversation with me in late 2008. Brauchli was one of the editors during the decade who led hard-hitting coverage that asked tough questions about what was going on.

> We pointed out the risks for a long period of time. And there were a lot of people in the financial world who knew what the risks were. But the history of manias is that people won't be stopped by the reality of the possibility that they may ultimately get wiped out, because the prospect of riches is a powerful attraction.[13]

Reporter Erin Arvedlund's article in the 7 May 2001 issue of *Barron's* is a classic example of what Brauchli is talking about. Her story, titled 'Don't Ask, Don't Tell', questioned the secrecy behind the hedge fund operations of Bernard Madoff. 'Some on Wall Street remain skeptical about how Madoff achieves such stunning double-digit returns using options alone,' Arvedlund wrote.[14] Her story should have touched off a round of investigations into Madoff's operations, but it failed to arouse the interest of regulators. It wasn't until 2008 that Madoff admitted he had been running nothing more than a scheme to defraud investors, who lost billions.

The problem with most of the critics of today's business journalism is that they are living in the past. For most of the past 100 years, business journalism has been blamed – and rightly so in some cases – for providing weak reporting and analysis that contributed to and caused many of the problems that have confronted the US economy and business world.

In 1938, business journalist Howard Carswell, writing in the *Public Opinion Quarterly*, noted the preponderance of business news that focused on the stock market at a time – the Great Depression – when fewer than 10 per cent of all households owned stock. 'The New York Stock Exchange is treated as the fountainhead of all news of the business and financial world,' he wrote. Carswell called for business news to expand itself to other areas of industry and finance. 'Anything within the purview of business affairs should be eligible,' he argued. 'The editing should be reader-minded and not investor-minded.'[15]

Writing in the *Harvard Business Review* in 1950, William Pinkerton noted the strain between business journalists and businessmen at a time when the economy was growing fast. The common complaints of businessmen who did not like the way they got into the news ran like this: 'The papers never get things right'; 'You can't trust reporters'; 'They didn't put in half of what I told them'; 'They missed the whole point of it'; 'I didn't say that at all.'[16]

Famed investor Gerald M. Loeb, who in 1957 created a series of awards that today are considered the Pulitzer Prizes of the field and that honor the best of business and financial journalism, lamented the quality of business reporting compared with other fields, such as sports and politics, in a 1966 commentary in *Columbia Journalism Review*. Loeb wrote,

> Many errors derive from superficial or erroneous reading of basic materials, like annual reports. The other day I saw the annual report of a company that showed earnings per share about the same as the year before. Examination of the footnotes, however, made it clear that had the same accounting been used in both years this company would have been several million in the red in the current reporting period. I rarely see this kind of explanation on the financial pages I read, and I read the best.[17]

Less than a decade later, business journalist Chris Welles, for whom this author worked at *Businessweek* in the 1990s, wrote in *Columbia Journalism Review* about the 'bleak wasteland of financial journalism'. Welles noted in 1973 that

> Too many business writers are mediocre rejects from other fields of journalism. The few ambitious and imaginative business editors struggle in vain against impassive superiors for more space, more money to hire better reporters. (Lacking any budget for financial news, radio station WCBS in New York recently recruited the editor of *Dun's Review* to give business commentaries in return for ads for his magazine.) Few senior editors willingly permit their careers to be sullied by a tour on the financial desk, which is widely regarded as a dead end.[18]

Two years later, Herbert Stein, former chairman of the President's Council of Economic Advisers, complained about how journalists wrote about the country's economy. 'Not only do the media concentrate on the short-term aspects of the economy, they also dramatize them in ways that further exaggerate their performance,' said Stein.[19]

In 1980, University of Missouri journalism professor William McPhatter, a former reporter for *Businessweek*, quoted an insurance company chairman as stating, 'Most of us are fed up with the glib, shallow, inaccurate reporting and editing – tired of journalistic tastes which prefer sensationalism above the fundamentals that allow a Thespian to pose as a newsman. We've had enough crudity and rudeness.'[20]

By the fall of 1991, Richard Cheney, chairman emeritus of the public relations firm Hill and Knowlton, changed the tone of criticism to one that took business journalists to task for being too soft on their subjects. 'The business pages in the '80s particularly appeared to be written in one dimension, like *Citizen Kane* without Rosebud, sometimes even without last week,' he wrote in *Nieman Reports*.

> Scoundrels hoodwinked the public and the best of the media too rarely sounded the alarm until it was too late. Indeed, they rooted them on with puffery, detailing, day by day, tender offers and counter-tender offers, breathlessly

following the bidding like hicks at Sotheby's. Hardly anybody stepped back to examine the consequences for the country.[21]

Merrill Goozner continued this theme in 2000, writing in *Columbia Journalism Review* that

> coverage of the current prosperity can read like a sports page when the home team is on a roll: cheerleading can drown out the occasional story pointing out weaknesses in the squad or the challenges coming up in the schedule. Journalistic scorn is reserved for the players – or in this case stocks – that don't make their numbers.[22]

And by the beginning of the twenty-first century, business journalists were used as target practice, blamed for everything from the tech bubble to the dramatic rise in the stock market to the creation of companies such as Enron and WorldCom, which were allowed to grow into Fortune 500 companies using faulty accounting because reporters and editors were asleep at the wheel. *New York Times* financial writer Diana Henriques put it best when she stated, 'I submit that there is no form of ignorance more widely tolerated in the American newsroom than ignorance about business and finance. For some inexplicable reason, it falls outside the category of common knowledge that any literate journalist is expected to possess.'[23]

But this is not your father's financial reporting. The tech bubble bursting was a wake-up call for financial journalism. The pendulum of fawning and favorable coverage began to swing back to where, for the first decade of the twenty-first century, the coverage has been critical and skeptical, as we'll see through many examples.

The paradox of increasing criticism of business journalism as the reporting and writing was getting better should be obvious. It's also easy to understand. The job of business reporters became much more complex and sophisticated during the latter half of the twentieth century, as they were required to understand arcane accounting strategies, and read income statements, cash-flow statements, and balance sheets in order to fully explain what was going on.

That's not an easy job, and some performed better than others. Business news consumers demanded more and more information as interest in the stock market and companies increased due to their growing influence in society, putting more pressure on business journalism to assess and analyse the big picture. The error mentioned by Loeb – of failing to see the effect of an accounting change on a company's earnings – would not occur today in any respectable business publication.

The powerful players in business journalism include the *Wall Street Journal*, the business sections of the *New York Times* and the *Washington Post*, and business magazines such as *Businessweek* and *Fortune*. These are the news outlets with the power to direct the conversation. Readers who care about business and the economy – from investors to regulators to company executives – read these publications.

An examination of their work before spring 2007, when the first cracks began to appear in housing and investments, reveals ample coverage of the dangers that lay ahead.

And it wasn't just the business-media elite. A number of smaller news organizations distinguished themselves by spotlighting the rampant problems. The *Charlotte Observer*, for example, ran a series in March 2007 about an unscrupulous home-building firm that caused the company to stop making loans and leave the area. In fact, 11 winners in the 2008 Society of American Business Editors and Writers' Best in Business contest – for material published in 2007 – focused on the mortgage mess or credit problems. Regional and metro papers, for the most part, covered the housing and credit issues well, but did so from a local angle and didn't convey the broad perspective that the national business media provided.

Let's start with the *Wall Street Journal*, considered the top business newspaper in the country, if not the world. Brauchli returned to the United States at the end of 1999 after reporting from China to become the *Journal*'s national editor. He immediately took an interest in the *Journal*'s coverage, then overseen by Constance Mitchell-Ford, of government-backed housing lenders Fannie Mae and Freddie Mac, two of the largest lenders in the country. The first page-one story questioning the lenders' practices ran on 14 July 2000.[24] Brauchli was called to Fannie Mae's headquarters in 2001 to meet with CEO Franklin Raines, who was upset about the tone of the articles. 'He felt we were unduly critical,' Brauchli remembers. 'We were just reporting the facts.'[25]

The *Journal* published numerous stories about the lenders, hammering away at the excesses it uncovered – often on the front page. On 2 January 2002, reporters Jathon Sapsford and Patrick Barta wrote about the dramatic increase in consumer lending.[26] On 6 August of that year, Barta followed up with a 2,400-word examination of Fannie and Freddie that asked, 'With homeownership already so high, are Fannie and Freddie running out of room to grow?' In the fifth paragraph, he wrote, 'The huge size and rapid growth, coupled with their concentration in a single industry, has brought concern about possible risk to the U.S. economy should one of them ever fail.'[27]

A month later, on 17 September, a Barta story on the front of the *Journal*'s 'Money & Investing' section pointed out the increased risk on Fannie's financial statements because of falling interest rates.[28] On 19 August 2003, Barta and fellow reporter Ruth Simon wrote a front-page story on the hidden closing costs for mortgages.[29]

And a month later, a 3,000-word bombshell on Freddie, written by Barta, John D. McKinnon, and Gregory Zuckerman, appeared on the *Journal*'s front page. They wrote:

> Far from the sleepy mortgage company of its carefully cultivated reputation, Freddie Mac in recent years has evolved into a giant, sophisticated investment company, running a business laden with volatility and complexity. That change has sent risks soaring, not just for investors but for U.S. taxpayers, who likely would be on the hook if the federally chartered company stumbled.[30]

Stories about the increasing uncertainty in the real estate market appeared regularly in the *Journal* for the next several years until the market imploded. A May 2005 front-page story focused on homeowners who took on too much debt while buying real estate.[31] An August 2005 front-page story examined the fact that lenders were selling more mortgages because investors wanted the securities that backed them.[32] James Hagerty wrote a front-page story on 11 March 2006 about the dangers of adjustable-rate mortgages.[33] In December 2006, a front-page article about the increase of delinquent sub-prime mortgages appeared, noting, 'If late payments and foreclosures continue to rise at a faster-than-expected pace, the pain could extend beyond homeowners and lenders to the investors who buy mortgage-backed securities.'[34]

Another *Journal* reporter, Jesse Eisinger, wrote extensively during this period about the risks posed by derivatives. After joining *Portfolio* in 2006, Eisinger repeatedly wrote about how derivatives might cause turmoil on Wall Street, going as far as to predict in a November 2007 cover story that Bear Stearns and Lehman Brothers would struggle to remain independent.[35]

Meanwhile, the *New York Times* and the *Washington Post* were sounding warnings of their own. In the *Times* on 3 October 2004, in a story headlined 'A Coming Nightmare of Homeownership?', Morgenson wrote, 'The most damaging legacy of Fannie Mae's years of unchecked growth may not be evident until the next significant economic slump.'[36] Alongside Morgenson's story that day was another on Fannie Mae, by Timothy L. O'Brien and Jennifer S. Lee, that said, 'If the company encounters serious setbacks, the impact on homeowners and the world's financial markets could be unpleasant.'[37]

When she wasn't writing about housing, Morgenson was detailing the continued excesses of executive compensation and the credit markets, two other areas widely covered with a critical eye by business journalists.

The *Times*' Henriques wrote a series of articles exposing instant lenders who preyed on military households, pushing high-cost loans with interest rates much higher than the norm.[38] Unlike many other pieces, her reporting set off a firestorm. Congress held hearings on the practice and passed laws to ban it.

Henriques believes she knows why regulators paid attention to her stories but ignored others about lending practices that were far worse because they were hurting investment portfolios. A friend of hers who works for a big institutional investor was called to Washington, DC, to speak to lawmakers before the first vote on the Bush administration's bailout plan in September 2008. The friend noticed that all of the televisions in Congressional offices were tuned to coverage of Capitol Hill on C-SPAN, not to CNBC or Fox Business Network. 'He said nothing had struck him so powerfully about how lawmakers had been cut off from what was happening on Wall Street,' Henriques says. 'As a business journalist, we were talking to a glass window. They were sealed off from what we were writing.'[39]

Also exploring the dangers on the horizon was the *Times*' Floyd Norris, whose coverage of creative accounting during this period was prescient. Time after time, he wrote about how companies, including Fannie Mae, were pushing regulators to relax standards and stretch the rules as far as they could, just a few years after

Enron's manipulation of accounting regulations helped push the company into bankruptcy court.[40]

The *Post*'s Pearlstein also shed light on the economy's pitfalls. At least someone noticed his work: Pearlstein won a 2008 Pulitzer Prize in commentary – the first ever given to a business columnist – for a series of columns about the impending economic turmoil.

These reporters weren't alone. Their colleagues at business magazines burrowed into the dangerous financial landscape and unearthed alarming stories as well.

Shawn Tully at *Fortune* raised serious questions about the housing market as far back as October 2002, when he wrote, 'U.S. housing prices are stretching the outer limits of what's reasonable and sustainable. Instead of cooling down, prices keep hurtling upward, defying the laws of economic gravity just as grievously as those unmentionable dot-coms once did.'[41]

In September 2004, Tully was back with a big story. The headline blared, 'Is the Housing Boom Over? Home Prices Have Gone Up for So Long That People Think They'll Never Come Down. But the Fundamentals Tell a Different Story – a Scary One.'[42] And in July 2005, Tully offered advice for how people near retirement could get the most from selling their houses in the 'overheated real estate market'.[43] In May 2006, Tully wrote about the beginning of the decline of the housing market.[44]

Not to be outdone, *Fortune*'s Bethany McLean – one of the first to expose Enron's problems – wrote two stories highly critical of Fannie Mae in early 2005.[45] And then there's Loomis' prophetic 1994 story about derivatives – the magazine trotted it out in mid-2008 and posted it on its home page.[46]

At *Businessweek*, banking and finance editor Mara Der Hovanesian chipped away as well. Her 11 September 2006 cover story, 'Nightmare Mortgages', was illustrated by a snake slowly squeezing the life out of a home. It covered everything from deceptive loan practices to investors willing to buy risky loan portfolios.[47] The previous year, Der Hovanesian wrote about derivatives, essentially warning about a pending credit meltdown. 'Surprises similar to Enron and WorldCom – large, investment-grade companies that fall from grace overnight – could roil markets,' she wrote in a May 2005 story.[48]

Other *Businessweek* articles hit Wall Street equally hard. An April 2006 piece titled 'Mortgage Lenders: Who's Most at Risk' exposed the sub-prime lending problems likely to face many finance companies.[49] A June 2006 *Businessweek* cover story raised warnings about Wall Street's enthusiastic embrace of risk.[50] And the magazine regularly published shorter stories about potential economic problems on the horizon.

So if business journalists did such a good job sounding the alarm about the nation's economic house of cards, why did its collapse seem to come as such a shock? Why wasn't anyone listening? The reading public wants to read only what it wants to believe. 'The notion that the business press wasn't paying attention is wrong, and the assertion that we were asleep at the switch is wrong,' noted Brauchli. 'We were attentive. We were aggressive. We were aware. We wrote abundantly. But it is very hard to get the public's attention for stories warning of complex financial risks in the middle of a roaring, populist bull market.'[51]

I believe that some readers – not all – now understand that business journalists can give them the information they need. That's why financial news services such as Bloomberg, Reuters, the *Financial Times*, and the *Wall Street Journal* have continued to grow and expand during the last five years while other media have scaled back.

The strong coverage continued through the crisis. In 2009 alone, the Pulitzer Prize selection committee picked five finalists in various categories that produced coverage related to the economy. The *New York Times* was lauded in the public service category for 'its comprehensive coverage of the economic meltdown of 2008, setting a standard for depth and sophistication while making the arcane world of finance and banking accessible to an often bewildered public'. Robert O'Harrow Jr and Brady Dennis of the *Washington Post* were finalists in the explanatory reporting category, in which the judges noted 'their vivid, richly documented explanation of why AIG, the insurance industry giant, nearly collapsed and what lessons the crisis holds for the nation's policymakers'.

In national reporting, the *Wall Street Journal* staff was praised for 'its highly detailed coverage of the collapse of America's financial system, explicating key decisions, capturing the sense of calamity and charting the human toll', while columnist Paul Krugman of the *New York Times* was a finalist in the commentary category for 'his prophetic columns on economic peril during a year of financial calamity, blending the scholarly knowledge of a distinguished economist with the skill of a wordsmith'. In editorial writing, Charles Lane of the *Post* was a finalist for 'his succinct and insightful editorials on the nation's economic collapse, zeroing in on problems and offering solutions with a steady voice of reason'.[52] In no other year has one topic dominated the Pulitzer finalists.

Despite the strong reporting about business and the economy, I worry about future coverage. Most mainstream media outlets have cut back on their coverage of business and the economy. Even some of the publications mentioned in this chapter, such as *Fortune*, have downsized and cut back on the number of issues they'll publish. The fear is that fewer stories – particularly investigative stories – will get published. Daily newspapers have virtually given up on aggressive, hard-hitting business journalism by eliminating their business sections and chunks of their business news desks.

Those fears are soothed by the growth of non-traditional business media such as blogs and websites, which seem to be taking up the slack. Matt Taibbi's 2009 writing about Goldman Sachs in, of all places, *Rolling Stone* shows that hard-hitting business journalism can appear anywhere.[53] In addition, wire services such as Reuters and Bloomberg have remained strong and have added staff. Reuters created in 2009 a team of reporters and editors to do investigative work, and the Associated Press produced an ambitious series of stories spanning five weeks examining how the economic meltdown and the Great Recession have changed everything from Wall Street to Main Street.

I'm bullish on business journalism. It has covered the most important story in the world for the past decade with great analysis and prescience. To say otherwise is to ignore what is happening in newsrooms across the country, and to ignore other factors.

Notes

1 Chris Roush (2009) 'Unheeded Warnings', *American Journalism Review*, January, pp. 34–9.
2 Dean Starkman (2009) 'Power Problem', *Columbia Journalism Review*, June, pp. 24–30.
3 Stieg Larsson (2009) *The Girl With the Dragon Tattoo*, New York: Vintage Books, p. 102.
4 Catherine Rampbell (2010) 'Lax Oversight Caused Crisis', *New York Times*, 3 January, p. A1.
5 Simon Dumenco (2008) 'Punish Wall Street? Yes. But What About Its Partner in Crime, the Kool-Aid-Drinking Financial Media?', *Advertising Age*, 29 September, p. 30.
6 Howard Kurtz (2008) 'Press May Own a Share in Financial Mess', *Washington Post*, 6 October, p. C1.
7 Carol Loomis (1994) 'The Risk That Won't Go Away', *Fortune*, 7 March, pp. 40–50.
8 'Fannie Mae Enron?', *Wall Street Journal,* 4 October 2004, p. A16.
9 Gretchen Morgenson (2007) 'Mortgages May Be Messier Than You Think', *New York Times,* 4 March, p. C1.
10 Steve Pearlstein (2007) 'Credit Market's Weight Puts Economy on Shaky Ground', *Washington Post*, 1 August, p. D1.
11 Allan Sloan (2008) Personal interview, 17 October.
12 Gregory S. Miller (2006) 'The Press As a Watchdog for Accounting Fraud', *Journal of Accounting Research*, December, 44 (5), pp. 1001–33.
13 Marcus Brauchli (2008) Personal interview, 20 October.
14 Erin Arvedlund (2001) 'Don't Ask, Don't Tell: Bernie Madoff Is So Secretive, He Even Asks Investors to Keep Mum', *Barron's*, 7 May, p. 26.
15 Howard J. Carswell (1938) 'Business News Coverage', *Public Opinion Quarterly*, October, 2 (4), pp. 613–21.
16 W.M. Pinkerton (1950) 'Businessmen and the Press', *Harvard Business Review*, May, 28 (3), pp. 25–32.
17 Gerald M. Loeb (1966) 'Flaws in Financial Reporting', *Columbia Journalism Review*, Spring, pp. 37–9.
18 Chris Welles (1973) 'The Bleak Wasteland of Financial Journalism', *Columbia Journalism Review*, July/August, pp. 40–9.
19 Herbert Stein (1975) 'Media Distortions: A Former Official's View', *Columbia Journalism Review,* March/April, pp. 37–41.
20 William McPhatter (1980) 'Introduction', in William McPhatter (ed.) *The Business Beat: Its Impact and Its Problems*, Indianapolis: Bobbs-Merrill Educational Publishing, p. xii.
21 R.E. Cheney (1991) 'Cheering on the Scoundrels', *Nieman Reports*, Fall, 45 (3), pp. 18–19.
22 Merrill Goozner (2000) 'Blinded By the Boom: What's Missing in the Coverage of the New Economy?', *Columbia Journalism Review*, November/December, pp. 23–7.
23 Diana B. Henriques (2000) 'What Journalists Should Be Doing About Business Coverage – But Aren't', *Harvard International Journal of Press/Politics*, 5 (2), pp. 118–21.
24 Patrick Barta (2000) 'Fannie Mae Posts 15% Earnings Gain for the Quarter — Solid Results Are Clouded By Questions Involving Methods of Accounting', *Wall Street Journal,* 14 July 2000, p. A2.
25 Marcus Brauchli (2008) Personal interview, 20 October.
26 Jathon Sapsford and Patrick Barta (2002) 'Precarious Balances: Despite the Recession, Americans Continue to Be Avid Borrowers', *Wall Street Journal*, 2 January 2002, p. A1.
27 Patrick Barta (2002) 'Saturation Scenario: Will Fannie Mae, Freddie Mac Hit Limits in Growth?', *Wall Street Journal*, 6 August, p. A1.
28 Patrick Barta (2002) 'Mortgage Mismatch: Home Refinancings Widen Fannie's Risk', *Wall Street Journal*, 17 September, p. C1.
29 Patrick Barta and Ruth Simon (2003) 'Furor Greets Bid to Alter System of Closing Costs on Mortgages', *Wall Street Journal*, 19 August, p. A1.
30 Patrick Barta, John D. McKinnon, and Gregory Zuckerman (2003) 'Behind Freddie Mac's Troubles: A Strategy to Take on More Risk', *Wall Street Journal*, 22 September, p. A1.
31 James R. Hagerty and Ruth Simon (2005) 'As Prices Rise, Homeowners Go Deep in Debt to Buy Real Estate', *Wall Street Journal*, 23 May, p. A1.

32 Ruth Simon, James R. Hagerty and James T. Areddy (2005) 'Housing-Bubble Talk Doesn't Scare Off Foreigners', *Wall Street Journal*, 24 August, p. A1.

33 James Hagerty (2006) 'The Home-Mortgage Muddle; Some Borrowers Are Confused by Terms of Adjustable-Rate Loans', *Wall Street Journal,* 11 March 2006, p. B4.

34 Ruth Simon and James R. Hagerty (2006) 'More Borrowers With Risky Loans Are Falling Behind', *Wall Street Journal*, 5 December, p. A1.

35 Jesse Eisinger (2007) 'Wall Street Requiem', *Condé Nast Portfolio*, November, pp. 178–81.

36 Gretchen Morgenson (2004) 'A Coming Nightmare of Homeownership?', *New York Times*, 3 October, p. C1.

37 Timothy L. O'Brien and Jennifer S. Lee (2004) 'A Seismic Shift Under the House of Fannie Mae', *New York Times*, 3 October, p. C1.

38 Diana B. Henriques (2004) 'Needing Cash, Veterans Sign Over Pensions', *New York Times*, 29 December, p. C1.

39 Diana B. Henriques (2008) Personal interview, 21 October.

40 Floyd Norris (2004) 'A Possible Case Of Fudging Profit to Match Desires', *New York Times*, 24 September, p. B6.

41 Shawn Tully (2002) 'Is This House Worth $1.2 Million?', *Fortune*, 28 October, pp. 58–72.

42 Shawn Tully (2004) 'Is the Housing Boom Over?', *Fortune*, 20 September, p. 106.

43 Shawn Tully (2005) 'Is It Time to Cash Out?', *Fortune,* 11 July, pp. 54–60.

44 Shawn Tully (2006) 'Welcome to the Dead Zone', *Fortune*, 5 May, pp. 94–102.

45 Bethany McLean (2005) 'The Fall of Fannie Mae', *Fortune*, 24 January, pp. 122–40.

46 Carol Loomis (1994) 'The Risk That Won't Go Away', *Fortune*, 7 March, pp. 40–50.

47 Mara Der Hovanesian (2006) 'Nightmare Mortgages: They Promise the American Dream', *Businessweek*, 11 September, pp. 70–2.

48 Mara Der Hovanesian (2005) 'Taking Risks to Extremes: Will Derivatives Cause a Major Blowup in the World's Credit Markets?', *Businessweek*, 23 May, p. 96.

49 Mara Der Hovanesian (2006) 'Mortgage Lenders: Who's Most at Risk?', *Businessweek*, 24 April, pp. 50–2.

50 Emily Thornton (2006) 'Inside Wall Street's Culture of Risk', *Businessweek*, 12 June, pp. 52–8.

51 Brauchli (2008) Personal interview, 20 October.

52 The 2009 finalists are listed at www.pulitzer.org/awards/2009

53 Matthew Taibbi (2009) 'The Great American Bubble Machine', *Rolling Stone*, 9 July, pp. 52–4, 58–61, 98–101.

3

THE US MEDIA AND THE 2009 STIMULUS PACKAGE

Anya Schiffrin

The US financial crisis of 2008 was the biggest economic story to hit the media in years, putting subjects like unemployment, inequality, and Keynesian economics on the front page for months. But the conversation was deeply divided, with the liberal wing of the Democratic Party pushing for a government stimulus package to restart the economy focusing on increased expenditures, and Republicans supporting tax cuts. Centrists in both parties supported a bank bailout, while conservatives and liberals were sceptical. In this situation, the way the media understood the policy debate and framed the options that were available gives us insight into how US policies are debated and shaped.

One of the standard criticisms of the business press is that, like journalism generally, the coverage is too focused on day-to-day events, and does not devote enough space to analysis and the big picture. This chapter is based on a study carried out by Anya Schiffrin and Ryan Fagan analysing press coverage of the American Reinvestment Act of 2009. Examining articles in the mainstream US media about the $787 billion government spending package that was passed soon after President Obama took office, we found that the press mostly reported on the political process rather than the economics of the stimulus.[1] Government and businesses sources were quoted the most, and media came a bit late to reporting on the important role that government spending can play in helping troubled economies. They focused on subjects like waste, executive pay caps, green energy, and protectionism, all matters that economists generally feel are of second-order importance compared with the more important issue of whether such spending could prevent a deep economic downturn.

Historic criticism of the role of the business press

While the media generally is lauded for its important role as a Fourth Estate, the business press has been viewed as the 'stepchild' (Henriques, 2000). For decades, business and financial journalists have been accused of being captured by sources and of parroting the conventional wisdom of the free market and the investment community, which has historically been its readership (Parsons, 1989).[2]

More recent critiques argued that the journalists covering economics did not understand the issues they covered, neither the larger macro indicators that economists actually look at nor basic macroeconomic principles (Parker, 1997).

Added to concerns over lack of competence are accusations that the average business journalist becomes tainted by constant exposure to Wall Street and comes to share its mindset. The fact that many business journalists lack the analytic training to critique prevalent business perspectives makes intellectual capture easier, as does a dominant orthodoxy in the business community. Moreover, print media depends on readership, and readership of specialized business outlets is disproportionately drawn from investors who share similar views and biases. The result is that the business press is often unable to educate the wider public (Doyle, 2006).

Like their readers in the markets who look at daily stock prices and quarterly returns instead of at the long-term prospects of the businesses whose shares they trade, business journalists are too focused on reporting short-term events. This mindset naturally is carried over when they look at broader policy issues. And when journalists do write longer features, the emphasis is on people rather than ideas, including human interest stories that are short on analysis. The business press has been criticized, too, for ignoring the common man in favour of stories that glorify successful businessmen. In the run-up to the crisis, many journalists produced glowing profiles of corporate CEOs whose fortunes – and the companies that they had been allegedly managing so brilliantly – were quickly reversed once the crisis started (Fraser, 2009; Starkman, 2009).

Press critiques during the financial crisis

The economic crisis that began in 2008 led to increased interest in the role of the press. While some journalists defended the role of the business press, others launched into withering self-criticism, just as many did after the collapse of Enron and the bursting of the tech bubble in the late nineties. Indeed, crises concentrate the mind: as ordinary investors lose money in real estate or the stock market, there is often an outcry in which the press is accused of not having seen it coming (Doyle, 2006) or, worse, of having actively served to cheerlead the bubble, as was the case after the housing and tech bubbles of the nineties (Madrick, 2002; Sherman, 2002).

Since the business media has gained readership/viewership, there is now even more interest in its performance, in part because as more Americans invested in stocks they became more interested in following companies (Doyle, 2006). The *Wall Street Journal* (Fitzgerald, 2010) has, for instance, become a national newspaper, with a readership of 4.3 million, and CNBC, a cable station focusing on business news, has an average viewership of 215,000 (Insider's Blog, 2010).[3] The rise of the business media has naturally been accompanied by a spate of articles examining its performance (Starkman, 2009). The Internet has also made it easier for journalists to publish immediate critiques of the day's press coverage at sites like *The Audit*.[4]

Unique opportunity

Despite the widespread anecdotal criticism, there is not much academic research on business/economic journalism. The literature that exists is mainly impressionistic, and there is a dearth of content analysis aimed at testing the hypotheses put forward in this literature. Because of the extensive coverage of the financial crisis, press coverage of the US stimulus provided a unique opportunity to examine press coverage of economic issues and, with many publications covering the same event over several years, we can begin to look for patterns.

Questions we tried to answer were: could the assertions of the critics of the business press be substantiated? Was the press biased? Did it examine alternatives to the policies pursued by the government? What were the sources used? Who did journalists quote? Did journalists examine the substance of the macroeconomic policies or focus more on the political process, such as whether the stimulus would get through Congress? A secondary point of interest was whether the media played an agenda-setting role rather than following the discussion already taking place, e.g. within Congress.

Our study examined press coverage of the stimulus package from 2 January to 5 March 2009 and then from 1 July to 1 September 2009. We chose these time periods in order to assess coverage before the American Reinvestment and Recovery was passed on 16 February, and a few months after to see how the coverage had changed, once it was clear that the US economy had not improved much. All the major papers and wire services were included.

Overview findings

The findings were consistent with the scant literature on the subject and, for the most part, with our hypotheses. Unsurprisingly, the wire services were the most fact-based and the least opinionated about the stimulus. The bread and butter of their coverage was their reporting on the events of the day. Also unsurprising was the fact that the *Wall Street Journal* editorial page and *Barron's* columnists (McTague, 2009a, 2009b) came out against the stimulus, mostly preferring tax cuts and warning of a possible upsurge in protectionism as a result of the 'Buy America' provisions within the bill. By contrast, the *New York Times* was broadly in favour of the stimulus, although its most high-profile writer on economics, the renowned op-ed columnist Paul Krugman, said repeatedly that it needed to be much bigger. *Financial Times* writer Clive Crook (2009a, 2009b) also argued that the stimulus should be bigger, quicker acting, and 'front loaded'.

The study classified the articles as news or editorial, but some subcategories emerged. First were spot news stories that were blow-by-blow accounts of the news that broke each day (Cowan, 2009; Fritze and Wolf, 2009). These overlapped with the second category, which consisted of stories that emphasized the process and politics of the passage of the American Recovery Act, such as Democrats' attempts to garner Republican support (Knowlton and Baker, 2009; Otterman, 2009). The third category was news stories that gave a detailed breakdown of the contents of the bill. These stories often looked at different sectors, such as high tech or education, to see how they would fare (Fox, 2009), or at different regions to see how much funding they would get (Deines, 2009; Jayakrishna, 2009; Kocieniewski, 2009; McCabe, 2009).

The fourth category was big-picture economic analyses that explained how stimulus packages are supposed to work, questioned whether they are effective, and discussed the ideas of economist John Maynard Keynes and the evidence as to whether government spending helps get countries out of recessions (Andrews and Herszenhorn, 2009). The fifth were editorials, op-eds, columns, and other opinion pieces (Crook, 2009a–b; Krugman, 2009a–e; Mankiw, 2009) that often came out for or against the bill, and in some cases suggested that tax cuts would be more effective than increasing government spending. Many of these opinion pieces warned against protectionist measures in the bill, and some urged lawmakers not to include caps on executive compensation (*Chicago Tribune*, 2009a). There were also miscellaneous articles such as those that discussed the market reaction to the news of the stimulus (Read, 2009) or the overseas response to the prospect of a US stimulus.

The wire service coverage was mostly focused on the first category. Reuters, AP, and Bloomberg tended to cover the ins and outs of the daily news events, while providing some analysis and opinion pieces. Newspapers such as the *Boston Globe*, *Chicago Tribune*, and the *New York Times* looked at how their localities would be affected. *Businessweek* also examined sectors such as high tech or green energy. *Time* magazine did some big-picture macroeconomic pieces (Grunwald, 2009a, 2009b; Sachs, 2009) and *Newsweek* ran some columns by big names. There were also several columns that took a scolding tone, warning of the dangers of a bill loaded down with pork or unnecessary spending and noting that the stimulus would not immediately inject much money into the economy (*Wall Street Journal*, 2009a). 'The stimulus package is turning into a big, opaque mess with questionable job-creation impact,' Jack and Suzie Welch (2009) cautioned in an opinion piece in *Businessweek*.

In general, the media tends to report the news rather than anticipate it, and this is certainly true of the coverage of the stimulus. The study suggests the press did not play much of a role in setting the agenda for the national debate. Instead of discussing the likely effectiveness of the stimulus, most of the articles before passage simply focused on whether or not it would pass, ignoring whether it would be effective and the limited effectiveness of the Bush tax cut. But months after the bill was passed, when the recession continued, the conservative press renewed its criticism of the stimulus. However, these critiques did not look at what unemployment or output would have been but for the stimulus. Much of the press coverage consisted of repeating conservative criticisms, rather than engaging in a deeper analysis.

In keeping with the ideology of the *Wall Street Journal*'s editorial page, a 24 February op-ed in the *WSJ* by Tom Hayes and Michael S. Malone (2009) pronounced the bill a failure *just one week* after it was passed. They wrote:

> The passage of the $787 billion stimulus bill has so far failed to stimulate anything but greater market pessimism. This suggests to us that the strategy

behind the American Reinvestment and Recovery Act is wrong – and worse, that the weapons it is using to fight the recession are obsolete.

After the stimulus was passed in February 2009, unemployment continued to rise.[5] As it crept higher in the first half of 2009, the press began to focus more on whether the stimulus had been effective. More articles in July focused on this point than in the earlier part of 2009 that we studied.[6] Although there were fewer articles in July than earlier in the year, the coverage that did exist was more contemplative.

Even so, relatively few of these pieces pointed out that only a small percentage of the stimulus money had been spent by then so it was premature to judge whether it was effective. An exception was a *Financial Times* piece by Bruce Bartlett (Bartlett, 2009). Instead, a number of the articles argued that since the stimulus had not worked, the US government should not consider a second one (Marshall, 2009).

Even when conceding that it was too early to tell if the stimulus would work, the *Chicago Tribune* (2009b) ran an editorial against a second one: 'Last winter, our leaders bet $787 billion they could alleviate our economic woes. If that wager pays off, another wager won't be needed. If it doesn't another won't be wise.' Bloomberg also ran an article quoting economists who were opposed to a second stimulus, and other news organizations published surveys finding that the majority of economists surveyed were opposed to a second stimulus.

There was a spate of articles looking at specifics and saying the money had not been well spent. One example is the coverage of a July report by the Government Accountability Office saying the money was not used as intended. An article in *USA Today* (Kelley, 2009) led with: 'Under pressure to spend stimulus money quickly, many states are using the federal funds for short-term projects and to fill budget gaps rather than spending on long-term improvements, according to a report by congressional investigators.'

An article by Jane Sasseen (2009) in *Businessweek* lamented that businessmen were 'unnerved' by the 'flawed legislation' that had resulted from the stimulus. 'The $787 billion stimulus program has been derided as a grab bag of initiatives that haven't stemmed job losses,' Sasseen wrote. Paul Krugman was one of the lone voices who kept pushing for more spending.

The differences between the perspectives of Sasseen and Krugman, as well as the underlying economic models, received scant attention. Krugman, like most Keynesian economists, argued that government spending would stimulate the economy *even if the investment projects were not well designed*. The failure to design the projects optimally might affect long-run growth, but not short-run job creation. Sasseen reflected the financial press's concern over 'confidence' – a notion that the press and financial markets are preoccupied with but which Krugman and many economists have largely discredited.[7] Interestingly, those in the financial press *never* responded to these critiques. It was seemingly a one-sided debate. But since the press was dominated by those from the business and financial community, their views prevailed for a long time.

In keeping with the tendency of the media to report daily events rather than look forward or do agenda-setting, we noted a drop-off in coverage in July compared with the earlier part of the year when the stimulus bill was being passed.[8]

Taking into account the op-eds and editorials, the *New York Times* ran the greatest number of articles on the stimulus, and was largely for it. Conversely, the *Wall Street Journal* was against it. But outside of these two publications, the coverage was fairly balanced (see Table 3.1).

As well as several supportive editorials, the *New York Times* ran analysis pieces by David Sanger, and economics writers David Leonhardt and Edmund Andrews, among others.

Columnists and op-ed writers in the Murdoch-owned *Barron's* and *Wall Street Journal* were almost uniformly opposed to the stimulus.[9] Before the ARA was signed into law, their editorials and columns warned that it was not going to help the economy recover and would merely run up the country's deficit. The editorial page argued that Keynesian ideas of stimulus don't work in general and that, even if they did, this particular piece of legislation was poorly designed. The *WSJ* cited economist Robert Barro's argument that a dollar of government spending merely replaces a dollar of private-sector spending and therefore does not add to the total amount of stimulus. However, the page (*Wall Street Journal*, 2009a) omitted to mention that Barro's theory was meant to apply to economies with full employment – a situation that was not the case during the Great Recession of 2008.

TABLE 3.1 Overall bias by publication: articles and editorials

Newspaper	Total articles	Articles w/net bias	% Negative
USA Today	45	10 (22.2%)	6 (60%)
AP	147	19 (12.9%)	14 (73.6%)
Bloomberg	42	6 (14.2%)	0 (0%)
Dow Jones	55	2 (3.6%)	2 (100%)
FT	51	10 (19.6%)	7 (70%)
LA Times	11	7 (63.6%)	5 (71.4%)
Reuters	52	2 (3.8%)	2 (100%)
WSJ	72	33 (45.8%)	31 (93.9%)
Chicago Tribune	35	16 (45.7%)	13 (81.2%)
NY Times	123	53 (43%)	16 (30.1%)
Boston Globe	61	29 (47.5%)	16 (55.1%)
Barron's	11	8 (72.7%)	8 (100%)
Businessweek	4	4 (100%)	2 (50%)
Fortune	2	0 (0%)	0 (0%)
Newsweek	4	3 (75%)	2 (66.6%)
Time	2	0 (0%)	0 (0%)
TOTAL	717	202 (28.1%)	124 (61.4%)★
TOTAL W/O NYT	594	149 (25%)	108 (72.5%)★★
TOTAL W/O WSJ	645	169 (26.2%)	93 (55%)

★Statistically different from 50% at the 5% level (p=.020)
★★Statistically different from 50% at the 1% level (p<.0001)

Using the feisty tone that is characteristic of the section, the *WSJ*'s editorial page (2009b) called the stimulus 'a political wonder that manages to spend money on just about every pent-up Democratic proposal of the last 40 years'. A few days later, US Senator Tom Coburn (2009) wrote that the bill 'is loaded with old-fashioned pork ... the bill not only fails to stimulate the economy, but could seriously delay economic recovery'. The *Journal* also focused on the things it cared about, such as the 'Buy America' provision, pork, pay caps for executives, and the need for tax cuts (Solomon and Maremont, 2009).

As well as the *Wall Street Journal* and *Barron's*, the *Chicago Tribune* was a major critic of the proposed stimulus, but its criticisms were mainly confined to the editorial and op-ed sections. As early as January 2009, the paper called for tax cuts and later in the month said there was little evidence that stimulus works. In a February editorial, the *Chicago Tribune* said that President Obama had exaggerated the dangers of the downturn in order to persuade Congress to vote for the stimulus. As an alternative, the paper counselled patience: 'The down-turn may do the economy some long-run good ... the most important asset Americans have is patience, keeping in mind that bad as things are they will eventually get better' (*Chicago Tribune*, 2009a). Interestingly, the *Chicago Tribune* was very much against the New Deal in the 1930s when it was owned by Colonel McCormick (Smith, 1997). Despite the paper's optimism about the downturn, it too felt the effects, filing for bankruptcy in April 2010.

Sources

The dependence of business/economics journalists on sources within the business community has been blamed for much of the poor reporting on the economic crisis (O'Connor, 2009). As mentioned, business/economic reporting is dominated by short-term stories about economic indicators, corporate earnings, and the financial markets, and not by stories about the larger social implications of the events being described. For these kinds of short-term stories, the sources that journalists call upon and quote are traders, fund managers, government officials, analysts, businessmen, and endless PR people, often referred to derisively as 'flacks'. The relationships journalists cultivate can and do lead to scoops and exclusives. However, the need to keep supply lines of information open, as part of the newsgathering process, also breeds a coziness that naturally inhibits hard-hitting, critical reporting.

Given that the stimulus was a story generated by the government, and that the media focused a lot on whether the Act would be passed, it is not surprising that government sources were quoted most frequently. Their comments were often confined to predictions as to whether the stimulus would pass, and they provided details on the negotiations taking place in Washington. However, there was also a tendency for government sources to push their agenda with respect to the stimulus package.

Table 3.2 provides a complete breakdown by publication of the types of sources quoted. Unsurprisingly, government sources were quoted the most frequently, followed by sources from business. There were two main types of business sources.

TABLE 3.2 Use of sources by publication: non-editorials

Newspaper	Total articles	Market/ Business		Economist/ Academic		Government		NGO		Public	
USA Today	37	11	(29.7%)	9	(24.3%)	29	(78.3%)	3	(8.1%)	1	(2.2%)
AP	147	20	(13.6%)	11	(7.4%)	107	(72.2%)	5	(3.4%)	4	(2.7%)
Bloomberg	40	9	(22.5%)	7	(17.5%)	35	(87.5%)	0	(0.0%)	3	(7.5%)
Dow Jones	55	11	(20.0%)	4	(7.2%)	37	(67.2%)	0	(0.0%)	0	(0.0%)
FT	38	7	(18.4%)	11	(28.9%)	28	(73.6%)	2	(5.2%)	0	(0.0%)
LA Times	3	0	(0.0%)	0	(0.0%)	3	(100.0%)	0	(0.0%)	1	(33.3%)
Reuters	52	15	(28.8%)	4	(7.6%)	33	(63.4%)	3	(5.7%)	1	(1.9%)
WSJ	43	11	(25.5%)	5	(11.6%)	34	(79.0%)	0	(0.0%)	1	(2.3%)
Chicago Tribune	22	5	(22.7%)	3	(13.6%)	21	(95.4%)	7	(31.8%)	3	(13.6%)
NY Times	87	22	(25.2%)	16	(18.3%)	76	(87.3%)	27	(31.0%)	9	(10.3%)
Boston Globe	40	8	(20.0%)	10	(25.0%)	33	(82.5%)	12	(30.0%)	4	(10.0%)
Barron's	4	3	(75.0%)	2	(50.0%)	1	(25.0%)	2	(50.0%)	0	(0.0%)
Businessweek	2	2	(100.0%)	1	(50.0%)	1	(50.0%)	1	(25.0%)	0	(0.0%)
Fortune	2	0	(0.0%)	2	(100.0%)	2	(100.0%)	1	(50.0%)	0	(0.0%)
Newsweek	2	0	(0.0%)	0	(0.0%)	2	(100.0%)	0	(0.0%)	0	(0.0%)
Time	2	1	(50.0%)	0	(0.0%)	1	(50.0%)	2	(100.0%)	0	(0.0%)
All Weeklies	12	6	(50.0%)	5	(41.6%)	7	(58.3%)	6	(50.0%)	0	(0.0%)
LAT, CT, NYT, BG	152	35	(23.0%)	29	(19.0%)	133	(87.5%)	46	(30.2%)	17	(11.1%)
Daily Financials (FT, WSJ)	81	18	(22.2%)	16	(19.7%)	62	(76.5%)	2	(2.4%)	1	(1.2%)
Financial Wires (Bloom., DJ, Reuters)	147	35	(23.8%)	15	(10.2%)	105	(71.4%)	3	(2.0%)	4	(2.7%)
TOTAL	**576**	**125**	**(21.7%)**	**85**	**(14.7%)**	**443**	**(76.9%)**	**65**	**(11.3%)**	**27**	**(4.7%)**

The first consisted of representatives of business associations and large businesses who had views (and lobbied as such) on the stimulus package. These sources were particularly interested in funding for infrastructure spending, much of it green, that could end up in the hands of their businesses.

The second category of sources, which we defined as being from Wall Street, a corporation, or professional association, was overwhelmingly opposed to the stimulus. Of those that were biased one way or another (29.1 per cent), 59 per cent were opposed. In this context, it might seem that academic economists would be a good source of information for journalists covering the stimulus. But although the journalists may have spoken with economists, they did not quote them very often. Economists were quoted less than most other kinds of sources. Unsurprisingly, when they were quoted it was for their opinions and analysis rather than straight news. Economists expressed an opinion either for or against the stimulus in 44.9 per cent of the articles we looked at, and in 45.5 per cent of those articles economists expressed opinions that were critical of the stimulus. By contrast, only 27.9 per cent of the quotes from government sources were critical.[10]

This slant in coverage ultimately put political pressure on the government, limiting any further measures the government could take. As US job growth didn't return, with unemployment remaining around 9 per cent, and the economy showed few signs of returning to growth, the government and Federal Reserve tried different measures. Given Republican opposition, a second stimulus was not an option and Obama's attempt to get a job bill passed in October 2011 failed to pass the Senate. The Federal Reserve continued with its policy of quantitative easing. Ironically, with fiscal stimulus off the table, both of these measures were often referred to as 'stimulus' measures by journalists, who, in their writing, noted that Republican opposition was going to doom the jobs bill.

Conclusion

The US press coverage of the 2009 stimulus, by and large, confirms existing critiques of business journalism. It mostly focused on day-by-day news events and the details of the proposed package, relied largely on mainstream sources, and in many cases reflected a pro-business mindset. There was some exceptional reporting that tried to look at big-picture economics questions and lay out possible alternatives for an economic recovery. Indeed, a close reading of the *Financial Times* and the *New York Times* would certainly have given readers an understanding of many of the key economics questions at stake. But much of the coverage focused on the political process and the familiar debates about tax cuts and protectionism, and so came across as fairly pedestrian and predictable. Partly due to the short length of many of the articles, there was little deep analysis and the press did not do very much to advance the debate or lay out a new agenda for discussion. Some reporters even felt that although the stimulus coverage was lacking in the months we studied, it got even worse after the stimulus was passed. Said one:

> The coverage since the stimulus was passed was spectacularly awful. It ranged from meaningless 'gotcha' stories to insignificant 'gotcha' stories. You can argue that the stimulus is a sugar rush and too short-term but you can't say that stimulus spending doesn't stimulate. Saying that goes against what all economists know. But as a reporter you need to present both sides and so you have these he-said/she-said stories with people quoting what is total lunacy.
> *(Author interview, June 2010)*

In retrospect, coverage of the politics, the economics, and the details of the bill did not raise issues that should have been central to the policy debate in 2008, and these deficiencies in coverage may have contributed to weaknesses in the subsequent policy debate. It should have been clear that there was considerable uncertainty about the length and depth of the downturn. For obvious reasons, both those in the financial markets responsible for the crisis and those in the Administration responsible for steering a recovery wanted to act as cheerleaders for a recovery. Hence, forecasts from these sources should have been treated with scepticism. Analysis should have focused on the best way of designing policies in response to such uncertainties, and exploring alternative contingencies. That was why some economists had focused on automatic stabilizers – programmes such as unemployment insurance and state financial aid that would release money if and only if the economy was weak.

Journalists should have asked: if the downturn is longer and deeper than the optimists believe, what will the consequences be? What happens if it is shallower and shorter? There's an asymmetry: presumably spending could be cut, or interest rates, if it appeared that the economy was becoming overheated. But if things turned out worse, it would be difficult to get money going into the pipeline.

This, in some sense, turned out to be the biggest failure of the political coverage: the recognition that, given the political divide, it might be very difficult to pass a second stimulus. This was to be Obama's only shot. In that context, having a stimulus that was too small, too short, and not well enough designed was a critical flaw.

Looking over the coverage, it is remarkable how much of it focused on details of political importance (the 'Buy America' provision) relative to those that were of economic importance. Here, the two essential issues were (a) the speed with which the money would get into the system; and (b) the relative size of the different 'multipliers', i.e. some kinds of spending (or tax cuts) stimulated the economy more than others. An analysis of these multipliers, and the speed with which money entered into the system, should have been at the core of all of the economics coverage.

Good coverage, too, would have made it clear why economists differed, and why making economic judgments was so difficult. There hadn't been a downturn as deep or long-lasting since the Great Depression, and the economy had changed in important ways in the subsequent 80 years. Coverage, especially analytic work, should have emphasized why making inferences from other experiences in the US was of limited relevance. Increasing government spending when the economy is at or near full employment has to lead to a decrease in some other spending.

Typically, the Fed, worried about an increase in inflation, raises interest rates. But when there is unemployment, government spending doesn't need to crowd out other spending, especially if, as now, the Fed is committed to maintaining interest rates at record low levels.

Almost none of the articles focused on the counterfactual, i.e. what would have happened had there *not* been a stimulus, especially after the stimulus was passed. The Administration had been overly optimistic in its predictions that unemployment would peak at 10 per cent, and that the stimulus would bring unemployment down to 8 per cent or less. The Administration made a mistake, but it wasn't with the claim about the effectiveness of the stimulus – it was with their estimate of the severity of the downturn. The press should have made this clear, perhaps with a wider discussion of the reasons for the mistaken forecasts.

So, too, much of the discussion of waste in spending didn't focus on the counterfactual: not stimulating the economy would have led, according to the advocates of the stimulus, to a massive waste of resources, as the economy performed below its potential. The presumption in much of that debate was that the private sector was efficient, the government inefficient. That this presumption was still held, especially by less ideologically driven media, is remarkable, given that the private financial sector had just wasted hundreds of billions of dollars in misallocation of capital and mismanagement of risk – with an eventual total cost in the trillions of dollars. One might have hoped for at least an articulation of this interpretation.

This raises another set of criticisms. While many of the assessments of the details were important, especially in discussions before the bill was passed, the critical question in a democratic process of compromise is this: was the stimulus, flawed as it was, better than no stimulus at all? Too few of the articles attempted to make that kind of *bottom line* analysis.

Finally, we have repeatedly noted our disappointment with the failure of the press to take an agenda-setting role. It could and should have asked: how could the stimulus be used to help restructure the economy in a way that promoted long-run goals? Given that America was consuming too much before the crisis, did it make sense to have a third of the stimulus designed to encourage more consumption? If one were going to have to have tax cuts, would it have made more sense to have tax cuts to encourage investment? Among the underlying problems responsible for the crisis were the country's high level of inequality and the structural transformation that it was going through as it made the transition from manufacturing to a services-based economy. Could one design a stimulus that would at least help address these two issues?

By 2011, it became increasingly evident that the economy was still weak, and that another stimulus would be needed. But by then, the popular image of such measures had become so discredited that the Administration refused to use that term. The bill that it introduced, only small parts of which were eventually passed, was called the American Jobs Act of 2011.

As the economic slowdown ground on for years, there was a resurgence of interest in the broader question of whether stimulus packages work and whether the alternative, austerity, was the solution. Journalists looked overseas for examples.

The *New York Times* published articles saying that the austerity programmes in Greece and the United Kingdom failed in that they did not restart the economy. Columnists Krugman and Nick Kristof made some of the same points and the *New York Times* began weighing in with several editorials (2011b), even calling austerity a 'harmful quack cure' (2011a), and saying the 'bitter medicine is killing the patient' (2013).

As we read these pieces – and others like them – we wondered why it took so long for these opinions to appear in major newspapers. Had the journalists and editors on the news pages looked earlier for examples from history or for similar experiences around the world, their coverage might have been more insightful and informative. The Asian crisis of 1997–8, the Latin American banking crises of the 1980s, and Japan's decade of stagnation were obviously not the same as the 2007 Great Recession, but examples from those periods could certainly have informed the coverage of the American Reinvestment Act of 2009 and helped journalists write more expertly on the questions of stimulus and austerity.

Acknowledgements

Ryan Fagan, from Columbia University, was responsible for the quantitative work upon which much of this chapter is based. We'd also like to thank Morgan Korn for coding and assisting with some of the references for this article, and Carolyn Stauffer for doing some of the coding. Danfeng Wu, Jonathan Hulland, Eamon Kircher-Allen, and Matthew Purcell also did much of the research. Samantha Marshall and Joseph E. Stiglitz edited versions of this chapter.

Notes

1 For a complete breakdown of what was spent and when, please go to *recovery.gov* at: www.recovery.gov/Pages/default.aspx
2 Criticism of the business press dates back more than a century and has remained remarkably consistent over the last 100 years (Roush, 2010).
3 CNBC personalities Jim Cramer, host of the show *Mad Money*, and Rick Santelli garnered special criticism for being cheerleaders for the bubble. Jon Stewart famously provided a set of clips of poor CNBC coverage before the crisis, which seemed markedly incongruous with what subsequently happened – and how CNBC reported it. See the 4 March 2009 edition of *The Daily Show With Jon Stewart*, available online at www.thedailyshow.com/watch/wed-march-4-2009/cnbc-financial-advice (accessed 29 April 2013).
4 *The Audit*, published online by the *Columbia Journalism Review* at Columbia University in New York: www.cjr.org/the_audit/
5 It was 8.2 per cent in February, 9.4 per cent in July, and 9.7 per cent in August 2009, and hovered around that level for the next 12 months (United States Department of Labor, 2010).
6 84.3 per cent in July versus 41.2 per cent in earlier periods for articles and editorials; 88.9 per cent versus 37.4 per cent in earlier periods for non-editorials.
7 It is not that they necessarily deny the role of confidence, but that they seek to explain confidence in terms of, say, the level of unemployment or other 'real' economic variables. They are not sanguine that a speech asserting that the future is bright will have any lasting effect on the level of economic activity. This is important, because critics of

stimulus measures often emphasize that such spending will increase the deficit, and the increase in deficit will erode confidence. By contrast, austerity will reduce the deficit, and the reduction in the deficit will increase confidence and economic activity. While *none* of the standard models (including those used by the Administration, the Federal Reserve, or any of the macroeconomic forecasters) support this latter view, it has remained remarkably popular among those in the financial community and in conservative political circles.

8 Two articles per day compared with 21 per day in the earlier part of the year.

9 An exception was the column by Robert Shiller on 27 January 2009, which called for a bigger stimulus than the $825 billion being proposed (Shiller, 2009).

10 These are different with Chi-Square = 12.74 (2 degrees of freedom), p = .0017.

References

Andrews, E. and Herszenhorn, D. (2009) 'A Plan to Jump-Start Economy With No Instruction Manual', *New York Times*, 10 January.

Bartlett, B. (2009) 'We Do Not Need a Second Stimulus Plan', *Financial Times*, 5 July.

Chicago Tribune (2009a) 'Reverse Economics', *Chicago Tribune*, 17 February.

——(2009b) 'Stimulus II? No Way', *Chicago Tribune*, 7 July.

——(2009c) 'How Not to Fix Business', *Chicago Tribune*, 17 February.

Coburn, T. (2009) 'The Stimulus Package Is More Debt We Don't Need: Can Obama Really Defend This "Line By Line"?' *Wall Street Journal*, 4 February, p. A11.

Cowan, R. (2009) 'US Economic Stimulus Bill Moves Ahead in House', *Reuters*, 27 January.

Crook, C. (2009a) 'Obama's Shot in the Arm Is Too Small', *Financial Times*, 12 January, p. A10.

——(2009b) 'Raise the Stimulus', *Financial Times*, 28 January, p. A8.

Deines, K. (2009) 'Federal Stimulus Plan Projected to Create Or Save 11,000 Jobs in Montana Over Next 2 Years', *Associated Press*, 13 February.

Doyle, G. (2006) 'Financial News Journalism: A Post-Enron Analysis of Approaches Towards Economics and Financial News Production in the UK', *Journalism: Theory, Practice & Criticism*, 7 (4), pp. 433–52.

Fitzgerald, M. (2010) 'Media Audit: *Wall St. Journal* Readership Up Big Since Murdoch Takeover, While *N.Y. Times* Stays Flat', *Editor & Publisher*, 26 May.

Fox, M. (2009) 'Analysis – U.S. Stimulus Plan Would Pour Billions Into Health', *Reuters*, 29 January.

Fraser, M. (2009) 'Five Reasons for Crash Blindness', *British Journalism Review*, 20 (4), pp. 78–83.

Fritze, J. and Wolf, R. (2009) 'House, Senate Quickly Reaches $790B Stimulus Deal: Compromise Slashes Spending, Reduces Tax Cuts', *USA Today*, 12 February, p. A4.

Grunwald, M. (2009a) 'How to Spend a Trillion. One. Trillion. Dollars', *Time*, 26 January.

——(2009b) 'How to Spend the Stimulus', *Time*, 16 February.

Hayes, T. and Malone, M. (2009) 'Entrepreneurs Can Lead Us Out of the Crisis', *Wall Street Journal*, 24 February, p. A15.

Henriques, D. (2000) 'What Journalists Should Be Doing About Business Coverage – But Aren't', *Harvard International Journal of Press/Politics*, 5 (2), pp. 118–21.

Insider's Blog (2010) 'CNBC Is Bleeding Viewers', *StreetInsider*. Available at: www.street insider.com/Insiders+Blog/CNBC+Is+Bleeding+Viewers/5568261.html [Accessed 3 March 2012].

Jayakrishna, N. (2009) 'Mass. Gets $22 Million for Use in Energy-Saving Projects', *Boston Globe*, 22 July.

Kelley, M. (2009) 'Report: States Aren't Using Stimulus Funds As Intended', *USA Today*, 8 July.

Knowlton, B. and Baker, P. (2009) 'White House Pushing Stimulus Package', *New York Times*, 26 January.

Kocieniewski, D. (2009) 'Many Failing Roads, Little Repair Money', *New York Times*, 26 July.

Krugman, P. (2009a) 'The Obama Gap', *New York Times*, 9 January.
——(2009b) 'Ideas for Obama', *New York Times*, 12 January.
——(2009c) 'The Destructive Center', *New York Times*, 9 February.
——(2009d) 'That '30s Show', *New York Times*, 3 July.
——(2009e) 'The Stimulus Trap', *New York Times*, 10 July.
McCabe, K. (2009) 'Effects of Stimulus Plan Kick In: From Schools to Roads to Arts, Federal Funds Coming to Communities North of Boston', *Boston Globe*, 30 July.
McTague, J. (2009a) 'Too Big to Flail', *Barron's*, 12 January, p. B21.
——(2009b) 'Where's the Stimulus?' *Barron's*, 2 February.
Madrick, J. (2002) 'A Good Story Isn't Always the Right One to Tell', *Nieman Reports*, 56 (2), pp. 6–7.
Mankiw, G. (2009) 'Is Government Spending Too Easy An Answer?' *New York Times*, 11 January.
Marshall, S. (2009) 'Another Stimulus? The First One Has Barely Kicked In', *USA Today*, 14 July.
New York Times (2011a) 'Britain's Self-Inflicted Misery', *New York Times*, 14 October.
——(2011b) 'Britain's Failed Experiment, Repeated', *New York Times*, 3 December.
——(2013) 'Europe's Bitter Medicine', *New York Times*, 14 April.
O'Connor, R. (2009) 'Embedded Business Press Misses the Story of the Century', *Huffington Post*, 21 March. Available at: www.huffingtonpost.com/rory-oconnor/embedded-busi ness-press-m_b_167860.html [Accessed 27 January 2012].
Otterman, S. (2009) 'Republicans Are Resistant to Obama's Stimulus Plan', *New York Times*, 26 January.
Parker, R. (1997) *Journalism and Economics: The Tangled Webs of Profession, Narrative, and Responsibility in a Modern Democracy*. Discussion Paper D-25. Cambridge, MA: Joan Shorenstein Center, Harvard University.
Parsons, W. (1989) *The Power of the Financial Press*, New Jersey: Rutgers University Press.
Read, M. (2009) 'Stocks Fall As Investors Ask: Will Stimulus Work?' *Associated Press*, 12 February.
Roush, C. (2010) 'The Financial Press: It's Not As Bad As Its Reputation', in Schiffrin, A. (ed.) *Bad News: How the Business Press Missed the Story of the Century*, New York: The New Press, pp. 54–71.
Sachs, J. (2009) 'The Case for Bigger Government', *Time*, 19 January.
Sasseen, J. (2009) 'Obama Hurries, Business Worries: Executives Fret the Administration's Rush to Pass Reforms Will Produce Flawed Legislation', *Businessweek*, 27 July, p. 26.
Sherman, S. (2002) 'Enron: Uncovering the Uncovered Story', *Columbia Journalism Review*, 40 (6), pp. 22–8.
Shiller, R. (2009) 'Animal Spirits Depend on Trust: The Proposed Stimulus Isn't Big Enough to Restore Confidence', *Wall Street Journal*, 27 January, p. A15.
Smith, R. (1997) *The Colonel: The Life and Legend of Robert R. McCormick, 1880–1955*, Illinois: Northwestern University Press.
Solomon, D. and Maremont, M. (2009) 'Bankers Face Strict New Pay Cap – Stimulus Bill Puts Retroactive Curb on Bailout Recipients; Wall Street Fumes', *Wall Street Journal*, 14 February, p. A1.
Starkman, D. (2009) 'Power Problem', *Columbia Journalism Review*, 48 (1), pp. 24–30.
United States Department of Labor (2010) *Labor Force Statistics from the Current Population Survey*. Available at: http://data.bls.gov/PDQ/servlet/SurveyOutputServlet?series_id= LNS14000000 [Accessed 2 March 2012].
Wall Street Journal (2009a) 'The Stimulus Time Machine: That $355 Billion in Spending Isn't About the Economy', *Wall Street Journal*, 26 January, p. A14.
——(2009b) 'A 40-Year Wish List: You Won't Believe What's in That Stimulus Bill', *Wall Street Journal*, 28 January, p. A14.
Welch, J. and Welch, S. (2009) 'For a Fast-Acting Stimulus Plan … Washington Needs to Face Three Facts – About Banks, Pork, and Revenge', *Businessweek*, 16 February, p. 78.

4

THE BRITISH MEDIA AND THE 'FIRST CRISIS OF GLOBALIZATION'

Steve Schifferes and Sophie Knowles

The City of London, the largest and most international financial centre outside of New York, was quickly engulfed by the collapse of the global financial system in September 2008. From an early stage British journalists were on the front line, trying to cover and interpret the rapidly evolving events, as the banking system and the economy went into free fall. The events in Britain signalled that the crisis that began on Wall Street had assumed a global dimension, had become what Prime Minister Gordon Brown described as 'the first crisis of globalisation' (Brown, 2010).

This paper analyses four crucial episodes as the financial crisis unfolded in the UK: the collapse of the Northern Rock bank in August 2007; the debate on the prospects for the UK economy during the following year; reactions to the collapse of the UK banking system in October 2008; and, finally, the growing consensus around austerity in the run-up to the General Election in May 2010. It evaluates the effectiveness of the UK press in covering each of these episodes, which posed different challenges in understanding and interpretation.

Promoting the boom

Before the crash the business media generally endorsed the idea that the UK had entered into a new era of strong economic growth and low unemployment that could continue indefinitely. This was the ideology of the newly elected Labour government, which came to power in 1997. Labour had abandoned its traditional support for nationalization and proclaimed the benefits of 'light touch regulation' of the financial sector. This helped revitalize the City and led to a property and stock market boom. As the economy continued to grow steadily, the Labour chancellor, Gordon Brown, proclaimed 'the end of boom and bust', a view echoed by the governor of the Bank of England, Mervyn King, who coined the term the

'NICE' decade (non-inflationary, consistently expansionary growth) in 2003 (Brown, 1997; Rawnsley, 2001; King, 2003).

The financial sector's role in expanding mortgage lending contributed to the rapid rise in house prices, which was the focus of personal finance pages and dinner party conversations alike. Banks encouraged people to take on more debt by offering large mortgages based on very high multiples of income (four to five times), self-certification of income for the self-employed, and a high loan-to-value ratio (up to 95 per cent of the property's purchase price). Some, including Northern Rock, even offered mortgages for more than the value of the property (up to 125 per cent). With rapidly rising property prices, banks also encouraged homeowners to take on another mortgage to buy a second home to let, expecting the profit from capital gains to offset any initial expenses (Brummer, 2009; Elliott and Atkinson, 2009; Mason, 2010; Peston, 2013).

Business journalism itself also expanded during the boom years. The leading daily newspapers expanded business sections, hired more columnists, and increased their coverage of personal finance (Parsons, 1989; Henriques, 2000; Roush, 2006; Budd Report for the BBC Trust, 2007). The BBC created a new personal finance programme (*Working Lunch*) and consolidated all its coverage in a large business and economics centre; while ITV and Channel 4 News hired new economic correspondents. New entertainment format programmes on television focusing on the property market proliferated, such as *Location, Location, Location* and *A Place in the Sun* (Kelly and Boyle, 2011). Circulation boomed at specialist newspapers like the *Financial Times* and *Economist*, especially internationally (Chyi, 2013). And local newspapers benefited from increased property advertising, which made up a substantial proportion of their overall advertising revenue.

The run on the Rock

The first signs that all was not well in the UK's financial world came in September 2007, when it emerged that the UK's second largest mortgage lender, Northern Rock, could no longer borrow funds on the wholesale money market, due to the collapse of the $4 trillion securitized mortgage market the month before. The dramatic news that the Bank of England was preparing a rescue plan for the stricken bank was broken by the BBC's business editor, Robert Peston: the first of many scoops he was to have during the crisis. He was careful to reassure the public: 'There was no reason for people with Northern Rock savings accounts to panic,' he said on the BBC News website. '[T]his does not mean that the bank is in danger of going bust.'[1] But by the next morning, on 14 September 2007, as the news dominated the TV news bulletins and the front pages, long queues of depositors formed outside Northern Rock branches, desperate to withdraw their savings. The debacle offered the kind of powerful scenes not usually available for stories on the economy and was described by Michael Wilson, business anchor at Sky News, as 'a gift for television' (Wilson, 2008, p. 61). It was the first run on a UK bank for more than a century and it was being played out in the full glare of the 24-hour news cycle.

The dramatic pictures of the queues outside Northern Rock were viewed with dismay by the chancellor, Alistair Darling, and the governor of the Bank of England, Mervyn King, who were watching the drama unfold on television while attending an EU meeting in Portugal. They immediately understood the powerful impact these images were having on public confidence in the banking system – and the credibility of the government – and were deeply distressed by the role played by the BBC. The chancellor thought that the coverage 'set in train a course of events that was disastrous for confidence in the government's ability to manage the crisis' (Darling, 2011, p. 13). Within days he was forced to announce a government guarantee of all retail deposits held by Northern Rock savers, reforming the inadequate system of UK deposit insurance, as he struggled to restore confidence in the banking system and the government.[2] The Bank of England, also deeply distressed by the turn of events, sought a clause in legislation that would allow the Bank to prohibit the publication of such information in the future (King, 2007).

The BBC argued the public had the right to know if a major bank was in trouble, pointing out that Northern Rock's flawed funding model meant that it was bound to fail whatever the BBC had said. Robert Peston, the BBC business editor, had the authority – and unimpeachable sources – to back up his scoop. He had been following the fortunes of Northern Rock for years with growing scepticism about its business model and the aggressive leadership of its chief executive, Adam Applegarth. In fact, his reporting had forced the Treasury to 'up its game' and take much more decisive action than had originally been planned in regard to deposit insurance (Darling, 2011, p. 26).[3]

The collapse of Northern Rock was a harbinger of a much larger danger to the entire financial system, which few journalists understood at the time. One distinguished exception was Gillian Tett, the then capital markets editor of the *Financial Times*, who, as early as January 2007, was warning that according to industry sources 'there has never been a time in history when such a large proportion of the riskiest credit assets have been owned by such weak financial institutions'.[4] But her warnings on this highly specialized area had little resonance among journalists covering the banking sector or other areas of the economy. Instead of heeding the potential problems that faced the financial system as a whole, further coverage focused on the political problems that Northern Rock had created for the Labour government. The government did not want to be seen as returning to its old policy of government ownership, and therefore wanted to sell it to the private sector: they failed to find a buyer and eventually had to assume nearly £100 billion in liabilities (Brummer, 2009; Elliott and Atkinson, 2009).

Meanwhile, the attention of the financial markets, and the banking correspondents, had turned to a titanic struggle between two UK banking giants – RBS and Barclays – for control of the Dutch banking group ABN Amro – the largest cross-border banking merger ever made. This single moment revealed how little the systemic nature of the crisis was understood. The victory of RBS in the autumn of 2007 was celebrated as a great triumph, and a vindication of the dynamic leadership of RBS boss Fred Goodwin. But, just a year later, this acquisition led his bank to the brink of collapse and Goodwin soon found himself a target of the press's vitriol.[5]

From credit crunch to recession

As banking correspondents celebrated RBS's merger victory, by the beginning of 2008, a real debate about the seriousness of the crisis had begun among policy-makers – a debate that was increasingly being echoed in the opinion and commentary columns of the British press. The weakness of the US financial sector, following the freezing up of the market for credit derivatives, was becoming increasingly apparent, with huge losses being announced by the major US banks. However, whilst the US Treasury secretly started preparing plans for a $1 trillion bailout fund for the banks, the Bank of England remained sceptical of the dangers to the UK financial sector and was convinced that any further guarantees of a government bailout would make the banks more reckless.[6]

In this period of great uncertainty, the 'commentariat' of pundits, analysts, and editors argued openly about whether the boom was really over and, if so, what framework of analysis might replace it.[7] One way this was played out was through the language used to describe the economic situation. A number of terms were in circulation, such as 'credit crunch', 'downturn', 'financial crisis', and 'recession'. Calling the crisis a recession instead of a downturn implied a wider impact on the economy, and the need for more concerted government action. At BBC News, the terminology used to describe the crisis was debated at great length, down to the title words used in the graphic projected behind television news stories about the economy. This was only changed from 'downturn' to 'recession' in January

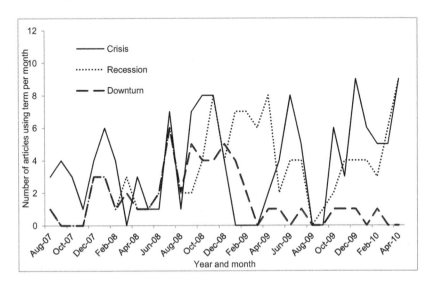

FIGURE 4.1 Frequency of terms used to describe the economic situation
Source: Articles from six major UK news publications accessed through Factiva and analysed using NVivo.

2009, after official figures confirmed two quarters of negative growth of GDP (Schifferes, 2010).

With this in mind, the authors analysed the language used by key economic and political commentators from the five major UK broadsheets (and *The Economist*) from August 2007 to April 2010 (for full methodology see the Appendix). The word 'crisis' is the word used most frequently until June 2008. By this point more commentators also begin to speak of the 'downturn' – implying a broader economic effect of the crisis. It is only after September 2008 that 'recession' begins to be used more frequently, and from then until April 2009 it dominates the discourse. Other words – 'credit crunch' and 'meltdown' for instance – are used far less and did not come to characterize the period in the same way as the words 'crisis' and 'recession'.

A number of well-known columnists were critical of any use of the word 'recession' in describing the situation.[8] Writing in *The Guardian*, the former *Economist* editor Bill Emmott took the press to task and said, 'we risk talking ourselves into recession through media scaremongering'.[9] One of the *Financial Times*'s most well-known columnists, Samuel Brittan, wrote, 'I feel like saying Buck Up … There is no need to talk ourselves into a recession.'[10] Another distinguished economics commentator, Anatole Kaletsky of *The Times*, also downplayed the possibility of a recession in the UK, claiming that 'the global credit crisis, far from taking a turn for the worse, is almost over'.[11] Even as late as August 2008, Hamish McRae wrote in *The Independent* that 'The R-word has such resonance and is bound to send a shiver through people's spines … yet, I can find no mainstream forecaster who predicts an annual contraction for the economy for 2009 or 2010. The housing market may be as bad as the early 1990s, and it is looking more and more as though it will be, but the economy as a whole should do better.'[12]

Although a number of distinguished commentators were lulled into a false sense of security, there were others who were sharply critical from the beginning. Martin Wolf was admirably early in drawing attention to the problematic role that the 'clever intermediaries' (the banks and investment houses) played in packaging up risky debt and selling it to gullible investors.[13] The further development of this critique of the crisis by such commentators showed the vigour of the debate going on in the UK media before the crisis broke. In March 2008 Jeff Randall wrote in the *Telegraph* that 'the collapse of once-mighty Bear Stearns is another reminder that the unwinding of the Great Debt Delusion still has a long way to go and many more victims to claim'.[14] Larry Elliott, writing in *The Guardian*, warned that 'times for most of us are tougher than they were a year ago: food costs more; fuel costs more; mortgages are hard to find and expensive. As usual after years of excess, there is the unmistakable sense of belts being tightened.'[15]

The collapse of the City

The speed and intensity of the global financial crisis took politicians and journalists on both sides of the Atlantic by surprise. The bankruptcy of Lehman Brothers on 15 September sent shock waves throughout the global financial system – with

Lehman's $687 billion in liabilities affecting banks around the world and pictures of Lehman employees leaving their office in London's Docklands flashing across TV screens. Within weeks, two of the UK's biggest banks needed massive injections of government cash to prevent their collapse. Just as in the case of Northern Rock, the press was able to break many of the key news stories as the crisis developed, including: the shotgun merger of Lloyds and HBOS, two leading mortgage lenders; the collapse of a major building society, Bradford and Bingley; and the partial government takeover of two of the UK's biggest banks, RBS and Lloyds (Peston, 2008a–c; Darling, 2011; Rawnsley, 2010).

Many of these stories were broken by the BBC's Robert Peston, whose blog became required reading for bankers, politicians, and the public alike during the crisis (Schifferes and Coulter, 2013). As the crisis deepened, he and other business journalists faced a storm of criticism, with bankers, businessmen, and politicians all blaming them for the panic. Even Richard Lambert, the former editor of the *Financial Times*, who was running the employers' group the CBI, accused the press of spreading rumours as facts and called for an investigation by the industry regulator, the Press Complaints Commission.[16] An MP, David Gauke, complained plaintively that 'the most striking thing about the last 13 months or so, about the various developments in this crisis, has been that practically every interesting bit of information has been revealed by Robert Peston on the BBC News'.[17] The criticisms led to a Parliamentary inquiry into the conduct of journalists amid fears that the freedom of the press might be curbed, an approach that was ultimately rejected by the Treasury committee (see Chapter 19).

In fact, although financial markets were understandably rattled by the banking crisis, the government had learned its lessons from its failure to manage the media during the Northern Rock debacle. News of the covert support operation by the Bank of England – which provided £61.5 billion to HBOS and RBS in early October to ensure that they did not run out of cash – did not leak out to the press. As a result, there was no run on the banking system in the way there had been during the Northern Rock crisis (Peston, 2009; Darling, 2011; Plenderleith, 2012).

Nor was the UK media aware of the key role played by Chancellor Alistair Darling in the negotiations over the collapse of Lehman Brothers on the weekend of 13–14 September. He rejected a last-ditch plan for Barclays to rescue the stricken US investment bank – arguing that the UK taxpayers could not be expected to take responsibility for the debts of Lehman. This left US Treasury Secretary Hank Paulson with no alternative but to put Lehman in bankruptcy (Paulson, 2010; Sorkin, 2010; Darling, 2011).

Bashing the bankers

In contrast to its earlier admiration for wealth creation and praise for the bankers' role in the property boom, after the crash the UK media – the popular press in particular – swung to the other extreme. As the crisis broke, 'greedy bankers' became the watchword of the press as the public came to realize how far the much-praised UK financial system had collapsed. The attack on the bankers personalized the crisis, always an attractive approach for the mass-market press, and allowed non-specialist journalists to weigh in with their comments. The leader of the Anglican Church, the Archbishop of Canterbury, Rowan Williams, became a much-quoted critic of the overly materialistic society that had led to the crisis.[18] Conversely, the moralizing of the crisis in the press allowed popular anger to focus on individuals, rather than on the financial system as a whole, or on the politicians and regulators who had created the structures that had permitted abuse of the financial system. In August 2008 the *Daily Mail* commented,

> Britain's embattled bankers and financial regulators must feel like they have been subjected to a modern day Spanish Inquisition ever since their sins and omissions unleashed the credit crunch. … But preventing another financial implosion will require a radical rethink by the real villains of the piece – the bankers themselves.[19]

And in September 2008 the *Daily Express* thundered in an editorial, 'In any other walk of life the negligence displayed by the greediest bankers would be classed as criminal.'[20]

There was one figure that stood out in popular opprobrium: Sir Fred Goodwin, the disgraced former chief executive of the largest bank to fail, RBS. When it was revealed that he had left the bank with his £700,000 per year pension intact the press frenzy knew no bounds. After making an abject public apology to Parliament's Treasury committee, Sir Fred fled to his holiday home in the south of France after vandals attacked his car and broke windows at his house in Scotland. 'Where lies the moral compass of this greedy little man?' wrote Carole Malone in the *News of the World*.[21] And *The Sun,* writing after the vandalism incident, editorialized, 'The yobs who vandalised Sir Fred's home and Mercedes have no excuse' but 'Greedy Goodwin and his £700,000 pension is simply the focal point of a groundswell of fury … if Britain is angry, we all know why.'[22] The quality press also joined in, with political columnist Andrew Rawnsley writing in *The Observer,* 'Bankers like Sir Fred Goodwin are lucky not to be in jail.' In the ultimate sign of establishment displeasure, Sir Fred was eventually stripped of his knighthood.[23]

The idea that the crisis had been caused by the moral failings of bankers implied that a renaissance of morality was needed instead of structural changes to the financial system as a whole. Talking about bankers' greed also distracted from discussions about the role of politicians in encouraging the development of the City as a freewheeling financial centre – and the dependence of the government on the City's huge profits, which had funded its social programmes. Greedy bankers were a far more exciting topic for the popular press than the complete failure of the system of banking regulation, and stories about their bonuses have continued to feature regularly. But no clear consensus has emerged on how to restrain bankers' pay and bonuses. More radical ideas about breaking up the banks struggled to find a voice, and it was not until 2011 that these ideas gained any traction in the policy debate (Independent Commission on Banking, 2011; UK Treasury, 2011; D'Ancona, 2013).

The politics of austerity

While the moral compass of the bankers was under the spotlight, a far bigger debate, on how to deal with the collateral damage the crisis had caused the UK economy, was gathering steam. The failure of Gordon Brown's global Keynesian approach weakened his credibility at a time when the effects of the recession on the economy and the public finances were increasingly evident. This debate ultimately pitted Prime Minister Gordon Brown against his own chancellor, much of his Cabinet, the Opposition parties, and most of the press. By the autumn of 2009, the result was a new framing of the crisis in terms of austerity, which shaped the terms on which the looming general election of 2010 would be fought.

When the crisis first broke in the autumn of 2008, the prime minister seemed to be at the height of his powers. He was widely praised in the press for his skill in managing the meltdown. Steve Richards in *The Independent* wrote that Brown 'was well-positioned to deal with the financial crisis' as he 'was never uncritically in awe of the market',[24] while Philip Stephens in the *Financial Times* argued that 'Gordon Brown has been gifted a financial crisis.'[25] Some, such as Jeff Randall and Hamish McRae, blamed the policies of the Labour government for the crisis;[26] others saw the UK's actions as a model for how other countries should deal with the financial crisis, and argued that it was 'fatuous' to blame Gordon Brown personally for a global crisis not of his own making.[27]

Brown's prestige reached its apogee at the G20 London summit in April 2009, as world leaders announced a $1.1 trillion stimulus plan to revive the world economy. Carefully managing the UK press corps, he appeared to have convinced other governments to embrace global Keynesianism, expanding global spending to boost their economies rather than cutting spending to narrow Budget deficits. Writing in *The Times*, the usually sceptical Anatole Kaletsky said that 'the G20 summit ended up as a triumph – for the world economy, for financial markets, and for Gordon Brown'.[28]

However, the triumph at the G20 summit soon proved illusory, and its effect on the global recession was limited. Key European countries, such as Germany, refused to sign up to the global stimulus plan. And the much vaunted $1.1 trillion rescue package, which was largely made up of credit facilities from the IMF, was never taken up. Meanwhile, the problems of the UK economy were deepening, with economic output declining rapidly and the government's Budget deficit swelling to an unprecedented £175 billion, or 12.6 per cent of GDP. The difficulty for Gordon Brown was that to acknowledge the depth of the UK recession, or the need for major cuts in public spending, was tantamount to repudiating his economic legacy and his international standing (Brown, 2010; Seldon and Lodge, 2010; Darling, 2011).

This put the prime minister on a collision course with his chancellor, Alistair Darling, most economic experts, and the bulk of the financial press, and ultimately weakened his authority in the Labour Party and in the country. The prime minister had been critical of Alistair Darling's pessimism even before the crisis, unleashing his 'attack dogs' to discredit the chancellor after he admitted in an interview in *The Guardian* newspaper in August 2008 that the UK economy was 'facing its worst crisis in 60 years'.[29] By April 2009, the prime minister was in open conflict with the chancellor over his planned Budget measures and his gloomy economic forecasts. The rift became unbridgeable when Mr Brown tried but failed to replace Mr Darling as chancellor in a botched Cabinet reshuffle later that month (Mandelson, 2010; Rawnsley, 2010; Darling, 2011; McBride, 2013).

Our qualitative analysis of the rise and fall of Gordon Brown across the key commentators in the quality press is shown in Figure 4.2. Praise for Brown and Labour is intermittent, with a small peak during October 2008, and a high point during the G20 summit in April 2009. From this point it drops to an insignificant level from where it never fully recovers. In contrast, the rise of the Tories and Cameron is evident through the period and mirrors the pattern seen for the fall of Brown and Labour – the rise is most evident from September 2009 onwards and in the months before the 2010 election.

In July 2009 Jeff Randall wrote in the *Telegraph* that 'with his boss at the G8 summit in Italy, having another crack at saving the world, Mr Darling was left to pick through the rubble of Labour's own making'.[30] Six months later, Danny Finkelstein in *The Times* describes Brown as 'at the head of the spending rebels' and 'far from backing his Chancellor in what needs to be done, he forces him to water down his proposals, making clearly inadequate plans to deal with the crisis'.[31] By this point commentators were also attacking Brown's credibility as the future prime

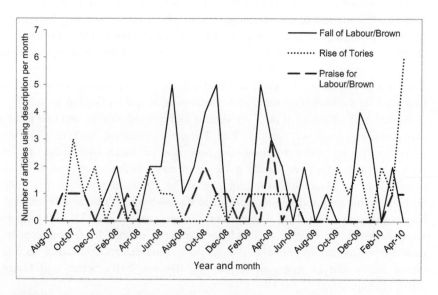

FIGURE 4.2 Sentiment relating to Gordon Brown and David Cameron
Source: Articles from six major UK news publications accessed through Factiva and analysed using NVivo.

minister. Writing in the *Financial Times*, Philip Stephens proclaimed in December 2009 that 'Gordon Brown's government has lost Britain's coming election.'[32]

While Mr Brown resisted frantic appeals from his advisers to come clean on the economic problems facing the country, by the autumn of 2009 his Conservative rival David Cameron, after some hesitation, had concluded that the Conservatives would have to accept the need for sweeping deficit reductions. 'If we win this election, it is going to be tough. There will have to be cutbacks in public spending, and that will be painful,' he told delegates at the Conservative Party conference in October (Cameron, 2009). This played an important role in persuading a number of newspapers to support Mr Cameron at the general election. *The Economist* explicitly endorsed the Conservatives because of their stance on austerity: 'He [Cameron] has been clearer for longer about the fiscal squeeze required than Mr Brown. At the party conference in October Mr Osborne was commendably ahead of the pack in outlining some specific measures to reduce the fiscal deficit.'[33]

There is a very close link between the growing chorus of criticism of Gordon Brown, the changing stance of the Conservatives, and the framing of the crisis in terms of austerity. By using the word 'austerity', commentators were signifying that the crisis had wider implications, with reductions in living standards and cuts to public spending on the cards. This is shown by a further analysis of the use of the words 'deficits', 'cuts', and 'austerity' by our panel of commentators – shown in Figure 4.3. It shows each of these words building momentum throughout the period. In particular, they start to gain in frequency from September 2008 onwards: the moment Lehman Brothers collapsed and – incidentally – the moment from which the word 'recession' is used more frequently (see Figure 4.1). The word 'austerity' is used most frequently from November 2009 and, along with the words

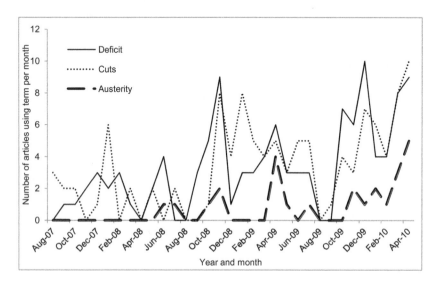

FIGURE 4.3 Frequency of terms relating to austerity

Source: Articles from six major UK news publications accessed through Factiva and analysed using NVivo.

'deficit' and 'cuts', 'crisis', and 'recession', indicates the kind of language that came to characterize the financial crisis in its later stages.

Explicit support for framing the crisis in terms of austerity was demonstrated by the widespread criticism of Alistair Darling's November 2009 pre-Budget report as not going far enough – with *The Economist* calling it 'timid'.[34] Analysis shows that of the six newspapers analysed, the *Telegraph*, *Times*, and *Economist* were most consistent in their support of the Tories and their portrayal of Gordon Brown as unfit for office in the months before the 2010 elections. But by the end of 2009 both left- and right-wing commentators broadly supported the need for austerity, and David Cameron was seen as more likely to implement it than Gordon Brown.

The events that were playing out in Europe – and especially the possibility of a Greek default – added to the concerns about the Budget deficit, a point pressed home by the Opposition. In an op-ed piece written for the *Daily Telegraph* on 21 December 2009, Shadow Chancellor George Osborne equated the UK economy with that of Greece, suggesting that the UK might be in danger of defaulting on its debts.[35] The Greek crisis deepened the pessimism of many commentators about the economic prospects of the UK. Hamish McRae argued in *The Independent*, 'We are worse than Greece, worse than Ireland, worse than Spain. The choice is between what services to cut and what taxes to raise.'[36]

The elephant in the room: the 2010 General Election

However, austerity proved a double-edged sword for politicians as the General Election approached in May 2010. The parties began to pull back from giving specifics of how they intended to implement spending cuts, which were barely mentioned in their manifestos or press releases (Gaber, 2011). A Conservative Party official commented that 'there was a sort of mutual pact among the parties about not being too upfront about future pain' (Kavanagh and Cowley, 2010, p. 347). The political logic was clear, as polls showed the UK public believed efficiency savings could accomplish the cuts without any damage to front line services (Ipsos MORI 2009).

As it turned out, the campaign was dominated by the three televised leader debates – the first ever in a British General Election – and the instant analysis of who had won or lost each debate.

The issue of the economy played a minor role in these debates, and was squeezed out as an electoral issue.

Leading commentators criticized the lack of discussion around the economy and spending cuts. Steve Richards wrote in *The Independent* in April that the leader debates shrouded the importance of the financial crisis: 'Almost forgotten in the excitement about the debates is that this campaign is taking place in the midst of an economic crisis.'[37] His colleague Hamish McRae in *The Independent* pointed out that none of the main parties had actually detailed their plans to tackle the deficit: 'The core problem … is that none of the three main parties has given any detail as to how it might achieve its overall deficit-cutting target.'[38] Writing in the *Financial*

Times, Philip Stephens echoed Richards and McRae in his concern that politics had overtaken economic priorities:

> An election that was supposed to be about the condition of Britain's economy has turned into one about the state of its politics ... The politicians have conveniently forgotten the country faces the fiercest squeeze on its public finances in modern memory.[39]

As one academic study has put it, although the press did not entirely ignore the economy, 'there was a collective failure of imagination, ambition, and independence which left the electorate poorly positioned to anticipate the scale, severity and radicalism of the statecraft that was to follow' (Deacon and Wring, 2011, p. 301).

Conclusions

The first crisis of globalization presented the UK media with some unique challenges and marked a key turning point in its relationship with the financial sector and the government. The many journalistic scoops, from Northern Rock onwards, were in sharp contrast to the cosy relationship that the press had enjoyed with the City and economic policymakers before the crisis. The speed of this shift may explain the fierce torrent of criticism directed at the media for causing unnecessary panic during the acute phases of crisis. It is unlikely that downplaying the crisis could have prevented households, businesses, and markets from noticing the serious consequences of the near collapse of the banking system, even if there is evidence that press reports do affect market sentiment (Kleinnijenhuis et al., 2013; Schifferes and Coulter, 2013).

The UK media was criticized in the period before the crisis for its dependence on a limited number of sources, its ideological identification with the City, and its groupthink – although the UK press never quite reached the level of unfettered admiration for business leaders that was a prominent feature of US business coverage (Mair and Keeble, 2009; Davis, 2011). And the relative size and scale of the City of London in the UK economy may have heightened the enthusiasm with which the press celebrated its expansion. Additionally, when it is compared with the US, the UK press has a weaker investigative tradition, particularly in the financial press.

But balancing out some of these failings was the UK media's long-standing tradition of informed commentary and analysis. This led to an early and vigorous debate on the seriousness of the crisis from early 2008 onwards, before the Lehman crash, which paralleled the debate among economic policymakers and helped articulate the nature of the problem more clearly in its global dimensions. Also striking in the UK context is the traditional role of the tabloid press and their attempt to find villains and scoundrels (Tumber, 1993). This arguably fed the tendency to blame the crash on the moral failings of bankers and distracted from a serious analysis of the causes of the crash and possible remedies, including the need for tougher financial regulation. The press also played a key part in reframing the crisis after its fiscal consequences became clear. Here the debate narrowed after the collapse of Labour's economic credibility and the apparent lack of viable economic alternatives to Budget cuts (Pirie, 2012).

Was the media guilty of institutional and ideological bias in its coverage of the crisis, as many of its academic critics allege? Did it fail to consider alternatives because of its reliance on a limited number of sources with a narrow range of views that were dictated by a coterie of business and political elites (Lewis, 2010; Berry, 2013; Knowles, Phillips, and Lidberg, 2013; Manning, 2013)? There were in fact several periods (2007–8 and early 2009) where there was no clear framing of the crisis, and the ideological landscape was more open, after the boom was discredited and before austerity became the new paradigm. But, to provide a real debate, the media needed politically credible alternatives, and this is what was lacking. The real puzzle of the crisis was its failure to trigger a wider political debate about alternative policies and, for this, the polity, not the media, must bear the primary responsibility.

Appendix: Methodology

To capture a mix of both political and economic commentary the following commentators were used: Martin Wolf (*Financial Times*); Philip Stephens (*Financial Times*); Hamish McRae (*Independent*); Steve Richards (*Independent*); Jeff Randall (*Telegraph*); Jeremy Warner (*Telegraph*); Larry Elliott (*Guardian*); Patrick Wintour (*Guardian*); Anatole Kaletsky (*Times*); Daniel Finkelstein (*Times*); and all articles on the UK economy, financial markets, and politics from *The Economist*. The articles were collected using the Factiva database. The chosen time frame was August 2007 to April 2010 and the sample included at least one relevant article per month by each journalist. The following terms, which describe the financial crisis and the debate on austerity, were used to collect a 256-article data set: austerity, cuts, budget deficit, Gordon Brown, Darling, Cameron, Osborne, King, recession, credit crunch, market crash, meltdown, downturn, and financial crisis. Several themes and sub-themes were then analysed qualitatively – (by a single coder) using NVivo – about the Labour Party and Gordon Brown, the Conservatives and David Cameron, the blame for the financial crisis, and the terms used to describe the financial crisis, and debate on austerity.

Notes

1 BBC News website (2007) 'Northern Rock Gets Bank Bail Out', 13 September. See also R. Peston (2007), 'Rock or Crock?' *Peston's Picks,* BBC News website, 14 September: www.bbc.co.uk/blogs/thereporters/robertpeston/2007/09/rock_or_crock.html

2 UK deposit insurance was introduced on a limited basis in 1991 following the BCCI scandal. A more comprehensive scheme of deposit insurance, with the same minimum standards across the EU, was introduced in 2008. See Mervyn King's testimony to the House of Commons Treasury Committee, session 2006–7, uncorrected oral evidence, 20 September 2007.

3 For Robert Peston's views see: House of Commons Treasury Committee (2009) oral evidence, 4 February 2009, q1510.

4 G. Tett (2007) 'The Unease Bubbling in Today's Brave New Financial World', *Financial Times*, 19 January.

5 P.T. Larsen (2007) 'Sir Fred's Heady Firsts', *Financial Times*, 4 October.

6 King had warned that the banks were overleveraged in his Mansion House speech (see King, 2007). See L. Elliot (2012) 'We Did Too Little to Warn of the Financial Crisis', *The Guardian*, 2 May; and M. Wolf (2013) 'Mervyn King: Lunch With the *FT*', *Financial Times*, 14 June.

7 See note on commentators in the Appendix.

8 Further commentary used during the financial crisis was drawn from Oldfield (2009), which covers the period to March 2009.

9 B. Emmott (2009) 'I Wasn't Right. But That's OK: My Economic Predictions Were Overly Optimistic – Yet Forecasts of Recession Can Make Matters Worse?' *The Guardian*, 3 January.

10 S. Brittan (2008) 'High Time for All of Us to "Buck Up"', *Financial Times*, 1 February.

11 A. Kaletsky (2008) 'Slower and Slower? Yes. Crash and Burn? No', *The Times*, 10 January.

12 H. McRae (2008) 'We're on Course for a Recession But There Are Reasons to Stay Positive', *The Independent*, 7 August.

13 M. Wolf (2007) 'Questions and Answers on a Sadly Predictable Debt Crisis', *Financial Times*, 5 September.

14 J. Randall (2008) 'A World Addicted to Easy Credit Must Go Cold Turkey; Banks, Governments and Consumers Have Become Borrowing Junkies and Cash Injections by Central Banks Only Prolong the Craving', *Daily Telegraph*, 16 March.

15 L. Elliott (2008) 'G2: A Cut Above the Rest: Designers Have Been Parading Dresses Costing £50,000 at the Paris Couture Collections This Week', *The Guardian*, 3 July.

16 See Richard Lambert (2008) *Speech at the Reform Media Group Dinner*, 2 December. Details on his comments are available in the following House of Commons Report (2009): www.publications.parliament.uk/pa/cm200809/cmselect/cmtreasy/519/519.pdf

17 See MP David Gauke's comments in the 2008 debate on banking regulation: www.publications.parliament.uk/pa/cm200708/cmpublic/banking/081021/am/81021 s06.htm

18 See Rowan Williams's interview on BBC TV's *Newsnight*'s 'Aftershock Special' on 18 September 2009, the first anniversary of the Lehman crash: http://news.bbc.co.uk/2 /hi/programmes/newsnight/8260059.stm

19 S. Fleming (2008) 'Treasury Man Tramples on Toes; The Crunch Interview', *Daily Mail*, 7 August.

20 *Daily Express* (2008) 'Jail Rogue Fat-Cats Who Caused Financial Turmoil', 30 September.

21 C. Malone (2009) 'A Rich Idiot's Still An Idiot!' *News of the World*, 1 March.

22 *The Sun* (2009) 'Britain's Angry', 26 March.

23 A. Rawnsley (2009) 'These Bankers Are Lucky That They Are Not Going to Jail', *The Observer*, 1 March.

24 S. Richards (2008) 'Brown Warned Us That Markets Fail', *The Independent*, 14 October.

25 P. Stephens (2008) 'Irresponsibility Ushers in the Age of Control', *Financial Times*, 14 October.

26 H. McRae (2008) 'Consumers Can Earn Their Way out of Trouble but Public Debt is the Problem', *The Independent*, 25 November.

27 L. Elliott (2008) 'The Markets Are Clear: Britain Is Mutton Dressed Up As Lamb: Labour Has Failed Over 11 Years to Build An Economy Fit for the 21st Century', *The Guardian*, 29 October.

28 A. Kaletsky (2009) 'Backslapping, Congratulations – But Surprising and Impressive Results Too', *The Times*, 3 April.

29 *The Guardian*'s controversial interview with Darling in 2008, conducted by Decca Aitkenhead, was published as 'Storm Warning' on 30 August. Brown's 'spin doctors"

response was reported in P. Webster (2008) 'Darling's Job on the Line After Recession Blunder', *The Times*, 1 September.

30 J. Randall (2009) 'You Can Bank on the Hand of Gord to Create Another Disaster: Labour's Financial Reform Paper Highlights the Problems of Having a Failed Chancellor As PM', *Daily Telegraph*, 10 July.

31 D. Finkelstein (2010) 'The Same Old Row. But With One Big Difference; This Labour Split Is Not About Style Or Strategy But Spending Cuts', *The Times*, 13 January.

32 P. Stephens (2009) 'Cameron's Choice: A Tory Or a Radical?' *Financial Times*, 15 December.

33 *The Economist* (2010) 'An Interview With David Cameron; David Cameron Is Still Favourite to Be the Next Prime Minister of Britain: The Sting in the Falklands Tale', 27 April.

34 *The Economist* (2010) 'Alistair Darling's Budget; An Intensely Political Budget will Merely Tinker Around the Edges', 27 April.

35 G. Osborne (2009) 'The Threat of Rising Interest Rates Is a Greek Tragedy We Must Avoid: Britain Needn't Look Far to See the Crisis in Store If We Allow Our Debts to Mount', *Daily Telegraph*, 22 December.

36 H. McRae (2009) 'Fiscal Credibility Is on a Knife Edge – and This Spring Could Be Nasty Indeed', *The Independent*, 13 December.

37 S. Richards (2010) 'Talk of Revolution is Still Premature', *The Independent*, 24 April.

38 H. McRae (2010) 'Growth, Not Government, Is the Way to Fix the UK's Economic Mess', *The Independent*, 25 April.

39 P. Stephens (2010) 'Sometimes the unthinkable is unavoidable', *Financial Times*, 27 April.

References

Berry, M. (2013) 'The *Today* Programme and the Banking Crisis', *Journalism*, 14 (2), pp. 253–70.

Brown, G. (1997) *Pre-Budget Statement By the Right Honourable Gordon Brown, MP*, 25 November. Available at: http://hansard.millbanksystems.com/commons/1997/nov/25/pre-budget-statement [Accessed 7 March 2014].

——(2010) *Beyond the Crash: Overcoming the First Crisis of Globalisation*, London: Simon and Schuster.

Brummer, A. (2009) *The Crunch: How Greed and Incompetence Sparked the Credit Crisis*, London: Random House.

Budd Report for the BBC Trust (2007) *Report of the Independent Panel for the BBC Trust on Impartiality of BBC Business Coverage*, chaired by Sir Alan Budd, London: BBC. Available at: http://downloads.bbc.co.uk/bbctrust/assets/files/pdf/review_report_research/impartiality_business/business_impartiality_report.pdf [Accessed 2 December 2013].

Cameron, D. (2009) *Speech to the Conservative Party Conference*, Manchester, 8 October. Available at: www.theguardian.com/politics/2009/oct/08/david-cameron-speech-in-full [Accessed 27 January 2013].

Chyi, H.I. (2013) 'World News Organizations' Web Strategies for the China Market: The Cases of the *Wall Street Journal*, *Financial Times*, and the *New York Times*'. Paper presented to the International Association for Media and Communication Research Conference, Dublin, 25 June.

D'Ancona, M. (2013) *In It Together: The Inside Story of the Coalition Government*, London: Penguin.

Darling, A. (2011) *Back from the Brink: 1,000 Days at Number 11*, London: Atlantic Books.

Davis, A. (2011) 'News of the Financial Sector: Reporting on the City Or to It?' *Open Democracy*, 31 May. Available at: www.opendemocracy.net/ourkingdom/aeron-davis/news-of-financial-sector-reporting-on-city-or-to-it [Accessed 10 December 2013].

Deacon, D. and Wring, D. (2011) 'Reporting the 2010 General Election: Old Media, New Media – Old Politics, New Politics', in Wring, D., Mortimore, R., and Atkinson, S. (eds.), *Political Communication in Britain: The Leader Debates, the Campaign and the Media in the 2010 General Election*, Basingstoke: Palgrave Macmillan, pp. 281–303.

Elliott, L. and Atkinson, D. (2009) *The Gods That Failed: How Blind Faith in Markets Has Cost Us Our Future*, London: Nation Books.

Gaber, I. (2011) 'The Transformation of Campaign Reporting', in Wring, D., Mortimore, R., and Atkinson, S. (eds.), *Political Communication in Britain: The Leader Debates, the Campaign and the Media in the 2010 General Election*, Basingstoke: Palgrave Macmillan, pp. 261–80.

Henriques, D. (2000) 'Business Reporting: Behind the Curve', *Columbia Journalism Review*, 39, pp. 18–21.

House of Commons Treasury Committee (2008) *Banking Crisis, Oral Evidence*, Volume I, HC 144–I, 1 April, Ev 197–Ev 211. Available at: www.publications.parliament.uk/pa/cm200809/cmselect/cmtreasy/144/144i.pdf [Accessed 7 March 2014].

Independent Commission on Banking (Vickers Report) (2011) *Final Report and Recommendations*, September. Available at: http://webarchive.nationalarchives.gov.uk/+/bankingcommission.independent.gov.uk [Accessed 12 February 2014].

Ipsos MORI (2009) *Voters Not Ready for Spending Cuts*. Available at: www.ipsos-mori.com/researchpublications/researcharchive/2473/Voters-not-ready-for-spending-cuts.aspx [Accessed 15 December 2013].

Kavanagh, D. and Cowley, P. (2010) *The British General Election of 2010*, Basingstoke: Palgrave Macmillan.

Kelly, L., and Boyle, R. (2011) 'Business on Television: Continuity, Change and Risk in the Development of Television's "Business Entertainment Format"', *Television and New Media*, 12 (3), pp. 228–47.

King, M. (2003) *Speech Given by Mervyn King at the East Midlands Development Agency/Bank of England Dinner*, 14 October. Available at: www.bankofengland.co.uk/archive/Documents/historicpubs/speeches/2003/speech204.pdf [Accessed 12 February 2014].

——(2007) *Speech Given by Mervyn King at the Lord Mayor's Banquet for Bankers and Merchants of the City of London at the Mansion House*, 20 June. Available at: www.bankofEngland.co.uk/archive/Documents/historicpubs/speeches/2007/speech313.pdf [Accessed 10 December 2010].

Kleinnijenhuis, J., Schultz, F., Oegema, D., and van Atteveldt, W. (2013) 'Financial News and Market Panics in the Age of High-Frequency Sentiment Trading Algorithms', *Journalism*, 14 (2), pp. 271–91.

Knowles, S., Phillips, G., and Lidberg, J. (2013) 'The Framing of the Global Financial Crisis 2005–2008: A Cross-Country Comparison of the US, UK and Australia', *Australian Journalism Review*, 35 (2), pp. 59–72.

Lewis, J. (2010) 'Normal Viewing Will Be Resumed Shortly: News, Recession and the Politics of Growth', *Popular Communication*, 8 (3), pp. 161–5.

McBride, D. (2013) *Power Trip: A Decade of Policy, Plots and Splits*, London: Biteback.

Mair, J. and Keeble, R.L. (eds.) (2009) *Playing Footsie With the FTSE? The Great Crash of 2008 and the Crisis in Journalism*, Bury St Edmunds: Abramis Academic.

Mandelson, P. (2010) *The Third Man: Life at the Heart of New Labour*, London: Harper.

Manning, P. (2013) 'Financial Journalism, News Sources, and the Banking Crisis', *Journalism*, 14 (2), pp. 173–90.

Mason, P. (2010) *Meltdown: The End of the Age of Greed*, London: Verso.

Oldfield, C. (2009) *The Credit Crunch Commentariat*, London: Editorial Intelligence.

Parsons, W. (1989) *The Power of the Financial Press: Journalism and Economic Opinion in Britain and America*, New Brunswick: Rutgers University.

Paulson, Henry (2010) *On the Brink: Inside the Race to Stop the Collapse of the Global Financial System*, New York: Business Plus.

Peston, R. (2008a) 'Lloyds to buy HBOS', BBC News website, 17 September. Available at: www.bbc.co.uk/blogs/thereporters/robertpeston/2008/09/lloyds_to_buy_hbos.html [Accessed 8 March 2014].

——(2008b) 'B&B to be nationalised', BBC News website, 27 September. Available at: www.bbc.co.uk/blogs/thereporters/robertpeston/2008/09/bb_to_be_nationalised.html [Accessed 8 March 2014].

——(2008c) 'Humbling of our Banks', BBC News website, 12 October. Available at: www.bbc.co.uk/blogs/thereporters/robertpeston/2008/10/humbling_of_our_banks.html [Accessed 8 March 2014].

——(2009) 'Why Did Bank of England Keep Shtoom?' BBC News website, 24 November. Available at: www.bbc.co.uk/blogs/thereporters/robertpeston/2009/11/why_did_bank_of_england_keep_s.html [Accessed 1 February 2014].

——(2013) *How Do We Fix This Mess? The Economic Price of Having It All, and the Route to Lasting Prosperity*, London: Hodder and Stoughton.

Pirie, I. (2012) 'Representations of Economic Crisis in Contemporary Britain', *British Politics*, 7 (4), pp. 341–64.

Plenderleith, I. (2012) *Review of the Bank of England's Provision of Emergency Liquidity Assistance in 2008–09*, Bank of England, October. Available at: www.bankofengland.co.uk/publications/Documents/news/2012/cr1plenderleith.pdf [Accessed 1 January 2014].

Rawnsley, A. (2001) *Servants of the People: The Inside Story of New Labour*, London: Penguin.

——(2010) *The End of the Party: The Rise and Fall of New Labour*, London: Viking.

Roush, C. (2006) *Profits and Losses: Business Journalism and Its Role in Society*, Illinois: Marion Street Press.

Schifferes, S. (2010) 'Aftershock: How the BBC Called the Crisis', in *Covering the Crisis: The Role of the Media in the Financial Crisis*, Brussels: European Journalism Centre.

Schifferes, S. and Coulter, S. (2013) 'Downloading Disaster: BBC News Online Coverage of the Global Financial Crisis', *Journalism*, 14 (2), pp. 228–52.

Seldon, A. and Lodge, G. (2010) *Brown at 10*, London: Biteback.

Sorkin, A.R. (2010) *Too Big to Fail: The Inside Story of How Wall Street and Washington Fought to Save the Financial System – and Themselves*, London: Penguin.

Tumber, H. (1993) 'Selling Scandal: Business and the Media', *Media, Culture and Society*, 15 (3), pp. 345–62.

UK Treasury (2011) *The Government Response to the Independent Commission on Banking*, prepared for the Department for Business, Innovation and Skills, December. Available at: https://www.gov.uk/government/uploads/system/uploads/attachment_data/file/228757/8252.pdf [Accessed 1 December 2013].

Wilson, M. (2008) 'Crisis? What Crisis? But It's Great TV', *British Journalism Review*, 19 (3), pp. 57–61.

5

FROM WALL STREET TO MAIN STREET

Australian finance and business journalism and the crisis

Michael Bromley

Just weeks prior to the beginning of what was known in Australia as 'the global financial crisis' (GFC), the veteran journalist and media commentator Mark Day (2007) celebrated the buoyancy of Australian finance and business journalism. Not only was Rupert Murdoch, the (originally Australian) founder, chairman, and chief executive of the global company that ultimately owned the largest single chunk of Australia's media, about to fold the *Wall Street Journal* (*WSJ*) into his holdings, but the country's most visible business journalist had launched two websites; another leading journalist had established an online presence aimed at small and medium enterprises; and the only general interest national daily newspaper, *The Australian*, had hired additional business editorial staff. Day declared business journalism to be 'the hot new industry sector', and, in particular, the 'spearhead' for newspapers. This bullish mood reflected three interconnected long-term trends: 1) the mainstreaming of the specialism of finance and business journalism;[1] 2) the support of major media conglomerates from the 1980s for the ideological turn to neo-liberalism; and 3) an increasingly urgent requirement for the press in particular to bolster its advertising-based business model. At its simplest, profit-driven news media needed to publish or broadcast journalism that drew in audiences who were attractive to advertisers, who in turn paid for that journalism, and more, by advertising in those media. Over the first decade of the twenty-first century, finance and business journalism seemed to many to hold out the promise of being that journalism.

It has been argued that during this period finance and business journalism was 'naturalized' – so mainstreamed that it no longer appeared distinctive but was embedded within general journalistic communication as Australia became 'a finance-led nation' (Greenfield and Williams, 2007, pp. 416, 418). Perhaps reflecting this requirement for Australians to assume personal responsibility for areas of finance previously fulfilled by government, spanning the onset of the GFC, between 2005/06 and 2009/10, the average personal assets of Australians, representing holdings in property, savings, superannuation, and stocks, rose in value by 14 per cent. Prior to that, between 2003/04 and 2005/06, they had grown by more than 12 per cent. Overall, in a period of six years, the average Australian was notionally almost 30 per cent better off. Moreover, while discrepancies in the distribution of wealth undoubtedly increased, those with a middle range of net worth experienced double-digit growth – 11.25 per cent between 2005/06 and 2009/10 (Australian Bureau of Statistics, 2013). It was reasonably safe to assume that a large potential consumer base existed for journalism that addressed topics such as home ownership, savings, pensions, and, to a lesser extent, stock investments, as well as consumerism, employment, commerce, business, and the economy in general. From the 1980s a succession of Australian governments had set the context through the adoption of neo-liberal (known in Australia as economic rationalist) policies that promoted free trade, the superiority of private enterprise, and indirect taxation as mechanisms for wealth creation and greater wealth distribution (see Quiggin, 2003). Arriving from Ireland, one business journalist found business journalism in Australia to be 'very, very big' and 'very advanced' (Kirby, 2010).

Initially, the crisis added impetus to the trend. The blogs editor of the *Business Spectator* noted that 'citizens are beating a path to the business media. Financial dailies and news websites have boosted their output … There's nothing like a meltdown to focus the mind' (Crook, 2008). This chapter explores how *The Australian* sought to make business, in its broadest sense, more widely accessible and comprehensible in journalism as the GFC became a major news concern.

The resistible rise of Australian finance and business journalism[2]

The systematic application of journalism to business and finance information was evident from the nineteenth century as European settlement in Australia expanded. The *Sydney Gazette*, the first newspaper printed in Australia (from 1803), concentrated on banking, while *The Australian* (1824–48) specialized in trade. The *Sydney Herald* promised in its first editorial in 1831 a focus on the 'commercial … relations of Australia' and 'The well being of the merchant, manufacturer, farmer …' (Anon, 1831). By the 1850s, papers were publishing market and commodity prices, shares listings, banking and company data, industry intelligence, and 'commercial news', as well as advertisements for stocks and shares. The New Financial Journalism, reaching out to a wider audience, and developed in the US in the 1880s, must have found its way to Australia (Porter, 2000, pp. 73–4). The *Daily Commercial News*, which first appeared in 1891, focused on shipping, trade, transport, and logistics.[3] By 1901, in addition to market data and shipping news, the Melbourne *Argus* (1846–1957) was publishing columns with headings such as 'Mining Intelligence and Stock and Share Market' and 'Monetary and Commercial'. Newspapers responded to Australians who were investing in joint-stock companies, saving with banks, taking out insurance, and trading on State stock exchanges. In a review of journalism published at this time, the *Sydney Morning Herald* (*SMH*) noted the existence of 'publications devoted to one or other of the chief interests of the colony – mining, agriculture, the pastoral industry, shipping, banking, and so on'. Its own 'commercial and mining information ... [was] a prominent feature' (Anon, 1901). Almost 30 years later, the reporting of trade, transport, markets, tourism, mining, and agriculture appeared throughout both the *SMH* and *The Argus*. In 1929, the *SMH* headed a page of various items 'Monetary and Commercial'. *The Argus* had part-page spreads of 'Commercial Intelligence' and shipping. Over the next 25 years the situation changed only insofar as newspapers began to collate material in dedicated business sections.

Nevertheless, boom–bust cycles, scandals and collapses, and the nature of the Australian economy, with its reliance on inward investment from the UK and State-led economic development, were problematic. The popular press in particular believed that business and finance news remained of interest chiefly only to 'City types' and wealthy private investors. The business section in *The Bulletin* weekly magazine was sceptically headed 'Business, Robbery, etc.' until the 1960s (Suich, 1988). A new concentration on business journalism proved to be one of the hallmarks of a widespread modernizing tendency in the press after World War Two, as cheaper newsprint became more globally available, advertising boomed, and there was a greater diffusion of affluence. In the 1950s in particular, business journalism began to change (Fahy, O'Brien, and Poti, 2010, p. 7; Jacobini, 2008, pp. 178–80; Slaata, 2007, p. 35; Tunstall, 1996, p. 358). Business in its broadest sense started to become 'big news' and business journalism a major growth area, shifting from the margins of journalism towards the centre and developing from an arcane specialism into a more generalist field (Lloyd and Walton, 1999; Matheson, 2007; Slaata, 2007, p. 68). Business journalists embarked on the journey from 'a desk in the corner' to editors' chairs (Fay, 2011, pp. 48–9).

When Rupert Murdoch's news organization established *The Australian* in 1964, a self-declared objective was to mainstream business:

> Reporting business will be big business for *The Australian* ... business is an important factor in our daily lives ... In today's Australia business and government are ever more closely entwined ... every day the financial pages of *The Australian* will publish informed interpretation of the meaning of the day's financial news ... For *The Australian*, therefore, reporting and interpreting the trend of business and finance will not be a matter for some half-forgotten section of the paper. It will be a key responsibility of *The Australian* and one of the areas in which the ideal of a national daily newspaper will be carefully filled.
> *(News Limited, 1964)*

Murdoch himself was disdainful of the technical coverage of the *Australian Financial Review (AFR)*, which had been established as a weekly in 1951, changed to bi-weekly in 1961, and to a daily in 1963, and was owned by his direct newspaper rivals, Fairfax (Schultz, 1993, p. 7). Possibly influenced by the success of general interest papers in the UK in appealing to business people, the short-lived *Sunday Australian* promised 'a large and authoritative business and finance section' (Cryle, 2005, pp. 226, 230). In 1971, *The Australian* recruited specialist staff from other papers to launch *Finance Week*, aimed at 'businessmen and investors', although it lasted only 14 weeks (Cryle, 2008, pp. 275–6). Business content was shaped by contemporaneous approaches to journalism – human interest, profiles, high visibility sectors (including television), and an interpretive edge (Cryle, 2005, p. 235; Cryle, 2008, pp. 270–2). Australian business reporting had changed from the dry noting of directors' reports and company results to the presentation of stories with additional material, journalistic emphases, and 'the liberal use of adjectives' (Schultz, 1993, p. 5). Yet very little of this was 'penetrating reporting' (Tiffen, 1989, p. 41). Business journalists still operated as a kind of guild. Schultz (1993, pp. 5–8), who worked for the *AFR* in the 1970s, recalled that 'the overwhelming sense was one of talking to members of a club'. Only a small number of journalists were prepared to challenge the prevailing orthodoxies. As proprietor of *The Australian*, Murdoch influenced the paper's business journalism until, by the 1970s, the business section became part 'promotional vehicle for corporate expansion' (Cryle, 2008, pp. 271, 278; House of Representatives Select Committee on the Print Media, 1992, pp. 268–71).

The immediate backdrop to this state of affairs was largely set by three overlapping factors. First, there was the emergence of global media corporations, to some extent led by Murdoch's News Corp. They became objects of business reporting. The interdependent relationship between advertising, corporate expansion, and business journalism was completed with the spread of home ownership, consumerism, and individual shareholding promoted by governmental economic rationalist policies (Cryle, 2008, pp. 270–3). Furthermore, corporate public relations (PR) grew exponentially. By the early years of the twenty-first century it was reckoned that in Australia there were 10 PR practitioners to every journalist (Kitchener, 2005, pp. 51–2; West, 2008/09, p. 23). In the 1990s it was estimated that 84–93 per cent of what appeared as business journalism in the Australian press originated in PR (Zawawi, 1994, p. 67).

There was another side to this, however. The amount of investigative journalism undertaken in Australia increased continuously from the 1950s to 2010. In the 2000s the *AFR* published as much investigative work as the major metropolitan 'quality' newspapers, the *SMH* and *The Age*. Among the winning entries to the annual Australian awards for journalism excellence, corporate affairs was the second most common topic after crime. Of these winners, approximately a half were investigations. Investigative journalism into corporate matters dominated in the 1970s and experienced a resurgence in the 2000s (Carson, 2013). At its beginning, *The Australian* was seen as 'a breath of fresh air' (Schultz, 1998, pp. 177–8).

All the same, business journalism also drew many reproaches for its timidity and failures, particularly in the 1960s, 1980s, and 1990s (Carson, 2013). High-profile instances of socially, financially, and environmentally damaging and even illegal business practices and corporate misconduct, as well as cyclical market fluctuations, intensified the criticisms (see Nash, 2001). Such was the dissatisfaction with the performance of business journalists in a 1960s mining boom that a subsequent Australian Senate inquiry led to them having to register their financial interests

(Schultz, 1998, pp. 2–4). Two decades on, more than a quarter of Australian business journalists believed that making personal financial gains from privileged access to information remained widespread, reasonably common, or quite usual, and a third said they would be more inclined to censor themselves when reporting on their own media owners (Schultz and Matolcsy, 1993, pp. 21, 25). In another survey conducted later, half the journalists reported experiencing improper managerial interference in their work (Henningham, 1997, p. 53). The biographer of *The Australian* argued that by the 1980s the paper had become more open in promoting Murdoch's business interests (Cryle, 2008, pp. 279–80).

Changes occurred in the 1980s that set in motion trends which characterized business journalism in Australia for the next 30 years (Greenfield, Williams, and Beadnell, 2004). Under the umbrella of economic rationalism, Murdoch was transformed from the smallest newspaper publisher in the country to controlling 60–70 per cent of all circulations (Manne, 2011; Schultz, 1998, p. 83). New specialist media appeared (see below), and personal finance, property, and consumerism featured more as a way of appealing to a more business-minded general population (Cryle, 2008, pp. 277–8). One former editor calculated that the number of business journalists in Australia trebled in less than a decade (Suich, 1988). Turner (1994, pp. 20–2) argued that Australian business journalists were self-referential, isolated, and captured by their sources in 'a complicit relationship with the highest flying sections of Australian business': 'high profile entrepreneurs were proffered as role models … despite their questionable business practices' (see also Carson, 2013). Schultz and Matolcsy (1993, p. 31) concluded that business journalists were also undertrained. More than 15 years apart, both Schultz (1993, p. 1) and Davies (2009) reported starting as business journalists with almost no knowledge of the field. Examining the collapse of the insurance company HIH in 2001, Kitchener (2002) found that *The Australian*'s business journalism was mainly uncritical, superficial, lacking in independent sources, and often just silent on the issue. More investigative journalism into corporate matters was undertaken by non-business journalists (Kitchener, 2005, p. 43); for example, Caroline Overington (2007), a former sports reporter and foreign correspondent, disclosed in *The Australian* the scandal of Australia's wheat exporter AWB Ltd paying about $AU300 million in bribes to the Saddam Hussein regime in the lead-up to the 2003 invasion of Iraq.

The censure of finance and business journalism elsewhere – that it had exchanged a journalistic virtuous cycle of scrutiny for a vicious circle of 'flabby reporting' (Longman, 2002) – appeared applicable in Australia, too. Business journalists ('fans of capitalism') were accused of being as voluntarily embedded with financial institutions as some reporters were with the military (Wilby, 2009). Whannel (2008) suggested that business journalism remained masculine, exclusive, devoid of investigation, dominated by PR, obscurantist about information, and indebted to 'powerful corporations'. Fraser (2009, pp. 79–81) believed that imperatives within the media led to a focus on 'daily dramas', scoops, short-sightedness, over-investment in bull markets, conformity, and the cult of the business personality. In their study of newspaper coverage of the Australian coal industry, Bacon and Nash (2012,

p. 250, pp. 256–7) found that business reporting relied heavily on corporate reports and aligned 'tightly' with the interests of industry, rendering opposing views largely invisible. The *SMH*'s Michael West (2008/09) blamed a failure to winkle out 'greed, leverage, risk, suspect corporate governance and complex corporate structures' on journalists, in part for failing to get on top of contemporary conditions where there were 'Too many press releases, too little time, too many promoters and PR people in the world, too much chipmonkery in the accounts and statutory documents, too little regulatory oversight.'

The popularization of business journalism

Notwithstanding Day's optimism, finance and business journalism was not immune from the circumstances of Australian journalism as a whole. Business journalists were among those who lost their jobs in a wave of cutbacks that swept the newspaper industry. Between 2006 and 2011, an estimated 13 per cent of print journalism jobs were eliminated.[4] Tiffen (2010a, p. 356) calculated that, following a period of growth in the amount of business journalism published in the 'quality' press starting in 1976, there was a reduction in the decade 1996–2006. Yet Australian business journalists lacked neither support nor opportunity. In 2012, the National Press Club established a prize for excellence in financial and business journalism, and Murdoch funded a business journalism award in honour of one of his Australian publishing executives. Alan Kohler and Michael Stutchbury (see below) were ranked respectively the fourth and twelfth most powerful journalists in Australia (www.thepowerindex. com.au/journalists-a-editors/).

As of 2009, all the major media – the two national papers already referred to; 20 state/territory daily and Sunday newspapers; 37 regional dailies and 470 other regional and suburban newspapers; the Australian Broadcasting Corporation (ABC) two-channel national television service; ABC Radio National, NewsRadio, and TripleJ, and 54 local radio stations; the Special Broadcasting Service (SBS); the network commercial television channels Seven, Nine, and Ten; a number of regional commercial networks; and Sky News Australia – produced news that included business segments, items, and programming.[5] From the mid 1960s to 1999, as noted, of Australia's three national daily newspapers, two specialized exclusively in business journalism, and the third covered business extensively. Between 1971 and 1991, the proportion of items relating to finance etc. published in the 'quality' press rose by almost 20 percentage points, and the number by more than 80 per cent (Greenfield et al., 2004). The 1980s was a period of growth in the publication of business magazines (*Business Review Weekly* [*BRW*], *Australian Business*) (Henningham, 1997, p. 45), and of television and radio programmes (Greenfield and Williams, 2007, p. 421); the 2000s brought the introduction of web-based business journalism (*Business Spectator*, *Eureka Report*).[6] The latter were founded by Kohler, a former editor of the *AFR*, who simultaneously presented finance on ABC television news and hosted ABC 1's *Inside Business* programme. ABC 1 also broadcast a weekday *Lateline Business* show from 2006 (Knott, 2013), and employed a Wall Street correspondent from 2007 to 2010.

On commercial television, the breakfast news and current affairs presenter for the Seven Network, David Koch, was one of the pioneers of contemporary business journalism in Australia, founding the Australian Financial Press in 1988. Prior to joining the 'family-friendly' *Sunrise* show, he was Seven's finance editor. He specialized in accessible popular business journalism, presenting 'A Minute on Your Money' and 'A Minute on Your Business', which were carried by more than 50 radio stations, and utilizing this approach in business and finance segments in *Sunrise*. In 2007, Seven began broadcasting his *Business Builders* programme aimed at SMEs (see http://au.smallbusiness.yahoo.com/), the same year he was named Australia's best finance journalist. Nine's competitor breakfast show *Today* paralleled this with 'Money Minute' presented by finance editor Ross Greenwood. Between 2007 and 2009, *Today* had up to four finance presenters. In 2009, Sky News Australia launched a new 24/7 business channel in collaboration with Fox Business Network in the USA. The GFC, it appeared, had helped propel business, and especially finance, as a topic into the mainstream of popular (mainly television) journalism.

Australia also existed within a wider media environment with access to business journalism from around the world. BBC World's *World Business Report* was available both directly and through re-transmission by NewsRadio. CNBC Asia broadcast programming made in Sydney. Bloomberg TV produced up to six Asian shows. *The Economist*, *Financial Times*, *Fortune*, *Forbes*, *WSJ Asia*, and the *International Herald Tribune* all circulated, some in significant numbers – and their websites were accessible – in Australia (Fumagalli, 2009). Although it was not possible to be certain, up to 25 per cent of Australian 'opinion leaders' may have accessed *The Economist* and 10 per cent the *Financial Times*.

These factors presented challenges for the traditional bastion of business journalism other than specialist magazines – the 'quality' broadsheet newspapers. Newspaper publishing in Australia was dominated by two corporations: News (then controlling aggregate circulations of more than 17 million) and Fairfax (more than 6 million). The 'quality' newspaper sector comprised only four titles: the *AFR*, *SMH*, *The Age* (all Fairfax), and *The Australian*.[7] Fairfax also owned *BRW*, and its raft of media properties included eight business publications and 12 business websites, many of them spin-offs from the *AFR*. The Financial Review Group relied heavily on Australia's 75,000 senior business executives as both readers and website visitors. *The Australian*, therefore, was uniquely positioned as the only nationally circulating general interest title in the country.

Murdoch, journalism, and the GFC

Although as many as 100 jobs were lost at the *WSJ* following its acquisition by Murdoch, later an additional 75 journalists were hired (Auletta, 2011, p. 27; Bercovici, 2009; La Monica, 2009, pp. 9–10). 'Some serious money' was spent at *The Australian*, too, in part to rebrand its business section to include content from the *WSJ* (Hartigan, 2009). The paper launched a new business magazine the following year (Day, 2008). Murdoch declared business journalism to be 'a great central franchise' in News's ambition to establish 'a digital dynasty' embracing newspapers and television (Robinson, 2010).[8] He insisted that 'The future of journalism is more promising than ever', and that 'even amid challenging economic times there are opportunities to improve and expand journalism'. News, he argued, 'believe[d] fiercely that the key to competing during difficult times is to invest more in journalistic content not less', and to encourage users to pay for 'quality'. In Australia, the chairman and chief executive of News said: 'We need more [journalists who are] specialists, more experts, more people who can provide compelling insights into what's going on' (Hartigan, 2007).

Murdoch's confidence that the GFC presented an opportunity for a cash-rich News to buy cheaply (even though it was widely believed that News paid about $US2 billion over the odds for the *WSJ*), and to begin to shift newspapers from a dependency on advertising to a subscription-based business model (Day, 2008; Rowland, 2008), appeared to be based on the impact of the crisis on the media themselves. Both a decline in advertising and a drift from print to the Internet accelerated. Many media in Australia were reportedly 'staggering under debt burdens of historical proportions'. Share prices fell (*7.30 Report*, 2009).[9] Murdoch's recipe for success was to make his papers 'populist'. He drew on the examples of *The* (London) *Times* and *Sunday Times*, which he had acquired in 1981 (Beahm, 2012, p. 36). In these terms, 'populist' meant 'combining an essentially serious approach with techniques derived from the popular tabloids', which some regarded as 'vulgarisation' (Leapman, 1992, pp. 77–9).

In 2007 the newest site for this tactic was the *WSJ*. Under Murdoch's proprietorship the paper moved to present 'a stronger focus on general news' with an 'emphasis on shorter stories ... and ... [a] de-emphasis of deeper reporting and analysis ... its focus on business' (Carr, 2012; Chittum, 2011). A survey of the front pages of the paper three months into News's ownership detected a significant increase in political coverage at the expense of business news, which had declined by half. A second study covering four years to 2011 found that business coverage had fallen by about a third, and some categories, such as media and transport, had disappeared from the paper. The paper was so much more Main Street, it was reported that Murdoch was even contemplating changing its title to omit Wall Street (Anon, 2011; Jurkowitz, 2008; Ro, 2012).

Popular business journalism and the GFC

A $AU42 billion economic stimulus plan announced in 2009 was a core response of the Australian Labor government to the GFC (Novak, 2009, p. 33). Two of the elements were a 'building the education revolution' (BER) capital works programme for schools, costing in excess of $AU14 billion, and a $AU2.4 billion home insulation initiative, known as the 'pink batts' scheme (Lewis, 2010, pp. 153–4). Whether these initiatives were successes on one or more of many fronts fuelled continuing debate (Austin, 2013),[10] but the focus of this chapter is how, as fiscal measures, they were popularized through journalism. Government appeared to be aware of the risk that journalism's drive for 'a good story' could overwhelm the economic rationale behind the schemes (Watson, 2010).

For Kevin Rudd (2009), the prime minister whose administration introduced the stimulus package, it had an ideological underpinning: social democratic governments, he argued, had to 'save capitalism from itself' through intervention. This jarred with Murdoch's belief in 'the free market system', the market's innocence in the sub-prime lending and subsequent banking collapse, and the limited utility of stimulus packages (Beahm, 2012, pp. 109–10). This was a signal for News's Australian newspapers, led by *The Australian*, to go 'to war' (Mayne, 2013). The paper's central message was that 'bureaucracies are ill-suited to doing what businesses do better' (*The Australian*, 2010). In February 2010, *The Australian* likened the Labor government to the regimes of the Soviet Union (Manne, 2011). What had started out as an economic, fiscal, business, and labour stimulus was transformed into something political, personalized, polarized, confrontational, and popularized through a focus on the pink batts and BER schemes (Manne, 2011; Neighbour, 2011). Tiffen (2010b) argued that this promoted 'unexamined assumptions about cause and effect' in reporting the stimulus, and demonstrated

> the stultifying and misleading narrowness of the news agenda. It was depressing testimony to how seldom a complex or rounded picture emerges ... The media controversy was framed almost entirely by the political conflict ... media pursues controversies with little curiosity about history and a defiant innumeracy.

One former financial journalist called it 'a wilful beat-up' (Parker, 2010).[11] An *Age* journalist blamed 'careless, pack-hunting journalists' (Watson, 2010). Pink batts in particular were made to define the stimulus effort, circumventing debate about economics, fiscal policy, or employment. The GFC as such simply slipped from Australian popular memory (Berg, 2013).

Conclusion: Wall Street to Main Street

In the 1960s, when *The Australian* began publication, business journalists in the UK, Ireland, and elsewhere were playing a prominent part in newspapers' coverage of government (Fahy, O'Brien, and Poti, 2010, pp. 6–7; Tunstall, 1996, p. 361). Over the next 40-plus years the reporting of business and politics not only became more 'closely entwined', but, in the case of *The Australian*, one subsumed the other (Manne, 2011). Topics of business, finance, and economics were popularized within a recognizable and traditional adversarial political (party) frame. The issues for *The Australian* and its reporting were the broader ones of the role of government in public life – social and cultural, as well as economic – and the meaning of pink batts was constructed primarily as one of governmental unfitness rather than of success or failure in identifying 'the path to economic recovery' from the GFC (Rudd cited in Shanahan, 2009). In this regard, *The Australian* mirrored the *WSJ* under News's control in shifting its centre of journalistic gravity from Wall Street to Main Street.

In an interesting postscript, in 2011 the editor-in-chief of the *AFR*, Stutchbury, who had previously been *The Australian*'s economics editor, declared an intention to realign his paper – more general and international news – to bring it closer to *The Australian*, citing the example of the direct competition between the *WSJ* and *New York Times* (*Lateline Business*, 2011). In coming into the mainstream, finance and business journalism had been subsumed within a broader political concentration and lost its distinctiveness. Ironically, finance and business journalism per se was again corralled in the ghetto of the specialist pages dedicated to the narrowest interests.

Notes

1 The terms 'finance and business journalism', or just 'business journalism', are used here to indicate journalism that addresses not just finance and business but economics, fiscal policy, commerce, consumerism, etc.
2 This section is taken in part from Bromley (2014, forthcoming).
3 The newspaper ceased publication in 1999 when it was merged with *Lloyd's List Australian Weekly*, which since 2011 has appeared as *Lloyd's List Australia*.
4 The losses intensified in 2012 and 2013 when it was said that 1,200 jobs in journalism were lost across newspapers, magazines, television, and the national news agency. Fairfax created a business unit, which incorporated the *AFR*, *BRW*, and *Smart Investor*, and signalled the end of separate business reporting at *The Age* and *SMH*. *BRW* ceased print publication to become an online-only entity.
5 The list excludes ABC News 24, which began broadcasting in 2010, nor is it intended to be comprehensive.
6 Australian Independent Business Media, owner of *Business Spectator* and *Eureka Report*, was acquired in 2012 by News Limited.
7 In 2007 and 2008, Fairfax launched online-only newspapers in Brisbane and Perth in the face of News monopolies in those cities.
8 As noted, as well as *The Australian* and the *WSJ* this initiative included the establishment of both the Fox Business Network and the Australian Sky News Business Channel, although the *WSJ* was regarded as the jewel in the crown (Wolff, 2013).
9 See also Beahm (2012, pp. 31, 33) for Murdoch's views on the future of newspapers and newspaper indebtedness.
10 The pink batts scheme was implicated in four deaths, several injuries, 120 house fires, and about 200,000 homes with inadequate insulation, and required a spend of $AU1 billion in rectification (Garnett and Lewis, 2010, pp. 183–4).
11 To 'beat up' is to sensationalize and exaggerate importance, or to make a journalistic story out of very little substantiating evidence.

References

7.30 Report (2009) 'Media Companies Struggling in Tough Times', ABC TV, 18 May. Transcript available at: www.abc.net.au/7.30/content/2009/s2574058.htm [Accessed 20 November 2013].

Anon (1831) '"Sworn to No Master, of No Sect Am I"', *Sydney Herald*, 18 April, p.2.

——(1901) 'Journalism and Literature', *Sydney Morning Herald*, 1 January, p.9.

——(2011) 'The *Wall Street Journal* Under Rupert Murdoch', *Project for Excellence in Journalism*, 20 July. Available at: www.journalism.org/commentary_backgrounder/wall_street_journal_under_rupert_murdoch/ [Accessed 31 October 2012].

Auletta, K. (2011) 'Murdoch's Best Friend: What Is Robert Thomson Doing at the *Wall Street Journal?*' *New Yorker*, 11 April, pp. 23–31.

Austin, A. (2013) 'We Really Must Talk About the Pink Batts', *Independent Australia*, 13 August. Available at: www.independentaustralia.net/politics/politics-display/we-really-must-talk-about-the-pink-batts [Accessed 25 November 2013].

Australian Bureau of Statistics (2013) *6554.0 – Household Wealth and Wealth Distribution, Australia, 2011–12, Summary of Findings.* Available at: www.abs.gov.au/ausstats/abs@.nsf/Latestproducts/6554.0Main%20Features22011–12?opendocument&tabname=Summary&prodno=6554.0&issue=2011–12&num=&view= [Accessed 28 October 2013].

Bacon, W. and Nash, C. (2012) 'Playing the Media Game', *Journalism Studies*, 13 (2), pp. 243–58.

Beahm, G. (ed.) (2012) *The Sun King: Rupert Murdoch in His Own Words*, Richmond, Vic: Hardie Grant Books.

Bercovici, J. (2009) 'Cuts Coming Next Week at the *Wall Street Journal*', *Portfolio.com*, 30 January. Available at: www.portfolio.com/views/blogs/mixed-media/2009/01/30/cuts-coming-next-week-at-the-wall-street-journal [Accessed 17 October 2011].

Berg, C. (2013) 'The GFC Debate We Never Had', *The Drum*, 2 July. Available at: www.abc.net.au/unleashed/4794186.html [Accessed 15 November 2013].

Bromley, M. (2014, forthcoming) 'Reporting Business and Finance', in Griffin-Foley, B. (ed.) *A Companion to the Australian Media*, Sydney, NSW: Australian Scholarly Publishing.

Carr, D. (2012) 'For the *Journal*, Leadership at a Crossroads', *New York Times*, 9 December. Available at: www.nytimes.com/2012/12/10/business/media/for-the-wall-street-journal-leadership-at-crossroadshtml [Accessed 10 December 2010].

Carson, A. (2013) 'Hold the Front Page: Despite Money Woes, News Outlets Doing MORE Investigative Journalism Not Less', *The Citizen*, 24 July. Available at: www.the citizen.org.au/media [Accessed 15 November 2013].

Chittum, R. (2011) 'Murdoch's *Journal*, Joe Nocera, and Fox-ification', *Columbia Journalism Review*, 18 July. Available at: www.cjr.org/the_audit/murdochs-journal-nocera-and-fo.php [Accessed 31 October 2012].

Crook, A. (2008) 'A Financial Crisis Is No Time to Trust Finance Journalists', *Crikey*, 20 October. Available at: www.crikey.com.au/2008/10/20/a-financial-crisis-is-no-time-to-trust-financial-journalists/ [Accessed 15 November 2013].

Cryle, D. (2005) '"A Second-Rate *Sunday Times*?": Murdoch's *Sunday Australian* (1971–1972)', *Media History*, 11 (3), pp. 225–38.

——(2008) *Murdoch's Flagship: Twenty-Five Years of the 'Australian' Newspaper*, Carlton, Vic: Melbourne University Press.

Davies, K. (2009) 'Follow the Money: How to Introduce Students to Business Journalism'. Paper presented to the Journalism Education Association conference, Perth, 30 November–3 December.

Day, M. (2007) 'Online Shift Signals Boom in Business Journalism', *The Australian*, 21 June. Available at: www.theaustralian.com.au/news/online-shift-signals-boom-in-business-journalism/story-e6frg6n6-1111113791340 [Accessed 28 October 2013].

——(2008) 'Rupert Murdoch Positive in the Face of Financial Crisis', *The Australian*, 20 October. Available at: www.theaustralian.com.au/news/gloom-and-doom-is-for-wimps/story-e6frg99x-1111117794388 [Accessed 8 September 2013].

Fahy, D., O'Brien, M., and Poti, V. (2010) 'From Boom to Bust: A Post-Celtic Tiger Analysis of the Norms, Values and Roles of Irish Financial Journalists', *Irish Communication Review*, 12 (2), pp. 5–20.

Fay, S. (2011) 'Big City, Bright Lights', *British Journalism Review*, 22 (1), pp. 48–53.

Fraser, M. (2009) 'Five Reasons for Crash Blindness', *British Journalism Review*, 20 (4), pp. 78–83.

Fumagalli, A. (2009) *The Pan Asia–Pacific Cross Media Survey*, London: *Financial Times*. Available at: www.docstoc.com/pass/68435961 [Accessed 15 January 2014].

Garnett, A. and Lewis, P. (2010) 'The Economy', in Aulich, C. and Evans, M. (eds.) *The Rudd Government: Australian Commonwealth Administration 2007–2010*, Canberra, ACT: Australian National University, pp. 181–98.

Greenfield, C. and Williams, P. (2007) 'Financialization, Finance Rationality and the Role of the Media in Australia', *Media, Culture & Society*, 29 (3), pp. 415–33.

Greenfield, C., Williams, P., and Beadnell, C. (2004) 'The Rise and Rise of Journalism Pertaining to Finance', in Nolan, S. (ed.) *When Journalism Meets History: Refereed Papers from the Australian Media Traditions Conference 2003*, Melbourne, Vic: RMIT Publishing, pp. 143–9.

Hartigan, J. (2007) 'Andrew Olle Media Lecture', Sydney, 19 October.

——(2009) 'The Future of Journalism', Address to the National Press Club, Canberra, 1 July.

Henningham, J. (1997) 'Characteristics and Attitudes of Australia's Finance Journalists', *Economic Analysis & Policy*, 27 (1), pp. 45–58.

House of Representatives Select Committee on the Print Media (1992) *News & Fair Facts*, Canberra, ACT: The Parliament of the Commonwealth of Australia.

Jacobini, M.L. de P. (2008) 'Economic Journalism and the Conception of Market: A Content Analysis of the Economy Sections of *Folha de S. Paulo* and *O Estado de S. Paulo*', *Brazilian Journalism Research*, 4 (2), pp. 176–94.

Jurkowitz, M. (2008) 'How Different Is Murdoch's New *Wall Street Journal*?' *Project for Excellence in Journalism*, 23 April. Available at: www.journalism.org/node/10769 [Accessed 31 October 2012].

Kirby, J. (2010) 'Australia and Me: Journalism', *Irish Echo*, 5 May. Available at: www.irishecho.com.au/2010/05/05/australia-and-me-journalism-3371 [Accessed 24 October 2013].

Kitchener, J. (2002) 'Business Reporting at the Beginning of the 21st Century: Is It Getting Any Easier?' Paper presented to the Australian and New Zealand Communication Association conference, Gold Coast, Qld, 10–12 July.

——(2005) 'Investigative Business Journalism in the Age of the Internet', *Australian Journalism Review*, 27 (1), pp. 41–56.

Knott, M. (2013) 'It's Just Business: Kohler's Axed Sunday Slot Leaves Coverage Gap', *Crikey*, 3 October. Available at: www.crikey.com.au/2013/10/03/its-just-business-kohlers-axed-sunday-slot-leaves-coverage-gap [Accessed 25 October 2013].

La Monica, P.R. (2009) *Inside Rupert's Brain: How the World's Most Powerful Media Mogul Really Thinks*, London: Penguin.

Lateline Business (2011) '*AFR* "Learning" From Online Paywall', ABC TV, 29 November. Transcript available at: www.abc.net.au/lateline/business/items/201111/s3379607.htm [Accessed 19 November 2013].

Leapman, M. (1992) *Treacherous Estate: The Press After Fleet Street*, London: Hodder & Stoughton.

Lewis, C. (2010) 'A Recent Scandal: The Home Insulation Program', in Dowding, K. and Lewis, C. (eds.) *Ministerial Careers and Accountability in the Australian Commonwealth Government*, Canberra, ACT: Australian National University, pp. 153–76.

Lloyd, C. and Walton, P. (1999) 'Reporting Corporate Crime', *Corporate Communications*, 4 (1), pp. 43–8.

Longman, P. (2002) 'Bad Press: How Business Journalism Helped Inflate the Bubble', *Washington Monthly*, October. Available at: www.washingtonmonthly.com/features/2001/0210/longman.htm [Accessed 9 October 2002].

Manne, R. (2011) 'Bad News: Murdoch's *Australian* and the Shaping of the Nation', *Quarterly Essay*, 43.

Matheson, C. (2007) 'Profile: Rupert Murdoch', BBC News, 1 August. Available at: www.bbc.co.uk/2/hi/business/69257_38.stm: [Accessed 3 April 2010].

Mayne, S. (2013) 'Kevin Rudd and Rupert Murdoch: A Brief History', *The Guardian*, 2 September. Available at: www.theguardian.com/commentisfree/2013/sep/02/rupert-murdoch-australia [Accessed 26 November 2013].

Nash, C. (2001) *Media Dimensions*, episode 3, ABC TV, 20 August.

Neighbour, S. (2011) 'The United States of Chris Mitchell: The Power of Rupert Murdoch and *The Australian*'s Editor-in-Chief', *The Monthly*, July. Available at: www.themonthly.com.au/issue/2011/july/1315015434/sally-neighbour/united-states-chris-mitchell [Accessed 25 November 2013].

News Limited (1964) *The Australian*, Sydney: News Limited.

Novak, J. (2009) 'Bailout Bonanza!' *IPA Review*, March, pp. 32–4.

Overington, C. (2007) *Kickback: Inside the Australian Wheat Board Scandal*, St. Leonards, NSW: Allen & Unwin.

Parker, J. (2010) 'The Numbers Game', *Failed Estate*, 20 September. Available at: http://the failedestate.blogspot.co.uk/2010/09/numbers-game.html [Accessed 25 November 2013].

Porter, D. (2000) '"Where There's a Tip There's a Tap": The Popular Press and the Investing Public, *c*.1900–1960', in Catterall, P., Seymour-Ure, C., and Smith, A. (eds.) *Northcliffe's Legacy: Aspects of the British Popular Press, 1896–1996*, London: Macmillan, pp. 71–96.

Quiggin, J. (2003) 'Economic Rationalism', *johnquiggin.com*, 13 June. Available at: http://johnquiggin.com/2003/06/13/economic-rationalism/ [Accessed 28 October 2013].

Ro, S. (2012) 'MURDOCH: "We Might Change *Wall Street Journal* to *WSJ*"', *Business Insider*, 28 June. Available at: www.businessinsider.com/murdoch-wall-street-journal-wsj-2012-6 [Accessed 31 October 2012].

Robinson, P. (2010) 'Rupert Murdoch: The Future of Newspapers', *Uncommon Knowledge*, Fora.tv, 5 February. Transcript available at http://fora.tv/fora/fora_transcript_pdf.php?cid=11524 [Accessed 14 February 2014].

Rowland, M. (2008) 'Murdoch Says Financial Crisis Hurting News Corp', ABC, 18 October. Available at: www.abc.net.au/news/2008-10-18/murdoch-says-financial-crisis-hurting-news-corp/545644/ [Accessed 18 September 2013].

Rudd, K. (2009) 'The Global Financial Crisis', *The Monthly*, February. Available at: www.themonthly.com.au/issue/2009/february/1319602475/kevin-rudd/global-financial-crisis [Accessed 26 November 2013].

Schultz, J. (1993) 'Reporting Business – A Changing Feast', in Schultz, J. (ed.) *Reporting Business*, working paper no. 5, University of Technology Sydney: Australian Centre for Independent Journalism, pp. 1–8.

——(1998) *Reviving the Fourth Estate: Democracy, Accountability & the Media*, Cambridge: Cambridge University Press.

Schultz, J. and Matolcsy, Z. (1993) 'Business Boosters or Impartial Critics?' in Schultz, J. (ed.) *Reporting Business*, working paper no. 5, University of Technology Sydney: Australian Centre for Independent Journalism, pp. 9–32.

Shanahan, D. (2009) 'Intimate Dinner Between Kevin Rudd and Rupert Murdoch Covers Biggest Issues', *The Australian*, 22 September. Available at: www.theaustralian.com.au/business/news/intimate-dinner-between-kevin-rudd-and-rupert-murdoch-covers-biggest-issues/story-e6frg906-1225777971451 [Accessed 20 November 2013].

Slaata, T. (2007) 'The Nordic Business Press and the New Field of Business Journalism (1960–2005)', in Kjaer, P. and Slaata, T. (eds.) *Mediating Business: The Expansion of Business Journalism*, Copenhagen: Copenhagen Business School Press, pp. 35–71.

Suich, M. (1988) 'Scepticism Lacking in the Fast Lane', *Sydney Morning Herald*, 15 November. Available at: www.paged.com.au/paged-articles/1988/11/15/scepticism-lacking-in-the-fast-lane/ [Accessed 15 April 2010].

The Australian (2010) 'Pink Batts Debacle Teaches Government Costly Lessons', 18 October. Available at: www.theaustralian.com.au/opinion/editorials/pink-batts-debacle-teaches-government-costly-lessons/story-e6frg71x-1225939909818 [Accessed 25 November 2013].

Tiffen, R. (1989) *News and Power*, North Sydney, NSW: Allen & Unwin.

——(2010a) 'Changes in Australian Newspapers 1956–2006', *Journalism Practice*, 4 (3), pp. 345–59.

——(2010b) 'A Mess? A Shambles? A Disaster?' *Inside Story*, 26 March. Available at: http://inside.org.au/a-mess-a-shambles-a-disaster/ [Accessed 25 November 2013].

Tunstall, J. (1996) *Newspaper Power: The New National Press in Britain*, Oxford: Oxford University Press.

Turner, G. (1994) *Making It National: Nationalism and Australian Popular Culture*, Sydney: Allen & Unwin.

Watson, J. (2010) 'Insulation Fire Risk Was Worse Before Rebate', *Sydney Morning Herald*, 4 March. Available at: www.smh.com.au/federal-politics/political-opinion/insulation-fire-risk-was-worse-before-rebate-20100303-pivv.html [Accessed 25 November 2013].

West, M. (2008/09) 'The Pom-Pom Effect', *Walkley Magazine*, 54, pp. 22–3.

Whannel, G. (2008) 'Information and Authenticity: Financial Information and the Media in the Age of Replication'. Paper presented to The End of Journalism? Technology, Education and Ethics conference, University of Bedfordshire, 17–18 October.

Wilby, P. (2009) 'When Business Journalism Gets in Bed With the Financial Institutions', *Online Journalism News*, 8 October. Available at: www.journalism.co.uk/articles/536070.php [Accessed 12 May 2010].

Wolff, M. (2013) 'Murdoch Tries for New Legacy', *USA Today*, 2 June. Available at: www.usatoday.com/story/money/columnist/wolff/2013/06/02/michael-wolff-rupert-murdoch-legacy/2382917/ [Accessed 18 September 2013].

Zawawi, C. (1994) 'Sources of News: Who Feeds the Watchdogs?' *Australian Journalism Review*, 16 (1), pp. 67–71.

PART II
The Euro-crisis and the media

6

THE IRISH PRESS, POLITICIANS, AND THE CELTIC TIGER ECONOMY

Mark O'Brien

The release by Independent Newspapers of the 'Anglo tapes' in July 2013 was in many ways a cathartic occurrence. More than any other event, the audio recordings from Anglo Irish Bank's telephone system capture the hubris that lay at the heart not only of the bank but of the entire Celtic Tiger economy.[1]

The conversations, which occurred in 2008, record for posterity the mentality that helped create the largest property collapse in history. The language used by the bank's executives sharply demonstrates the fact that the property boom had been built on nothing other than arrogance and an infallible sense of entitlement. Realizing that the bank needed a bailout, its chief executive David Drumm is heard announcing that he does not want 'any fucking bolloxology' from the Central Bank. The strategy to get the Central Bank to commit €7 billion to Anglo was simple: he would go there 'with arms swinging [and say] we need the moolah, you have it, so you're going to give it to us and when would that be?' When asked how the €7 billion figure had been calculated, another Anglo executive, John Bowe, is heard explaining: 'I picked it out of my arse.' Bowe is also heard acknowledging that Anglo needed more than €7 billion but the strategy was to 'pull them [the Central Bank] in, you get them to write a big cheque and they have to keep, they have to support their money, you know'. Although expressed in crude terms, the strategy worked – at a horrendous cost to the taxpayer. In September 2008, the Irish government announced a blanket guarantee for the banking system and in November 2010 was forced to accept an €85 billion rescue package from the EU and the IMF. The arrival of an IMF team to oversee a succession of austerity budgets was the harsh wake-up call that all was not as it had seemed in Ireland's banking sector.

Indeed, the language captured on the Anglo tapes is a far cry from the refined public relations strategy that characterized the rapid growth of the bank during the Celtic Tiger years. The entire episode – the unquestioned expansion of the bank during the boom followed by a hard-hitting exposé after its collapse – is starkly illustrative of the relationship between journalists, financial institutions, and the public. As Davis (2000, p. 284) has pointed out, wide audience interest in business and financial stories generally only occurs 'if a sensational negative story is being reported'. While strong criticism was directed at the former Anglo executives for their behaviour and role in creating an unsustainable banking sector, much criticism was also directed at the Irish media by the government-appointed commission of inquiry into the banking sector. Listing the conditions necessary for a systemic financial crisis to occur, the report (Nyberg, 2011, p. 5) included 'media that are generally supportive of corporate and bank expansion, profit growth and risk taking, while being dismissive of warnings of unsustainable developments'. The report found that Anglo Irish Bank had been 'lauded by many investors, consultants, analysts, rating agencies and the media as a role model for other Irish banks to emulate' (p. ii). It also noted what it referred to as the 'relentless media attention' given to the property market and concluded that 'much of the media enthusiastically supported households' preoccupation with property ownership' (pp. ii–iii and 50).

This chapter presents an exploratory analysis of the world of Irish financial journalism in which eight financial journalists report their views on how they conceptualize their professional roles, routines, and work practices during and after the economic boom. The professional lives of financial journalists in other jurisdictions have been thoroughly examined within the literature. Davis (2000, pp. 285–6) contends that as business is one of the main patrons of media organizations through advertising and information provision, business news, in effect, is paid for by business advertising and is largely for business consumption. As a result, financial journalists tend to move in small, exclusive circles, and their journalism reflects the views and values of a narrow business-elite. He concludes that 'the corporate sector, combining PR with its advertising and news source advantages, has "captured" business and financial news', and notes that even though some journalists may be active in their reportage, in the final analysis 'business news will always follow corporate agendas and ignore non-corporate interests' (p. 286).

Similarly, Doyle (2006, p. 443) found that while financial journalists 'are generally highly sceptical about "spin" and strongly inclined towards highlighting instances of corporate underperformance and mismanagement', their professional routines and the constraints under which they work 'make it unlikely that financial irregularities obscured within company accounts will be detected on a routine or consistent basis'. She concludes that the complicated nature of financial markets and the limited interested audience for in-depth analysis means that the capture of financial journalists by corporate elites has less to do with the tenor of individual news items than with how such coverage is framed and the values that such coverage serves to reinforce (p. 446).

In his interviews with British financial journalists, Tambini (2010, p.158) found that no consensus existed about their 'watchdog role in relation to markets and corporate behaviour'. He also found that they agreed on the key challenges facing them – including the fact that interested parties, including corporate executives and analysts, were sometimes the only source of relevant information – but that they were uncertain on how to respond to these challenges. More bluntly, Marron (2010, pp. 73–4) concludes that the Irish media 'failed to probe, to exercise scepticism about what is done and said by those in political and financial power'. Describing both general and financial journalists as 'cheerleaders for Wall Street and the City', she notes that they 'failed to serve as a watchdog on the powerful, to anticipate and predict'. Likewise, Manning (2013, p. 173) found that 'most financial journalists and most international news agencies simply failed to report much of the emerging evidence of the growing possibility of collapse', and notes that among the explanations put forward were 'the complexities of the evidence, the manipulative power of financial public relations, and the difficulties of undertaking investigative journalism when newsrooms cut staff'.

The key question for this chapter is whether and to what extent these findings apply to the Irish case. The eight journalists interviewed were sampled to ensure variability in type of media organization (print, broadcast, wire service), length of financial journalism experience, and position in their organization's editorial hierarchy, and were granted anonymity on the grounds that they were critiquing their peers and employers, and that the views expressed were their own and not those of their news organizations. The journalists, hereinafter identified by the letters A to H, were overwhelmingly experienced: six had been reporting on financial matters for between five and ten years, one for between one and five years, and one for more than ten years. All were questioned on how they viewed the role of financial journalist, sources relationships, professional constraints, how their organizations treated financial stories, whether financial journalism had been unduly uncritical during the economic boom, whether this had changed in light of the crisis, and whether, in light of the crisis, they felt they now could freely critique the financial sector.

Perceived roles and work practices

In terms of roles and work practices, almost all the interviewees viewed the role of the financial journalist as being the same as other reporters who cover a specialist area. Journalist E believed the specialism's 'basic role should be the same – to keep the audience regularly informed of developments and act as a form of watchdog for wrongdoing', though he concluded that 'it often acts as a cheerleader for capitalism, distributing company news but rarely critiquing what's going on beyond basic profit/loss and investment return figures'. Journalist A believed its role was 'holding business people and organisations to account and explaining complex events to people who are not experts in the field'. However, Journalist H noted that the role was very different in that financial journalism is largely:

> reporting on private activity that is not automatically open to media scrutiny, like the business of government ... Finance itself is a relationship in the main between the buyers and sellers of assets; the journalist is an intruder into that relationship ... the financial journalist is not paid to consider the wider social

consequences of commercial decisions, so hence the financial journalist has to be able to zone in on the strict commercial merits of big decisions.

Some interviewees noted that in addition to the usual tensions on all reporting beats – the constant aims of being competitive, fair, accurate, balanced, and avoiding defamation – financial journalists faced particular newsgathering constraints. Several of the interviewees identified access to information and sensitivity surrounding information as being major constraints of the specialism. Journalist H noted that 'company accounts are by definition historical in nature and commercial information is routinely denied to financial journalists by a whole plethora of organisations and individuals'. Several of the interviewees pointed out that they operate under strong legal constraints: they are constrained by stock market regulations concerning the public disclosure of market-sensitive information that affects share prices. Journalist D stated that journalists were conscious of the impact of their stories on share prices. He noted that 'market behaviour is more often than not influenced by rumours and interpretations of trends so the weight of such consequences is in our minds when reporting potentially incendiary stories'. While Journalist B criticized daily financial journalism for being 'almost entirely press release and stock exchange disclosure based', Journalist E noted that the opportunity to undertake investigative financial reporting – of company performance, for example – is severely limited because of a lack of resources. Moreover, it emerged that the threat of legal action is particularly acute, since they are writing frequently about well-funded companies that could afford expensive litigation. While Journalist B noted that 'very often a threat of an injunction is enough to have a story pulled', according to Journalist H many legal actions by wealthy individuals or companies are 'executed purely to stifle genuine inquiry'.

When questioned about their sources it emerged that the financial community served as the major pool of sources for business news. As Journalist E observed: 'the routine sources of information are company results, company announcements, regulatory businesses e.g. consultations, analysts' reports and company spokespeople. Company spokespeople often brief for their client, but also against their competitors.' The interviewees also routinely consulted documentary sources, including material filed with regulatory and statutory bodies, and, as observed by Journalist F, senior journalists have built up a network of senior financial sources and do not rely on company spokespeople as frequently as junior colleagues. However, he also conceded that because of the need for regular contact with financial sources, 'some journalists are reluctant to be critical of companies because they fear they will not get information or access in the future'. Journalist E was more forthright. He believed that during the boom some journalists had become 'far too close to their sources':

> They viewed them as friends and allies and essentially became advocates for them. Their approach was justified editorially because many developers and bankers limited access to such an extent that it became seen to be better to write soft stories about them than to lose access. Extremely soft stories would

be run to gain access too – indeed, [developer] Seán Fitzpatrick was a particularly coveted source among some journalists.

Most of the interviewees mentioned that they are careful to move routinely outside the financial community for sources of information. Two interviewees noted that there has often been considerable pressure from public relations professionals to influence the content of financial news. Disturbingly, Journalist F noted, it was 'well known that some PR companies try to bully journalists by cutting off access or excluding journalists from briefings', while Journalist E stated that there existed 'an unofficial blanket ban on any engagement with the trade union movement, despite their obvious role in the economic system. I have been told by editors in the past that they had no place in the business section.' He also recounted how he had witnessed 'the lack of critical scrutiny of information provided by sources – a fair amount of which was deliberate misinformation, particularly surrounding the banks'. In a detailed exposition of his work during the boom he recounted how a prominent state source for banking stories contacted his editor to complain about how a story had supposedly criticized the individual's office. He was warned about how his story had damaged the newspaper's relationship with the office and was 'informally banned' from writing about that office. The newspaper was then given access to a senior official from the office 'who briefed my colleagues on the "correct" position'. Looking back on the affair, Journalist E concluded that 'basically they trusted the banks, the developers and the regulator and never suspected that they were misleading them or hiding potentially improper acts from them'.

In terms of the stories they produced, all eight interviewees believed that differences existed in the treatment of financial stories depending on the intended audience or readership. They all agreed that the style of writing differed for reports written for the news, rather than the business, pages of a newspaper. Journalist A noted that there existed 'a greater tendency to avoid technical financial terminology outside the business pages', while Journalist F noted that he would have regularly been told to cleanse his articles of 'jargon and financial terms'. According to Journalist H, such stories tended to more crudely point out who the 'good' and 'bad' guys were in a particular development, and, as noted by Journalist E, this process of making stories more readable sometimes caused tension between the news and business desks:

> It also brings its own tensions: the news section is generally interested in the most sensational angle on a story, based on their limited knowledge of the field, regardless of accuracy. This generally results in a compromise where the story isn't as precise as a business story but it's in the right ballpark. It is preferable to getting general reporters to write the stories as they lack the understanding of terminology and financial structures that underpin modern capitalism.

These tensions were also noted by Journalist F, who observed that it was 'not uncommon for news-desks to change business copy to make it more "punter friendly'". Several of the interviewees observed that the process of a story transferring from the business to the news pages often involved the story referring to why the development was important to the average citizen. A commonly used angle was that of consumer or taxpayer impact. Journalist G highlighted stories about mortgage rates or stories that involved a cost to the taxpayer as 'extreme examples' of the general newsworthiness of specialist financial stories. He also noted that big company losses or stories involving well-known businessmen might also transfer to the general news pages due to their high public profiles.

Reporting the boom

No consensus emerged when the interviewees were asked whether financial journalists had been sufficiently critical in their coverage of financial institutions' practices and government policy during the Celtic Tiger years. Several of the interviewees believed that a systematic analysis of the published or broadcast reports would demonstrate that financial journalists 'did not shirk' their responsibilities. They argued that they performed their role within the constraints of the specialism, and pointed to the pronouncements of high-profile commentators and journalists, such as the columnist David McWilliams and former RTÉ economics editor George Lee, as examples of critical journalism. However, one journalist dissented strongly from this view: Journalist G observed that

> for the most part they were not critical enough and even those that were [critical] in private conversation didn't express those views in their stories. There were some reporters who did criticise policies, but they were in a minority and no matter how vocal they were, there is an argument that no one wanted to hear it.

Some interviewees argued that critical coverage did not receive the prominence in newspapers and broadcasts that it warranted. Journalist H observed that 'business and economic journalists constantly questioned the sustainability of the Celtic Tiger economy, but it was not always given proper foregrounding. Criticism of government policy was rife throughout the period of the boom.' The same journalist noted 'there was too much acceptance' of what the banks said about their commercial property lending, but journalists who covered this sector 'found no regulators or outside forces suggesting the problem was as big as it later became'. Furthermore, some interviewees felt they had been constrained in their newsgathering by the lack of information provided by financial institutions. Referencing the property boom, Journalist B said there was 'a dearth of publicly verifiable information on the rise in indebtedness'. Likewise, Journalist A noted that there 'was no requirement on the main players to publicly declare their financial performance and virtually all of them exploited the rules governing companies with unlimited liability to avoid public scrutiny of their accounts. This was pointed out at the time, repeatedly.' Nonetheless, the annual reports of banks showed the huge reliance on foreign borrowing and high loan-to-deposit ratios, which may not have received sufficient critical coverage. However, it must also be remembered that some banks 'adjusted' their loan books prior to the annual auditing process. Anglo Irish Bank temporarily moved €87 million of loans to Irish Nationwide Building Society every year. These circular loans misled not just journalists but also auditors, shareholders, and the banking regulator.

Some of the interviewees mentioned the tensions involved in reporting on business for news organizations that were heavily reliant on advertising revenue from property and financial organizations. Journalist C noted that

> much of the mainstream media seems to me to be very conflicted because of their reliance on real-estate and recruitment advertising. That doesn't mean reporters consciously avoid writing bad news stories, but it's hard to run against the tide when everyone is getting rich.

The importance of property advertising to media organizations was illustrated in 2006 when the *Irish Times* paid €50 million for the property website *myhome.ie*. Indeed, in their study of the *Irish Times*'s housing and property issues, Preston and Silke (2011) found that coverage was biased in its selection of sources – the majority came from the mortgage, real-estate, building and banking industries – and uncritical in terms of how such statements were utilized in reportage. Significantly, Journalist F believed that journalists 'were leaned on by their organisations not to talk down the banks [and the] property market because those organisations have a heavy reliance on property advertising'. At its most public, this became manifest in the well-publicized departure of *Sunday Tribune* business editor Richard Delevan in 2007, when he reported that a prominent estate agent was struggling to sell his own house amid what his company was calling a bullish housing market in its press statements (Cullen, 2007).

On top of all these pressures there existed a consensus among the interviewees that journalists who took a critical view of the boom were excluded from receiving off-the-record information, and were often 'shouted down' by politicians or special interests. The comment by former Taoiseach (Prime Minister) Bertie Ahern in 2007 in which he wondered why those who were criticizing the economy did not 'commit suicide' (RTÉ, 2007) was mentioned in several interviews as being symptomatic of this process of marginalization. The comment was prompted by a late 2006 *Irish Times* article by university economist Morgan Kelly who predicted a property crash (Kelly, 2006). Alongside politicians, property developers were also vocal in demonizing those who critically examined the boom. In early 2006, high-profile developer Seán Dunne criticized those in the media whom he referred to as 'the harbingers of doom and gloom' (McDonald and Sheridan, 2008, p. 268). Crucially, the interviewees linked the tone of coverage to experience and expertise, with Journalist F noting that few journalists had business or economics degrees. Journalist E was harsher in his assessment, noting that 'a lot of the journalists involved didn't have specific knowledge of their sectors and lack the interest to educate themselves on them'.

Journalist C observed that the more financially literate journalists were the ones that were the most critical, as relatively few financial journalists 'really understand the numbers and the trends, so there doesn't tend to be much independent thinking'. Notably, the two journalists most referenced by the interviewees as evidence of critical thinking within the specialism, George Lee and David McWilliams, are both economics graduates and worked as economists before becoming journalists.

Reporting post-boom

Significantly, all eight interviewees agreed that the type and tone of financial reporting changed when the scale of the global financial crisis and scandals in the Irish banking sector emerged. Journalist A noted that it was 'inevitable that reports on an economic meltdown and corporate malfeasance have their own style and tone. The tone was no different in past scandals and past crises.' Journalist D noted that 'suddenly the stakes became far greater. Banks overtook politicians as sources of scandal and financial news became far more relevant to a general audience.' Interestingly, Journalist G noted that while coverage changed, this suited news outlets because, for such institutions, bad news is good news:

> Yes, financial reporters have become much more critical of regulations and regulators as well as those that are seen to be to blame for the crisis. The tone of financial journalism has become angrier – in print, but particularly in broadcast – but this can be partly explained as capturing the mood of the people. Financial journalism has become much more closely read in the last two years, in my opinion – partly as people try to understand what happened, but also because newspapers are pushing financial news more – bad news sells.

Journalist B noted that while business journalists had been critical of certain aspects of the boom before the crash, 'the tone turned negative as the scale of incompetence, at both the regulator and at the banks' executive level, was exposed'. Journalist C noted that 'the economy and business has become the new sport or politics, dominating the front pages. The tone has clearly changed as well.' Coverage, he believed, was now 'far more critical and economists have become the new celebrities'. Likewise, Journalist F noted that 'reporters have become much quicker to question figures presented by either government or companies and to ask whether the information has been independently audited as accurate'. Journalist H believed that coverage 'became more critical, more investigative and more sceptical'. Journalists, he believed, have developed 'a healthy scepticism' towards the business community. However, one interviewee, Journalist E, dissented from this new 'healthy scepticism' belief. He noted that 'most of the top bankers are gone, the regulator is gone but the financial journalists who so woefully reported their sectors remain in place. And they still aren't holding industry to account.'

Asked whether they now felt they could be more critical of the financial system, all eight interviewees agreed that they could be, though many questioned the degree to which critical analysis had been or could be carried out. Journalist A noted that comment pieces, rather than straight reporting, allowed journalists to be critical, while Journalist B observed that journalists could be critical 'by writing about the bonus culture that fuels short-termism, by challenging broker recommendations, by pointing out conflicts of interest and by having the courage to take a stand on certain issues'. Journalist C noted that journalists should be 'questioning', but queried what he saw as the increasingly blurred lines between reportage and comment. But some interviewees viewed such developments as too little too late, and again questioned whether they had been sufficiently critical during the boom years. According to Journalist E:

> The problems that we have seen in Irish financial journalism in recent years have been due largely to its unquestioning support for the elite consensus. There have been critical financial journalists but they have largely been marginalised by their profession. For instance, during the property boom, the journalists shouldn't have been just reporting what the developers said, they should have been asking 'where's the demand for all these houses?' and 'how do you propose servicing your debt?'

Journalist F expressed similar sentiments by noting that 'during the boom years very few reporters asked critical questions for fear their access would be denied by PR people or [they] didn't have the knowledge to ask detailing and probing questions'. But he concluded 'that has changed and, if anything, most reporters now distrust everything they are told'. However, several interviewees pointed out that even with the crash, the news production process has not changed that much. Journalist D observed that 'there is little space for in-depth questioning and analysis in a sound-bite driven, conveyor-belt news environment', while Journalist G acknowledged that financial journalists 'operate within that system and within [or] on the fringes of certain circles of knowledge. If they are overly critical of those within those circles, they can lose out on access to that knowledge and therefore they lose stories. They have to tread a fine line.'

However, this newfound sense of public scepticism on the part of journalists has not gone down well with politicians or business moguls. In a 2010 speech the then minister for finance, Brian Lenihan, called for journalists 'to be aware of the self-fulfilling nature of doomsday scenarios', because media coverage could 'undermine or promote confidence in our economy'. Negative reports at home were, Lenihan declared, 'beamed around the world and can influence the decisions of foreign investors and multinationals' (Cullen, 2010). In response, Fintan O'Toole (2010) of the *Irish Times* pointed out that Lenihan's complaint sounded very like the situation in 2007 and 2008 when, as it became clear that an economic crash was looming, the government, the financial regulator, and the Central Bank insisted that there was nothing to worry about, that Irish banks were robust, and, if anything, we were heading for a soft landing. As O'Toole saw it, journalists are now critically engaged because they had 'learned the hard way not to trust emollient assurances that everything will be okay'. Politicians were now 'the opposite to the boy who cried wolf – even when the politicians insist there is no wolf, journalists listen for the howling in the woods'. In a similar vein to Lenihan, in a radio interview, former Taoiseach Bertie Ahern (Edwards, 2011) called for an investigation into the media for what he claimed was the failure of journalists to properly report an overheating economy. This had happened, Ahern alleged, because journalists had focused all their attention on him and the investigation into his financial affairs by a government-appointed tribunal of inquiry. As he bluntly put it:

> The government were following the economy but the media weren't. It was a very poor job by the media really. They were shown to be incompetent and that was the trouble, everything was on me ... There should be an investigation into it. They should have been following the economy from August 2007, but they weren't, they were following me. I think a lot of these guys really should have looked at themselves.

Business and media moguls have also joined the chorus of condemnation. In 2009, one of Ireland's leading businessmen and media moguls, Denis O'Brien (2009), declared that 'some journalists are anti-business and anti-enterprise'. It must, however, be noted that O'Brien was a participant in the Moriarty Tribunal established to investigate payments to politicians by businessmen. The tribunal found that O'Brien had made two payments totalling half a million Irish pounds to a politician, Michael Lowry, and that Lowry, while minister for communications, had 'secured the winning' of the 1995 mobile telephone licence for O'Brien's company Esat Telecom (Keena, Lally, and Collins, 2011).

Discussion and conclusion

This study demonstrates that the professional tensions at the heart of business journalism in other jurisdictions are also present in the professional roles, routines, and work practices of Irish financial journalists. First, no consensus emerged regarding the role or function of financial journalism: while some interviewees viewed it as explaining complex financial developments to the public, others viewed it as essentially reporting developments in what are (or were) private businesses. Second, there existed tensions and constraints in relation to accessing information, concerns about the market sensitivity of certain information, a fear of expensive litigation, and a lack of time and resources to conduct detailed long-term analysis or investigations. Third, there existed effective source capture in that the journalists operated in a closed network of information sources. While they largely disagreed that they were part of an elite communication network, they stated that their sources were largely drawn from the broad financial community, which in turn comprised a large part of their readership/audience. Moreover, the responses indicate that the tendency for financial journalists to operate within closed networks was more pronounced during the boom years, as the lack of criticism from regulatory, economic, or policy sources contributed to the lack of criticism in news coverage. For the most part, the journalists operated within a tightly knit circle of powerful interest groups that all stressed the positive aspects of light-touch regulation. The gatekeeping tactics of public relations professionals only added to this tight circle of established sources. Fourth, there existed a strong awareness of the intended audience for stories, with tension sometimes emerging as stories migrated from business to general news pages.

Fifth, there existed no consensus on whether financial journalism had been sufficiently critical during the boom years. There existed a belief that dissenting views did not receive sustained prominence in coverage during the boom, and that anyone who dissented from the view that the good times would last forever would be shouted down and demonized. The tension between analysing an economic boom and property corruption, and the dependence of media outlets on property advertising revenue, was instanced by several journalists as a potential conflict of interest that could have compromised media credibility. Lastly, there existed a strong consensus that the crisis empowered journalists to be more critical of the financial system. However, there also existed a belief that the news production process had not been radically altered since the crisis, as the instantaneous nature of journalism meant that there was little time or space for in-depth analysis. The fact that such limited criticality arises only in the wake of an economic crisis (and arguably in response to a heightened public demand for accountability) is worrying. It may be that all concerned – the business community, educators, media institutions, journalists, and the public – need to change the perception that financial news is of relevance to the public only when things go wrong.

Note

1 The tapes can be heard on www.independent.ie

References

Cullen, P. (2007) 'Tribune Business Editor Loses Post After Article', *Irish Times*, 8 November, p. 7.
——(2010) 'Lenihan Critical of Doomsday Media Coverage', *Irish Times*, 25 September, p. 4.
Davis, A. (2000) 'Public Relations, Business News and the Reproduction of Corporate Elite Power', *Journalism*, 1 (3), pp. 282–304.
Doyle, G. (2006) 'Financial News Journalism: A Post-Enron Analysis of Approaches Towards Economic and Financial News Production in the UK', *Journalism*, 7 (4), pp. 433–52.
Edwards, E. (2011) 'Ahern Says "Incompetent" Media Should Be Investigated', *Irish Times*, 19 October, p. 3.
Keena, C., Lally, C., and Collins, S. (2011) 'Tribunal Finds That Lowry Secured Licence for O'Brien', *Irish Times*, 23 March, p. 1.
Kelly, M. (2006) 'How the Housing Cornerstones of Our Economy Could Go Into Rapid Freefall', *Irish Times*, 28 December, p.14.
McDonald, F. and Sheridan, K. (2008) *The Builders: How a Small Group of Property Developers Fuelled the Building Boom and Transformed Ireland*, Dublin: Penguin.
Manning, P. (2013) 'Financial Journalism, News Sources and the Banking Crisis', *Journalism*, 14 (2), pp. 173–89.
Marron, M.B. (2010) 'The Scorecard on Reporting of the Global Financial Crisis', *Journalism Studies*, 11 (2), pp. 270–83.

Nyberg, P. (2011) *Misjudging Risk: Causes of the Systemic Banking Crisis in Ireland: Report of the Commission of Investigation into the Banking Sector in Ireland*, Dublin: The Stationery Office. Available at: www.bankinginquiry.gov.ie/

O'Brien, D. (2009) Address at Connacht Tribune Centenary Conference, NUIG, 2 October. See also Kenny, C. (2009) 'A Lecture from Denis O'Brien on Media Standards', *Sunday Independent*, 4 October, p. 16.

O'Toole, F. (2010) 'Confidence in Action: Speech by Minister for Finance Brian Lenihan', *Irish Times*, 29 September, p. 11.

Preston, P. and Silke, H. (2011) 'Market "Realities": De-coding Neoliberal Ideology and Media Discourses', *Australian Journal of Communication*, 38 (3), pp. 47–64.

RTÉ (2007) 'Ahern Apologises for Suicide Remark', Available at: www.rte.ie/news/2007/0704/90808-economy/ [Accessed 13 December 2013].

Tambini, D. (2010) 'What Are Financial Journalists for?', *Journalism Studies*, 11 (2), pp. 158–74.

7

THE SPANISH PRESS

No illusions

Ángel Arrese

The media and the crisis

The current global financial and economic crisis is generating a number of studies about its media coverage. One of the recurring ideas is that in the years before the crisis, news organizations were unable to warn of existing risks in the financial industry. As the crisis progressed, the media are often criticized for their simplistic and alarmist view of the economic and financial problems.

However, research carried out on those issues does not provide a unanimous answer to the question of how far the media has failed, and there is a wide variety of opinions on the matter, both professional and academic.

Professional criticism

Even though there is no single view among professionals on the topic, there are many out there who consider that news organizations could have done more, especially when it comes to connecting and interpreting signals of risk seen in several economic indicators, which in the end had consequences both in the whole economy and in the financial system. Many journalists have identified several issues that prevented the media from properly researching and publishing those risk indications: the lack of education among professionals, their attitude towards accepting official consensus, and their uncritical praise of markets and their main characters during boom times (Banda, 2009; Caplen, 2009; Fuller, 2009; Harber, 2009). At the same time, there were problems related to the organizational structure of news organizations, which made it more difficult to accomplish a more critical and in-depth coverage of general economic matters (Kurtz, 2008; Stuller, 2008; Luscombe, 2009; Satija, 2009; Chittum, 2011).

But there are also those who refuse to accept the idea that media companies failed, or at least failed to some extent. Usher (2013) describes that resistance among business journalists at *The New York Times*. Francesco Guerrera, a former *Financial Times* editor, does not accept the idea that insufficient work was done by business journalism during the crisis as a consequence of some sort of 'Stockholm Syndrome': a syndrome in which media, in theory, end up being too close to those whom their economic and reporting luck depends on, especially advertisers and news sources (Guerrera, 2009). Other renowned journalists, such as Larry Ingrassia of *The New York Times*, and Robert Peston of the BBC, have also excused the media, particularly when their role is compared with that played by other institutions (Peston, 2009; Sposito, 2009).

In any case, all of them acknowledge that news organizations could have done more, although they were less well placed to understand the situation than other economic agents, including financial research analysts, regulators, public authorities, and experts, none of whom were able to predict the size of the problem. In Paul Krugman's words, 'Just a few economists forecast the crisis' (Krugman, 2009).

Now, in the middle of the crisis, it is widely accepted that the media have made an enormous effort to devote both time and space to economic news, which, seemingly overnight, turned out to be the most important story in newsrooms (Fernández, A., 2008). Even in specialized media, such as the *Financial Times*, content was reorganized to devote almost half the pages to topics related to the crisis (Thompson, K., 2008).

Regarding alarmism, most professionals think that there are isolated exaggerations, but that, in general, those journalists and media that try to produce good financial journalism are aware of how sensitive that information is. In Spain, no particular *mea culpa* has been perceived related to sensationalism. Magis Iglesias, chairman of the Spanish Journalists Association, said: 'In Spain, media coverage about the economic crisis is good. There is evidence of some journalists embracing yellow journalism in order to sell more newspapers, but those are isolated cases' (cited by Fernández, D., 2008). Joaquín Estefanía, a veteran Spanish business journalist, recently said:

> News organizations and journalists must work on this issue within very narrow boundaries: on the one hand, we must report and explain what happens, regardless of how serious and alarming those facts are (and the current economic crisis is very deep, long and its consequences are terrible for the Spanish society) and on the other hand, we must avoid injecting fear to citizens that read, listen or watch us.
>
> (cited by Pérez Oliva, 2012)

Other countries also dealing with a difficult economic environment, such as Ireland, confirm the idea of business journalists showing more decision-making and professionalism in their coverage of this crisis compared with previous years (Fahy, O'Brien, and Poti, 2010).

Academic thinking

A review of published research and studies about the role of the media during the crisis shows an outstanding critical vision while most academics consider that economic journalism has not lived up to expectations, for several structural and professional reasons.

Within the structural analysis, it is worth pointing out those who consider that business journalism was unable to reveal and warn of the economic crisis because of its own capitalist nature. Media companies, in this analysis, were conditioned by the economic interests of both owners and advertisers, and were therefore unable to adopt a critical view about the functioning of the market economy, which inevitably led them to praise the system's kindness, to promote prosperity ahead of the crisis, and to not warn enough about the risks. A full acceptance of the notion, 'the market is good', led the media to avoid questioning or seriously criticizing the cracks in the economic system (Chakravartty and Downing, 2010; Chakravartty and Schiller, 2010; Hope, 2010; Lewis, 2010; Sandvoss, 2010). In Spain, de Mateo, Bergés, and Garnatxe (2010) mention the lack of economic independence of the media, who are limited by their financial obligations, a lack that triggered a shortage of both good stories and analysis about the problems in the banking and financial industries. That perspective is also shared by other authors (Almiron, 2008; Lits, 2010).

In line with that structural view, there are other approaches to explaining the inadequate coverage of the crisis, including that of Stiglitz (2011), who describes how the information economy and existing incentives in the markets distort the message, and that of Thompson, G. (2009), who applies Herman and Chomsky's propaganda model to the production and distribution of financial news. Additionally, several authors have criticized the growing 'politicking' of journalism, which has led the media to give up on both analysis and insightful interpretation, and to embrace partisan views of the whole situation (Becerra and Mastrini, 2010; Caruso, Cepernich, and Roncarolo, 2012).

Other authors explain the theoretically inadequate coverage of the economic crisis by reference to professional reasons rather than structural ones. From this perspective, the failures of business journalism are not so much a consequence of the economic or market structure as of factors related to professional experience, such as journalists' lack of economic and financial education, the controversial relationship with news sources, and the trend of telling current stories as if they were episodes (Davis, 2005; Doyle, 2006; Tambini, 2008, 2010; Fraser, 2009; Marron, 2010).

To sum up, almost all published theoretical studies about the role of the media in condemning market practices and alerting people to the crisis consider that the coverage has been very inadequate: 'the truth is that when businesses and finance became the best story in the world, almost all journalists did not notice it' (Fay, 2011: 53).

Empirical research

Empirical studies about this role of the media are very scarce and those that do exist present contradictory results or lead to different conclusions. The reason for the lack of a consensus is probably due to the fact that both the methodologies and the nature of the subject under analysis are very different and are therefore really difficult to compare. As an example, it is worth noting two of the first studies that were written in the US, those by Chris Roush (2008) and Dean Starkman (2009), which were published by *American Journalism Review* and *Columbia Journalism Review*, respectively.

Roush states that news organizations published enough stories to warn people of certain financial risks, but that those stories did not get much credit (Roush, 2008, 2011). Starkman analysed a sample of 730 stories published from 2000 to 2007 in some of the most influential US media outlets (The *Wall Street Journal*, *The New York Times*, *The Washington Post*, *Bloomberg News*, *Financial Times*, *Fortune*, *Businessweek*, and *Forbes*). According to this author, even if there was news that condemned some risks in the system, from 2003 to 2006 this news disappeared, and he concluded that the media did not fulfil their role of being watchdogs in the most crucial period (Starkman, 2009).

More recent research by Chernomas and Hudson (2011) about the coverage by the *New York Times* draws the conclusion that the newspaper did a fine job during the years before the crisis, thanks especially to its critical view on financial deregulation. However, the daily was unable to extend its analysis beyond the specific problems faced by the real-estate, banking and financial sectors, and to connect those with more general ones such as the freeze of salaries and the growing income gap that led to a dwindling of consumption among US households (Chernomas and Hudson, 2011: 165).

After analysing the coverage of the US stimulus package of 2009 in 16 different media outlets, Schiffrin and Fagan (2013: 16) note that the media did not play an important role in setting the agenda as they were too dependent on government sources. Their analysis 'confirms criticism towards business journalism. This focuses almost exclusively on daily events and details of proposals, based mostly on official sources and which in the vast majority of cases shows a pro-business mindset'.

It is in Germany perhaps where there can be found the most solid empirical research about this topic, particularly thanks to work by Arlt and Storz (2010). Their research monograph, 'Wirtschaftsjournalismus in der Krise', looks into the coverage by five quality newspapers (*Frankfurter Allgemeine Zeitung*, *Financial Times Deutschland*, *Handelsblatt*, *Süddeutsche Zeitung*, and *Die Tageszeitung*) from 1999 to 2005. The authors conclude that newsrooms were lured by the exaltation of increasing freedom and deregulation in the financial markets, and barely warned of the risks that would eventually have a deep impact on the economic system.

More positive results stem from analysis such as that carried out by Schranz and Eisenegger (2011), in which they compare coverage of the crisis undertaken by three prestigious international dailies (the Swiss *Neue Zürcher Zeitung*, the British *Guardian*, and the American *New York Times*). In this study, the period under analysis is 2007 to 2009, and what stands out is how, until the middle of 2007, there was a strong presence of general alerts about the real-estate bubble in the US, Spain, and the UK. Quiring and Weber (2012) also conclude that the coverage by German media on government measures to combat the crisis was 'prudent and balanced', a very positive judgement taking into account that their study focuses on TV news. On the other hand, Schifferes and Coulter (2013), in their study of the online coverage by the BBC, point out that it was not as superficial as is sometimes supposed.

Other more particular features of the crisis coverage, linked to traditional criticism of business journalism, show much clearer evidence. For instance, Bähr (2009) has described the predominance of negative news and pessimistic views about the crisis in the German press, a finding that had already been confirmed in economic news in other periods of time without a crisis (Lowry, 2008). Tracy (2012) has spoken out against clichéd and simplistic views provided by the US media on the Greek crisis and the reasons behind it because, according to him, they focus on cultural and peculiar features of the Greek people, and leave aside other more institutional reasons, which implicate other European and US leaders. From a more linguistic perspective, Lits (2008), through an analysis of eight French dailies and magazines, confirms the excessive use of dramatic terms that appeal to emotions. And Horner (2011), in the US, criticizes the abuse of using metaphors that are full of ideological content both in media that were in favour of the Wall Street bailout in 2008, and those that were against.

One last field of study concerns whether or not there is a predominance of sources and frameworks of official analysis in contrast to the possibility of giving a more important role to alternative voices. In this area, Schranz and Eisenegger (2011), in their previously mentioned study, concluded that the well-known media they looked at did not present alternatives to the ruling capitalist model, although, in many cases, they spoke out against some specific sectors, such as the financial. Mylonas (2012) reaches a similar conclusion when analysing the coverage by German newspaper *Bild-Zeitung*, as does Berry (2013) on the coverage of the banking crisis in the BBC's *Today*, and also Titley (2013), after studying alternative journalism actions established in Ireland to respond to the submissive acceptance by the media of the unavoidable bailout of the country. All those studies, as well as other more specific ones about the usage of specialized sources (e.g. Sarabia-Panol and Sison, 2010), show the limited range of voices used to explain and interpret current news, with most of them representing the political, economic, and financial systems.

Regarding Spain, there are only very few studies about the role of the media in the coverage of the crisis. It may be worth citing the doctoral project started by Stefanie C. Müller – *The Role of the Press in the Biggest Economic Crisis in Spanish Democracy* – in which she analyses the front pages of Spain's newspapers *El País* and *El Mundo* from 1996 to 2009. Müller concludes that the two newspapers

> did not fulfill their role of reporting on events in an objective, analytical or informative way [...] The power of Spanish media to warn and control democracy has failed. The most influential media groups have accepted the usage of their news platforms to boost the real estate 'boom'.
>
> *(2010: 101)*

To sum up, no final conclusions can be drawn from this bibliographic analysis about the role of the media in the economic turmoil. There exists some kind of consensus saying that news organizations – especially the high-quality press – could have done a better job in accomplishing their commitment. But the role performed by the media has not been very different from that performed by many other political and financial institutions, whose actions in defence of public interest were as limited as those of the press. This has particularly been true in the Spanish case.

The Spanish media and the financial crisis

There was an old Spanish tourism slogan, that people might still be familiar with, that read, 'Spain is different'. It has been a while since it was used because Spain stopped being a different country once the political transition to democracy in the 1970s was complete. However, that idea of a different Spain has now been used once again during the current economic and financial crisis, and it still continues to be valid, at least when referring to the role of the media in this crisis.

The next pages will explain why we believe that the Spanish media coverage of this crisis doesn't deserve, perhaps, as much criticism as that of other countries, particularly when it comes to comparing the behaviour and attitude of other institutions and people involved, which include the government, businessmen, and experts. First, we will try to shed some light on the special state of the economic and financial press in Spain; second, we will talk about the media coverage and its attitude during the different stages of the crisis; finally, a few conclusions and final remarks will be made.

The special reality of economic and financial journalism in Spain

The history of economic journalism in Spain is very brief, nothing comparable to that of other countries, especially the Anglo-Saxon ones. The first professional economic newspaper was opened in 1978. But it was only in the eighties, after Spain joined the European Union in 1986, that economic journalism became relevant within the media context, both in general and specialized news. There has not been enough time for the emergence of truly influential newsrooms in the industry. So the first important idea is that Spain's economic and business journalism is quite immature (Arrese, 2008).

The development of business journalism since 1986 began as our country was going through deep economic changes, but it also took place amid an optimistic environment, with positive news prevailing during the so-called Spanish 'economic miracle' that lasted almost two decades.

Perhaps as a consequence of the last two ideas, it cannot be said that the media has had a critical attitude towards current economic issues. In general, all financial, business, and economic news organizations worked more as 'cheerleaders' of prosperity than as 'watchdogs' of potential problems resulting from the economic boom. An example of this is investigative journalism, which has failed to develop significantly in this particular field, unlike in others such as politics (Arrese and Baigorri, 2011).

A final idea to contextualize the state of Spanish business journalism just before the crisis unfolded is that Spaniards' interest in economic and financial issues has traditionally been rather low. A survey carried out in the European Union in 2007, before the crisis began, said that only 18 per cent of the Spanish population had a high interest in news about those issues, a figure that is higher than that of only Italy (17 per cent), and Portugal (5 per cent). The average of the 27 countries of the Union was 28 per cent, with highlighted cases such as Sweden and Finland, where interest levels were higher than 40 per cent (Eurobarometer, 2007).

In such conditions, one could not expect that the attitude of the Spanish media during the crisis would be outstanding. And, certainly, the media did not anticipate the crisis, did not thoroughly investigate the economic and financial imbalances that were later proved to be perverse, did not condemn the huge risk that certain financial practices entailed, and so on. To sum up, they probably did not work as 'canaries in a coalmine', as might have been expected of them.

But, at least in the case of Spain, we don't think that that attitude throws outright discredit on their coverage, or conclude that their behaviour during the crisis could be assessed as a failure. On the contrary, and as we will try to explain now, both prior to the crisis and during the crisis itself business and economic journalism has kept a more critical and more sceptical attitude than many other institutions, especially governments, but also businessmen, bankers, and many others. In our opinion, even if they haven't actually behaved as 'soothsayers of doom', they have reported about the real situation of the Spanish economy during the whole crisis with more honesty and more rigour than many other public servants have.

The media and the different stages of the crisis

Spain has lived through the current economic and financial crisis in a different way from that of other countries (you know, 'Spain is different'). On the one hand, the financial crisis emerged later and with less virulence than in other places (in Spain we haven't had a Northern Rock or a Lehman Brothers, and still in 2007 we were regarded as a 'miracle economy'). On the other hand, when the crisis came, it was an economic crisis, characterized by an extraordinary deterioration of the economy and labour activities, and the wreckage of public finances. Finally, when both realities converged, the intensity of the crisis was much greater than that of other countries, which makes Spain a country that could still have to be bailed out.

Without a doubt, the epicentre of the Spanish crisis can be located in the 'real-estate' bust, whose consequences for economic activity, the financial system, and public and private finances have been catastrophic. It could be no other way in a country in which, according to experts – although this is arguable – the construction industry accounted for about 18 per cent of gross domestic product.

The whole story of the crisis hasn't yet been told, mainly because it is not over yet. But it is still possible to analyse specific issues during each stage, especially from the perspective of its discussion in public opinion. In Spain, taking the years prior to the crisis and the period of 2008 to 2010, it is possible to point out some events and some topics that summarize its development and how citizens perceived it through their consumption of the media coverage.

Following the tradition of fixing phases or stages of the crisis, which is very common in financial meltdowns (Kindleberger, 1978), an approach for Spain would be to focus the analysis on five debates that took place, and that to some extent explain scenes of our particular 'narrative' or 'story' of the crisis – following the idea of economic 'stories' described by Akerlof and Shiller (2009: 51–58), or the more popular 'narrative' described by Thompson, G. (2009). Moreover, in the particular case of Spain, those debates have been focused on issues of public opinion that were, and are still, a synthesis of the state of the crisis.

The six scenes or stages are: a) the debate on the 'real-estate bubble' (2003 to 2007); b) the 'Champions League economy' (2008); c) the 'green shoots' (2009); d) 'Spain isn't Greece' (2010); e) 'Maybe the banking industry isn't such a model' (2011); and f) 'Waiting for a bailout' (2012).

Is there a 'real-estate bubble'? (2003 to 2007)

From 2003, there was a strong debate about whether or not a 'real-estate bubble' was taking place in Spain, mostly as a consequence of alerts about that phenomenon from some international media (in particular *The Economist*), and from institutions such as the International Monetary Fund. Ministers from the Conservative government led by José María Aznar – in particular Rodrigo Rato – as well as industry experts, businessmen, and bankers, among them Banco Santander Chairman Emilio Botín, all denied that the increase in housing prices in Spain could be called a bubble, which would have meant recognizing the extremely serious risks that its rupture could cause. The Socialists, the opposition party back then, talked about the bubble, but after winning the 2004 general election they also tried to avoid using that concept or admitting its existence, while at the same time trying to defend against – as the creation of a Housing Ministry shows – the possibility of a slowdown in housing prices.

That institutional refusal to recognize the existence of a bubble, and thus not speak about the perverse consequences of a potential burst, did not prevent the media from using that concept and having regular discussions about it. A study carried out at the University of Navarra's School of Communication showed that from 2003 to 2008 there were about 2,500 stories that used the term 'real-estate bubble' published by influential daily newspapers (the three largest general news ones, *El País*, *El Mundo*, and *ABC*, and the economic and financial papers, *Expansión* and *Cinco Días*). There were of course many more stories about the real-estate industry, housing prices, etc. Although the debate eased from 2004 to 2006, the potential threat of a bubble never waned in the minds of some commentators and experts, as those newspapers showed (Arrese and Vara, 2012).

José García Montalvo, arguably the best expert on the real-estate bubble – and a kind of a Robert Shiller in Spain – acknowledged the important role of the media in the bubble debate during those years, and said that the Spanish economic crisis, in that sense, may be one of the most announced crises in history (García Montalvo, 2008).

The 'Champions League' economy or an economy in crisis (2008)

From late 2007 to the beginning of 2008, and concurrent with the mortgage crisis in the United States, the Spanish real-estate bubble burst, as housing sales sank 72 per cent in the first quarter of 2008, and Martinsa-Fadesa, the country's biggest builder, filed for bankruptcy in July. In February of that year, the media was openly speaking about the real-estate market collapse, and about its dire economic consequences.

For almost a year, the public economic debate was about the bleak outlook for the Spanish economy. In September 2007, Prime Minister José Luis Rodríguez Zapatero delivered the famous phrase that the Spanish economy was in the 'Champions League' of the world's economies. He portrayed the image of a robust economy during the general election in 2008, when he argued that there was no risk of an economic crisis. In June that year, as news organizations and public opinion explicitly talked about the crisis, Zapatero said that 'it was arguable that there was actually a crisis' (El País, 28 June 2008), and pleaded for the avoidance of doom-laden and unpatriotic statements. In July, as reporters persisted in using the term, 'crisis', Zapatero, in a televised interview, finally acknowledged that there was an economic crisis, 'as they called it' (El Mundo, 9 July 2008). Of course, the Lehman Brothers collapse came soon afterwards.

Green shoots (2009)

In October 2008, once the crisis was accepted, and with the financial collapse caused by Lehman, Prime Minister Zapatero met with editors from Spain's mainstream media to lobby for moderation and the avoidance of doom-laden overstatements of the situation – such as the ones they were already spreading, according to the government (González and Lobo, 2008). At the same time, Zapatero said, news organizations needed to emphasize the strength of the Spanish banking industry – unlike that of other countries – and the Spanish economy's ability to respond to the crisis. A crisis that he predicted would be a brief one.

Perhaps the best metaphor for that idea was the quick usage by Spain's finance minister, Elena Salgado, of the image of existing 'green shoots' of economic recovery in May 2009, right before the European elections. Salgado said: 'Let's wait a few weeks and green shoots will be seen' (El País, 20 May 2009). That statement came after a €50 billion public spending plan to boost demand, and with more than 4 million people already unemployed.

Both the media and a growing number of experts and politicians from the opposition party immediately started to criticize the idea that a recovery was under way. El Mundo newspaper published in May 2009 an editorial with the following headline: 'Obvious dry shoots in the economy' (El Mundo, 26 May 2009). The foreign press also echoed that unfortunate expression, and its deep meaning. *The Economist* wrote: 'Spain's decade of growth has come to a painful end. In contrast to much of Europe, which is home to a few green shoots, Spain's economy still looks as arid as the meseta' (*The Economist*, July 2009).

In fact, the 'green shoots' reference became the basis for the debate about the gravity of the crisis. From May to December 2009, the three largest Spanish dailies (*El País*, *El Mundo*, and *ABC*) published 1,000 stories that openly referred to that term. Of course, the concept spread, and crossed borders. It has since been used ironically to refer to the government's false vision of the crisis in its early stages. In Conservative circles, and with a sense of humour, it became very popular to say that the government smoked those green shoots ... but they were green shoots of marijuana.

Spain is not Greece (2010)

By 2010, the depth of the recession was already clear to everybody, problems related to Spanish sovereign debt spread, and the extra yield demanded by investors to persuade them to hold on to 10-year Spanish bonds instead of German ones, were front page issues. In February that year, doubts over Greece's solvency set alarms off, and the comparisons between Spain, Greece, and Portugal did not stop, particularly within the foreign press. Spain's membership of such an unpopular group as the PIIGS touched the national sensitivity, and a new slogan emerged, which actually was approved by everybody – including government, media, and other institutions – that read 'Spain is not Greece'.

In May 2010, Spain was on the brink of collapse and of being bailed out, and the patriotic consensus within public opinion that 'Spain is not Greece' – this time with support from mainstream media – emerged at a time when there was an emerging critical sensitivity towards foreign countries, towards the easy and stereotyped image of our country in the foreign media, towards credit rating agencies, which were regarded by some as potential 'international speculators', towards the evil markets and, in general, towards the structural perversion of a political and economic system incapable of coping with social outcry. The government even decided to investigate the role of the 'Anglo-Saxon media' in fomenting the crisis (*Der Spiegel*, 15 February 2010; *The Economist*, 9 February 2010).

After more than a year of becoming steadily conditioned to swings in bond yields, the reaction against external factors eased, and there was a more balanced perspective about the circumstances of the Spanish crisis – even as new scapegoats were emerging, such as the so-called 'Merkozy' alliance.

Maybe the banking industry isn't such a model (2011)

Maybe the aspect of the Spanish economic and financial crisis about which the media was blindest was the strength of the banking system. There is little surprise in this, bearing in mind that the press in Spain has traditionally kept an almost deferential attitude towards this industry. Both Spain's biggest banks and the regional savings banks, or *cajas*, cultivated close and good relationships with the media, thanks to their roles as big advertisers, providers of loans for highly indebted companies, and sometimes even as shareholders. All this, obviously, acquired an even greater weight in such difficult business situations as the ones media companies were now going through.

From the beginning of the crisis, the government, the banking industry, and experts protected the power of Spanish banks. At the end of 2008, a historic television story by *Informe Semanal* – the best-known TV news magazine in the country, which is broadcast by state-owned television – showed five chairmen from Spain's biggest banks and savings banks, along with the then finance minister Pedro Solbes, the Bank of Spain's governor, and the Spanish deputy prime minister, making a solemn statement on the trust that everybody should have in the strength and solvency of Spanish banks. That idea, based on the fact that Spain did not experience any bankruptcy or a banking panic, unlike in other countries, caught on in both the media and public opinion for quite a long time.

Over time, little by little, and even as the media couldn't boast about having engaged in any special activism, the banking industry, especially the savings banks or *cajas*, started to see the light in a controlled way, and a wide political consensus on how to confront the crisis emerged, following technical directions from the Bank of Spain. Some entities merged, public subsidies were set up, *cajas* – owned by regional governments – were transformed into commercial banks, and some of them were taken over by Spain's bank rescue fund, known as FROB.

Finally, in 2010, the European Banking Authority's stress tests surprisingly showed that some banks, which were thought to have served as models, actually failed. Spanish media have since then sharpened their criticism of these entities – mainly the former savings banks – and it is now more common to find investigative reporting pieces that question bad management practices, outrageous executive salaries, balance sheets infected by overvalued real-estate assets and bad debt, etc. Nonetheless, those investigations usually focus on small banks rather than on the big ones.

Waiting for the country's bailout (2012)

As a new Conservative government led by Mariano Rajoy was elected, the truly critical state of the Spanish economy was revealed. After the revelation of a bigger than expected budget deficit, the sovereign debt crisis deepened. At the same time, the banking crisis exploded with the bankruptcy of Bankia, the fourth-largest Spanish bank, which has recently been nationalized, and the conditions of the economy worsened – particularly unemployment – after tough spending cuts were approved by the new cabinet.

Amid this new context, and with risk premium out of control, the main topic under discussion was the possible bailout of the Spanish economy by the European Union. In June 2012, a banking bailout of as much as €100 billion was approved, and in the second half of the year the main topic was the possibility of Spain requesting a bailout for the whole economy.

The vast majority of the national media, as well as many international media – especially the British – announced 'imminent' bailouts several times. In August 2012, for instance, *El País* said on its front page: 'BCE pushes Spain to another bailout' (Doncel, 2012). There were times when it was stated that a bailout was just a matter of hours away: The *Financial Times* said in October: 'Spain ready to make rescue request' (Johnson, 2012). In December, *El País* again – in an editorial – asked for an 'Urgent Bailout' (*El País*, 10 December 2012). *Reuters*, on the other hand, mentioned several specific dates for that event, such as the first weekend of October, and, later on, November.

In general, news organizations announced and analysed in detail a bailout that never happened, and whose final phase took place on 19 December, when Spanish Prime Minister Mariano Rajoy said in parliament that, in the end, Spain had made the decision not to request a bailout.

For several months, newspaper pages and broadcast news were full of rumours, speculation, and predictions whose tone, in general, was more catastrophic than that used by the government. Though it is true that the government contributed in part to that confusion, particularly Mariano Rajoy, the so-called 'Mysterious Mariano' (*The Economist*, 6 October 2012).

Final remarks and conclusions

As was explained at the start of this chapter, it's hard to say that the Spanish press, particularly the country's economic and business journalism, delivered extraordinary critical work, alerting and condemning in an exemplary fashion, before and during the current financial and economic crisis. The very immaturity of the industry probably made that task impossible.

However, given that economic content has dominated the news during the last five years, it could be said that, in general terms, the media did indeed work as a *watchdog*, balancing the powers, providing a voice of criticism in a context in which both public authorities and the most influential businessmen tried to minimize the seriousness of the situation. Some would even say that at certain times there was the intention of misleading the population, with the goal of not carrying out the enormous austerity measures needed to get the country out of the crisis. Within that environment, as we have shown and explained, the press has maintained a critical and sceptical stance towards the official statements, and has kept public opinion alerted about these issues.

There are of course many remaining issues about which Spain's business journalism needs to think carefully as a consequence of its role in this crisis. Its lack of ability to challenge the financial world has been noted already, especially due to that quasi-reverential and too respectful attitude towards some almost untouchable sectors, such as banking. The well-known alignment of certain Spanish media with certain ideas, and even with political parties, could also be criticized, because those relationships excessively affect such news fields as the economic and financial. But this needs more objective analysis, and to be based on technical arguments and evidence.

However, in this crisis at least, even with their limits, the media have in our opinion been more worthy of admiration, and have served society far better, than other institutions with a serious and greater public responsibility. It could be said that in this crisis the Spanish press has been the one-eyed in the land of the blind, or at least in a country where many didn't want to see at all.

It is difficult to establish a direct connection between the media coverage and the behaviour of citizens, but probably its influence on public opinion is in part responsible for the spectacular political shift that took place at the last general election, held on 20 November 2011. Citizens punished the former government for its mismanagement of the crisis with the worst election results for the Socialists since Spain returned to democracy in 1978. People's Party leader Mariano Rajoy won the biggest parliamentary majority in a Spanish election in 29 years, betting on a radical change in economic policy, fortunately, without waiting until this had been directly imposed by the European Union.

References

Akerlof, G. and Shiller, R.J. (2009) *Animal Spirits: How Human Psychology Drives the Economy, and Why It Matters for Global Capitalism*, Princeton: Princeton University Press.

Almiron, N. (2008) 'Crisis Financiera, Economía y Medios de Comunicación', *Mientras Tanto*, vol. 108–109, 83–90.

Arlt, H.-J. and Storz, W. (2010) *Wirtschaftsjournalismus in der Krise*, Frankfurt/Main: Otto Brenner Stiftung.

Arrese, Á. (2008) 'Prensa Económica y Financiera en España. Apuntes para una Historia Reciente', in J.J. Fernández (ed.), *Prensa Especializada: Doce Calas*. Madrid: McGraw-Hill, 1–36.

Arrese, Á. and Baigorri, M. (2011) 'Corporate Reputation and the News Media in Spain', in Craig E. Carroll (ed.), *Corporate Reputation and the News Media Around the World*. New York: Routledge, 168–192.

Arrese, Á. and Vara, A. (2012) '¿Canarios en la Mina? La Prensa y los Riesgos de la « Burbuja Inmobiliaria » en España', in 'Comunicación y Riesgo', *III Congreso Internacional de la Asociación Española de Investigación en Comunicación*, AE-IC, Tarragona, 20 December 2012.

Bähr, H. (2009) 'The World Economy Crisis and Its Actors in the Online Publications of German newspapers and Journals', *Journal of Media Research*, 4, 56–64.

Banda, F. (2009) 'When Journalism Is a Blunt Knife', *Rhodes Journalism Review*, 29, 10–13.

Becerra, M.A. and Mastrini, G. (2010) 'Crisis. What Crisis? Argentine Media in View of the 2008 International Financial Crisis', *International Journal of Communication*, 4, 611–629.

Berry, M. (2013) 'The *Today* Programme and the Banking Crisis', *Journalism*, 14 (2), 253–270.

Caplen, B. (2009) 'Mea Culpa: Why We Missed the Crisis', *Ethical Space: The International Journal of Communication Ethics*, 6 (3/4), Special Issue, 28–32.

Caruso, L., Cepernich, C., and Roncarolo, F. (2012) 'Le Rappresentazioni Mediali della Crisi tra Bisogni Informativi e Strategie Político-Comunicative', *Rassegna Italiana di Sociologia*, 1, 137–168.

Chakravartty, P. and Downing, J.D.H. (2010) 'Media, Technology and the Global Financial Crisis', *International Journal of Communication*, 4, 693–695.

Chakravartty, P. and Schiller, D. (2010) 'Neoliberal Newsspeak and Digital Capitalism in Crisis', *International Journal of Communication*, 4, 670–692.

Chernomas, R. and Hudson, I. (2011) *The Gatekeeper: 60 Years of Economics According to the New York Times*. Boulder: Paradigm Publishers.

Chittum, R. (2011) 'Missing the Moment', in A. Schiffrin (ed.), *Bad News: How America's Business Press Missed the Story of the Century*. New York: The New Press, 71–93.

Davis, A. (2005) 'Media Effects and the Active Elite Audience: A Study of Media in Financial Markets', *European Journal of Communication*, 20 (3), 303–326.

de Mateo, R., Bergés, L. and Garnatxe, A. (2010) 'Crisis, What crisis? The Media: Business and Journalism in Times of Crisis', *tripleC: Cognition, Communication, Co-Operation*, 8 (2), 193–204.

Der Spiegel (2010) 'A Media Plot against Madrid? Spanish Intelligence Reportedly Probing "Attacks" on Economy', *Der Spiegel*, 15 February.

Doncel, L. (2012) 'Draghi empuja a España a solicitar un nuevo rescate', *El País*, 3 August.

Doyle, G. (2006) 'Financial News Journalism', *Journalism*, 7 (4), 433–452.

El Mundo (2009) 'Evidentes "brotes secos" en la economía', *El Mundo*, 26 May.

El País (2009) 'Salgado augura los primeros "brotes verdes" en una semana', *El País*, 20 May.

——(2012) 'Rescate urgente', *El País*, 10 December.

Eurobarometer (2007) *Scientific Research in the Media*, Special Eurobarometer, 282, December. Brussels: European Commission.

Fahy, D., O'Brien, M., and Poti, V. (2010) 'Combative Critics or Captured Collaborators? Irish Financial Journalism and the End of the Celtic Tiger', *Irish Communications Review*, 12, 5–21.

Fernández, A. (2008) 'La Crisis Se Populariza en los Medios', *El Mundo*, 27 October.

Fernández, D. (2008) 'Callar, Nunca', *El País*, 24 December.

Fraser, M. (2009) 'Five Reasons for Crash Blindness', *British Journalism Review*, 20 (4), 78–83.

Fay, S. (2011) 'Big City, bright lights', *British Journalism Review*, 22 (1), 48–53.

Fuller, J. (2009) 'Why Journalists Need to Relearn the Old Habits of Scepticism, Fearless Questioning and Digging for Information', *Ethical Space: The International Journal of Communication Ethics*, 6 (3/4), Special Issue, 87–91.

García Montalvo, J. (2008) *De la Quimera Inmobiliaria al Colapso Financiero: Crónica de un Desenlace Anunciado*. Barcelona: Antoni Bosch.

González, A. and Lobo, J.L. (2008) 'Pacto de Silencio: Los Grandes Editores de Prensa Se Comprometen a Apoyar a Zapatero Ante la Crisis', *El Confidencial*, 16 October. Available at: www.elconfidencial.com/cache/2008/10/16/comunicacion_33_pacto_silencio_grandes_editores_prensa_comprometen_apoyr.html [Accessed 8 January 2010].

Guerrera, F. (2009) 'Why Generalists Were Not Equipped to Cover the Complexities of the Crisis', *Ethical Space: The International Journal of Communication Ethics*, 6 (3–4), Special Issue, 43–49.

Harber, A. (2009) 'When a Watchdog Doesn't Bark', *Rhodes Journalism Review*, 29 (1), 20–21.

Hope, W. (2010) 'Time, Communication and Financial Collapse', *International Journal of Communication*, 4, 649–669.

Horner, J. (2011) 'Clogged Systems and Toxic Assets: News Metaphors, Neoliberal Ideology, and the United States "Wall Street Bailout" of 2008', *Journal of Language and Politics*, 10 (1), 29–49.

Johnson, M. (2012) 'Spain prepares to make a rescue request', *Financial Times*, 24 October.

Kindleberger, C.P. (1978) *Manias, Panics, and Crashes: A History of Financial Crises*. New York: Basic Books.

Krugman, P. (2009) 'How Did Economists Get It So Wrong?', *The New York Times*, 6 September.

Kurtz, H. (2008) 'Press May Own a Share in Financial Mess', *The Washington Post*, 6 October.

Lewis, J. (2010) 'Normal Viewing Will Be Resumed Shortly: News, Recession and the Politics of Growth', *Popular Culture*, 8, 161–165.

Lits, M. (2008) 'Les Médias Face à la Crise', *Médiatiques*, 43, 3–7.

——(2010) 'Pourquoi les Médias N'ont-ils Rien Vu Venir?', in V. Dujardin, Y. De Cordt, R. Costa, and V. de Moriamé (eds.), *La Crise Économique et Financière de 2008-2009: L'entrée dans le 21e Siècle?* Paris: Peter Lang, 81–94.

Lowry, D.T. (2008) 'Network TV News Framing of Good vs. Bad Economic News Under Democrat and Republican Presidents: A Lexical Analysis of Political Bias', *Journalism & Mass Communication*, 85 (3), 483–498.

Luscombe, B. (2009) 'Business Journalism: A Vanishing Necessity?', *Time*, 20 July.

Marron, M.B. (2010) 'British/Irish Media Excel in Episodic Coverage, Fail in Probing', *Journalism Studies*, 11 (2), 270–274.

Müller, S. (2010) *El Papel de la Prensa en la Mayor Crisis Económica Que Ha Vivido la Democracia Española*, DEA, Universidad Complutense de Madrid. Available at: www.scm-communication. com/files/dea16.pdf [Accessed 5 March 2011].

Mylonas, Y. (2012) 'Media and the Economic Crisis of the EU: The "Culturalization" of a Systemic Crisis and *Bild-Zeitung*'s Framing of Greece', *tripleC: Cognition, Communication, Co-Operation*, 10 (2), 646–671.

Pérez Oliva, M. (2012) '¿Contribuyen los Medios a la Crisis?', *El País*, 29 January.

Peston, R. (2009) 'In the New Digital World, There Is a Stronger Need Than Ever for Subsidised, Public-Service News', *Ethical Space: The International Journal of Communication Ethics*, 6 (3/4), Special Issue, 10–21.

Quiring, O. and Weber, M. (2012) 'Between Usefulness and Legitimacy: Media Coverage of Governmental Intervention During the Financial Crisis and Selected Effects', *The International Journal of Press/Politics*, 17 (3), 294–315.

Roush, C. (2008) 'Unheeded Warnings', *American Journalism Review*, October/November, 35–39.

——(2011) 'The Financial Press: It's Not as Bad as Its Reputation', in A. Schiffrin (ed.), *Bad News. How America's Business Press Missed the Story of the Century*. New York: The New Press, 54–70.

Sandvoss, C. (2010) 'Conceptualizing the Global Economic Crisis in Popular Communication Research', *Popular Communication*, 8, 2010, 154–161.

Sarabia-Panol, Z. and Sison, M. D. (2010) 'Who's to Blame for the GFC? Insights from Southeast Asia', *Journalism Studies*, 11 (2), 274–278.

Satija, N. (2009) 'Why Did Financial Journalists Miss the Financial Crisis?', *Huffington Post*, 22 April. Available at: www.huffingtonpost.com/neena-satija/post_304_b_190057.html [Accessed 6 June 2010].

Schifferes, S. and Coulter, S. (2013) 'Downloading Disaster: BBC News Online Coverage of the Global Financial Crisis', *Journalism*, 14 (2), 228–252.

Schiffrin, A. and Fagan, R. (2013) 'Are We All Keynesians Now? The US Press and the America Recovery Act of 2009', *Journalism*, 14 (2), 151–172.

Schranz, M. and Eisenegger, M. (2011) 'The Media Construction of the Financial Crisis in a Comparative Perspective – An Analysis of Newspapers in the UK, USA and Switzerland Between 2007 and 2009', *Swiss Journal of Sociology*, 37 (2), 241–258.

Sposito, S. (2009) 'Coverage of the Meltdown: Did We Blow It?' Available at: http://sabew. org/2009/08/coverage-of-the-meltdown-did-we-blow-it/ [Accessed 2 January 2010].

Starkman, D. (2009) 'Power Problem', *Columbia Journalism Review*, May/June, 24–30.

Stiglitz, J. E. (2011) 'The Media and the Crisis: An Information Theoretic Approach', in A. Schiffrin (ed.), *Bad News: How America's Business Press Missed the Story of the Century*. New York: The New Press, 22–36.

Stuller, J. (2008) 'The Changing World of Business Journalism', *The Conference Board Review*, July/August, 41–47.

Tambini, D. (2008) *What is Financial Journalism For? Ethics and Responsibility in a Time of Crisis and Change*. London: Polis-School of Economics.

——(2010) 'What are Financial Journalists For?', *Journalism Studies*, 11 (2), 158–174.

The Economist (2009) 'When Good Politics is Bad Economics', *The Economist*, 30 July.

——(2010) 'Spain Shoots the Messenger', *The Economist*, 9 February.

——(2012) 'Mysterious Mariano', *The Economist*, 6 October.

Thompson, G. (2009) 'What's in the Frame? How the Financial Crisis is Being Packaged for Public Consumption', *Economy and Society*, 38 (3), 520–524.

Thompson, K. (2008) 'Reshaping the Financial Times' Newsroom for the Credit Crisis', *editorsweblog.org*, 9 October.

Titley, G. (2013) 'Budgetjam! A Communications Intervention in the Political-Economic Crisis in Ireland', *Journalism*, 14 (2), 292–306.

Tracy, J. F. (2012) 'Covering "Financial Terrorism": The Greek Debt Crisis in US news media', *Journalism Practice*, 6 (4), 513–529.

Usher, N. (2013) 'Ignored, Uninterested, and the Blame Game: How *The New York Times, Marketplace*, and The Street Distanced Themselves from Preventing the 2007–2009 Financial Crisis', *Journalism*, 14 (2), 190–207.

8

EUROPEAN MEDIA VIEWS OF THE GREEK CRISIS

Stylianos Papathanassopoulos

Introduction

Informing the citizenry is fundamental to democratic governance (Schudson, 2008; Aalberg and Curran, 2012). A considerable number of studies demonstrate the significance of the media in agenda-setting and creating images of society (Altheide and Snow, 1979; DeFleur and Ball-Rokeach, 1989; McCombs, 1997). In fact,

> the media's role in a nation's political, economic, social, and intellectual life and their influence on a person's cultural and religious values, sexual and leisure norms, work and play behavior may be far greater than the agenda setting theory ... defines it.
>
> *(Shaw, 1979, p. 101)*

Effective participation in the political process presupposes an electorate informed about public affairs and political choices, and actively engaged in expressing informed preferences. Such informing is achieved, to some degree, through the news media, which the electorate rely on as their primary source of information, a reliance that raises questions about media coverage to do with news agendas, objectivity, and accuracy. Although the news media compete with other sources (for example, personal contacts and experiences), their influence may be particularly significant when an issue is nationally or internationally salient, and beyond the personal experience or knowledge of most people (Norris, 2000; Alarcón, 2012; Azrout, van Spanje, and de Vreese, 2012). Nevertheless, a large majority of Europeans feel that they are ill-informed about the European Union (EU). Europeans tend to regard the coverage of the EU by the various media as 'insufficient' (Eurobarometer, 2011, pp. 24–5). Whichever medium is considered, significant minorities of respondents believe that there is 'too little' information about the EU (p. 24).

This chapter aims to trace the reaction of the international press to the Greek and eurozone financial crisis. More precisely, it tries to record the financial crisis that Greece faced in 2010, as well as the impact on the eurozone, especially in the period from 23 March 2010 to 6 May 2010, when Greece applied for its international financial rescue under the auspices of the International Monetary Fund (IMF), the European Central Bank (ECB), and the European Commission (EC). This analysis includes both the outlook of the international press with respect to the performance of the Greek and EU efforts to 'save' the Greek economy, and the press's general evaluation of the country concerning its economy.

Reporting Europe, reporting financial crises

Since the 2007 crisis in the US, there has been a growing interest in the media research field with respect to the role of the media in the global crisis, given that the news media play a critical role in covering and commenting on social and political crises, natural disasters, and financial recession (Cottle, 2009; Chakravartty and Downing, 2010, p. 693). Broadly speaking, the media coverage of the economy is important for at least three reasons. First, because it can affect the public agenda. Second, because it may influence, in certain circumstances, public attitudes toward existing or proposed policies, especially with respect to the economy (Carroll and McCombs, 2003). Third, it may also affect citizens' behaviour in various sectors of the economy, such as consumer behaviour, financial activities, professional and investment decisions, and their commercial transactions, and so on (Kollmeyer, 2004).

Although news concerning the economy does not usually get extensive coverage in comparison with news related to domestic and foreign policy, societal issues (for example, unemployment, health, pensions, education, etc.), and human interest stories (Kollmeyer, 2004), a major financial crisis usually attracts the attention of the news media for various reasons. In this situation, media coverage is influenced by factors that are related to the coverage of the economy and the depth of the financial crisis. Moreover, a financial crisis is considered as a negative outcome per se, and subsequently the related topics get extensive coverage in contrast to any other financial news stories.

As in other cases, the news media increase their attention and subsequently their focus on financial news when the latter is concerned with negative stories such as financial problems, reduced growth rates, increased cost of living, etc. (Soroka, 2006). This phenomenon becomes more apparent in cases where isolated negative developments in the economy (such as an increase in fuel prices) are associated with other aspects of the economy (such as an increase in transport fares or in the prices of basic goods). News media tend to overemphasize the prevalence of negative stories as well as to give more coverage to bad economic trends than to good economic trends (Kollmeyer, 2004).

The media coverage of negative financial stories (for example, a sharp drop in stock prices) increases, in most cases, for two reasons: first, the story relates to other sectors of the economy; and second, the story has a significant impact on society, leading, for example, to an increase in unemployment, poverty, and social exclusion, etc. (Cottle, 2009; Chakravartty and Downing, 2010; Hope, 2010). This is because, in such cases, the crisis is perceived as a general economic crisis, or even as a general social and political crisis, and not just as a negative development in an isolated part of the financial realm (Scheufele, Haas, and Brosius, 2011). Within this context, the negative media coverage 'increases with signs of economic deterioration, but does not consistently decrease with signs of economic improvement. And only in one case – positive inflation coverage – is there any sign that news adjusts reliably as the economy improves' (Soroka, 2006, p. 376).

The news media are crucial buffers in the articulation of issues of common concern in the European public sphere (Papathanassopoulos and Negrine, 2011). Through their coverage they tend 'to dominate the European public sphere' (Zografova, Bakalova, and Mizova, 2012, p. 68). On the other hand, though European institutions make important decisions and adopt directives and policies that directly affect citizens, 'European news is dwarfed in comparison with national and regional issues' (Veltri, 2012, p. 355). Another problem for news media and journalists is to make the European Union more attractive to their readers. The difficulty that the news media have is to make people understand the directives and policies as well as to make them realize the importance of the EU, and the role it plays in their daily lives (Alarcón, 2010). Generally, the main challenge of the journalist, regardless of the medium, is to create adequate public awareness of significant European issues. Particularly in the case of television, media organizations play a crucial role in defining the scope and content of the attention paid to European affairs. However, the focus of media on authentic EU events is considered cyclical, peaking during the events but fading before and after them (de Vreese, 2001; de Vreese and Boomgaarden, 2006).

More specifically, research has shown that although issues related to Europe have recently increased their presence (if not visibility) in the European news media, they actually receive relatively little coverage compared with other news stories (Kevin, 2004; Peter and de Vreese, 2004; Trenz, 2004).[1] By and large, news on European issues has a small presence in the European media (de Vreese, 2002). In most cases, the European news media pay attention to, and subsequently increase their coverage of, significant events such as the EU summits (Kevin, 2004; Peter and de Vreese, 2004). One has to admit, however, that it is difficult for a journalist or a news medium to make complex institutions understandable, especially when they are perceived by the public as detached and without much connection to their lives – one of the elements directly contributing to the communication deficit in the EU. According to Trenz (2004), there are three types of European affairs reported in the European press: a) European news characterized by the shared meaning of European events and issues, such as the EU summits or the European elections; b) Europeanized news characterized by the secondary impact of European events and issues on national news coverage, such as the financial crisis in the US; and c) national news on domestic events and issues characterized by evolving forms of European monitoring and rhetoric.

In other words, the EU is a difficult topic for media coverage. But if it is, the economic crisis of a country and how it affects and is affected by the capitalist system, and also how it is related to the globalization process and the eurozone, and what its implications are for the European project, are much more difficult issues. In the present crisis, journalists were invited to refer to complex technical and political issues with various possible implications for the euro area and, by extension, their own economies, while, in practice, they had no idea about such issues.

While EU policies are characterized by bureaucratic language and plenty of acronyms, the potential default of a eurozone country is a news-intensive and high-interest story, because a major crisis in one eurozone member state may affect the other member states. It is possible that, as a result of the obfuscatory terms in which the EU leaders discussed the Greek situation, the news media of the other member states misconstrued the financial crisis as an external crisis or as a negative development of the European integration project.

As is known, Greece entered a deep recession in 2008 and is struggling to emerge. The Greek economy featured high levels of public debt, a large trade deficit, 'undiversified industries, an overextended public sector, militant trade unions, widespread corruption, uneven payment of taxes, an overvalued currency, consumers expecting rising living standards, and euro membership based on inaccurate data' (Manolopoulos, 2011, p. xi). The debt crisis has led the government to adopt several harsh, multi-billion-euro austerity packages, accompanied by higher taxes and higher unemployment, to tackle its fiscal imbalances, part of a fiscal stabilization programme designed to achieve lasting economic recovery. At the same time, the Greek fiscal crisis is linked to the rest of the eurozone member states in various ways. The Greek economy is interlinked to the common currency, and to the participation of Greece in the eurozone, as the country has to comply with the terms of the Stability Pact. Under the Stability Pact, the member states of the eurozone have to remain within certain financial limits, and not to exceed certain levels of indebtedness. Beyond those limits, financial systems become overly exposed (Jordan and Schout, 2006).

Therefore, a key aspect of the coverage of the Greek crisis in the European media was the impact the crisis could have on the euro and the eurozone. As the focus on the EU's common currency and the eurozone is a political as well as a national choice, it was possible that the news media would approach the issues related to the crisis from both a political and a national perspective. As de Vreese has noted, European financial issues are largely covered under a national perspective (de Vreese, 2002, 2007), but it is questionable whether media coverage reflects or shapes the EU agenda. A majority of Europeans in autumn 2010 believed that the news disseminated by national media about the European Union was objective (Eurobarometer, 2011, p. 25).

The economic as well as the political significance of the euro for the EU is likely to mean a greater prevalence of those voices that suggest EU intervention in the economy or elsewhere, such as in federal European monetary policy or a bank. In effect, an intervention by the EU or its institutions or by the larger EU member states in financial aspects that are closely related to the sovereignty of the member states may accelerate the EU integration project or, on the contrary, may lead to a growth in Eurosceptic tendencies (Taggart and Szczerbiak, 2004; Crowson, 2006). The Greek financial crisis, apart from exposing domestic weaknesses (Featherstone, 2011), also exposed some of the weaknesses of the eurozone financial project in a globalized world. Thus, it may not be a coincidence that, in the aftermath of the

2007 US crisis, concerns about the impact of the fiscal crisis in one eurozone member kept the news media around the world busy with a small and single southern European country, or, as Hahn and Jaursch point out, 'this business journalistic storytelling became "re-Grecized"' (Hahn and Jaursch, 2012, p. 98). In other words, the Greek crisis, to a certain extent, has confirmed Bauman when he noted that in our 'negatively globalized planet … there cannot be local solutions to globally originated and globally invigorated problems' (Bauman, 2007, pp. 25–6).

Situating the study: research design

Greece, like various other European countries, is neither a Third World country nor a powerful nation in either political or financial terms. It is usually placed somewhere in between. This would imply, then, that the coverage of the Greek fiscal crisis in major European newspapers would fall somewhere between Euroscepticism and the peddling of a negative image of the country. A negative image of Greece might be the result not only of negative coverage of the country, but also of bias on certain topics, such as the usual stereotypes of the country and its people. Such bias may have been evident in the fact that the complex issue of financial recession triggered journalists to bring to the surface the vulnerabilities of Greek society at large (for example, corruption, unemployment, hyper-expanded public sector).

By and large, one can say that usually Greece does not get much coverage in the international press, because it is a small nation and thus not an influential nation. The image of Greece in the international media is one of non-importance. It could obviously be expected that the types of items receiving the most coverage would be those that directly concerned the international community, and countries with the size and scope of Greece usually receive the attention of the international press only in cases of political crises or upheavals or natural disasters. This was the case with Greece: from the beginning of the crisis, Greece received extensive coverage in the international press. The emergence of Greece as a serious case of financial instability within the eurozone challenged the EU to find a solution to a problem inside its own structures.

The goal of our research was to trace the reaction of the European press to the 2010 Greek financial crisis. More precisely, we tried to monitor the financial crisis that Greece faced in 2010 and also the impact on the eurozone, especially in the period of 23 March to 6 May 2010, when Greece applied for its international financial rescue under the auspices of the IMF, the EU, and the European Central Bank. This study includes both the outlook of the international press with respect to the performance of the Greek and the EU efforts to 'save' the Greek economy, and the press's general evaluation of the country with respect to its economy.

The aim of the project was to examine how selected and elite newspapers in different countries have represented the Greek crisis and how the journalists approached this case. More precisely, we tried to monitor:

- What did the newspapers say about Greece as a case that needed help?
- Did they see it as a deserving case or not?

- Did they see the Greek problem as part of inherent problems with the EU and the eurozone? Was the Greek case seen as a positive or negative dimension of the eurozone?
- Did the papers comment on the future of the eurozone and the euro?
- Was the EU seen as a saviour of Greece and as a legitimate source of help?
- Were divisions between EU member states identified in the coverage?

We monitored the positions of the following newspapers, by reference to their website versions:

TABLE 8.1 The newspapers surveyed

Country	Title
Austria	*Die Presse*
Belgium	*Le Soir*
UK	*The Daily Telegraph*
	The Guardian
	BBC webpage
France	*Le Figaro*
	Le Monde
	Libération
Germany	*Frankfurter Allgemeine*
	Süddeutsche Zeitung
US	*The New York Times*
Spain	*El Mundo*
	El País
Italy	*La Repubblica*
Cyprus	*Phileleftheros*

The period of 23 March to 6 May 2010 was one of the most painful for the international image of Greece. The choosing of this time frame was led by the desire to acquire data in a period during which the Greek press was claiming that Greece was collapsing, and when the foreign press was extremely hostile to the salvation of Greece. We traced and analysed 723 items regarding Greece and the problem of the financial crisis. The research combines quantitative data and qualitative analysis. The unit of analysis was any newspaper article (presented as news) focusing on the Greek economic crisis and the euro area. The collected data were interpreted and structured according to the aforementioned objectives and categories, quantified when possible, and summarized. Broadly speaking, the analysis showed that the positions of the newspapers were less negative than originally supposed. Although there were differences, the newspapers had some common positions with respect to the Greek case:

- The German government adopted a tougher policy approach with respect to the financial support for Greece.

- Achieving agreement on the economic aid to Greece was an act contributing to the stability of the euro.
- The design of the financial aid to Greece, including loans from the EU and the IMF, indicated the leading role of Germany and France.
- The financial support of Greece should inevitably be supplemented by strict austerity measures.
- The agreed financial aid was offered to Greece as the last alternative of the country.
- Bloody riots resulted in a tragedy (the loss of life of three bank employees).

Findings

In the period studied, the German newspapers on the panel, *Süddeutsche Zeitung* and *Frankfurter Allgemeine*, devoted a considerable number of news items to the Greek recession (14.7 per cent and 13.3 per cent respectively of the total examined). This is not a coincidence when one considers that Germany was the country that would put its hand deeper into its pocket than any other country for the salvation of Greece. From a comparative perspective, with respect to the number of news items, the German newspapers published more articles than any other paper on the panel (Figure 8.1).

Most papers referred to Greece in medium-sized items (44.8 per cent) and, in many cases, in large ones (37.1 per cent), demonstrating the importance and seriousness of

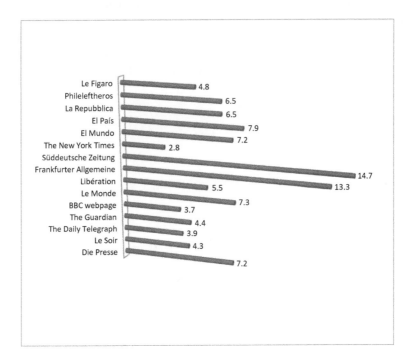

FIGURE 8.1 Number of news items per newspaper (%)

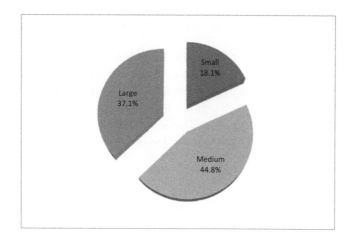

FIGURE 8.2 News items by size (%)

the issue of the crisis, a problem transcending – from the outset – national borders (Figure 8.2).

The topic of the Greek crisis and the subsequent reputation of Greece was primarily approached through feature articles (44.7 per cent) and secondarily through simple news stories (36.1 per cent). Commentaries and opinion articles, although limited (14 per cent), were quite sharp and enlightening in some cases (Figure 8.3).

The fact that Greece needed help at that difficult time was recognized by the vast majority of the newspapers on our panel (83.5 per cent). This finding is in itself an important indication of the seriousness of the Greek crisis (Figure 8.4).

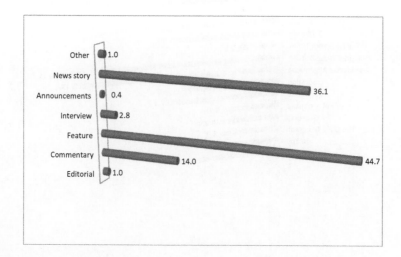

FIGURE 8.3 News items by type (%)

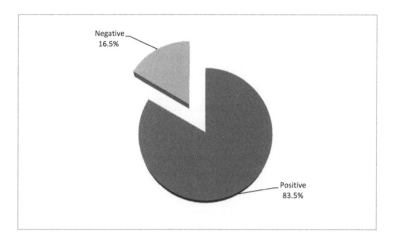

FIGURE 8.4 What did the newspapers say about Greece as a case that needed help?

The above finding, however, does not necessarily imply that aid would be given to Greece generously, as there were comments at the same time wondering about the worthiness of Greece to receive it. The data show that on the question of whether Greece was a deserving recipient of aid, a negative attitude (48.1 per cent) was more common than a positive (31.7 per cent). Although the negative positions prevailed over the positive ones, the latter did indicate that there were European voices that condemned and resisted the theory that Greece should be abandoned to its fate (Figure 8.5).

The Greek crisis was associated in 49.8 per cent of the items with the problems of both the eurozone and the EU, which indicated the scale and the scope of the general problem. The newspapers' coverage was not only of the eurozone, but also of the structural weakness of Greece. However, it is interesting to note that in

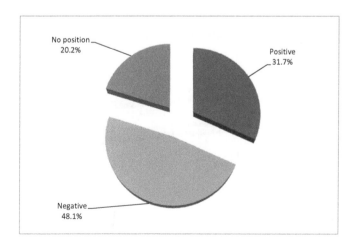

FIGURE 8.5 Did the newspapers regard Greece as a deserving case or not?

some publications (11.6 per cent) the Greek problem was to a certain extent linked to the dysfunctions of the eurozone. In other words, though it was the case of Greece that was being considered, it was the eurozone that appeared to be the main concern. Needless to say, Greece was considered to have a traditionally poor record in financial matters (Figure 8.6).

Possibly for this reason, Greece was regarded as a negative aspect of the eurozone (54.9 per cent), although the newspapers recognized the wider scope of the problem of the economic recession. On the other hand, there was a significant proportion of publications (42.2 per cent) that expressed neutral positions concerning the fate of Greece in the eurozone (Figure 8.7).

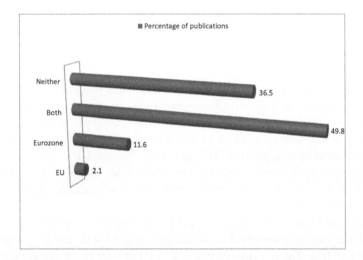

FIGURE 8.6 Is Greece part of the problems of the eurozone and the EU?

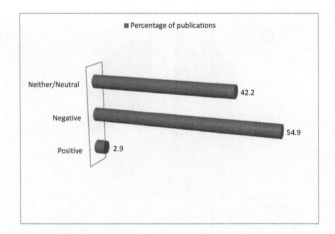

FIGURE 8.7 Is the Greek case seen as a positive or negative dimension of the eurozone?

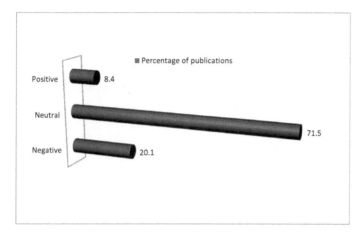

FIGURE 8.8 The position of the newspapers with regard to Greece's membership of the eurozone

Although Greece as a member of the eurozone was often associated with negative positions and commentaries, the overall position of the newspapers in our research was mostly neutral (71.5 per cent) (Figure 8.8).

On the question of whether Greece should seek and find salvation within the EU in the form of a legitimate source of economic support, there was not a clear position. A large proportion of publications (44.8 per cent) regarded the EU both as the saviour and as a legitimate source of help, but a slightly larger proportion (47.2 per cent) was either negative or neutral (Figure 8.9).

The future of the eurozone and the euro was not a main issue at that period, demonstrated by the fact that the vast majority of publications (77.2 per cent) avoided commenting on it (Figure 8.10). Of course, this question intensified during the following years.

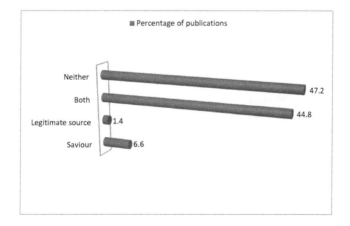

FIGURE 8.9 Is the EU seen as a saviour of Greece and as a legitimate source of help?

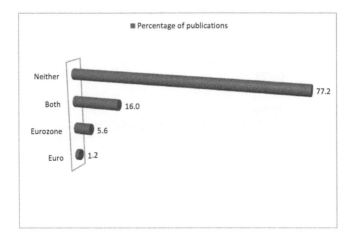

FIGURE 8.10 Did the newspapers comment on the future of the eurozone and/or the euro?

It is obvious that the persons/politicians/executives involved in the Greek fiscal crisis would vary due to the transnational scope of the issue. The interest of journalists was not the same for all players in the theatre of crisis. The majority of news stories focused, unsurprisingly, on Angela Merkel (26.4 per cent) and George Papandreou (21.4 per cent). They were the two main protagonists of the Greek drama in that period, leaving the secondary characters to other personalities (such as Sarkozy, Zapatero, Barroso, Trichet, Olli Rehn) (Figure 8.11).

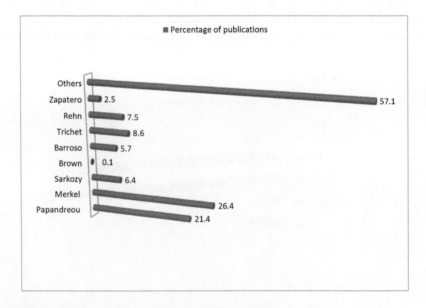

FIGURE 8.11 Personalities or politicians referred to most often

More precisely, the German chancellor – even in the German press – was presented as the most steadfast and uncompromising head of state in the discussion and negotiations concerning the financial rescue of Greece (Gammelin, 2010; *Süddeutsche Zeitung*, 2010). She was even referred to by the terms 'Iron Chancellor' (Kornelius, 2010) and 'Tough Lady' (Hank, 2010). This image of Mrs Merkel is not a surprise if one considers that she represented the country that raised the strongest doubts, if not resistance, with respect to financial aid for Greece, and when the idea was finally accepted it was after pressure from her European partners. Also, the equally strong focus on Papandreou is not surprising, since, as the prime minister of Greece, he became an object of negative comments, if not disrespect.

Concluding remarks

The Greek financial crisis has shown that the world is much more connected than we have so far believed. The world's economies are tied together more closely than most people could imagine. It is perhaps not a coincidence that while Greece has received billions of euros from the lenders overseeing its bailout, almost none of the money has gone to the Greek government to pay for vital public services, and the Greek economy has continued to decline.

The international image of Greece presented by the selected major newspapers during the two months before the first bailout of Greece was the image that might have been expected. Greece was not treated as a failed state in the period under examination (this impression may have been given in the months after the time frame of this research), but at the same time it was not treated as an important nation. On the other hand, the visibility of Greece increased tremendously, as it became a commonplace topic in the news media. This, to a certain extent, confirms the view that the old distinctions between 'domestic' and 'foreign' news may, in the era of globalization and interdependence of economies, become increasingly anachronistic (Cottle, 2011, p. 84). Yet there is still no pan-European publication that has as much influence as the national newspapers of the member states of the EU. Nor has anyone dared to make an attempt similar to that of Maxwell in the late 1980s with *The European*.

The media coverage of Greece during the months of our research period was tense, almost on a daily basis, especially in the German newspapers on our panel, but most of what was covered was informative, and some reports dealt with the complexities of Greek debt and fiscal crisis or with concerns about the social and political impact of the crisis and the austerity measures. I would however like to point out that the research shows that in the first phase of the crisis, Greece's international image was only to a certain extent affected. However, the image of a country is interlinked to its strategic management, implemented by the government of the day, and also to the real conditions its citizens experience and live in.

The frequent riots in Athens also gave the news media the spectacle they desperately wanted for their coverage, following programmes such as Channel 4's docusoap *Go Greek for a Week* on British television, and stories such as the one that appeared in the German magazine *Focus*, where a notorious cover featured the statue of the Venus de Milo giving readers the finger! As Simon Cottle has commented with regard to the global crisis and the news, the media:

> are not only capable of 'hiding' and 'forgetting' crises, they can also sensationalize them, literally investing "sensations" into their public elaboration and wider circulation. They can do so through spectacular visualization and by embedding personal narratives of tragedy, trauma and despair. The news media can also perform an indispensable role in amplifying mega-media events and transnational protests, events that originate in civil society and are designed to capture the public imagination and put pressure on governments to act. So too can the news media variously give vent to the contention and conflicts that surround and shape crises.
>
> *(Cottle, 2009, p. 166)*

Overall, the case of Greece is representative of how other countries in similar circumstances are being and will be reported by the international press. When countries such as Greece become trouble spots, it is to be expected that they will receive extensive coverage in the international media for only a certain period of time. Today's image of Greece in the international news media is directly linked to the failures of the government and the way in which the state manages its relations with its citizens and the society at large. A Greek state rarely 'bends' to hear the problems of the citizens. It is even more rarely honest with its citizens, often intimidating and blackmailing them. Sometimes it pushes them to immediate action to react, to go on successive strikes, to riot, or even to destroy their own cities. From there onwards everything is recycled in the international news media, in line with a negative image of the country.

Note

1 For example, in the past there were scholars arguing that the research field lacked adequate studies shedding light on the impact of European integration on domestic political news coverage (Semetko, de Vreese, and Peter, 2000).

References

Aalberg, T. and Curran, J. (2012) *How Media Inform Democracy: A Comparative Approach*, London: Routledge.

Alarcón, A.V.M. (2010) 'Media Representation of the European Union: Comparing Newspaper Coverage in France, Spain, and the United Kingdom', *International Journal of Communication*, 4, pp. 398–415.

——(2012) 'Newspapers Coverage of Spain and the United States: A Comparative Analysis', *Sociology Mind*, 2 (1), pp. 67–74.

Altheide, D. and Snow, R. (1979) *Media Logic*, Beverly Hills, CA: Sage.

Azrout, R., van Spanje, J. and de Vreese, C. (2012) 'When News Matters: Media Effects on Public Support for European Union Enlargement in 21 Countries', *Journal of Common Market Studies*, 50 (5), pp. 691–708.

Bauman, Z. (2007) *Liquid Times*, Cambridge: Polity Press.

Carroll, C.E. and McCombs, M. (2003) 'Agenda-Setting Effects of Business News on the Public's Images and Opinions About Major Corporations', *Corporate Reputation Review*, 6 (1), pp. 36–46.

Chakravartty, P. and Downing, J.D.H. (2010) 'Media, Technology, and the Global Financial Crisis', *International Journal of Communication*, 4, pp. 693–5.

Cottle, S. (2009) *Global Crisis Reporting: Journalism in the Global Age*, Maidenhead: Open University Press.

——(2011) 'Taking Global Crises in the News Seriously: Notes from the Dark Side of Globalization', *Global Media and Communication*, 7 (2), pp. 77–95.

Crowson, N.J. (2006) *The Conservative Party and European Integration Since 1945: At the Heart of Europe?*, London: Routledge.

DeFleur, M.L. and Ball-Rokeach, S.J. (1989) *Theories of Mass Communication*, 5th edn, White Plains, New York: Longman.

de Vreese, C.H. (2001) '"Europe" in the News: A Cross-National Comparative Study of the News Coverage of Key EU Events', *European Union Politics*, 2 (3), pp. 283–307.

——(2002) *Framing Europe: Television News and European Integration*, Amsterdam: Aksant Academic Publishers.

——(2007) 'A Spiral of Euroscepticism: The Media's Fault?', *Acta Politica*, 42, pp. 271–86.

de Vreese, C.H. and Boomgaarden, H.G. (2006) 'News, Political Knowledge and Participation: The Differential Effects of News Media Exposure on Political Knowledge and Participation', *Acta Politica*, 41 (4), pp. 317–41.

Eurobarometer (2011) *Information on European Political Matters Report. Standard Eurobarometer*, 74, Brussels: TNS Opinion & Social.

Featherstone, K. (2011) 'The Greek Sovereign Debt Crisis and EMU: A Failing State in a Skewed Regime', *Journal of Common Market Studies*, 49 (2), pp. 193–217.

Gammelin, C. (2010) 'Merkel allein zu Haus', *Süddeutsche Zeitung*, 22 March. Available at: www.Süddeutsche.de/geld/streit-um-hilfe-fuer-griechenland-merkel-allein-zu-haus-1.8369 [Accessed 5 May 2011].

Hahn, O. and Jaursch, J. (2012) 'Telling the Greek Story of Europe and the Bull Trap: How U.S. Correspondents Attribute News Value to a Topic-Oriented Country's Status Within the Eurozone's Debt Crisis', *Journal of Applied Journalism and Media Studies*, 1 (1), pp. 97–113.

Hank, R. (2010) 'Wie europäisch ist Angela Merkel?', *Frankfurter Allgemeine*, 29 March. Available at: www.faz.net/s/Rub3ADB8A210E754E748F42960CC7349BDF/Doc~E21C09387D8 AB4337AFE5CB075FA018CB~ATpl~Ecommon~Scontent.html [Accessed 5 May 2011].

Hope, W. (2010) 'Time, Communication, and Financial Collapse', *International Journal of Communication*, 4, pp. 649–69.

Jordan, A. and Schout, J.A. (2006) *The Coordination of the European Union: Exploring the Capacities of Networked Governance*, Oxford: Oxford University Press.

Kevin, D. (2004) *Europe in the Media*, Mahwah, NJ: Laurence Erlbaum Associates.

Kollmeyer, C.J. (2004) 'Corporate Interests: How the News Media Portray the Economy', *Social Problems*, 51 (3), pp. 432–52.

Kornelius, S. (2010) 'Eiserne Kanzlerin Merkel', *Süddeutsche Zeitung*, 25 March. Available at: www.Süddeutsche.de/politik/eu-griechenland-krise-eiserne-kanzlerin-merkel-1.10925 [Accessed 5 May 2011].

McCombs, M.E. (1997) 'New Frontiers in Agenda Setting: Agendas of Attributes and Frames', *Mass Communication Review*, 24 (1), pp. 32–52.

Manolopoulos, J. (2011) *Greece's 'Odious' Debt*, New York: Anthem Press.

Norris, P. (2000) *A Virtuous Circle: Political Communications in Postindustrial Societies*, Cambridge: Cambridge University Press.

Papathanassopoulos, S. and Negrine, R. (2011) *European Media: Structures, Politics and Identity*, Cambridge: Polity.

Peter, J. and de Vreese, C.H. (2004) 'In Search of Europe: A Cross-National Comparative Study of the European Union in National Television News', *Harvard International Journal of Press/Politics*, 9 (4), pp. 3–24.

Scheufele, B., Haas, A., and Brosius, H.B. (2011) 'Mirror or Molder? A Study of Media Coverage, Stock Prices, and Trading Volumes in Germany', *Journal of Communication*, 61 (1), pp. 48–70.

Schudson, M. (2008) *Why Democracies Need An Unlovable Press*, Cambridge, UK: Polity Press.

Semetko, H.A., de Vreese, C.H., and Peter, J. (2000) 'Europeanised Politics – Europeanised Media? European Integration and Political Communication', *West European Politics*, 23 (4), pp. 121–41.

Shaw, E. (1979) 'Agenda-Setting and Mass Communication Theory', *International Communication Gazette*, 25 (2), pp. 96–105.

Soroka, S. (2006) 'Good News and Bad News: Asymmetric Responses to Economic Information', *Journal of Politics*, 68 (2), pp. 372–85.

Süddeutsche Zeitung (2010) 'Europas Zahlmeister verriegelt die Kasse', 26 March. Available at: www.Süddeutsche.de/geld/eu-gipfel-in-bruessel-europas-zahlmeister-verriegelt-die-kasse-1.11957 [Accessed 5 May 2011].

Taggart, P. and Szczerbiak, A. (2004) 'Contemporary Euroscepticism in the Party Systems of the European Union Candidate States of Central and Eastern Europe', *European Journal of Political Research*, 43 (1), pp. 1–27.

Trenz, H.J. (2004) 'Media Coverage on European Governance: Exploring the European Public Sphere in National Quality Newspapers', *European Journal of Communication*, 19 (3), pp. 291–319.

Veltri, G.A. (2012) 'Information Flows and Centrality Among Elite European Newspapers', *European Journal of Communication*, 27 (4), pp. 54–75.

Zografova, Y., Bakalova, D., and Mizova, B. (2012) 'Media Reporting Patterns in Europe: The Cases of Construction of the EU and Reform Treaty', *Javnost – The Public*, 19 (1), pp. 67–84.

PART III

Challenges for the media

9

WHAT ARE FINANCIAL JOURNALISTS FOR?

Damian Tambini

Financial journalism: the debate

Criticism of financial and business journalists is not new.[1] They have faced their share of public criticism both before and since the 2007 credit crisis. The charge sheet is a long one: financial journalists are criticized for superficiality and for a failure to conduct investigations (Davis 2005, Wilby 2007, Doyle 2006), for inappropriate news values (Doyle 2006). They are criticized for being insufficiently sceptical (Doyle 2006), and captured (Starkman 2009). The following passage, from *Columbia Journalism Review* (Brady 2003), focuses on the role of CNBC during the first dotcom boom and bust in the US:

> Critics claim that CNBC's on-screen personalities led the charge into the speculative stocks of the 1990s, stocks that eventually imploded. There are professional questions, as well, about the network's cheerleading coverage of Wall Streeters who were extolling stocks that those same analysts were privately calling 'crap.' The Merrill Lynch analyst Henry Blodget, for one example, had been a frequent guest on CNBC. His Internet stocks all came crashing down, and eventually it was learned that he'd been recommending stocks on-air that he privately called 'junk.' ... Alan Abelson, the respected financial columnist of Barron's, comes down hard on the channel. 'CNBC,' he says bluntly, 'was a product of the stockmarket mania. They contributed to it, and they ate off it.'
>
> *(Brady 2003)*

Whilst questions should be asked about the complex ethical conflicts and more subtle conflicts of interest behind this 'bubble' journalism, most see financial journalism's weakness as cock up rather than conspiracy. Gillian Doyle (2006: 433) questions the level of training and skill among business journalists. Many of the financial journalists she interviewed said that as financial products become more complex it is difficult to find journalists with the expertise to adequately understand the material they are reporting on. Aeron Davis' research, based on interviews with fund managers, brokers, and other interested parties in 2002–4, similarly reports perception of a lack of expertise and of critical reflection by journalists (Davis 2007: 163–164).

Gillian Doyle argues that a lack of skills among journalists as markets become more complex undermines journalists' ability to hold companies to account (Doyle 2006: 442). According to a news editor interviewed by Doyle:

> financial journalists are generally good at analysing companies and interpreting and maintaining companies at arms length. Where they are less good, however, is in pro-actively investigating stories – in stepping back to see the wider picture and spotting things that deserve a closer look. This is because they don't have the time and the opportunity and perhaps the education and training needed to be more pro-active.
>
> *(Doyle 2006: 442)*

Similarly, several financial journalists and editors I interviewed for this article raised the issue of the lack of specialist training for financial analysis. 'The people that are really skilled go and make loads of money working in the financial sector. Not writing about it' one respondent said.

The challenges faced by financial journalists were well illustrated during 2007–9 when only a very few individuals, notably Gillian Tett of the *Financial Times*, spotted the crisis coming. Financial journalism is accused of giving a partial view of the business world. But is it a distorted one? Do the financial media, as Peter Wilby (2007) asserts, 'present the world through a middle-aged, middle-class prism'? Wilby's charge is that in reporting financial issues, for example house prices, there is a tendency to frame issues as though what was 'good news' was uncontroversial. As those who wish to buy, but not sell, houses know very well, price hikes are not good news for everyone. For those journalists that aspire to 'public interest' coverage, just what interest they should serve is a very complex issue: should they serve investors? Or the 'rationality' of the market? Only exceptional individuals will actively want to be the one that burst the bubble.

Critics of the current state of UK financial and business journalism thus tend to focus on the problem of a skills and resources gap. And whilst the shifting relationship of power between political journalists and politicians is much discussed (see John Lloyd (2004) and Nick Jones (1999)), the similar standoff that occurs between financial journalists and their sources has been subject to less discussion. One very real problem is that interested parties – including corporate executives and analysts – sometimes constitute the only repositories of relevant data and employ the main experts. With the help of proactive PR, information can be controlled despite the fact that – as we have found – ultimately the financial system is a public matter that affects us all. Dyck and Zingales describe the relationship between financial journalists and their sources in terms of a quid pro quo situation: access to information is granted; but only on condition that stories are presented in the required manner (Dyck and Zingales 2003: 1–6). Sources exert their control through granting/denying of access, the potential for treating, threat of lawsuits. ' ... Corporations vie with each other for the attention of a target audience mostly composed of investors. In so doing, they dominate or "capture" business and financial news agendas to the exclusion of all other interests' (Doyle 2006: 435; see also Davis 2005).

The charges levelled against current financial journalism: of capture and of superficiality, and of lack of skills, are of course based on the assumption that financial journalists should play an independent, 'watchdog' role. Since this is not a consensus view, even among journalists, it is worth making this explicit. Might the problem not be that markets are increasingly complex, or that journalists are insufficiently funded? Perhaps business and financial journalists themselves don't see themselves as engaged in 'public interest' reporting in the same way that political journalists do.

The interviews conducted for this project, perhaps surprisingly, showed a large degree of dissensus on whether, and to what extent, business and financial journalists should seek to serve a wider public interest. One way of examining this question theoretically is to ask what it is that our corporate governance structure asks of financial journalism. Obviously there are no formal, legal responsibilities placed on journalists; but after high profile failures such as Enron and Northern Rock, we might ask how financial journalism fits in to a general framework of checks and balances on business.

Financial journalism and corporate governance

Joe, Louis, and Robinson report a 2002 survey finding that US board members 'rank negative press as the greatest threat to corporate reputation, ahead of corporate unethical behaviour and litigation' (Joe et al. 2007: 4). Journalists thus have a potentially powerful position if they choose to hold companies to account. But whilst political journalists have a strong professional commitment to exposing wrongdoing and corruption, our interviewees reported that the notion of a watchdog role is less pronounced among business journalists, particularly where journalists see their main role as supplying investors with market-relevant information.

Understanding the role of financial journalism in a broader system of corporate governance means understanding how financial journalism is involved in holding corporations to account, and informing the public about the risks of the financial system. Regulators of course hold businesses – including banks – to account, but they are the first to admit that they cannot regulate every aspect of corporate behaviour. They rely also on the public and the media working together to expose wrongdoing and expose matters of public interest.

Michael Borden (2007) has analysed the role of financial journalists from the perspective of the overall system of corporate governance. His research focuses on the US but there seems to be no reason to expect the UK to differ. From this perspective, is has been argued (Klausner 2005, cit. Borden) that corporate law has inherent limitations and that in order to understand failures of regulatory systems, attention must turn to extralegal enforcement mechanisms. Borden's approach is to identify what he describes as 'gaps' in corporate law, arguing that the key issues of disclosure and investigation rely on the media. He sees the role of the media as: 'Uncovering and deterring fraud, and acting as an informational intermediary that catalyzes and informs legal action by Congress, the SEC, the courts, shareholders, or private litigants' (Borden 2007: 315). As Borden points out, journalists encounter conflicts of interest and challenges in relation to each of these roles. I return to this issue below.

This functional, systemic view of the role of financial journalists may well be rejected by journalists who invoke a narrow or market-based notion of their responsibilities. Several of the journalists interviewed for this research simply rejected the notion that they had such 'ethical' or 'social' responsibilities. These ethical minimalists saw their ultimate responsibility as being to respect the law and serve the shareholders of their companies, not to plug gaps in the system of corporate oversight.

I will return to this disconnect between a systemic view of business journalism and the reality of professional practice below. In the following section I shift perspective, looking at the direct and powerful impacts that financial news can have on market behaviour and the implications of this for the regulation, role, and responsibilities of financial journalists.

The effects of financial coverage: reflexivity and market impact

> Keynes compared financial markets to a beauty contest where the contestants' behaviour is based not only on their own beliefs but also on their expectations of the other contestants' beliefs ... accordingly ... the media is likely to play a disproportionate role in asset pricing.
>
> *(Joe et al. 2007: 2)*

One reason that a peculiar ethics and regulatory framework applies to financial journalism is that business news can have a very direct and powerful impact on market behaviour – with the '*City Slickers*' case the most pungent recent reminder. On one hand, the fact that journalists may be in a position to abuse their influence has led to detailed regulation, some of which will be examined in detail in the next section. On the other hand there is a more diffuse and less researched notion that journalists should avoid 'panicking' markets, or contributing to irrational behaviour, a notion much debated after the Northern Rock debacle.

Measurement of the impact of news on stock prices is a well-established field of research which involves a number of distinct approaches. The research originates mainly in discussions about what makes markets move – rather than discussions about what impact changing media technologies might have. And there are specific literatures on policy issues such as central bank transparency (Connolly and Kohler 2004; Reeves and Sawicki 2007). Some researchers treat events (announcements for example, release of information) as 'news', whilst others attempt to separate out the fact of coverage in news media as the key variable, asking whether the fact of coverage has an independent and measurable effect (Connolly and Kohler 2004; Dyck and Zingales 2003: 2).

There is, however, a danger of media centrism: of prioritizing the impact of media coverage beyond the range of other factors on market outcomes (see Dyck and Zingales 2003). Barber and Odean (2006) find that individual investors tend to be net buyers of shares on 'high attention days'. The important finding in this US-based research is that the tendency on such days is for institutional investors to be net sellers of those stocks whereas individual investors buy. The authors hypothesize that this is due to the limited information available to investors and 'bounded rationality'. Other research into the relationship between reporting and market behaviour examined the market impact of a survey of the 'Worst Boards' published in *Businessweek* in the US. Interestingly the results showed positive short-term share price gains even among companies identified as the worst boards. The short-term gains did subsequently reverse, however (Joe et al. 2006: 19). Other authors concern themselves with the problem of what influences investment decisions and the extent to which news reporting might be a factor.

It is useful to keep in mind these two systemic views of the role of financial journalists: first in terms of their role in corporate governance and secondly in terms of their role in relation to markets and particularly capital markets when considering the responsibilities of financial journalists. On one hand they indicate a wider watchdog role for journalists in the system of corporate governance; and on the other they show that the reflexive nature of the relationship with markets requires a particular ethical approach.

In the following sections I describe financial journalism as a combination of various hard-won rights and privileges that are granted in recognition of the social role that financial and business journalists are seen to play. This approach draws on Osiel's (1986) study of the professionalization of journalism in its understanding of the relationship between law, self-regulation and professional practices (see also Hallin and Mancini 2004). Whilst journalists themselves, particularly in the UK, often reject the notion that they have institutionalized professional responsibilities, I argue that such a position is untenable as it is possible to demonstrate that the legal and self-regulatory framework within which journalists work sets out and reinforces such responsibilities. In order to understand current challenges in the profession, it is useful to consider the longer-term context: business and financial journalism has evolved a clear set of professional rights and responsibilities which reflect (i) the macro role of financial journalism in the broader system of corporate governance; (ii) the reflexive relationship between news and markets; and (iii) the codification of the resulting set of roles and responsibilities in law and self-regulatory codes.

Financial journalism, regulation, and the law: Formal duties of journalists

In this section I will look at duties that are much clearer and less disputed than the broader 'ethical' responsibilities discussed above. My concern is with the legal obligations of business and financial journalists. In the following section I outline the legal privileges that apply to financial journalists. Here is an incomplete list of the main duties of financial journalists relating to market abuse:

1. Insider trading

Trading on the basis of information that is not in the public domain. Notoriously hard to define, this impacts journalists when they may be party to private information prior to publication, and may at that point take part in trades that would be illegal. Under the Financial Services and Markets Act: Market Abuse can involve 'behaviour [that] is based on information which is not generally available to those using the market but which, if available to a regular user of the market, would or would be likely to be regarded by him as relevant when deciding the terms on which transactions in investments of the kind in question should be effected' (s118.2.a).

2. Market manipulation

One variant of this, known as 'share ramping', was at the heart of the *Daily Mirror/ 'City Slickers'* case. Because of the strong influence that certain media can have on prices, it is possible for certain players to impact prices through recommendation and thereby profit by selling shares on in the short term. Readers who invest do so in inappropriately inflated stock and are likely to lose money when prices correct.

3. Conflicts of interest

All journalism has to face issues of conflict of interest, but such issues are particularly pronounced in relation to financial journalism. The interest of the reader, investor or market may be in conflict with the private interest of the journalist if for example the journalist or an associate has a shareholding or some other stake in a company they are reporting on. The temptation may be to withhold information that could hurt the company in question or publish information that favours it, or engage in profit-driven market manipulation.

4. Non disclosure

Where journalists do have an interest, they are obliged under relevant codes (such as The Market Abuse Directive) to disclose the identity of the producers of the recommendation, and any interests that the producer might have in the recommended investment. Most established financial news providers operate in addition a policy of *internal disclosure* whereby any stocks held are disclosed to a key manager or editor who can monitor whether the journalist is as a result placed in a conflict of interest as regards stories that are covered by that journalist.

For each of these there are layers of overlapping regulation and self-regulation including:

The Financial Services and Markets Act 2000
Industry codes such as the PCC Code and Guidance on Financial Journalism
The Investment Recommendation (Media) Regulations 2005 (Statutory Instrument 2005 No 382).

There are of course many other ethical issues. Some of these (such as accuracy, honesty) are covered by general journalism ethics codes, and some are contained within specialist codes such as the Press Complaints Commissions' (PCC) 2005 Best Practice Note on Financial Journalism. In addition, most established leaders in financial news have their own guidance and codes of conduct. These do cover issues relating to conflicts of interest, and independence of journalists, but also deal with other issues such as whether stock tipping is encouraged and working for other organizations.

Privileges of financial journalists

The law applied to journalists is in many respects the same as that applied to anyone else. But in some respects the regime for journalists is different. On one hand, the courts rely on the self-regulatory bodies such as the PCC to implement the rules, and this raises questions about the level of oversight and enforcement, particularly in the light of the extremely low level of PCC activity in this area, and the fact that it is almost always complaints-driven.[2] In the light of the exemptions for journalists by The Market Abuse Directive and the lack of PCC activity in this area, ethical responsibilities lie with journalists and their employers. Journalists were placed outside of the scope of some key aspects of the EC Market Abuse Directive – in recognition of the role they play in corporate governance and the fact that they operate their own codes of conduct. And on the other hand, journalists do have some informal immunities (for example in terms of their ability to protect their sources) in the light of the role they play in corporate governance.

Journalists are therefore treated as a special case, and in the UK they enjoy a system of formal and informal regulatory and legal privileges. On one hand, because of the particular role that news reporting plays, journalism is recognized in European Convention on Human Rights jurisprudence as worthy of special protection (Castendyck et al. 2008: 46). The fact that courts tend to afford a lower level of protection to commercial speech than political speech may be relevant to the framework for financial journalism: it may be that journalists who are obviously fulfilling a public interest role are more protected by free speech rights. Where issues of free speech are likely to arise, in the UK as in the US, is in relation to source protection (Osiel 1986). UK financial regulators have developed informal and formal procedures that go beyond the protection afforded by the European Court in terms, for example, of the protection of sources. This means that whilst non-journalists (and we might include bloggers in this category – though this is less clear) could be obliged to reveal sources to a regulator, professional journalists under the PCC or Ofcom regimes are much less likely to be. Research on the historical emergence of these privileges and duties is the subject of another paper, but it is useful to note two cases which illustrate the slow formalization of journalistic privilege in respect of one journalistic privilege: the right to protect sources.

Following a 2006 dispute with the *Wall Street Journal* over a case relating to Overstock. com, the U.S. regulator formalized its approach to working with journalists. Policy Document SEC 34-53638 sets out a set of rules and procedures that the SEC should follow before they subpoena a journalist to force her to reveal her sources. SEC officials should: try to obtain information first from alternative sources, determine if the information really is essential to the case, and contact the journalist's legal counsel in the first instance rather than the journalist directly, in order to ascertain how important the information is, and the extent to which other sources have been exhausted. In announcing this new doctrine the SEC director was quick to point out that the SEC strongly supported freedom of the press. Cox argued that his agency 'relies on aggressive investigative journalism to uncover wrongdoing in companies. Therefore, the SEC should do nothing to chill that work.' Cox said 'Financial journalists need to understand that the SEC considers them vital partners in our mission' (Orange County Register March 6 2006).

In the UK, the equivalent moment in which a line in the regulatory sand was drawn was in relation to the Interbrew case, in which *The Guardian* found itself in contempt of court after refusing to hand over documents relating to a leaked story about a merger involving a large drinks company. In this case too, the regulator (UK regulator the FSA) established a doctrine relating to protection of sources, but, in the case of the UK, this remains informal and unwritten.

Both regulators, in establishing these doctrines, recognized the public interest functions that journalists can play, such as holding companies to account and investigating illegal behaviour. Insofar as they do provide these benefits they should be helped by regulators rather than hindered, for example by scaring off potential sources; hence journalists are granted privileges of source protection.[3]

Protection of sources is only one aspect of the privileges that are extended to financial journalists in recognition – and this is the crucial point – of their role in corporate governance and the wider public interest. The majority of privileges that financial journalists enjoy are in fact those enjoyed by all journalists, and include the notion of qualified privilege as reflected in the 'Reynolds defence' in defamation cases. In a defamation case brought by the Prime Minister of Ireland against the *Sunday Times*, it was established that journalists should be permitted protection of speech if they worked ethically: if journalists work without malice, on a matter of public interest and were not reckless. Lord Nicholls set out a ten-point test of privilege, adding that:

> The press discharges vital functions as a bloodhound as well as a watchdog. The court should be slow to conclude that a publication was not in the

public interest and, therefore, the public had no right to know especially when the information is in the field of political discussion. Any lingering doubts should be resolved in favour of publication.

Whilst judges do tend to err on the side of free speech, the key implication here is whether financial journalists that reject both bloodhound and watchdog roles should enjoy privilege, and whether bloggers and others might also benefit.

So whilst interviews for this project uncovered a somewhat patchy notion among journalists of any social or ethical responsibility to act in a watchdog role, it is in recognition of this role that journalistic privileges have been granted. What is implied in this: whether rights and duties might be conditional on one another, for example, is a question that is too broad to be addressed in this short article. The interviews conducted for the project sought to elucidate exactly how journalists viewed their role, and the challenges they faced in the attempt to fulfil it. It is to this material that we now turn.

Key challenges for financial journalism

Between September 2007 and July 2008 researchers conducted more than 30 in-depth interviews with leading business and financial journalists, their editors and their lawyers.[4] The research focused primarily on the UK, with some US material included for comparison. The aim was to investigate the ethical and professional concerns of financial and business journalists, and the views of professionals on the key challenges facing the profession. The following sections of this paper report on the journalists' views of these key challenges.

Some of the challenges facing financial journalism are not new. The need for enhanced training and skills for financial journalists, and the unremitting daily struggle to treat stories with appropriate scepticism are the enduring themes of the trade, dating back to the emergence of financial journalism in the mid 20th century. But according to those interviewed for this report, new communications technology adds to these pressures and poses new challenges.

Speed

Pressure for increased productivity has led to journalists writing more stories in less time than before. Some things have got easier, such as the availability of data online and accessibility of sources, but, on the other hand, the expectation is that material will be published as soon as possible, regardless of print deadlines or broadcast bulletins. Most journalists agree that this leads to intense professional pressures: both in terms of the degree of senior editorial oversight before publication and in terms of the extent to which additional sources can be accessed and verification standards maintained. Many respondents claimed that journalists were forced as a result to rely on a narrower range of established news sources such as PR companies.

According to the editor of a web-based business news service:

> our readers want information at 6.00, 7.00 or 8.00 in the morning. ... On the newspaper the moment when a piece of news has been delivered to, say, the news editor, it'll go through the whole process of ... news editing, sub editing, copy proof, whatever, go through that process and sending to the print site, put it on the page. That'll take 2, 3 hours, OK (on our site), because we're a very small team using quick, light, web-based technology, the production process takes about 2 or 3 minutes. So, it's fast, ultra-fast. That again changes the way you write.

The processes through which facts are verified, judgements of news value reached, and reports are selected for publication are likely to have significant consequences for individual companies, investors, employees and potentially for the broader economy. There is a trade-off between speed and attention to ethics and it is one where financial journalism has yet to find a new equilibrium of accepted practices. Getting the balance wrong could lead to financial journalism as a profession becoming irrelevant. According to a leading fund manager:

> There is this ... vicious downward circle: you have fewer journalists paid less with less time and they don't have the luxury of spending the time you need to come up with information that is required. So it becomes less useful to people like me. We ignore it increasingly and it becomes sort of marginalised.

These pressures of time are not peculiar to business journalists, but are of course widely noted tendencies of contemporary journalism. Coupled with some of the other trends reported by interviewees, however, the increased pressures on journalists' time may be undermining the ability of business and financial journalists to fulfil an effective public interest function.

Complexity

Financial stories are more complex and specialist than ever before. In the hand wringing following the collapse of Enron, some journalists admitted that the degree of complexity in the structure of Enron's business baffled them. Those covering the Credit Crunch and the Northern Rock stories also required specialist knowledge if they were to form an independent view. The lack of skills of this type among journalists adds to the reliance on intermediaries and news professionals to 'interpret' and explain stories for journalists.

According to BBC Business Editor Robert Peston, the financial media could have done more to foresee some of the problems resulting from the credit crunch and complexity is part of the problem:

> The financial press has typically focused too much on equity markets and not enough on debt markets. ... For many months, I was very concerned about

the explosive growth of CDOs (Collateralized Debt Obligations) and I tried to explain them through my reporting. Doing so was a challenge, when even bankers creating the CDOs were unable to describe them in terms that make sense to non-specialists.[5]

Whilst non-journalist stakeholders agreed that complexity was a problem, there was some dissent from this view in the interviews conducted with journalists. Perhaps because of professional pride, they tended to point to some of the strengths and successes of the profession. Others were more ready to argue that the complexity of business and financial markets is putting a strain on reporting.

Strategy

Increasing pressures of speed, complexity and productivity add to the constant challenge for journalists: namely to ensure that they are not used in the service of someone else's interests, but report in the public interest or at least the interests of their readers. Business and financial PR has become much more important in the field in recent years.

Professional strategy advice, in the form of financial PR, has become a high-margin, rapid-growth industry in recent decades. In 1986, British companies spent £37m on financial PR. A decade later the annual figure had risen to £250m (Michie 1998: 26). The evidence is that the past decade has seen similar or perhaps larger rates of growth. Industry sources estimate that financial PR consultancies can command fees up to 1 per cent of the bid values in M&A deals (Miller and Dinan 2000).

The current credit crisis is considered to be the greatest challenge of the industry and the professionals predict that the merger business will pick up only at the end of the decade. Even so, the financial PR industry as a whole managed a revenue increase in 2007. On *PR Week*'s top 150 UK PR consultancies league, listed companies' fee income saw an average 22 per cent increase (*PR Week*, 2008). The industry is dominated by a few agencies. Brunswick tops the league in *Merger-market*'s 2006 table of pan-European PR advisers after advising on 146 deals worth £177.8bn. Brunswick, the largest financial PR company in the UK, had almost a third of FTSE 100 Companies on its books. Finsbury, Financial Dynamics, Citigate and Maitland hold the spots from the second to the fifth, all advising on deals worth over £100bn.

One editor with a long experience in the UK saw the rise of financial PR as the single most important change to have taken place in recent years:

> In the last ten, twenty years I suppose the biggest change has been the rise of the financial intermediary, financial public relations services. They are putting up barriers to information. I think they were always around but they've developed and become much more sophisticated. When I first came across them they were really kind of press cutting services. But now they are really

strategy advisors. And there are some company directors that do not talk or answer phone calls without consulting them. And they have enormous power. In many ways, they set the agenda. They are the access point. They are making these people available for interviews or they don't make them available for interviews. They release information in a, what's the word, in a way which is carefully orchestrated to happen. [...] Things are very controlled in a way compared with the way it used to be. ... The free flow of information has been interrupted and the kind of information we get can be very sanitized. It's very hard getting to the bottom of a story.

One former Financial PR professional claimed that there was increasing co-dependency between PR and journalists, as journalists are under time pressure to get stories, and PR now controls access to the larger companies that control most of the larger stories: 'the papers couldn't exist without financial PRs pushing stories to them everyday because they just don't have many stories'.

Journalists are of course aware of such strategies. The business editor of a national newspaper admitted: 'I love the leaks. Some of the leaks are obviously done to protect insider shares or to manipulate the share price. There is no question in my mind about that. But it is much more difficult to do today than ten years ago.' There is a clash here between different aspects of professional and ethical responsibility on the part of the journalist. The journalist must get the story, and the leak is great news from that point of view. Presumably, if the story is big enough, who cares that the journalist is being put to instrumental use? In that context, the journalist may reason, perhaps the fewer questions asked about why the leak has been made, the better.

The more seasoned journalists reveal a distaste for dealing with PR when pressed on the matter.

> Because if PR give it to you it means they want something. I don't particularly like it. If people give me stories I will be happy but I will stand them up. I try not to be used or manipulated. I don't want to be used. A lot of PR companies try to trade with journalists so it is always very subtle. They say 'we will give you this now' then they might want something nice written about their clients. It does happen. But I don't like it.

According to one former editor of a national newspaper: 'some financial PRs simply tell whoppers. ... Friendship is a potential corrupter so PR must be kept at arms' length.' London financial news is particularly susceptible to capture by PR. According to one financial journalist who had worked in several countries 'people are spoon-fed here in London. The financial PR industry is very developed. In Hong Kong journalists have direct access to people operating in the market.' ... 'PR can be a big problem for journalists. They [PR] selectively release information and then can block any further access. They can deny access to company briefings, AGMs and profit warning briefings.'

This would seem to support Gillian Doyle's description of business news production: 'corporations vie with each other for the attention of a target audience mostly composed of investors. In so doing, they dominate or "capture" business and financial news agendas to the exclusion of all other interests' (Doyle 2006: 435; see also Davis 2005).

Whilst problems of spin and bias do create challenges for journalists, one very real problem is that interested parties – including corporate executives and analysts – do sometimes constitute the main repositories of data and the main experts. Dyck and Zingales describe the relationship between financial journalists and their sources in terms of a quid pro quo situation, and one analogous to recent critical views of political journalism: Access to information is granted, but only on condition that stories are presented in the required manner (Dyck and Zingales 2003: 1–6).

The combination of increasing complexity and increasing impact of communications professionals is a powerful double whammy for financial journalists. According to a leading business editor:

> Well, I think, you know, there is a risk that any journalist can swallow lines from the […] public relations people and so on but you need to be sceptical. But you know it's about picking all the information hopefully from the source, and not to take it all so seriously.
>
> Interviewer: With all the complexity you talked about, has it become more difficult to do that?
>
> Editor: It is more difficult. Yeah. But, you know, there is a lot of going on which you don't understand and which we can't get at because of that complexity. That does make it a bit harder. But you know, what we are reporting on most of the time is takeovers, and companies' results, regular trading statements, and so on. We are all writing about the same statement. You need to ask all the right questions.

Sustainability: Business models for financial and business news

Many interviewees harked back to a golden age of financial journalism in which a few players (the *Financial Times* in London; the *Wall Street Journal* in New York) enjoyed a privileged monopoly provision as specialist business news providers. Supported by 'tombstone' announcement advertising by large corporate clients and steady sales, with little serious competition, times were easy. In the protected environment the professional ethics and responsibility of the profession were fostered and there was the financial stability to fund more investigations and longer-term risks.

The contemporary scene is quite different according to those interviewed. Competition from new entrants, some driven by new technology, and specialist subscription news and information terminals such as those provided by Bloomberg and Reuters have long ago upset the comfortable monopoly of the business press. Increasingly, previously bundled services providing data, information, news, analysis and comment are unbundled. Much of the value derived in financial and business news, particularly in the press, is now in analysis and comment rather than data, information and news, as updates are provided around the clock and, increasingly, as a free service online. Many of the journalists interviewed stressed that there is still considerable doubt about the sustainability of new business models for financial journalism in the new competitive environment. Intensified competition leads to questions about what in fact the market will provide. Whilst demand for quality business news remains high and business news readers' demographics are valuable to advertisers, some aspects of business journalism may suffer. In particular, expensive and risky ventures such as investigations are seen as increasingly difficult to fund:

> The huge investment of energy and uncertain outcome associated with investigative reporting means that, for most financial media in the UK at least, this is supported only on an occasional basis rather than as a routine activity. So long as this remains the case, the opportunities for media to play a role in uncovering frauds such as Enron will be limited.
>
> *(Doyle 2005: 443)*

A senior editor of a national UK financial news outlet agreed that:

> Putting two or three people onto a project for a month where at the end of it you might get nothing in terms of material is something that we would think very hard about doing, because it is expensive. [...] We used to have a small investigative unit, we don't really anymore.

A lack of resources would seem likely to impact quality and, in particular, accuracy. Standards of verification and sourcing vary outlet by outlet. Very few outlets will commit to the industry gold standard of two named sources for each story – for the simple reasons that sometimes one person in the right position is enough to verify a story, particularly if it involves that person – and time is scarce. It appeared that journalists are aware of the market impact of their reporting – both its impact on individual companies and on market sentiment more broadly. When journalists were questioned about whether this would affect their verification of a story there was a mixed response. Some indicated that they might be less inclined to publish a story at all until they were very sure of its veracity if they thought it may have an immediate impact on job losses, for instance. Others admitted that they might be inclined to adopt higher verification standards if the story was likely to have an immediate market impact.

Regulation and information

Defamation law was singled out as a key problem by several of those interviewed, as was the problem of the lack of publicly available information. Reform of the UK's plaintiff-friendly defamation law is a demand made by all journalists, not just business journalists. But many argue that business journalism faces particular challenges, in part, because of the imbalance of resources between struggling media companies and large companies with larger budgets for legal fees.

The law impacts not only in relation to structuring the profile of liability risk for publishers. It also structures the access to the basic materials that journalists transform into news. According to one interviewee, 'one of the key challenges for financial journalists is access to information'. In the view of these journalists 'what is publicly available information in the UK that journalists can get hold of does not compare well to the US or any other country. That surely has a role to play in relation to financial journalism.' Whilst freedom of information law has had an impact on access to data held by public authorities, journalists need better access also to that held by private bodies.

Professional closure: Who is the financial journalist?

To claim that the status of the business journalist comes with rights and responsibilities begs the question 'who is a financial journalist?' Whilst in the past it was relatively clear who was a financial/business journalist since they worked for the established news media, the rise of bloggers, social media, new kinds of newsletters and other news services, undermines the informal professional definitions. There has always been pseudo journalism in the form of tip sheets, rumour reports, and newsletters, and many bloggers do aspire to being financial journalists, describing themselves as such, but existing outside the ethical and professional – and to an extent, legal – constraints of the profession. The results of the interviews suggest that financial and business journalism is more than a job, or an activity. Like other specialist beats it is a set of rules of thumb, formal rules and an ethical attitude, albeit one that varies in some respects between outlets and a great deal between countries.

Online financial news should be separated between online versions and initiatives of old media – which tend to observe the same codes and standards – and pure play online financial news and information. This latter group appears to exist outside the existing framework.

Where broadcasting and newspapers once were the crucial media in terms of their market impact, new media now play a significant part. One editor recounts the case of a report on a rumour on his purely online news messaging service:

> There are rumours of private equity interest in a company called X. Now if it was true that the private equity group was going to buy X it would be on the front page of the newspaper because it would be confirmed, checked news. It would be a big story. But at the moment it is just among the market chatter. So, traditionally, this sort of information would be within the market reports. ... Because we are working online in this IM format, we print the same material but it HAS instant effects. Normally, the story which comes to the newspaper is printed in the middle of the night, turned over by the news wires. By the morning, people can take a view, a quite leisurely view on whether it's true or not true. Or the story might have moved on in some

way. When you print it live in IM conversation, nobody has any time to check. And so the story can have a sort of exaggerated effect in terms of moving the prices. That brings with it huge responsibilities. Because if the story is wrong you can be moving prices falsely. If you say something is true which is not true. [...] And it means you have to be 100 per cent squeaky clean. Because people automatically believe you can be guilty of manipulating the stock market. So you have to be completely open. You have to write your doubts of the story. [...] You have to make it very clear to the reader what sorts of information you are talking about, how firm the information is and literally you have to tell the reader everything you know. If there's any sense you're holding back the information you immediately look like you are manipulating the market in some way. You might not be actually doing anything bad but the perception would still be there. That means we could never be seen to have any investment of our own.

Interviewer: So you have to be very clean.

Editor: One hundred per cent, squeaky clean.

Interviewer: That means you don't own any stocks.

Editor: No. I only have debts.

The site being discussed is in fact subject to the PCC code as these kinds of sites are operated by a national newspaper. Others are not, and as the interviewee acknowledges, this could lead to pushing the regulatory and ethical boundaries. 'We abide by all the values which go with this newspaper. ... Yet at some point, somebody ... if (the site) sat under someone else's umbrella, we could be abused because the technology allows you to speak to a lot of people.' The implicit assumption here is that the (self-) regulatory framework that professional print and broadcast journalists are subject to is an effective foil against abuse of journalistic power, for example through market abuse. There is a need for more clarity about who is operating within the professional and ethical framework of financial journalism, particularly with regard to internet content.

Conclusions

Financial and business journalists, like other journalists, sometimes deny that they are part of an organized 'profession'. But this paper has sought to show that whilst financial journalists are reluctant to accept it, they do have a clear institutional role in the broader financial system. A simple way to understand this role is to see it as a framework of rights and duties that have been developed in the context of legal and regulatory disputes and which form the institutional framework which governs and shapes professional practice. In return for the social function they perform, financial journalists are granted professional privileges.

Interviews conducted for this research support the view that many financial and business journalists lack awareness about the professional and institutional framework they operate within. They hold a range of opinions about their ethical responsibilities and broader governance role. Interviewees' responses also show that financial journalism is under intense pressure because of the challenges of increased complexity of financial and business news, together with industry changes that put pressure on the funding of investigations and the time available to professionals in fulfilling their duties. The powerful role that strategic PR has come to play in the financial and business journalism sector constitutes another key challenge. And in addition the profession faces two key strategic questions. One is how to respond to the question of professional closure as bloggers and other new media services compete with established financial news sources. Another is the question of what role financial news journalism seeks in the broader settlement for corporate governance. As the regulatory response to the financial crisis of 2007–9 is designed, debate on the appropriate balance between legal and extralegal enforcement will entail a debate about the role of public – and therefore journalistic – oversight. The privileges extended to financial journalists – and the duties that are expected in return – should be part of that debate.

This could be an opportunity to revisit a broader debate about what role journalists should play in the overall framework of corporate governance: not only unearthing cases of fraud, but providing the balanced and sceptical news and comment that deflates bubbles and helps avoid market irrationality. In the current environment, pressures of time and resources are in danger of undermining business journalism in general, and the ability of financial journalists to find a way through the current impasse. The long-standing pressures on business journalism, such as sustainability, source dependency and pressure from PR, are exacerbated by the economic pressures that undermine risk taking, together with the increased complexity of financial markets and the pressure for rapid publication. The response to this impasse was beyond the scope of the interviews conducted for this phase of the research, but we might speculate about possible ways forward. Journalists could respond by seeking regulatory support to enable them to fulfil their role – for example by reducing defamation risk. Radical solutions are being discussed about new ways of funding journalism, and these will inevitably entail judgements about what constitutes good journalism, and whether business journalism qualifies. Given the range of the challenges they face, journalists will need to work together and pool resources if they are to strike a new compact about their rights and duties in the new environment, and to whom these rights and duties should be extended.

Notes

1 From Tambini, Damian (2010), 'What Are Financial Journalists For?', *Journalism Studies*, 11 (2), pp. 158–174; reprinted with kind permission of Taylor & Francis Ltd. An earlier version of this essay was published as a pamphlet by Polis/LSE in December 2008. I am grateful to Charlie Beckett, director of Polis and the participants in two workshops organized by Polis for comments. I am also grateful to Isabelle Cao Lijun, Terence Kiff, Eva Knoll, Judy Lin and Gladys Tang for research assistance.
2 Interviews were carried out with the PCC director and data on official complaints reveals a lack of complaints against this article of the code. In the first 10 Months of

2007, there were 2 complaints: one did not breach the Code and the other was dropped by the complainant. In 2006 there were 3, of which 2 did not breach the Code and 1 was dropped. In 2005 there were 4, 2 of which were not pursued by the complainant while 2 accepted some offer of action by the editor (information supplied by the PCC).

3 I am grateful for information provided by former *Wall Street Journal* general counsel Stuart Karle and Howard Davies, Director LSE and former Director, Financial Services Authority.

4 Methodological note: Semi-structured interviews were conducted mainly by the author, and some were conducted by researchers working with him according to a semi-structured interview guide focusing on the role of the business journalist and challenges faced in performing that role. They lasted between 30 and 65 minutes and were recorded and transcribed. Transcripts were analysed for the main themes they focused on, and the key challenges identified form the structure of the following report. Interviewees consisted of the most senior financial and business journalists in the UK, some of whom requested anonymity, which has been granted to all interviewees for consistency. The list of interviewees is available from the author. (Additional comparative material has been provided as background from interviews conducted with financial journalists in New York and Hong Kong, which will be published separately.)

5 Robert Peston quotes are from an interview conducted by Terence Kiff for an MSc dissertation, Department of Media and Communications, London School of Economics, July/August 2008. I am grateful to Terence for supplying the transcript.

References

Barber, Brad M. and Terrance Odean (2006) "All that Glitters: The Effect of Attention and News on the Buying Behavior of Individual and Institutional Investors". *EFA 2005 Moscow Meetings*, available at http://ssrn.com/abstract=460660

Borden, Michael J. (2007) "The Role of Financial Journalists in Corporate Governance". *Fordham Journal of Corporate and Financial Law.* Vol XII. 312–370.

Brady, Ray (2003) "MAKEOVER; CNBC Fell from Grace When the Bubble Burst. How Does It Look Now?" *Columbia Journalism Review.* November/December.

Butterworth, Siobhain (2008) "Open door – The readers' editor on … leaky ships and journalistic privilege". *The Guardian,* 1 September, available at www.guardian.co.uk/commentisfree/2008/sep/01/pressandpublishing

Castendyck, Oliver, Egbert Dommering and Alexander Scheuer (2008) *European Media Law.* Alphen aan den Rijn: Wolters Kluwer Law and Business.

Connolly, E. and M. Kohler (2004) "News and Interest Rate Expectations: A Study of Six Central Banks". Research Discussion Paper 2004–10, available at www.rba.gov.au/rdp/RDP2004-10.pdf

Davis, Aeron (2005) "Media Effects and the Active Elite Audience: A Study of Media in Financial Markets". *European Journal of Communication,* 20(3): 303–326.

——(2007) "Economic Inefficiency of Market Liberalisation: The Case of the London Stock Exchange". *Global Media and Communication,* 3(2): 157–178.

Deephouse, David I. (2003) "Media Reputation as a Strategic Resource: An Integration of Mass Communication and Resource-Based Theories". *Journal of Management,* 26(6): 1091–1112.

Doyle, Gillian (2006) "Financial News Journalism: A Post-Enron Analysis of Approaches Towards Economic and Financial News Production in the UK". *Journalism,* 7(4): 433–452.

Dyck, Alexander and Luigi Zingales (2003) "The Media and Asset Prices". Working Paper, Harvard Business School.

Hallin, Daniel C. and Paolo Mancini (2004) *Comparing Media Systems: Three Models of Media and Politics.* Cambridge: Cambridge University Press.

Joe, Jennifer, Henlock Louis and Dahlia Robinson (2007) "Managers' and Investors' Responses to Media Exposure of Board Ineffectiveness". *Journal of Financial and Quantitative Analysis*, forthcoming, available at http://papers.ssrn.com/sol3/papers.cfm?abstract_id=1014903

Jones, Nick (1999) *Sultans of Spin. The Media and the New Labour Government*. London: Orion.

Kiff, Terence (2008) *MSc Dissertation*. London School of Economics, Department of Media and Communications, July/August.

Klausner, Michael (2005) "The Limits of Corporate Law in Promoting Good Corporate Governance". In: *Restoring Trust in American Business* (Jaw W. Lorsch, Leslie Berlowitz and Andy Zelleke, eds. Cambridge, Mass: MIT Press.

Lloyd, John (2004) *What the Media are Doing to our Politics*. London: Constable and Robinson.

McGeehan, Patrick (2003) *MEDIA; CNBC Disclosure Stirs Ethics Debate in Business Media*. *New York Times*, 28 July 2003, available at http://query.nytimes.com/gst/fullpage.html?res=9C03E7DC1E3FF93BA15754C0A9659C8B63&sec=&spon=&pagewanted=all

Mergermarket (2007) Press release: *Mergermarket's Year End 2006 House League Tables of Financial PR Advisers to European M&A*, available at http://cnc-ag.com/pdf/en/Press-Release-for-PR-Advisers-Q4-2006-Europe.pdf

Michie, David (1998) *The Invisible Persuaders: How Britain's Spin Doctors Manipulate the Media*. London: Bantam.

Miller, David and William Dinan (2000) "The Rise of the PR Industry in Britain 1979–1998". *European Journal of Communication*, 15(1): 5–35.

O'Neill, Onora (2002) "Licence to Deceive". *BBC Reith Lecture* number 5, available at http://www.bbc.co.uk/radio4/reith2002/lecture5.shtml

Osiel, Mark J. (1986) "The Professionalization of Journalism: Impetus or Impediment to a 'Watchdog' Press?" *Sociological Inquiry*, 56(2): 163–282.

PR Week (2008) "2008 Top 150 PR Consultancies".

Reeves, Rachel and Michael Sawicki (2007) "Do Financial Markets React to Bank of England Communication?" *European Journal of Political Economy*, 23: 207–227.

Starkman, Dean (2009) "A Timely Academic Study Asks the Right Questions". In: *The Audit. A Blog of the Columbia Journalism Review*, January 2009, available at http://www.cjr.org/the_audit/post_153.php

Wilby, Peter (2007) "How to Play Footsie With Younger Readers". *MediaGuardian* 19 March.

10

THE MEDIA AND THE CRISIS

An information theoretic approach

Joseph E. Stiglitz[1]

The media have rightly been criticized for failing to adequately cover the crisis.[2] Some news outlets (such as CNBC) were active cheerleaders for the bubble as it grew. But even the more responsible press were insufficiently critical in their reports of official views ("there is no bubble, just a little froth";[3] the problem of the subprime mortgages has been contained;[4] the economy is on the way to recovery[5] – just weeks before the economy sank into deep recession).

How do we understand and explain these failures? What should the press have done? In the aftermath of the crisis, governments around the world grappled with the question of how to prevent a recurrence. Some in the financial market have taken the view that crises are inevitable. To impose more stringent regulation would risk dampening innovation – and in the end would be futile in preventing a recurrence. The wiser course is simply to accept such failures as part of the price we have to pay for a dynamic market. So too, some claim the problems are inevitable and inherent in a free and market-driven press.

In the case of the financial system, however, there is a broad consensus that the response of passive acceptance is wrong: we may not be able to prevent crises, but we can make them less frequent, less severe, with fewer innocent victims. But in the case of the press, the question of whether there is anything that can be done to improve significantly the quality of coverage remains unresolved.

I approach the problem from the perspective of the economics of information. The function of the press in our society is to convey information to readers. Information enables readers – whether as consumers, managers, workers, investors, home owners, or voters – to make better decisions. Better individual decisions would have led to better societal outcomes. If home buyers had a better sense that they were buying into a bubble, they might not have been so willing to pay so much, the bubble would thereby have been diminished, and so too the consequences of its breaking. If those running pension funds had a better sense of the risks associated with the financial products that they were buying—the toxic mortgages that polluted the entire global economy – perhaps fewer of them would have been produced, and perhaps America would not be facing the magnitude of the dislocation in its housing markets that it confronts today. If regulators had more of a sense of the bubble that was forming, perhaps they would have been less confident that it was just a little froth, and perhaps they would have done something to softly deflate it.

Of course, each of these parties has a responsibility for gathering the information required to make good decisions. The regulators have large staffs of economists who are supposed to inform them of what is going on in the economy; pension funds are supposed to gather information from a variety of sources before they put at risk the money that has been entrusted to them.

Still, each of these is part of its own "society" and part of a broader society, networks of individuals who share information and come to shared views, often in a too uncritical way. There is often a herd mentality underlying bubbles. Such a herd mentality can be especially strong in groups that do not have the checks and balances that can bring them back to reality – to say, for instance, that a price of $1,000 for a tulip bulb is not sustainable.[6]

A critical press might serve as one of the checks and balances, restoring sanity to markets that have lost touch with reality, providing the crucial pieces of information that might help remind market participants that what is going on is not sustainable.

But one of the central lessons of the modern theory of the economics of information[7] is that while good information is necessary for good decision making, markets for information often work imperfectly. There are incentives for providing distorted information. Market participants may even understand this, but even when all participants are fully rational in their understanding of these distorted incentives, the outcomes can be distorted relative to what would be the case with full information.

The media transmits information. Unlike the "private reports" that inform bankers and investors, the information transmitted is public. As a result, the media plays a key role in shaping widely held perceptions, for example, whether there is or is not a bubble. The media can, accordingly, play a central role in moving the herd – toward a bubble in the years before the crisis and into the deep pessimism that spread around the world after the breaking of the bubble. The fact that the media can and does play this role increases, of course, incentives to shape the media, by those in the markets and in the government, exacerbating the forces leading to distorted information.

Inevitably, the media is also engaged in a process of editing: there is an infinite amount of information that could be transmitted. What it transmits, and how it transmits it, affects beliefs; beliefs affect behavior – and how the economy and society perform.

Because the media has to be engaged in "editing," it is an active participant in the transmission of information and therefore, as we have noted, in the creation of beliefs.[8] Still, it is useful to make a distinction between two different roles: one in which it is (relatively) passive, simply "reporting" on news (or what it decides is newsworthy – itself an act of editing); and that in which it takes a more critical role of analysis. There were failures in both roles. This chapter suggests that these failures were understandable given the incentives and constraints confronting reporters and the media.

Of course, reporters and their editors do not stand apart from the rest of society. They too can easily be swept up in the herd mentality. Indeed, in this crisis many reporters and editors were. Our argument is that, unfortunately, there are at play strong incentives for the media not to serve as part of society's systems of checks and balances, not to "lean against the wind."[9] While the "failures" cannot be fully eliminated, changes in practices and institutions could ameliorate the problems.

Biases in sources

As Anya Schiffrin points out in her chapter, one of the major problems is that the natural sources for news stories are biased. For the business and financial press, the most important sources of information are the leaders and key personnel at the businesses and financial institutions upon whom they report. For the non-business press, one of the most important sources of information is the government (and especially the "administration"). Both of these sources have strong incentives to provide distorted information.

The business press

Businesses want to sell their products and want investors to pay more for their shares. They thus have an incentive to try to present the best news they can about themselves, their products, their balance sheets, and so forth, consistent with two constraints: fraud laws (they don't want to go to prison) and the loss of reputation (overt errors will undermine credibility). But these constraints are weak. Short-sighted firms care relatively little about their loss of reputation – so long as the returns in the short run are large enough to compensate. Indeed, the crisis has revealed the shortsightedness of financial institutions, and how their short-sightedness has "infected" so much of the rest of the economy, for example the increased focus on quarterly returns.

Business media naturally turn to business sources. They typically present the accounts as the businesses present the accounts to their shareholders. There are several reasons for this. A natural defense is that it is not their job to assess the accuracy of the accounts. That is the job of the accountants/auditors. If the auditors have approved the accounts after a thorough review, how is a lowly reporter to question it?

Moreover, there is a question of "responsible" journalism – especially when it comes to a firm that might be on the verge of bankruptcy (or facing a liquidity crisis). Announcing that such a possibility exists might precipitate the event. More troubling is that even inaccurate information – that a firm is on the verge of bankruptcy when it is not – can precipitate a bankruptcy when without that "information" it would not occur – a self-fulfilling prophecy.

Making matters more difficult is the threat of litigation. This is especially true in countries like the UK where there are imbalanced libel laws and even an accurate story may be subject to suit.

But there are two further problems. The first is that because business reporters depend on their sources, they have to please those sources. For example, if a reporter covering some company is excessively critical, he risks being denied access to information about the firm's plans for expansion. He will have to rely on publicly available information, and that will put him at a competitive disadvantage relative to rivals who can obtain "scoops."

In the highly competitive world of journalism, access to informants is critical, and a symbiotic relationship between the press and those they cover results – a relationship that does not necessarily serve the rest of society well. There is, of course, a trade-off between the speed at which information is delivered and its accuracy. Unfortunately, accuracy is often hard to assess – it took a long time before the inaccurate reports of those promoting the housing bubble and the banks' "prowess" were exposed; but it is easy to tell who is first with a given piece of information. Moreover, hubris can lead to the view by journalists that as recipients of information they can sort out the distortions and inaccuracies – so long as they can get the information. In a world in which information is power – and money – having information quickly is what matters. Indeed, much of the economic return in the market relates simply to that. The person who knows it will rain tomorrow can buy the umbrella today, while they are underpriced and underutilized. Even if he has no use for the umbrella, he knows that tomorrow, the price will be high. He gains a return simply because he had this information earlier than others. Indeed, there may be no social return to such early information – only a private return.[10] The gains by one party represent losses to another. But the private returns can be high, and the media responds to these private returns, not the social returns.

I have already alluded to the second problem, the "cognitive capture" of the reporter by those that they cover. It is not just that the reporter writes the story that the business wants him to write in order to gain or maintain access – an economic quid pro quo, a nonmonetary exchange – but also that the reporter comes to think like the business he covers. He becomes one of them. Being part of the club does give greater access, but it is more than that. Individuals come to adopt the views and perspectives of those with whom they interact. If they spend all day talking to business people, there is at least a risk that they come to think, at least to some extent, like business people. And if they do that, they may not be able to fulfill their critical role.

Of course, a good business reporter does not have to rely just on "sources." Listed companies have to file accounts that are publicly available. Accounting frameworks give considerable "flexibility" – and many of the financial innovations have been directed at increasing this flexibility – for instance, helping firms move losses and risks off the balance sheet.[11] Still, the tension between trying to minimize reported income for the tax authorities and maximizing reported income for investors can generate useful information that can be analyzed by reporters. One of the criticisms of the press in this crisis (as in the scandals earlier in the decade) is that they made insufficient use of this information, at the very least to raise questions. The fact that, for instance, anyone looking at Citibank's reported balance sheet as it managed its way through the crisis could not have predicted that this was a company on the verge of bankruptcy – net worth held steady year after year – provides evidence (if evidence was needed) of the extent of "manipulation" of the accounts.[12]

Financial press

Those covering the financial press have an even more difficult job. I described earlier the natural and understandable incentives of businesses: to increase sales (through good coverage of their products) and to increase share value (through favorable coverage of expected profitability). The incentives of those in the financial markets are not always so easy to decipher. They make money when prices change, but they can make money when prices go up or down, depending on whether they have a long or a short position. Anyone can potentially have a vested interest. No reporter can know whom to trust. But, unfortunately, in their coverage they often do not bring along the necessary dose of skepticism.

This applies both to the coverage of broad economic stories as well as particular events. For instance, the financial press faithfully repeats the adage that it is necessary for governments to reduce their deficits, and unless they do that, all manner of economic ills will follow. Many putting forth these views have large long-term bond positions. They stand to gain if governments pursue policies that lead to lower inflation, which leads in turn to lower interest rates. Bond prices will increase. Those making these pronouncements will, of course, deny that their views have anything to do with their own financial interests.

A story reported in the *Financial Times* in January 2010[13] illustrates the risks to which the media are prey. It reported that the Greek government had undertaken talks with China for financing their bonds. It appears that the story was not true, though a large financial firm as advisers to Greece may have suggested that as a course of action. If so, it was a suggestion that was turned down. It is also widely believed that the story was planted by the financial firm, who had shorted Greek bonds and stood to gain by the story (which resulted in the price of those bonds going down). If the story were true, it was newsworthy. It was a story that, if true, would probably be denied by government officials. Thus, verifying the story (other than by market participants who potentially had incentives to substantiate the story) would be difficult. It seems that the *Financial Times* may have been used.

While this is a dramatic case illustrating the risks confronting the financial press, in more mundane forms, it occurs every day – and it was a central part of the failure of coverage. The financial sector had financial incentives to keep the bubble going, and so had incentives to persuade the press (as well as the regulators) to go along with the prevailing wisdom: there couldn't be a bubble in a modern sophisticated economy (the tech bubble notwithstanding); we were not experiencing a bubble; one couldn't in any case be sure there was a bubble; even if one suspected a bubble, there were no instruments to deflate it – at least no instruments without serious adverse side effects (conventional wisdom held that the interest rate is a blunt instrument, but there were actually many other instruments in the arsenal of the Fed that it *chose* not to use); even if the bubble broke, the consequences would be minimal because risk had been so well diversified and distributed. Accordingly, it was far better to let the markets take their own course and clean up any minor problems that might emerge in the aftermath of the breaking of the bubble. The press repeated uncritically this kind of mantra, little noting that these views reflected the financial interests of those that were promulgating them.

While cognitive capture plays an important role in explaining the failure of the media to adequately cover the events leading up to the crisis, other explanations are required to understand the inadequacies in coverage after the crisis broke. What made coverage of the banking crisis so difficult is that the financial markets (the banks) had worked hard to develop a system of off-balance-sheet accounts that obscured what was going on; it allowed them to take on more leverage than any responsible bank should have done. But the complexity and nontransparency of the banks made providing an accurate depiction of the situation – or the consequences, for instance, of not bailing out the banks – difficult if not impossible. The press, like Congress, had to rely on banks' assertions that in the absence of the multi-trillion-dollar bailouts and guarantees, the financial system (and therefore the economy) would have collapsed.

But again, I believe that they could have played a more critical role. A single Bloomberg reporter, Mark Pittman, looked at the accounts carefully.[14] Only Bloomberg turned to the Freedom of Information Act to uncover hidden details of the bailouts, to find out where the money was really going.[15] Good reporting eventually uncovered that claims by the New York Federal Reserve that French law required AIG credit default swaps (CDSs) to be settled for 100 cents on the dollar were false.[16] There remains no good accounting of why the CDSs had, in fact, to be settled – especially if they were to be settled on such unfavorable terms. Much of what was uncovered by the inspector general and the Congressional Oversight Panel could have been uncovered by good investigative reporting but was not.

The non-business/non-financial press

The national press also failed in this crisis. Of course, they do not see themselves as experts in economics and business – that is a responsibility delegated to the business press. Their focus is normally on politics, on the one hand, and "human interest," on the other – covering the stories about the forces shaping the lives of their readers.

The result is that there is a gap in coverage, which only the largest and best-financed media can bridge: economics. While to many, economics is *just* business, there is a marked difference. The latter covers the fortunes of particular firms or sectors. A reporter covering the retail sector may cover what is happening to Wal-Mart, or the sector as a whole. But economics is about the performance of the entire economic system. Normally – when everything is going well – the economic story is fairly boring. The economy grows at say 3 percent a year, a little faster one year, a little slower another. Of course, investors worry intensely about how, say, the Fed is going to respond, for example by raising or lowering interest rates. But while for those who have millions at stake, a change in interest rates of one tenth of 1 percent can be a big deal, for most readers, such changes will not affect their lives. It is nice to know that everything is going on as it should be, but for most readers, that is all they want or need to know. It is only in times of crises that economics becomes a matter of everyday concern.

The problem is that it is expensive for newspapers to keep on reserve a reporter ready to provide this exciting coverage at the moment it is needed. And so typically they don't. Some of the coverage is done by business reporters who "convert" from covering the details of firms or sectors to covering the big economic story; some by political reporters who try to cover the underlying economics as they unravel the political implications of the changing scene; and some by "human interest" reporters who cover how the unfolding economic tale is affecting the lives of ordinary Americans. But few of these have the training to critically assess the pronouncements coming out of the administration or the Fed or the contrary pronouncements of the critics.

The result is that, too often, there is a "he said, she said" kind of coverage, a simple reporting of the different perspectives, with little balance, let alone analysis. It is as if, in covering a story about the color of the sky, a color-blind reporter gave equal weight to those who claim it is orange as to those who claim it is blue. Of course, it is more complex: it is perhaps more akin to how a reporter in the Middle Ages might have covered the story about the "discovery" that the world is round. With a majority of those interviewed still claiming that the world is flat, it would be natural for the critics to dominate.

This is understandable. What is less understandable is the seeming failure of so many in the press to understand (and convey) the incentives of those in the administration and Fed to provide distorted information. Increasingly, administrations have seen part of their task as "shaping" news coverage (or to use the less polite term, "spinning" the stories). In their quest to keep the poll numbers up, they want voters to believe that the administration is doing a good job, and a key metric for performance is how well the economy is doing. This is especially true in times of trouble, with an administration elected on a platform of restoring an economy that (allegedly) had been badly bruised by the misdeeds of the predecessor.

Here, the press consistently falls for what has come to be called presidential economics, where the performance of the economy under different presidents is compared and contrasted. The reality is that much of what goes on in the economy is outside the control of the administration (or even the Fed); and what is under their control typically affects the economy with a long lag. What we see today is as much the result of what happened in previous administrations as it is of actions taken today. The economic policies of an administration are important, but their effects *typically* take months or years to be fully realized. (An important exception is in the midst of a crisis, a point to which I shall return shortly.)

Thus, the Clinton administration rightly pointed out that the bottom of the income distribution had not been doing well for years, and that their plight had largely been ignored – and sometimes exacerbated – by its predecessors. But the improvement in their plight in the early years of the administration was only partially a result of what the White House did. The administration should have been given credit for the earned income tax credit, which made a big difference in the well-being of many lower income individuals; but the relative improvement in the before-tax income of unskilled workers was the result of complex forces, largely beyond their control.

In seeming to claim too much credit, political leaders also, of course, get too much blame for what goes wrong.[17] Political leaders, perhaps intuitively grasping that they have only limited ability to change the course of events, focus on what they do have some control over – perceptions of those events. This is especially so since they believe (and partially correctly so) that beliefs and perceptions do affect reality: the belief that a political leader is "powerful" can induce congressmen to support his position, and thus increase the likelihood of success of his initiatives. Power breeds power (and conversely for powerlessness).

So, too, in economics: the belief that the economy is going well ("confidence") can induce people to spend more, and that will help the economy to do well. In economics, there is a long-standing view that "animal spirits" matter,[18] and more recently, behavioral economists have tried to study the determinants of such animal spirits.[19] Administration pronouncements ("spin") can help induce confidence, in a self-confirming way.

Those in the financial community have always emphasized confidence. And, indeed, one of my long-standing complaints against the financial press is that they have paid too much attention to the financial community's perspectives, for example in the coverage of crises like that of East Asia. They typically did not even note that most economists disparage the role of confidence except as it affects short-term markets. Standard economic models for half a century have attempted to explain movements in output and employment without any reference to psychological variables such as confidence.

Of course, a statement by a finance minister can affect the exchange rate (or some other variable) for an hour, a day, or even a week. But economists focus on the underlying realities and believe that rational market participants do likewise. There is thus a major gulf between economists' perception of the functioning of the economy and that of the finance (and, to a lesser extent, business) community. Most reporters (including, or perhaps especially, those whose main job is covering finance) seem unaware of this, and this has impaired their ability to cover effectively economic stories, including the story of the crisis.

In March 2009, the Obama administration began talking about "green shoots," the nascent recovery of the economy. It seemed a blatant attempt to enhance confidence, which, it was hoped, together with the stimulus measure that the administration had just passed, would restart the economy's engine. If it worked, the enhanced confidence would reinforce the real effect of the stimulus. There was, of course, a real risk in this strategy: beliefs have to be tied to realities.[20] If the green shoots withered by the early summer, then confidence in the administration and its policies might erode.

The national press covering the administration is in much the same position as the business press covering businesses. They may be aware that those that they are covering have an incentive to distort information, but in covering (or uncovering) these distortions they face several problems.

First, like the business press, they need access. They do not want to lose access, and to retain access they have to provide favorable (or at least not too unfavorable) coverage. Those in the administration work hard to create an artificial scarcity of information so that they have something to trade in return for favorable coverage.[21]

Second, they have a problem of expertise: it is not always easy to challenge the administration's experts. In America's system, the job of challenging pronouncements is given to the members of the opposition party (and allied think tanks). That is why so much of the reportage is of the "he said, she said" form.

Thirdly, there is an element of "responsible journalism." They fear that to suggest that the economy is on the verge of collapse might precipitate the collapse itself.

Economists

While politics is important, and while different political parties had different economic theories – and therefore different interpretations of the likely efficacy of different policies – there needed to be better coverage of the underlying economics.

Here, the press faced an unusual problem. The mainstream of the economics profession had, in a sense, failed as badly as financial markets. They had provided the models used by those in finance which had gone badly awry; they had provided the theories that underpinned the deregulation movement and that provided succor to regulators who did not believe in regulation.[22]

I believe that the press should have taken this fact into account in its coverage of the crisis. It should have leaned more heavily on those who had predicted the crisis – their interpretation of the crisis and the remedies – and been more critical of others. So, for instance, in covering the impact of the stimulus, "Chicago" school economists were typically more skeptical of the effectiveness of the stimulus. But in describing these economists' position, it would have been of relevance to most readers to know that these economists not only did not predict the crisis: their models suggested that unemployment could not exist, or at least persist for long.

The difficulty the media had in turning to economists was thus not just that these were not their ordinary sources, but also that they had a difficult time sorting out different positions.

Market distortions

Most of this chapter has focused on the distortions in coverage that arise from the distortions in sources – the incentives that most sources have in shaping the news coverage in particular ways. I have also discussed some of the distortions in incentives of the reporters, which limit their drive to uncover these distortions.

But there are also well-known distortions in organizational incentives, which I briefly note. The media is (for the most part) a business, and it has to get subscribers and advertisers. Both of these respond to coverage, in ways that are not always helpful in ensuring accuracy.

Would readers have responded favorably to doom-and-gloom stories that suggested they were about to lose a large fraction of their net worth? Would bankers have responded favorably to business stories that suggested they were irresponsible in their risk management?

Such stories would have been uncomfortable. Revealed preference shows that those who acted as cheerleaders – such as CNBC – did better. The market responded to demands, even if those demands led to poorer quality information. (By the same token, many of those in the financial sector claim that they were just responding to the demand for leverage by their investors.)

In emphasizing the incentives for the provision of distorted reporting, I have perhaps paid too little attention to the countervailing incentives (weaker, admittedly, in a market dominated by shortsightedness): media has an incentive to gain a reputation for accuracy and anticipating stories before they occur. No one wants to have a reputation for being a mouthpiece of industry or finance or the administration. They at least want to seem to be critical.

The critical word, however, may be "seem." Alternative views and voices may be reported, but at the end of the story. An appearance of balance is thereby given, one that pleases the party wanting distorted news – his side gets prominence, and the fact that there is some criticism lends authenticity to the story that it might not otherwise have.

Remedies

Many of the problems that we have described are unavoidable, or almost so. The media is part of our society, and will therefore inevitably suffer to some extent from cognitive capture. If irrational exuberance captures society, it is unreasonable to think that reporters can stand fully apart.

But some of the problems can be alleviated. Part of the problem is a lack of training in *economics*, even for business reporters. And because economic debates are always evolving, the economics training has to be constantly updated. What is required is more than an undergraduate degree – but something different from the technical training afforded by most PhD programs. There needs to be a focus on ideas and policies, not on mathematics. Foundation support for the creation of a summer institute or a program along the lines of the Knight–Bagehot program at Columbia University's School of Journalism, which focuses on training business journalists, could bring this idea into fruition.

We noted, too, how the problem of access in business and finance might undermine reporters' incentives to be critical. Fair disclosure rules – ensuring that any information made available to one reporter be made available to all – will at least mitigate these problems.

So too, in the public sector, stronger and more effectively enforced right-to-know laws may mitigate some of the problems of access there, though to the extent that what matters is *early* access, it may have little effect.

Attempts to identify capture by particular reporters might have a salutary effect, for example studies that correlate "puff pieces," favorable coverage, and scoops. At the time I served in the Clinton administration, we had a sense of which reporters were "owned" by which members of the administration. If these perceptions could be quantified, verified, and publicized, it might have a chilling effect on this kind of capture.

Finally, there needs to be more independent financing of investigative and analytic reporting, with a recognition that reporting on economics is different from reporting on finance or business, and that such reporting requires specialized training. This problem may be getting worse as the Internet has undermined traditional business models.

Concluding comments

Certain aspects of the press coverage of the financial crisis were stellar, from the detailed accounts of the collapse of auction-rated securities markets to some of the investigative reporting surrounding the AIG bailout.[23] Yet, overall, the press acted more like a cheerleader as the bubble grew than like a check, like a warning light, like a critic of a set of fallacious ideas that underpinned the bubble. So, too, in the aftermath of the crisis, it has provided both less analysis and less investigative reporting than one might have hoped. Much of the coverage, both in the run-up to the crisis and its aftermath, was biased – reflecting more the distorted perceptions and beliefs of those in the financial sector that had helped create the crisis than the economists who had predicted its end and provided prescriptions for dealing with the havoc left in its wake. Better information might have led to better policies, but market participants had incentives to provide distorted information. The media may have served those interests better than it did the public interest. We have uncovered some of the reasons why this may have been so. Understanding these reasons is helpful in thinking about how we can ameliorate these problems – not prevent them, but at least mitigate the distortions.

Notes

1 University Professor, Columbia University and Chair, Brooks World Poverty Institute, University of Manchester. Financial support from the Hewlett and Ford Foundations is gratefully acknowledged. I am also indebted to Jonathan Dingle and Jill Blackford for research assistance.
2 From Stiglitz, Joseph E. (2009), 'The Media and the Crisis: An Information Theoretic Approach,' pp. 22–36, in Schiffrin, A. (2009), *Bad News: How America's Business Press Missed the Story of the Century* (New York: New Press); reprinted with kind permission of Joseph E. Stiglitz and New Press.

3 In 2005, Greenspan said: "There are a few things that suggest, at a minimum there's a little froth in this market." While "we don't perceive that there is a national bubble ... it's hard not to see that there are a lot of local bubbles" [Edmund L. Andrews, "Greenspan is Concerned about 'Froth' in Housing," *New York Times*, 21 May 2005, p. A1; Joseph E. Stiglitz, *Freefall* (New York: W.W. Norton, 2010), p. 310].

4 As late as March 2007, Federal Reserve Chairman Bernanke claimed that "the impact on the broader economy and financial markets of the problems in the subprime market seems likely to be contained." Statement of Ben S. Bernanke, Chairman, Board of Governors of the Federal Reserve System, before the Joint Economic Committee, U.S. Congress, Washington, DC, 28 March 2007 [J.E. Stiglitz, *Freefall* (New York: W.W. Norton, 2010), p. 19].

5 As the housing market fell to a fourteen-year low, Bush reassured the nation on 17 October 2007: "I feel good about many of the economic indicators here in the United States." Bush in November 2007: "The underpinnings of our economy are strong, and we're a resilient economy." Bush in October 2008: "We know what the problems are, we have the tools we need to fix them, and we're working swiftly to do so" [Stiglitz, *Freefall*, pp. 28–9].

6 The Dutch "tulip mania" of the 1630s was one of the most famous early bubbles. In this bubble, the price of tulip bulbs – a product that can be quickly reproduced at low costs – reached 2,500 florins, which would be worth more than $30,000 in today's prices. See Charles P. Kindleberger, *Manias, Panics, and Crashes: A History of Financial Crises*, New York: Basic Books, 1978 and Mark Hirschey, "How Much Is a Tulip Worth?" *Financial Analysts Journal*, Vol. 54, No. 4 (Jul.–Aug. 1998), pp. 11–17.

7 See, for instance, Preface and Introduction to *Selected Works of Joseph E. Stiglitz: Volume I: Information and Economic Analysis*. Oxford: Oxford University Press.

8 Though the role of "belief systems" has long been central to the understanding of sociologists and anthropologists of the functioning of society, until the recent crisis, the dominant school in economics focused on rational expectations, on models in which market participants digested all of the information that was available, using (somehow) the "correct" model of the world. Ironically, of course, what these economists asserted as the "correct" model was shown to be grossly flawed in the recent crisis. More recently, economists have attempted to incorporate broader perspectives concerning belief systems in their models – especially as they affect developmental processes. See Avner Greif, *Institutions and the Path to the Modern Economy: Lessons from Medieval Trade* (Cambridge: Cambridge University Press, 2006), Masahiko Aoki, *Toward a Comparative Institutional Analysis*, MIT Press, 2001, and Karla Hoff and Joseph E. Stiglitz, "Equilibrium Fictions: A Cognitive Approach to Societal Rigidity," *American Economic Review*, May 2010.

9 The usual advice given to central bankers, which many (including those in the United States) unfortunately did not heed.

10 See, e.g., Jack Hirshleifer, "The Private and Social Value of Information and the Reward to Inventive Activity," *American Economic Review*, 61(4), pp. 561–574, September 1971 and J.E. Stiglitz, "Using Tax Policy to Curb Speculative Short-Term Trading," *Journal of Financial Services Research*, 3(2/3), December 1989, pp. 101–115.

11 A point brought out forcefully by Lehman's infamous "Repo 105" transactions, which moved some $50 billion off its balance sheet. The use of "creative accounting" is not new; it was one of the distinctive aspects of the scandals of the early years of the century, epitomized by Enron. In the case of Lehman brothers, a firm that claimed to have a net worth of $26 billion just before their collapse turned out to have a negative net worth of -$200 billion. See J.E. Stiglitz, *Freefall* p. 156.

12 Remarkably, as Citibank went through its crisis, Citigroup shareholder equity (as reported) continued its growth: it went from $114b (Dec. '07), to $142b (Dec. '08), and on to $153b (Dec. '09) [www.google.com/finance?q=NYSE:C&fstype=ii].

13 Tony Barber, David Oakley, and Kerin Hope, "Chinese whispers drive up Greek yields," *Financial Times*, 26 Jan 2010, www.ft.com/cms/s/0/65ac74fc-0aaf-11df-b35f-00144feabdc0.html

14 Mark Pittman, "S&p, Moody's Mask $200 Billion of Subprime Bond Risk," Bloomberg, 29 June 2007, www.bloomberg.com/apps/news?pid=20601087&refer=home&sid=aIzzx2vC10KI and "S&P May Cut $12 Billion of Subprime Mortgage Bonds," Bloomberg, 10 July 2007, www.bloomberg.com/apps/news?pid=20601103&sid=aN4sulHN19xc

15 A U.S. district judge ordered the Federal Reserve to turn over records identifying the companies receiving money through its emergency lending programs in August 2009. Mark Pittman, "Court Orders Fed to Disclose Emergency Bank Loans," Bloomberg, 25 August 2009, at www.bloomberg.com/apps/news?pid=20601087&sid=a7CC61Z sieV4. In March 2010, the U.S. Court of Appeals in Manhattan upheld the decision that the Fed must disclose its documents. David Glovin and Bob Van Voris, "Federal Reserve Must Disclose Bank Bailout Records," Bloomberg, 19 March 2010, www.bloomberg.com/apps/news?pid=20601087&sid=aUpIaeiWKF2s

16 Jody Shenn, Bob Ivry and Alan Katz, "AIG 100-Cents Fed Deal Driven by France Belied by French Banks," *Bloomberg*, 20 January 2010, www.bloomberg.com/apps/news?pid=20601208& sid=a__.69Q8BR04

17 See, for instance, J.E. Stiglitz, *The Roaring Nineties* (New York: W.W. Norton, 2003).

18 John Maynard Keynes, *The General Theory of Employment, Interest, and Money* (London: Macmillan, 1936).

19 See George A. Akerlof and Robert J. Shiller, *Animal Spirits: How Human Psychology Drives the Economy, and Why It Matters for Global Capitalism* (Princeton: Princeton University Press, 2009).

20 George Soros has emphasized that while beliefs are an important part of economic reality, they are not untethered. See George Soros, *The New Paradigm for Financial Markets* (New York: Public Affairs, 2008).

21 See, in particular, J.E. Stiglitz, "Transparency in Government," in Roumeen Islam (ed.), *The Right to Tell: the Role of Mass Media in Economic Development* (Washington: World Bank Publications, 2002) and J.E. Stiglitz, "On Liberty, the Right to Know and Public Discourse: The Role of Transparency in Public Life," Chapter 8 in Ha-Joon Chang (ed.), *The Rebel Within* (London: Wimbledon Publishing Company, 2001), pp. 250–278. Also published in Matthew Gibney (ed.), *Globalizing Rights*, (Oxford: Oxford University Press, 2003), pp. 115–156. (Originally presented as 1999 Oxford Amnesty Lecture, Oxford, January 1999.)

22 See J.E. Stiglitz, *Freefall*.

23 See, for instance, Floyd Norris, chief financial correspondent for the *New York Times* and the *International Herald Tribune*, Gretchen Morgenson, who writes the Sunday "Fair Game" column for the *New York Times*, and the late Mark Pittman of Bloomberg.

11

WHY THE PUBLIC DOESN'T TRUST THE BUSINESS PRESS

Steve Schifferes

Interest in the global financial crisis has remained high but public trust in the journalists who covered it is low. Audience research in the UK suggests that many people don't think the media gave them an accurate picture of the financial crisis, nor did it explain how the crisis affected them personally. The research also suggests people think that the journalists who reported on the crisis failed to provide fair, balanced, and independent coverage. This lack of trust is a challenge for journalists who face the difficulty of telling a complicated story to an audience that is new to business news and has little prior knowledge of the subject.[1]

A major opinion poll by ICM for City University's Department of Journalism carried out in November 2011, three years after the crisis began, provides a unique insight into public attitudes towards the media coverage of the crisis in the UK.[2] In this wide-ranging survey, only half the public were satisfied with the media coverage of the economic crisis in general. Even more worrying, many people displayed a deep level of mistrust in the objectivity of business journalists, and criticized their reliance on biased sources and lack of understanding of the concerns of ordinary people. The poll demonstrated that public interest in news about the financial crisis had not diminished in the three years since it had begun – another reason to take seriously the public concerns. The difficulties that financial journalists face in reporting and explaining the crisis to the public have been exacerbated by the lack of financial literacy among a large section of the population.

Interest in the financial crisis undiminished

While the high level of interest in the global financial crisis is not unexpected, the fact that it remained at the same level three years after it began in 2008 is more remarkable. Our research shows the public's appetite for financial information increased dramatically between 2005 and 2011, and that up until 2011 there was little evidence of 'crisis fatigue'. This should be good news not just for major newspapers and broadcasters, but also for the specialist financial press and websites.

A key measure of audience interest is to ask how closely viewers are following a story. In October 2008, as part of a BBC audience research survey, 78 per cent said they were following the news about the economy closely or very closely – one of the highest figures the BBC said it had ever recorded for a news event. When the same question was asked in the City University poll three years later, the result was almost identical (75 per cent).[3] The fact that this figure was so close to that recorded at the absolute height of the crisis, when the international banking system was on the verge of collapse, suggests that the very strong interest in the crisis was sustained over time (BBC Audience Research, 2008; Schifferes and Coulter, 2013).

Our poll respondents not only *said* they were very interested in following the crisis. They also reported a major change in their media habits: they were seeking financial information much more often. Before the crisis, nearly half the population (40 per cent) said they rarely or never kept up with financial matters on a regular basis, while only one third were looking as much as weekly. By 2011, less than 10 per cent reported that they rarely or never kept up. Indeed more than 70 per cent now said they were keeping up weekly or daily. Of that total, four in 10 said they were checking financial information *daily* – a category not even asked in the 2005 survey.[4]

Other measures also show that the public interest in the financial crisis remained high between 2008 and 2011 and indeed continued well into 2013. Data from the

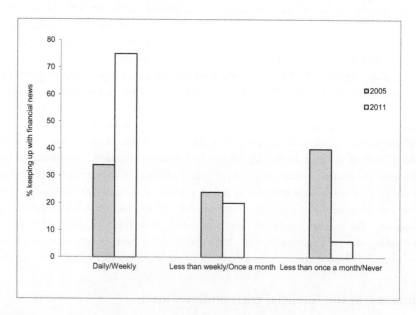

FIGURE 11.1 Changes in frequency of keeping up with financial matters, 2005–2011
City/ICM Question 2: How often do you keep up with financial matters generally, such as the economy and the financial services sector?
Sources: (2011): City/ICM Poll, November 2011; (2005): Baseline Survey of Financial Capability, Table 7.5, p. 116 (frequency of monitoring financial information).

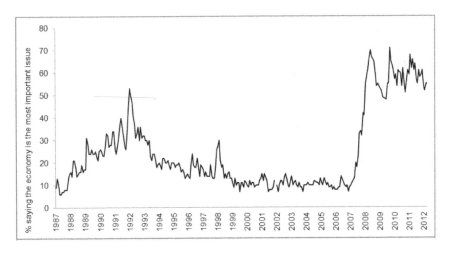

FIGURE 11.2 The most important issue facing Britain today, 1987–2012
Source: Ipsos MORI (2013), Political and Social Trends, Research Archive.

polling firm Ipsos MORI (2013) reveals that the economy was judged by far the most important issue facing Britain for a continuous period of 62 months between September 2008 and December 2013 – the longest run for any issue in the poll's 40-year history. This level of concern about the economy occurred only once before – during the Exchange Rate Mechanism (ERM) crisis in September 1992 – but in that case the economy stayed as the most important issue facing the country for just four months.[5]

A crisis of trust

The intense interest in the crisis has not been matched by satisfaction in the way the media has covered it. According to the City University poll, many people feel that the media failed to explain the crisis clearly in ways that were relevant to their day-to-day concerns. Even more worrying for the profession, few thought that business journalists were 'fair and balanced' in their coverage and many thought they were too close to their sources and too easily influenced by their proprietors.

The City poll had three questions designed to measure overall public satisfaction with the media's performance during the financial crisis. First, we asked how satisfied people were with the way the media had been covering the news about the economic crisis over the past few years. Just over half (52 per cent) said they were 'very' or 'fairly' satisfied, while the rest said they were either dissatisfied or neither satisfied nor dissatisfied. Those who were following the crisis closely and were better informed were less satisfied with the coverage.

Then – as the poll was carried out during a key moment in the economic crisis in Europe[6] – we asked how well the public felt they understood how the current economic events in Europe would impact on the UK economy. Only 55 per cent

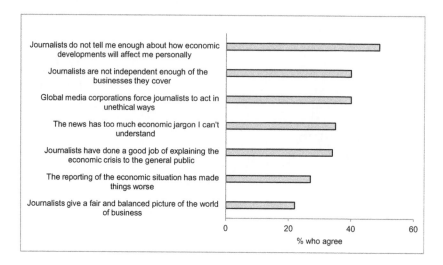

FIGURE 11.3 Lack of trust in business journalists
City/ICM Question 5: Can you tell me how much you agree or disagree with the following statements?
Source: City/ICM Poll, November 2011

felt they understood this 'a lot' or 'quite a bit', roughly the same proportion as those who were satisfied with the overall media coverage. Finally, in a separate question, only one in three of our sample agreed that journalists had done a good job overall explaining the economic crisis to the public.

But the public is not only concerned about the ability of business journalists to report on the crisis in a way that can be understood. There is a more fundamental lack of trust in business journalists. Our poll suggests there is a deep-seated mistrust of their objectivity, scepticism about their motivation and use of sources, and a belief that they are out of touch with the needs and wants of the ordinary public.

Half of the audience say that journalists do not report enough about how economic developments will affect them personally, and would like the coverage to have a different focus. Even more damning, only one in five believes that journalists 'give a fair and balanced picture of the world of business'. In regard to bias and use of sources, our polling shows that close to half the public also believe that business journalists are too close to their sources and 'are not independent enough of the businesses they cover'. Finally, nearly half of the population believe that 'global media corporations force journalists to act in unethical ways'. This last result may have been affected by the timing of our poll, which occurred at the height of the phone-hacking scandal.[7]

One key reason for the lack of trust is that the public don't believe that journalists share their concerns or point of view. Our poll gives further details of exactly where the public thinks the coverage falls short. Overall, people wanted less coverage of how the crisis affects affluent groups, such as shareholders and businessmen, and more of how it will affect jobs, government spending cuts, and their own personal finances. Clearly, the rise in unemployment and the austerity policies

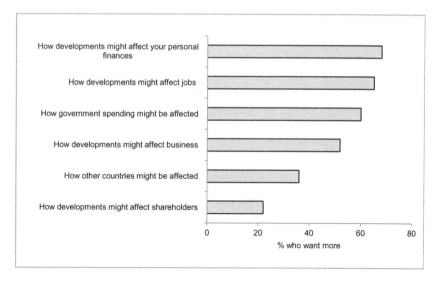

FIGURE 11.4 Audience news preferences

City/ICM Question 7: Thinking about the media coverage of the UK economy, which areas do you think should be covered MORE by the media, and which areas do you think should be covered LESS?
Source: City/ICM Poll, November 2011

of the Coalition government have made these issues more salient during our survey period. Significantly, those in our poll who felt they were financially stressed (who reported that their standard of living had gone down in the past year, and expected it to decline further) felt strongly that coverage had the wrong emphasis.

The changing audience for business news

One reason why the focus of coverage has fallen short of expectations is the changing nature of the audience itself. The audience interested in business and especially economic news has expanded greatly in the wake of the crisis. As the audience for news about the crisis grew, business journalists faced a particular challenge in pitching their stories to reach a more general audience, as well as retaining their specialist readers with different interests who were worried about the 'dumbing down' of coverage.

One way of understanding these two different audiences is to distinguish between those who are interested in 'economic news' and those who say that 'business and financial news' is important to them. These categories seem to broadly correspond to the general and the specialist audience for news about the crisis. We have demographic and comparative data from the Reuters Digital News Survey in 2013 that asked people to state 'what sort of news is important to you'. It found that across nine countries, twice as many people said economic news was important to them as business and financial news. In the UK, 44 per cent chose economic news (more than any other specialist news category, including sport, politics, and celebrity news), while only 20 per cent chose business and financial news. The demographic characteristics of the two groups were also very different. The group that said financial news was important was generally more affluent, better educated, and contained fewer women than the general population. Those interested in economic news were more broadly representative of the population as a whole in terms of social class, age, and gender, with the exception of younger women. It was also significant that the interest in economic news varied with the severity of the economic crisis, with the US and the UK at the top (Schifferes, 2012; Reuters, 2013).

Explaining the decline in trust

These striking findings about the lack of trust in British journalists covering the financial crisis need to be understood against a background in which trust in the media as a whole is in sharp decline. This has been paralleled by a decline in trust in politicians and, even more dramatically since the crisis, in business leaders and bankers.

Public opinion polls have been tracking the declining confidence in the media for over 30 years. The British Social Attitudes Survey (BSAS) has asked participants since 1983 'how well run' various institutions are. In 1983, 53 per cent said the press was well run, but that number had declined by half in 2012. For the BBC, the decline was less steep, from 75 per cent to 65 per cent (Park et al., 2013).

A variety of different measures suggest that this decline in trust has accelerated during the past decade, helped along by the impact of the hacking scandal.

For the last decade, we have a more fine-grained tracking poll that shows public trust varies substantially between different categories of journalists. The polling organization YouGov (2012) has asked respondents for a decade which professions they would 'trust to tell the truth'. The results show public trust in all journalists has declined sharply since 2003. The percentage of the population who said that tabloid journalists tell the truth 'a great deal' or 'a fair amount' dropped from 14

TABLE 11.1   Perceptions of how well major UK institutions are run, 1983–2012

% saying institution is 'well run'	1983	1986	1987	1994	2009	2012	Change 1983–2012
Banks	90	92	91	63	19	19	−72
The press	53	48	39	47	39	27	−26
The police	77	74	66	68	62	65	−12
BBC	72	70	67	62	49	63	−9
NHS	52	36	35	33	54	54	2
Trade Unions	29	27	27	47	35	33	5

Question: How well do you think the following institution is run?
Source: The 30th British Social Attitudes Survey, 2013, Table 0.1, p. xvi, www.bsa-30.natcen.ac.uk/downloads.aspx

TABLE 11.2 Trust in journalists to tell the truth, 2003–2012

% saying 'trust a great deal' or a 'fair amount'	Mar 2003	May 2006	Apr 2007	Mar 2008	Aug 2010	Jul 2011	Jan 2012	Oct 2012	Nov 2012	Change 2003–2012
BBC news journalists	81	71	62	61	60	58	60	57	44	−37
ITV news journalists	82	67	54	51	49	47	52	51	41	−41
Journalists on 'upmarket' newspapers (e.g. Times, Telegraph, Guardian)	65	62	43	43	41	35	41	43	38	−27
Journalists on 'mid-market' newspapers (e.g. Mail, Express)	36	36	20	18	21	16	20	19	18	−18
Journalists on red-top tabloid newspapers (e.g. Sun, Mirror)	14	12	7	15	10	6	10	10	10	−4

Question: How much do you trust the following to tell the truth?
Source: YouGov, 2012, Trust tracker: longitudinal survey results, http://cdn.yougov.com/cumulus_uploads/document/syrhatyofp/Trust_trends_Nov_2012.pdf

per cent in 2003 to an all-time low of 6 per cent in 2011 at the height of the hacking scandal. Trust scores were much higher for broadcast journalists and upmarket newspapers. But over 10 years, trust was halved for journalists on both mid-market and upmarket newspapers. The decline in trust in broadcast journalists to tell the truth was even sharper in absolute terms. By 2012 less than half the public trusted *any* journalist to tell the truth even 'a fair amount'.

These major differences between the levels of trust in different types of journalists and news organizations are also reflected in the outlets people turn to for business and financial news coverage. The City poll results show broadcasters as the most popular source of business and economic news, and that the BBC is most trusted of all in an economic crisis. Our poll showed that for most people television was their main source of news about business and the economy (46 per cent), followed by internet news (25 per cent) and newspapers (18 per cent). This broadly accords with the findings of other surveys looking at general news consumption (Ofcom, 2013; Reuters, 2013).

Looking at specific news brands also highlights the dominance of the broadcasters as providers of business news. Seven out of the top 10 news sources were broadcasters. BBC television news has the biggest monthly reach (54 per cent used it monthly), followed by ITV News (35 per cent), the BBC News website (35 per cent), BBC News 24 (30 per cent), Sky News (26 per cent), and BBC radio news (24 per cent).

The only newspaper group that could match these figures was the *Daily Mail*, with 32 per cent of the population viewing the printed newspaper and its associated websites (including thisismoney.co.uk) for business news, helped by its strong personal finance offering.

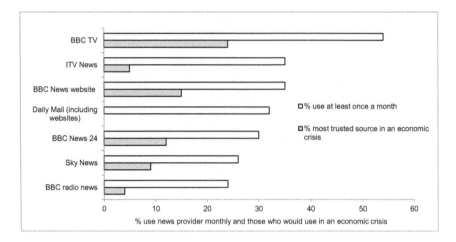

FIGURE 11.5 Most trusted news sources in an economic crisis

City/ICM Question 9: Which of the following sources, if any, do you use at least once a month to follow the news about business and the economy?

City/ICM Question 10: Regardless of which sources you use at the moment, which would you turn to for reliable and trustworthy information if there was a major economic crisis that was affecting you and your family?

Source: City/ICM Poll, November 2011

Even more striking differences emerged when we asked which source 'would you turn to for reliable and trustworthy information if there was a major economic crisis that was affecting you and your family?' Here the dominant position of the BBC stood out even more sharply. Over half the population (55 per cent) said they would go to one of the BBC sources (TV, radio, or online) first, far more than any other broadcaster or newspaper. Other broadcast channels were far behind (9 per cent for Sky News and 5 per cent for ITV). Figures for the print media (including their websites) were even lower. The importance of the *Daily Mail* as a source of business news did not carry over to its role as a trusted source in an economic crisis. This is not wholly unexpected: the dominance of the BBC as the UK's most trusted news source, especially for 'serious news' such as elections, is one of the most distinctive features of the British media scene (Ofcom, 2013; Reuters, 2013; Schifferes and Coulter, 2013).

The decline in trust: a secular trend?

One explanation for the decline in trust in the media is that it is part of a broader long-term secular trend across all Western countries towards greater scepticism towards all institutions, based on the rise of individualism and the decline of collectivism (Norris, 2000; Inglehart and Welzel, 2013; Park et al., 2013). There is certainly extensive evidence of a decline in trust in all major institutions, such as the press, government, and business, across much of Europe and the US (Wood and Berg, 2011; Pew Research Center, 2012, 2013; Eurobarometer, 2013a–c; Manchin, 2013).

The decline in trust in British politicians has been particularly well documented ever since the first studies of 'the civic culture' began in the 1950s (Almond and Verba, 1963). Some commentators have argued that the decline in trust in politics goes hand in hand with the decline in trust in the media, each reinforcing the other. But even in 1983, only 38 per cent of Britons trusted the government 'to put the needs of the nation above the interests of their own political party', and by 2000, only 16 per cent did so (Park et al., 2013). Kellner (2012) found similar results in relation to MPs. Only 15 per cent thought MPs were doing a good job (down from 38 per cent in 1954), while two thirds of the public thought 'politicians tell lies all the time' and they 'end up becoming remote from the everyday lives and concerns of the people they represent' – figures no doubt made worse by the 2011 expenses scandal.

Since the crisis, there has been an even sharper decline in trust in banks and financial institutions. Those who viewed banks as well run collapsed from 90 per cent in 1983 to only 19 per cent in 2009, as part of 'the most dramatic change of attitude registered in 30 years of the British Social Attitudes Survey' (Park et al., 2013, p. xv). The decline was across the board, affecting trust in all financial institutions (Gritten, 2011). Trust in banks also plunged in Europe and the US to all-time lows following the crisis (Wood and Berg, 2011; Crabtree, 2013; Eurobarometer, 2013a).

Looking at this data more closely suggests that a secular decline in trust across the board cannot be the whole story. The recent decline in trust in the media has been much more pronounced in the UK and the US than in Europe, where, although there have been dramatic falls in the confidence in governments and the central bank, there is relatively little decline in trust in the media (Pew Research Center, 2011; Eurobarometer, 2013a–c; Manchin, 2013). This suggests that there may be factors that are specific to the UK and the US, such as the increasingly aggressive tabloid press in the UK, the political polarization of the media in the US, and indeed perhaps the extent of the damage caused by the financial crisis in both countries (Pew Research Center, 2009a, 2013; Coleman, 2012; Golding, Sousa, and van Zoonen, 2012).

It is also possible that the decline in trust is cyclical, relating to economic conditions, and not a long-term secular trend. In this case, trust in all institutions, including the media, will have gone down during the recession, but will return when economic conditions improve (Stevenson and Wolfers, 2011).

Problems in understanding: jargon and financial literacy

If part of the problem for financial journalists is the general decline in trust in the media, another barrier to trust that is very specific to business journalism is the complexity of the issues involved and the difficulty in explaining them clearly. From sovereign debt to CDOs to sub-prime mortgages, these were terms that had rarely appeared in the general press before the crash. This is reflected in the findings of our poll, where half said that they didn't understand how broader economic

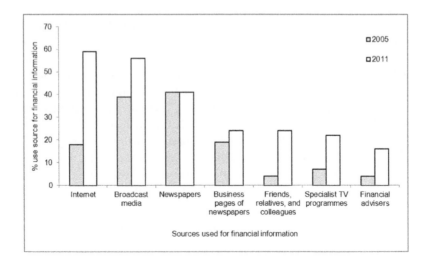

FIGURE 11.6 Changes in sources used for personal financial information, 2005–2011
City/ICM Question 3: Which of the following sources, if any, do you use to get advice on personal financial matters?
Sources: (2011): City/ICM Poll, November 2011; (2005): Baseline Survey of Financial Capability, Table 7.4, p. 115 (sources used to monitor financial information).

events would affect them – and one in three said the news had too much economics jargon that they can't understand. Journalists should not under-estimate the limits to public understanding of economic or financial concepts.

One way the public is dealing with this problem of understanding is by seeking more sources of financial information. There is some evidence that the public is no longer solely relying on the mass media. Compared with 2005, our sample in 2011 used a more diverse group of sources. There was a big shift to using the Internet, which may be connected with increased searching for information and explanation. Even more striking was the growing reliance on personal sources of information, such as advice from friends, colleagues, and financial advisers. This suggests a degree of scepticism about the reliability or usefulness of mainstream media sources.

But there are deeper barriers to public understanding of economic issues, which are not solely due to the inability of journalists to explain things clearly. Research has shown that few people can explain even basic economic concepts, such as GDP, interest rates, inflation, and bond markets. In a recent UK survey, one in 10 thought Bank of England interest rates were 10 per cent (when they were actually 0.5 per cent); and in the US only 27 per cent of young people could answer three basic financial literacy questions (Lusardi, 2008; Peston, 2008; Lusardi and Mitchell, 2009; Pew Research Center, 2009b; Money Advice Service, 2013).

Underlying these specific difficulties are the broader problems of 'financial literacy' and 'financial capability'. International surveys show that a substantial proportion of the public not only have a very limited understanding of many key concepts, but they also lack both 'financial literacy' (relevant financial knowledge) and the broader 'financial capability' to effectively save, plan, and budget their money. In the UK in 2005 a Financial Services Authority survey found one third of the population overall having weak financial capability (Atkinson et al., 2006). This figure is broadly unchanged in 2013, when the government agency the Money Advice Service (2013) estimates that 37 per cent of the population lack the knowledge they need to manage their finances. Similar surveys in the USA, Canada, and Australia have yielded similar results, while comparative studies have shown that the gender gap in financial knowledge is particularly large in the UK (Lusardi and Mitchell, 2009, 2011; Pew Research Center, 2009a–b; Jappelli, 2010; Taskforce on Financial Literacy, 2010; ANZ, 2011; Atkinson and Messy, 2012; FINRA Investor Education Foundation, 2013; Nicolini, Cude, and Chatterjee, 2013).

In the wake of the financial crisis, which has weakened the welfare state, governments have become increasingly concerned that their citizens lack the financial capability to take more responsibility for their own financial decisions (OECD, 2005; Hecklinger, 2006; Mishkin, 2008; Brookings Institution, 2009). Longitudinal research from the British Household Panel Survey has shown that individuals with high financial capability are better off, happier, and have a more secure retirement, even taking into account variables such as social class and education (Taylor, Jenkins, and Sacker, 2009; Taylor, 2011). But recent attempts to provide financial education at the secondary level, and to provide more advice about money matters, seem to have had a limited effect (Atkinson, 2008; Lusardi, 2008; Kempson and Collard, 2010).

More recent research, drawn from behavioural economics, has highlighted the problem that people may not always make the best decisions for their financial future, because of assumptions they are not aware of, such as wishful thinking, overconfidence, and oversimplistic shortcuts. This has led governments to adopt 'nudge' strategies, such as auto-enrolment in private pension plans, to encourage 'rational' behaviour (De Meza, Irlenbusch, and Reyniers, 2008; Thaler and Sunstein, 2008; Collard, 2009; Elliott et al., 2010; Kahneman, 2011).[8]

Financial journalists could make an important contribution in helping to tackle this issue, which would help rebuild trust in their profession. But it would take a major effort to reshape the way personal finance is currently covered by journalists given the widespread criticism of their standards during the financial crisis; which, according to the public, were biased, lacking in independence, and failed to explain how the crisis would take its toll on their personal finances (Peston, 2008; Olen, 2012).

Conclusion: blaming the messenger?

What light can audience research shed on the broader criticisms that have been made of the media's performance during the financial crisis? The results can only be suggestive but they raise the possibility that the public has a more nuanced view of the role of the press in the crisis than some of its critics.

At the height of the crisis, some of the fiercest criticism of the media came from politicians, businessmen, and bankers who claimed that the media coverage of the crisis was causing panic and was 'talking ourselves into a recession' (see Chapter 19). However, when asked whether the reporting of the economic situation has made things worse, only one in four of our sample agreed. Although this is still a significant minority, it suggests that the fears of press scaremongering have been overdone.

A second area of concern is how the crisis was framed, with a number of commentators arguing that news organizations only used conventional sources instead of those who would provide a critique of existing policy. A related criticism is that there was not enough coverage of how ordinary individuals were affected. Our results are certainly consistent with the view that the public wanted more rather than less coverage of the crisis, but a different kind of coverage, particularly in areas that they felt were of personal concern to them. The poll data also suggests that the public is sceptical of the sources used by business journalists, although it is not clear if that means they want to hear a radical alternative.

A third major criticism is that the press failed to warn the public of the impending disaster until it was too late and was a 'lapdog not a watchdog'. However, our polling suggests that overall the UK public does not blame the media for causing the crisis. When we asked our sample to rank different groups in order of blame for the financial crisis, journalists were at the bottom of the list, while bankers and politicians came top. It is telling that journalists were ranked below not just bankers, politicians, civil servants, and regulators, but were even seen as less culpable than ordinary members of the public who had behaved irresponsibly by borrowing too much.

Our review of financial literacy shows the deep-seated challenges that journalists face in trying to explain complex financial events to the general public, and the potential benefits that would follow if they were able to do more to tackle this problem. It is also clear that any notion of a general breakdown in trust has to be more nuanced, as during the financial crisis some journalists (and some media organizations) were more trusted than others.

We do not have longitudinal data on the level of trust in financial journalists before the crisis. But it is a reasonable hypothesis that one of the main reasons that trust has broken down is that the promise of an economic golden age – endorsed by bankers, politicians, and journalists alike – has proved to be a painful illusion. The biggest challenge for business journalists posed by the economic crisis is how to rebuild the trust of the public. It is only when this happens that the media will be able to help shape the debate about our economic future.

Notes

1 The author would like to acknowledge the support of City University's early-stage researcher grant in funding the poll, and the invaluable help of his research assistant Sophie Knowles.
2 ICM interviewed a representative sample of 2,000 UK adults on 2–4 November 2011 using one of its omnibus online panels. The panel was stratified by age, gender, and

social class. The margin of error is +/-3 per cent. Full details of the poll methodology, top line questions, and the full data set are available from the author.

3 The BBC data comes from their daily 'Pulse' online panel survey of 20,000 people who are asked to complete a survey to say what they watched and listened to and rate it on a scale of 1 to 10. The Appreciation Index (A1) is the average rating multiplied by 10. Since the BBC weekly audience reach is 91 per cent of the population, and our own poll showed that BBC News was by far the largest source of business news, these results are likely to be compatible. For BBC methodology, see http://downloads.bbc.co.uk/aboutthebbc/reports/pdf/audience_0711.pdf

4 This comparison is based on the Baseline Survey of Financial Capability (BSFC) carried out by Bristol University for the FSA in 2005 (Atkinson et al., 2006). Such comparisons need to be seen as broadly indicative, due to several methodological differences in the way the polls were conducted, although wherever possible identical question wording was used. The BSFC survey was based on face-to-face interviews, not online polling; it included a larger sample but was GB-only, as opposed to the UK-wide ICM poll (thus excluding Northern Ireland), and was done on the basis of stratified geographical districts, and prompted respondents by listing specific types of financial data such as interest rates before asking how often this information was being monitored or where it was sourced.

5 Ipsos MORI has used its monthly UK omnibus survey since 1974 to ask 'What would you say is the most important issue facing Britain today?' using a set of showcards. More than 50 per cent chose 'economy' as the answer between September 2008 and July 2013. The number choosing 'economy' fell below 50 per cent in August 2013 and by December was just ahead of immigration (39 per cent v. 37 per cent). See www.ipsos-mori.com/research-publications/researcharchive/2905/Issues-Index-2012-onwards.aspx?view=wide

6 On 27 October 2011 the EU agreed a second bailout of Greece following all-night negotiations amid market turmoil. On 30 October Greek Prime Minister Papandreou said he would not accept the deal unless it was approved in a referendum by the Greek people. This plan was dropped on 3 November and Mr Papandreou resigned on 10 November. The City poll was carried out 2–4 November.

7 The phone-hacking scandal came to a head in the summer of 2011 when *The Guardian* newspaper revealed that the *News of the World* had hacked into the phone of the murdered schoolgirl Milly Dowler. The Leveson Inquiry, which began in November 2011, held a series of public hearings that revealed widespread phone hacking of celebrities, politicians, and members of the public. It made its final recommendations in November 2012 (Leveson, 2012).

8 The UK government has created a behavioural economics unit in the Cabinet office to advise the government on how to 'nudge' citizens into financially sensible decisions, such as savings (see www.gov.uk/government/organisations/behavioural-insights-team). Since October 2013, most UK employers have been required to offer an occupational pension scheme that features auto-enrolment.

References

Almond, G. and Verba, S. (1963) *The Civic Culture: Political Attitudes and Democracy in Five Nations*, Princeton: Princeton University Press.

ANZ (2011) *Adult Financial Literacy in Australia*, Australia and New Zealand Banking Group Limited (ANZ). Available at: www.anz.com.au/resources/3/d/3dbcd380493e8b9395e5 d7fc8cff90cd/2011-Adult-Financial-Literacy-Summary.pdf.pdf?MOD=AJPERES [Accessed 3 December 2013].

Atkinson, A. (2008) *Evidence of Impact: An Overview of Financial Education Evaluations*, consumer research 68, prepared for the Financial Services Authority by the Personal Finance Research Centre, University of Bristol, Financial Services Authority, July.

Atkinson, A., McKay, S., Kempson, E., and Collard, S. (2006) *Levels of Financial Capability in the UK: Results of a Baseline Survey*, consumer research 47, prepared for the Financial Services Authority by the Personal Finance Research Centre, University of Bristol, Financial Services Authority, March.

Atkinson, A. and Messy, F.A. (2012) *Measuring Financial Literacy: Results of the OECD/International Network on Financial Education (INFE) Pilot Study*, no. 15, OECD Working Papers on Finance, Insurance and Private Pensions, Paris: OECD Publishing.

BBC Audience Research (2008) *The Lehman Crash: Analysis of BBC News Coverage*, BBC, November, unpublished report in possession of the author.

Brookings Institution (2009) *Financial Literacy in Times of Turmoil and Retirement Insecurity: Conference Proceedings*, Washington, DC: Brookings Institution.

Coleman, S. (2012) 'Believing the News: From Sinking Trust to Atrophied Efficacy', *European Journal of Communication*, 27, pp. 35–45.

Collard, S. (2009) *Individual Investment Behaviour: A Brief Review of Research*, final report, Personal Finance Research Centre, University of Bristol, January.

Crabtree, S. (2013) 'European Countries Lead World in Distrust of Banks', *Gallup World*, 20 May. Available at: www.gallup.com/poll/162602/european-countries-lead-world-distrust-banks.aspx [Accessed 3 December 2013].

De Meza, D., Irlenbusch, B., and Reyniers, D. (2008) *Financial Capability: A Behavioural Economics Perspective*, consumer research 69, prepared for the Financial Services Authority by the London School of Economics, Financial Services Authority, July.

Elliott, A., Dolan, P., Vlaev, I., Adriaenssens, C., and Metcalfe, R. (2010) *Transforming Financial Behaviour: Developing Interventions That Build Financial Capability*, CFEB consumer research report 01, Consumer Financial Education Body (CFEB), July.

Eurobarometer (2013a) *Trust in Banks*. Available at: http://ec.europa.eu/public_opinion/cf/index_en.cfm [Accessed 10 December 2013].

——(2013b) *Trust in the Media*. Available at: http://ec.europa.eu/public_opinion/cf/index_en.cfm [Accessed 10 December 2013].

——(2013c) *Trust in Government Institutions*. Available at: http://ec.europa.eu/public_opinion/cf/index_en.cfm [Accessed 10 December 2013].

FINRA Investor Education Foundation (2013) *Financial Capability in the United States: 2012 Report of National Findings*, Washington, DC: FINRA Investor Education Foundation. Available at: http://usfinancialcapability.org/downloads/NFCS_2012_Report_Natl_Findings.pdf [Accessed 20 November 2013].

Golding, P., Sousa, H., and van Zoonen, L. (2012) 'Trust and the Media', *European Journal of Communication*, 27, pp. 3–6.

Gritten, A. (2011) 'New Insights Into Consumer Confidence in Financial Services', *International Journal of Bank Marketing*, 29 (2), pp. 90–106.

Hecklinger, R. (2006) 'Opening Remarks'. Paper presented at the G8 International Conference on Improving Financial Literacy, Moscow, 29–30 November.

Inglehart, R. and Welzel, C. (2013) *Modernization, Cultural Change, and Democracy*, Cambridge: Cambridge University Press.

Ipsos MORI (2013) *Political and Social Trends*, Research Archive: Most Important Issues Facing Britain Today 2007–2012. Available at: http://www.ipsos-mori.com/researchpublications/researcharchive.aspx?keyword=Issues+facing+Britain [Accessed 10 December 2013].

Jappelli, T. (2010) 'Economic Literacy: An International Comparison', *Economic Journal*, 120 (548), pp. F429–F451.

Kahneman, D. (2011) *Thinking, Fast and Slow*, London: Penguin.

Kellner, P. (2012) *Democracy on Trial: What Voters Really Think of Parliament and Our Politicians*, Oxford: Reuters Institute for the Study of Journalism and YouGov.

Kempson, E. and Collard, S. (2010) *Money Guidance Pathfinder: A Report to the FSA*, evaluation report 01, Personal Finance Research Centre, University of Bristol, April.

Leveson, B.H. (2012) *An Inquiry Into the Culture, Practices and Ethics of the Press*, London: The Stationery Office.

Lusardi, A. (2008) *Household Saving Behavior: The Role of Financial Literacy, Information, and Financial Education Programs*, NBER working paper no. 13824, Cambridge, Massachusetts: National Bureau of Economic Research (NBER).

Lusardi, A. and Mitchell, O.S. (2009) 'Financial Literacy, Retirement Planning, and Retirement Wellbeing: Lessons and Research Gaps'. Paper presented to the Financial Literacy Conference, Brookings Institution, Washington, DC, 20 March.

——(2011) 'Financial Literacy Around the World: An Overview', *Journal of Pension Economics and Finance*, 10 (4), pp. 497–508.

Manchin, A. (2013) 'Trust in Government Sinks to New Low in Southern Europe', *Gallup World*, 30 October. Available at: www.gallup.com/poll/165647/trust-government-sinks-new-low-southern-europe.aspx [Accessed 5 December 2013].

Mishkin, F. (2008) 'The Importance of Economic Education and Financial Literacy'. Paper presented to the Third National Summit on Economic and Financial Literacy, Washington, DC, 27 February.

Money Advice Service (2013) *The Financial Capability of the UK*, London: Money Advice Service (MAS), November.

Nicolini, G., Cude, B.J., and Chatterjee, S. (2013) 'Financial Literacy: A Comparative Study Across Four Countries', *International Journal of Consumer Studies*, 37, pp. 689–705.

Norris, P. (2000) *A Virtuous Circle: Political Communications in Postindustrial Societies*, Cambridge: Cambridge University Press.

OECD (2005) *Improving Financial Literacy: Analysis of Issues and Policies*, Paris: Organisation for Economic Co-operation and Development (OECD) publications.

Ofcom (2013) *News Consumption in the UK – 2013 Report*, London: Ofcom.

Olen, Helaine (2012) *Pound Foolish: Exposing the Dark Side of the Personal Finance Industry*, New York: Penguin.

Park, A., Bryson, C., Clery, E., Curtice, J., and Phillips, M. (eds.) (2013) *British Social Attitudes: The 30th Report*, London: NatCen Social Research. Available at: www.bsa-30.natcen.ac.uk/

Peston, R. (2008) 'The Big Stories of the Past Year'. Presentation to the Society of Editors: Fighting for Press Freedom, Bristol, 10 November. Available at: www.societyofeditors.co.uk/page-view.php?pagename=BigStoriesOfPastYear [Accessed 25 February 2014].

Pew Research Center for the People and the Press (2009a) *Political Knowledge Update Survey, Final Topline*, Washington, DC: Pew Research Center, 26–9 March. Available at: http://people-press.org/files/legacy-questionnaires/504.pdf [Accessed 24 February 2014].

——(2009b) *Public Knows Basic Facts About Financial Crisis*, Washington, DC: Pew Research Center, 2 April. Available at: www.people-press.org/2009/04/02/public-knows-basic-facts-about-financial-crisis/ [Accessed 20 November 2013].

——(2011) *Press Widely Criticized, But Trusted More Than Other Information Sources*, Washington, DC: Pew Research Center, 22 September. Available at: http://people-press.org/files/legacy-pdf/9-22-2011%20Media%20Attitudes%20Release.pdf [Accessed 5 December 2013].

——(2012) *Further Decline in Credibility Ratings for Most News Organizations*, Washington, DC: Pew Research Center, 16 August. Available at: www.people-press.org/2012/08/16/further-decline-in-credibility-ratings-for-most-news-organizations/ [Accessed 25 November 2013].

——(2013) *Public Trust in Government: 1958–2013*, Washington, DC: Pew Research Center, 18 October. Available at: www.people-press.org/2013/10/18/trust-in-government-interactive/ [Accessed 25 November 2013].

Reuters Institute for the Study of Journalism (2013) *Reuters Institute Digital News Report 2013: Tracking the Future of News*, Oxford: Reuters Institute for the Study of Journalism.

Schifferes, S. (2012) 'Austerity News: The Financial Crisis and the Digital Revolution', in *Reuters Institute Digital News Report 2012*, Oxford: Reuters Institute for the Study of Journalism.

Schifferes, S. and Coulter, S. (2013) 'Downloading Disaster: BBC News Online Coverage of the Global Financial Crisis', *Journalism*, 14 (2), pp. 228–52.

Stevenson, B. and Wolfers, J. (2011) 'Trust in Public Institutions Over the Business Cycle', *American Economic Review*, 101, pp. 281–7.

Taskforce on Financial Literacy (2010) *Canadians and Their Money: Building a Brighter Financial Future*, Ottawa: Department of Finance, Government of Canada.

Taylor, M. (2011) *The Long Term Impacts of Financial Capability: Evidence from the BHPS*, CFEB consumer research report 03, Consumer Financial Education Body (CFEB), February.

Taylor, M., Jenkins, S., and Sacker, A. (2009) *Financial Capability and Wellbeing: Evidence from the BHPS*, occasional paper series 34, Financial Services Authority, May.

Thaler, R. and Sunstein, C. (2008) *Nudge: Improving Decisions About Health, Wealth, and Happiness*, Michigan: Yale University Press.

Wood, J. and Berg, P. (2011) *Trust in Banks*, Washington, DC: Gallup Inc. Available at: www.gallup.com/strategicconsulting/157145/trust-banks.aspx [Accessed 1 January 2013].

YouGov (2012) *Trust Tracker: Longitudinal Survey Results*. Available at: http://cdn.yougov.com/cumulus_uploads/document/syrhatyofp/Trust_trends_Nov_2012.pdf [Accessed 1 January 2014].

12

THE MEDIATION OF FINANCIAL INFORMATION FLOWS

Traders, analysts, journalists

Peter A. Thompson

This chapter aims to provide an original perspective on the role of the media in the 2008 global financial crisis by focusing on information flows between reporters and finance professionals.[1] This requires a significant revision of the orthodox account of how information underpins financial market activity. As Hyman Minsky's Financial Instability Hypothesis (1977, 1982) presciently recognized, financial crises occur cyclically, not because of a lack of accurate information or transparency, but because markets become sensitized to their own price signals as asset values are expanding. This gives rise to self-reinforcing feedback loops that engender investor confidence but simultaneously increase systemic fragility. Drawing on the author's doctoral research into information usage by investors and their relations with financial reporters[2] (Thompson, 2010b), the chapter analyses the links between feedback loops and crises to show how different financial media perform different functions and information flows among traders, analysts, and journalists may be implicated in the recent credit crunch. However, this requires a revision of the orthodox economic assumption that information efficiently moves prices to their correct level in line with fundamentals (Fama, 1970). Rather, financial information actively shapes the market events it ostensibly describes and, as George Soros (1994) recognized, price movements feed back reflexively into the market expectations that underpin asset values.

Truth is never independent in financial news

This analysis also problematizes recent criticisms levelled at the financial media's ostensible failure to anticipate and critically investigate the recent crisis. Financial events are not directly accessible and amenable to independent verification by external observers. The relationship between financial reporters and expert sources in the investment community is therefore a crucial one. Indeed, the truth/accuracy of financial news is never independent of the prevailing knowledge frameworks within the investment community that permit meaning to be ascribed coherently to market events and financial values to be coordinated among investors. Consequently, it is difficult for the news media to critically report financial events in a meaningful way without implicitly reflecting the prevailing consensus within the investment community. However, the coherence of these knowledge frameworks can break down during periods of crisis, even to the point of redefining what factors are considered 'fundamentals'. This complicates the calculation of financial asset values and makes it impossible for reporters to determine which expert claims are accurate. Such an account challenges not only neoclassical economics but also orthodox conceptions of news production as providing an accurate account of an objective market reality.

Minsky's unsustainable bubbles

Hyman Minsky's (1977, 1982) Financial Instability Hypothesis suggests an important link between market information flows and crises. In contrast to the orthodox economic assumption that market instability is attributable to external non-market distortions (such as state regulation), Minsky's argument is that financial markets have a self-generating tendency toward periodic bubbles and crises. The central argument is that periods of stable financial growth engender creeping systemic fragility. Financial innovations (e.g. new investment instruments such as collateralized mortgage securities) attract investment capital and inflate market prices. The growth of asset values encourages market confidence and a discounting of risk. In turn, this enables access to cheap credit to fund the acquisition of financial assets (leveraging) offering returns higher than interest rates. These leveraged investments drive further increases in asset values, cultivating market expectations of even further growth. Crucially, the inflation of fictitious asset values is collectively interpreted as validation of prevailing valuation models and serves to obscure gradually increasing systemic fragility.

Minsky explains this creeping fragility as follows: initially, leveraged investment positions that are *hedged* allow the repayment of borrowed capital to be covered by existing cash flows, meaning investments and asset values are sustainable. However, as asset inflation based on borrowed capital continues, investments gradually become *speculative*, meaning credit repayments require continued increases in asset values. Eventually, investment positions enter a 'Ponzi' state, meaning credit repayments become dependent on yet further borrowing to maintain investment and leveraged asset prices.[3] At this point, there is an unsustainable credit bubble and inflated asset values become highly susceptible to shocks (e.g. in the form of defaults or interest rate hikes). Once this occurs, market confidence evaporates, risk levels are reassessed, and the availability of cheap credit evaporates. As the leveraged 'Ponzi' positions become unsustainable, panicking investors try to sell off toxic assets into an illiquid market, which simultaneously collapses their overinflated values and their capacity to serve as the collateral needed to sustain highly leveraged portfolios. Thus the process of fictitious asset inflation is thrown into reverse once expectations are recalibrated and market confidence evaporates.

Minsky's prescience in recognizing the central role of credit in financial crises has gained wider recognition since the 2008 credit crunch. However, the role of the media and communication processes in the self-reinforcing feedback loops that underpin bubbles and crashes is not addressed by the Financial Instability Hypothesis.

Market information, investors and the media

Integrating this into a communication-based framework requires both a theoretical critique of neoclassical conceptions of the role of information in markets and consideration of empirical evidence of how investors interact with the financial media. The neoclassical notion of market efficiency holds that publicly disseminated information is automatically incorporated into market prices, and that asset prices accurately reflect their respective fundamental values (Fama, 1970; also see Bryan and Rafferty, 2013). A concomitant assumption here is that financial news media function by verifying market facts and communicating these to investors. Thus price-sensitive news, such as company earnings reports or a shift in reserve bank interest rates, triggers recalculations of asset values and commensurate trading activity. However, financial news cannot be adequately understood as simply *representative* in the sense that valuations and prices directly reflect market facts in a more-or-less accurate manner. Although price movements do appear to be correlated with market news (e.g. Sant and Zaman, 1996; Vickers and Weiss, 2000; Busse and Green, 2002) the financial media should not be assumed to have a direct effect on trading behaviour (Davis, 2005, 2007).

As George Soros has usefully pointed out, fundamentals should not be regarded as the determinant of asset prices because fluctuating asset prices also influence investor expectations and valuations (Soros, 1994). This *reflexive* relation means that flows of information and the evolving models investors use to interpret them actively shape financial markets. Thompson (2003, 2010b) has differentiated between three key forms of reflexivity in financial markets.

Type of reflexivity

Transactional reflexivity is analogous to the process Soros describes. It primarily involves the crystallization of asset prices through the action of buying/selling and the feeding back of price signals into investor expectations of future values. As transactions register on trading screens around the globe, the symmetrical distribution of price information to all investors facilitates the real-time coordination of asset valuations across the market. However, these valuations do not reflect any natural set of fundamentals. Rather, they reflect investors' collective future expectations of value (see Pryke and Allen, 2000; Golding, 2003; Thompson, 2010a). Thus asset values are not intrinsic properties – they are valid relative to the prevailing frameworks of calculation that underpin current trading patterns. Movements in asset prices are price-sensitive and influence subsequent trading decisions. In line with Minksy, this feedback loop can confirm investor expectations based on current asset pricing models, thereby engendering increased market confidence, but when transactions begin to crystallize prices that fail to meet market expectations, this may trigger the onset of crisis.

Performative reflexivity, meanwhile, concerns the way in which financial knowledge frameworks and models not only describe but actively shape market reality when investors act on them. These frameworks are largely implicit but they enable investors to ascribe meaning to financial objects and events. This includes mutual recognition of price-sensitive fundamentals, the validation of new financial instruments (such as collateralized mortgage securities) as tradable objects, as well as models of asset value calculation (see MacKenzie and Millo, 2003; MacKenzie, 2004, 2012; see also Davis, 2006). During periods of financial stability when the variables driving trading behaviour are relatively predictable, the validity of these frameworks is largely taken for granted and market confidence grows as asset values are inflating. However, during periods of volatility or crisis, investors' expectations change and collective confidence in the prevailing models can break down. Although some fundamentals (such as price/earnings ratios) do have long-term salience, the validity of the variables underpinning current trading models may shift across cycles (see Thompson, 2010a; Bryan and Rafferty, 2013). As the subsequent discussion will outline, this was a key factor in the 2008 crisis when the ability of investors to coherently value mortgage securities failed.

Game reflexivity involves the sensitivity of investors to the anticipated patterns of trading behaviour of other market actors as they collectively interpret and respond to news/events. Essentially this process of second-guessing the market is what Keynes (1936) described in his well-known 'beauty contest' analogy.[4] Although 'herding' behaviour and simple self-fulfilling prophecies are atypical of professional investment practices, the monitoring of consensus expectations and market sentiment is nevertheless significant. The availability of real-time market information through financial wire services and globally interlinked trading screens makes it difficult to access fundamental market information before everyone else. Consequently, maintaining a trading advantage requires more rapid processing of news/information and also relevant *meta-information* (i.e. information about information) to anticipate what factors are liable to trigger trading activity. Particularly during a crisis, awareness of shifts in market sentiment and the price-sensitive variables driving investment decisions can be critical. Game reflexivity is implicated in the self-reinforcing feedback loops that engender collective investor (over)confidence during bullish periods when financial values are expanding and risk aversion/panic selling during bearish periods when bubbles of fictitious value deflate. Although expanding values may well be a critical indicator of increasing systemic fragility and imminent collapse, such interpretations may only become apparent *in hindsight*. This has implications for how the media's ostensible failure to critically report on the impending financial crisis in 2008 might be understood.

Minsky's Financial Instability Hypothesis (1977, 1982) and the reflexive aspects of information flows and feedback loops described above can be usefully applied to the 2008 global financial crisis. The collateralized mortgage securities based on risky sub-prime mortgage debt were given legitimacy as tradable asset forms through the application of complex new systems of calculation that ostensibly enabled the risk of mortgage defaults to be dispersed predictably across different grades or 'tranches' of security. The key ratings agencies (Moody's, Fitch, and Standard & Poor's) were thus persuaded to award investment-grade ratings. This ensured collective investor confidence in the value of mortgage securities, and investment banks were soon trading them in massive volumes. Initial returns confirmed market expectations and encouraged leveraging to maximize returns. However, as investment banks increased their debt-backed holdings of each other's securities, the potential for a devaluation across the entire class of mortgage debt securities to pose a systemic risk to the market was also growing. The credit crunch was attributable in part to a critical breakdown in investors' intersubjective trust in the validity of the credit ratings and the valuation models underpinning collateralized mortgage securities (Thompson, 2010a, 2010b; see also MacKenzie and Millo, 2003). Once the valuation and risk models underpinning collateralized mortgage securities broke down, institutions with significant holdings on their books attempted to offload huge volumes into an illiquid market (Thompson, 2010a). As heavily leveraged banks were left uncertain of the scale of each other's potential losses, game reflexivity played a role in shaping their responses. Collective recognition that any institution with significant mortgage security holdings might suffer the fate of Bear Stearns or Lehman Brothers drove the banking sector's mutual aversion to extending credit. There is an element of self-fulfilling prophecy here in that the crisis was not driven by a shift in objective market fundamentals but by the breakdown of mutual confidence in mortgage securities and the valuation models underpinning them. Insofar as the media's role in the mediation of meanings and collective perceptions in markets and crises can be understood in terms of self-reinforcing feedback loops, then their role in such events demands critical examination.

Journalists' sources

Financial crises and criticism of the financial media have a long history, and indeed events such as the 1873 crisis indicate that even global crises are not an especially recent phenomenon (see Parsons, 1989; Kindleberger, 1996; Winseck, 2010). Analyses of news reporting of the 1997 South East Asian currency crisis and the 2001 Enron collapse (Bryan, 2001; Sherman, 2002; Doyle, 2006) have raised questions about journalistic dependence on expert sources and the extent to which reporters have sufficient expertise to critically assess complex financial issues. Financial journalists rely on traders and analysts as expert sources even when their views are often shaped by vested interests in the markets they are commenting on (Kurtz, 2000; Golding, 2003; Davis, 2005). The criticisms of the financial media's performance in reporting the 2008 crisis should therefore be regarded not as an exceptional contemporary aberration, but as the latest manifestation of a problematic structural relation between journalistic practices and financial institutions. Prior to the 2008 crisis, several news reports did raise questions about the ethics and potential risk of the growing mortgage securities sector (e.g. Hudson, 2007; Tett, 2007). Subsequent reporting was also critical of exotic mortgage securities and bankers' bonuses (Thompson, 2009; Manning, 2012). However, the financial media did relatively little to critically investigate the institutional and deeper structural causes of the financial news and continued to privilege the voices of expert sources from within the financial sector. A range of factors have been suggested for these shortcomings.

As Starkman (2008, 2009) suggests, news reports did little to challenge powerful financial institutions and tended to treat the crisis more like a natural disaster than as a consequence of significant institutional failings. Although there was critical reporting on specific crisis-related issues, this never coalesced into a more systematic examination of the mortgage and banking sector. Inevitably, most reporters lacked the specialist expertise to analyse complex mortgage securities and therefore were reliant on expert sources (see Doyle, 2006; Tambini, 2010; Manning, 2012). However, the collateralized debt securities at the centre of the sub-prime mortgage meltdown were so complex that many financial analysts dealing with the media likewise misunderstood the potential for systemic risk (Cohan, 2009; Tett, 2009). This was exacerbated by the financial media's tendency to prioritize the investment community as the audience stakeholder over watchdog obligations to the general public (Tambini, 2010). The relation between reporters and financial actors therefore entails not only institutional dependency on expert sources for definitions of events; it extends to a kind of *knowledge dependency* whereby financial news as a genre comes to assume the investment community's prevailing frameworks and concepts in order to make sense *as* financial news (Manning, 2012; Thompson, 2013).

Examining the entrails

Despite the shortcomings in the financial media's reporting of the 2008 crisis, it is far from self-evident that more diligent investigative journalism would have uncovered the risks before the crisis became inevitable. Even the reporting of ostensibly objective, quantified market facts such as company earnings, fluctuating exchange rates, or the decline of a stock exchange index presuppose shared knowledge frameworks that define these as real for the investment community. Major investment institutions typically employ dozens of analysts with specialist expertise in different market sectors, and most professional traders will have a network of contacts who share tips, confirm or refute rumours, and help them interpret the flows of data on the trading screens. The role analysts play in assisting traders make sense of the constant flows of market news may have less to do with making accurate forecasts than with providing a context or frame to enable market data to be interpreted in a way that rationalizes investment decisions. Although more technically sophisticated, there is perhaps something analogous here to the soothsayer interpreting the entrails if they augur well. Analysts also play an important marketing role for their institutions, attracting corporate business (e.g. managing new share issues/IPOs) and ensuring the in-house view of the markets gains a profile both in public and elite market discourses. Journalist relations with senior analysts/economists in major investment banks are therefore significant here. Sell-side analysts are often influenced by vested institutional interests (e.g. corporate clients of their bank), and either 'talk their book' or conform to the prevailing analyst consensus (see Kurtz, 2000; Golding, 2003; Davis, 2007; Thompson, 2009; Manning, 2012).[5] There is competition among analysts for media profile, because this provides the opportunity to promote a particular frame or narrative that could shape market perceptions of events. As this comment from a senior bank trader explains, 'If you've got good relationships with Dominion, Herald, Dow Jones, Reuters, you can send them your new piece and they'll give it some coverage ... Because you want the credibility, you want the profile, and you want the influence on the market' (Trader C) (*see endnote 2*).

Several interviewees pointed out that sell-side analysts and brokers were motivated to spot new angles and 'stories' to push trading opportunities. Specifically, this entailed reinterpreting news events to identify a new trading frame or narrative, highlighting heretofore overlooked variables moving the market. There is clearly a rhetorical aspect to this, as the following comment from a senior bank analyst suggests: 'Your views are a portfolio – you might have a dozen views. ... So what you've got to try and do is, from all the information that's available, try and [identify] a story – and then use that story to generate business' (Analyst B). Another senior bank trader commented that there was a 'massive competitive advantage' in attracting routine media attention because this boosted their visibility and credibility among the investment community (Trader E). As a senior bank analyst confirmed, 'You want top business people to think we're a player in the markets. We want our view to be known to the people who are making decisions – like the Reserve Bank, for instance' (Analyst A).

A symbiotic relationship

There is evidently a symbiotic relationship between financial journalists and sources in the investment community (Manning, 2012). This raises questions about the potential for self-reinforcing feedback to arise from the flows of information from market to media and back to the market. Different traders will pay attention to those analysts whose views of the market align with their own way of thinking:

> You can ask [a trader] – all that economic information and the emails you're given – Is it valuable? And he'll say, 'Shit, no – I get bloody emails from 40 analysts. I only read 2 or 3' – Why do you read 2 or 3? – 'Oh, I find those really good because I'm on the same wavelength as those guys and they help me make my trades' – So why don't we fire the other 37? Well of course, the other 37 are hitting someone else.
>
> *(Trader D)*

The plurality of competing expert claims suggests no single voice will dominate. However, consensus indicators and public comments by top analysts still provide a common reference point and indicate the parameters of expert opinion:

Reuters, Dow Jones, and Bloomberg as well, they all release surveys of what the different banks are expecting for interest rate announcements. For every data release they'll say, 'Here's 10 banks, here's the expectations, this is the average, this is the last number' – So we all look at those. I don't need to worry what any one bank thinks – I'd rather just look at the averages.

(Trader B)

Analysts can nevertheless be prone to self-referentiality and the reliance of financial reporters on these actors means media representations tend to amplify and reinforce the prevailing market consensus (Rothkopf, 1999; Kunczik, 2002; Davis, 2005). As one bank analyst noted, reporters could inadvertently disseminate market rumours when they called different sources to double-check stories, although he regarded top analysts as more influential than any journalist: 'If you think a journalist has power, then the research analyst has incredible power – because their degree of knowledge will be much higher than the financial journalist's ... so their ability to spread those rumours must be very, very high' (Analyst E). In some cases it is possible for the stories/frames being touted by one institution to circulate widely, as this comment from a senior trader with a sell-side role suggests:

I might wake up with a particular theme in my mind, and of course I'll ring everyone and push that. ... If they like that idea, they'll say, 'That's a great idea' – So a rival bank will ring up and I'll say, 'Yeah, but what about this?' – As if it's their idea! Then I'll hear it coming back to me, and suddenly that might be the theme in the market. And it's something I sort of woke up with in my head.

(Trader B)

Although there are examples of market movements correlating with analyst comments in the media, notably from guests on CNBC (e.g. see Sant and Zaman, 1996; Vickers and Weiss, 2000; Busse and Green, 2002), this typically reflects the reactions of day traders rather than of major investment firms. Moreover, it is problematic to suppose correlations of news and market movements indicate any simple cause–effect relation. Insofar as financial media induce any kind of 'effects' in investment professionals, this must be understood in terms of how expert actors engage with the media to discern shifts in market consensus (Davis, 2005). The fact that traders are informed by analysts and real-time financial news flows, that analysts monitor each other and talk to the financial reporters, and that the financial reporters rely on analysts and traders as expert sources, means there is potential for feedback loops in market information flows. This is not to deny the plurality of market views or to assume that herd behaviour and self-fulfilling prophecies are an automatic outcome of the exchange of information between reporters and financial market sources. Although reporters may corroborate multiple analyst accounts, it is difficult to verify whose is more valid except in relation to consensus indicators.

The author's doctoral work (Thompson, 2010b) explored how traders and analysts in New Zealand prioritized different media and types of information in making investment decisions (*see endnote 2*). Although the data collected preceded the onset of the crisis, respondents were specifically asked about their media usage and information priorities during periods of volatility. As Minsky suggests, information flows during stable periods preceding crises are indicative of the feedback loops underpinning the formation of bubbles. The study found that although no media/information sources were regarded as irrelevant, those rated most important were limited in access to professional investor networks (including high-end wire services/trading platforms such as Thomson–Reuters and Bloomberg, and various informal channels/networks used to cross-reference news with colleagues or access specialist expertise). In regard to publicly available news media, there was minimal difference in the relative importance ascribed to those with a specific financial orientation (e.g. *Wall Street Journal*, CNBC) compared with general interest news media. A likely explanation for this is that most of the market information appearing in the public media would already have been made available on the real-time brokerage screens. Although fundamental and technical market data were regarded as important, so too were the perspectives/positions of other investors, which is consistent with the preceding observations concerning game reflexivity.

Analysts not the media

The significance of professional contacts and personal relationships to investment decisions was further underlined after statistical analysis identified a functional distinction between *public media* (i.e. information sources readily available to non-professional investors) and *institutional media* (i.e. specialist information sources primarily restricted to professional investors such as high-end wire services, subscription analyst services, bespoke trading analytics, and networks of contacts with other professional investors). The analysis also identified a distinction between *market information* (fundamental and technical data that neoclassical theory would regard as driving asset prices) and *reflexive information* (factors generally regarded as externalities in neoclassical theory, including market sentiment, non-market news, and the opinions/positions of other market actors). The pattern of information usage that emerged here suggested that investment decisions are informed by *both* the standard variables assumed in neoclassical models *and* factors indicative of some level of reflexive response to other market actors and market moods.

Further analysis identified significant statistical relationships between the relative importance investors ascribed to *public media* sources and *market* information, and between the relative importance they ascribed to *institutional media* sources and *reflexive* information. However, there was *no* statistical correlation between the relative importance ascribed to public media sources and reflexive information or between institutional media sources and market information. This suggests public and institutional media sources serve somewhat different informational functions. It was counter-intuitive to discover that institutional media sources were not primarily valued as a principal source of real-time market information. The probable explanation is that although brokerage screen displays and networks of trading contacts are indeed crucial sources of real-time price data, the simultaneous disclosure of most fundamental data such as company earnings means it confers no distinct trading advantage (although its absence would certainly be disadvantageous). Any edge in trading is therefore more likely to stem from accessing *meta-information* allowing the prioritization of data and also early identification of changes in the variables currently driving trading. Access to this kind of reflexive information is more likely to stem from professional contacts within institutional networks than from publicly accessible media.

Data from interviews conducted with traders and analysts supported this interpretation. These suggested that institutional networks of contacts were particularly important in identifying *flows* and *frame-shifts*. 'Flows' refers to the identification of the positions, strategies, and agencies of other market participants that permit forthcoming transactions and price movements to be anticipated (such as a high-volume trade likely to affect prices or liquidity). Operating in a large investment institution that offers brokerage services to clients also enables in-house analysts and traders to discern more flows in the sense of increasing the transparency of the trading patterns driving price movements. This leads to the second significant theme: the identification of shifts in the trading *frames* currently driving investment activity. Interviews confirmed that the factors driving market activity periodically evolved, particularly during periods of volatility. Although there was broad acceptance that core market fundamentals (e.g. price/earnings ratios) are the main determinants of value in the long term, over the short term, many other variables are incorporated into the frames/schemata used to inform trading decisions (see Beunza and Garud, 2005; Arnoldi, 2006). Traders need to be aware of how these frames change because they shape market expectations and asset valuations. Analysts are a key source of this meta-information because the frames and narratives they suggest help to contextualize and prioritize incoming data. One example of a shift in framing concerned a Reserve Bank statement about US payroll data, which many investors then began monitoring. As one trader openly acknowledged, this stemmed more from the perception that other market actors were paying attention to it than from any intrinsic market significance. Crucially, information about frames and flows is unlikely to be available through public news media. This is why the institutional media channels and networks of contacts play a key role in providing the flows of reflexive information needed to maintain an edge in the market.

Crisis news

In respect to media usage in periods of volatility/crisis, the majority of respondents indicated that their monitoring of information sources to keep track of the momentum of a crisis would intensify. However, the emphasis here was on institutional media (notably real-time wire services and professional networks) in order to double-check or correlate interpretations. It was also pointed out that most information would circulate through institutional networks and be picked up by the feeds from real-time wire services *before* becoming available through other public news media. As one senior trader commented, 'By the time that news hits the general media, we've probably heard it anyway' (Trader B). Determining price and liquidity in a volatile market was cited as a particular challenge. Several respondents suggested that tracking prices would necessitate increased monitoring of networks of contacts rather than just relying on screen prices. As one trader observed, 'The prices will get misaligned in volatile times, that's for sure. ... If things were volatile and there were no prices in the machine [trading screen], what are you going to do?' (Trader F). Another trader pointed out that during a crisis, analysis of fundamentals would take second place to cross-referencing the real-time news feeds across the main wire services, while others suggested that attention would shift away from news media towards cross-referencing expert opinion through institutional networks. Another senior bank trader pointed out that turmoil in the money markets (even before the credit crunch) had intensified the need to monitor short-term factors, for which his network of contacts accessed through his Bloomberg terminal were vital:

> The currency markets have had enormous volatility, so it indicates there's more going on in the short term. So it's [about] positioning, trying to find out from the people we talk to about flows. So our primary information source for the short term [is] discussions with all the banks that we talk to. ... So I guess, at the coalface, that's really the primary means of getting information – the whispers in the market, what's going on.
>
> *(Trader G)*

In contrast, several traders involved in fundamental stock-trading strategies over longer-term time-horizons indicated they would rely *less* on market noise, price momentum, and shifting market opinions and focus more on fundamental market data during a crisis. However, others noted the importance of identifying the variables driving price fluctuations, suggesting that the validity of prevailing fundamentals cannot be taken for granted in a crisis. This indicates a need to validate trading frames and identify new variables driving trading. As one trader observed, although fundamentals provide background context, 'If things are happening quite quickly ... the fundamental model may change. You've always got to be open to new information – you can't be a stick in the mud!' (Trader H). Indeed, the validation of trading frames and price-sensitive variables becomes problematic precisely during transition phases of market cycles or in crisis scenarios. Thus what counts as a 'fundamental' is liable to be renegotiated in a crisis. The 2008 crisis saw a massive implosion of the value and evaporation of the liquidity of mortgage securities after the investment-grade credit ratings that provided the basis for coherent valuation were rendered meaningless (Thompson, 2010a).

Public-private information nexus

The scale and complexity of different financial sectors and the plurality of analyst opinions and trading strategies dictate some caution about overgeneralizing theories of media and finance. Nevertheless, the evidence here broadly supports the argument that public media and institutional media/networks have different functions. In a global, informationally symmetrical financial market with real-time media systems providing news updates, trading advantages must be derived from superior anticipation and interpretation of the available data. This reflexive meta-information is more readily accessible from institutional networks and high-end financial sources/information systems. In a crisis, this is more important than market fundamentals for many investors. When market confidence in the validity of key financial indicators becomes destabilized, the need to monitor other market actors to confirm the intersubjective validity of trading schemata/frames is likely to intensify.

Although institutional networks are considered more important to investment decisions than publicly accessible financial news media, the latter are by no means irrelevant. However, the salience of public news media reports on financial markets stems not from any direct influence on trading decisions, but from providing contextual information about unfolding political and economic events against which more specific financial data is interpreted. Publicly available financial news media also provide a platform for market analysts to promote and contest frames and narratives concerning the variables driving trading activity and future expectations. Again, most individual analyst comments do not typically trigger trading responses, but collectively they help establish the parameters of market consensus and provide an index of the prevailing mood of the investment community. Journalistic relations with analysts and traders as expert sources provide a key point of interconnection or *nexus* through which reflexive meta-information can pass from the institutional networks into the public media, as Figure 12.1 illustrates.

This nexus between public media and institutional networks is potentially significant where received opinion is questioned or a previously firm view is reversed, confirming the point of inflection in a cycle where an upturn is liable to become a downturn (or vice versa) and the assumptions underpinning the prevailing

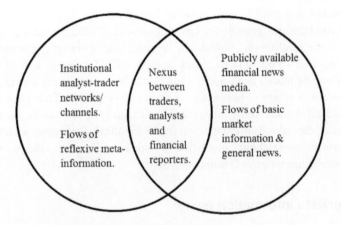

FIGURE 12.1 Financial information flows between institutional and public channels

consensus are likely to shift. As Lee's (1998) work on 'informational avalanches' suggests, investors do not always trade on price-sensitive information if there is uncertainty about whether other investors have received it and will act on it. This means market rumours may percolate over time, leading to a latent shift in market consensus, which is not yet expressed in trading behaviour and prices. This is consistent with Minsky's arguments about gradually increasing fragility and the process of game reflexivity described earlier. As Trader J observed,

> If the weight of money, corporate hedging, speculative positions are all positioned one way round, then all those buyers are potential sellers. ... It may not take an external event – or it could take a very small and otherwise benign external event – to render the system completely unstable.

The nexus between public and private media is a potential channel through which market rumours or shifts in market perceptions circulating through private institutional networks can become public, triggering a sudden shift in market expectations and valuations. Such a process would appear consistent with the sequence of events surrounding the collapse of Bear Stearns in 2008, particularly when CNBC went public with a market rumour about its routine financial transactions being declined by counterparties (see Cohan, 2009). Indeed, Burrough (2008) attributes the collapse of Bear Stearns directly to CNBC's coverage of rumours of failing liquidity (propagated by unscrupulous hedge funds), which obliged Bear to issue public denials that were interpreted as confirmation of the rumours. Sherman (2011) rightly points out that such a conspiratorial narrative understates the role played by Bear's high leverage and massive holdings of mortgage securities in making it vulnerable. Nevertheless, the public media confirmation of what had heretofore been rumours circulating through private investor networks certainly helped crystallize market suspicions that Bear was indeed in distress, and the strenuous denials issued by Bear executives merely served to confirm them. There was evidently an element of game reflexivity here as investors became aware of other investors' scepticism about Bear's liquidity and viability. Despite Bear's public assurances that it had significant liquid assets (Cohan, 2009), the loss of confidence and rapid withdrawal of creditors fatally undermined its leveraged position, thereby fulfilling the media prophecy of its imminent demise. The fire-sale 'rescue' of Bear, closely followed by the Lehman collapse and the rating agencies' revisions of the credit risk of collateralized mortgage securities, led to the onset of the credit crunch as inter-bank lending risks were revised and investor confidence across the entire mortgage and banking sector evaporated.

Market sensitivity to information flows

By extending Minsky's (1977, 1982) Financial Instability Hypothesis with an account of informational reflexivity, it becomes apparent why markets are sensitive to information flows generated by their own internal processes. The expansion of fictitious asset values feeds back into market optimism, encouraging a discounting of risk and cheaper credit. In turn, this fuels further speculation which increases the market's susceptibility to collapse once the momentum of value inflation falters. The relation between expert financial sources and reporters means that the media tend to operate within the investment community's prevailing knowledge frameworks and reflect and broadly reinforce the prevailing market consensus. Although there will always be competing expert opinions, it is difficult to independently verify claims about market risk and complex financial instruments without cross-referencing them with other sources within the financial system. Prior to the 2008 crisis, there were several news reports about growing risks in the mortgage securities sector (e.g. Hudson, 2007; Tett, 2007), and those growing concerns were doubtless shared privately by many expert commentators whose vested interests made them disinclined to comment publicly at the time. This analysis would explain why the *overall* pattern of reporting tended to reflect continued confidence that the markets would remain stable even while a growing number of market actors were privately becoming increasingly concerned about systemic risk. Public news media reports may have minimal *direct* effect on trading decisions, but they nevertheless feed into the broader climate of expectations against which market news is interpreted. This would also explain why periods of asset inflation tend to be framed as confirmation of market optimism rather than as a sign of increasing fragility, and also why, in hindsight, there are often recriminations about the failure to recognize the (now evident) signs of impending financial doom.

The nexus of exchanges between investors and reporters provides a key link between information percolating through institutional networks and financial news in public media. Media reports help reflect and reinforce periodic shifts in consensus once privately held uncertainties about the sustainability of the value inflation become widespread. Once that consensus has begun to shift, news reflecting the shifting perceptions of key financial experts feeds back into the market. As investors become aware that other market actors are publicly changing their expectations and positions, fundamentals can be renegotiated and a shift in collective market perceptions and expectations can arise. This does not mean the media directly trigger financial crises, but the public reporting of information heretofore confined to privately circulating rumours is likely to accentuate any shift in consensus. When the prevailing knowledge frameworks underpinning the current market consensus become destabilized, investors have to monitor each other for cues indicating the likely direction of trading activity. In such a context, there is potential for the frames and narratives of key analysts reported in the news to influence the course a crisis takes (see Bryan, 2001). In such a context, investor self-monitoring will tend to intensify as traders seek to validate trading frames and points of market consensus against a backdrop of ambiguous definitions and contested claims. For example, the efficacy of measures intended to resolve the 2008 credit crunch (notably government-backed guarantees of security, acquisition of toxic assets, and huge injections of capital into the banking sector) depended in no small part on how far the investment community collectively had faith in such measures and recommended lending and trading in mortgage assets.

Conclusions

Extending Minsky's Financial Instability Hypothesis by incorporating the reflexive processes implicated in financial information flows provides a more nuanced account of the role that the financial media play in crises. However, this also has implications for how financial market journalism should be understood. When the shared knowledge frameworks that permit the coherent valuation of assets become destabilized, it is not possible for reporters to verify which expert source claims are valid. Amidst the competing claims from expert sources seeking to impose their own frames on rapidly evolving events, there is no coherent financial reality, rendering the notion of objectivity meaningless. This occurs partly because the institutional networks through which the shifts in trading frames, market expectations, and asset valuations are negotiated are not directly accessible to reporters. On a deeper structural level, however, in crisis scenarios, performative reflexivity renders the very nature of market reality (ontology) inseparable from investors' prevailing knowledge frameworks (epistemology). If investors collectively believe that existing asset values will continue to increase or will collapse imminently, and they trade accordingly, then there is the potential for a kind of self-fulfilling prophecy. In a crisis, therefore, the truth value of financial information is not independent of how investors collectively interpret and respond to it. In respect to the 2008 credit crunch, once the breakdown in market confidence in the value of mortgage securities became widely manifested and inter-bank lending seized up, market events ceased to be driven by any coherent set of fundamentals, rendering verification of unfolding market facts impossible.

Although public news media are not the primary source of information investors use to make trading decisions, they provide a continuous flow of contextual information concerning unfolding political and economic events, and thereby shape the backdrop against which financial information circulating through institutional networks is interpreted by investors. The interactions among reporters, analysts, and traders also constitute a nexus through which rumours underpinning a latent shift in market consensus (e.g. growing concerns that asset inflation represents an unsustainable bubble that are not yet expressed in trading and market prices) can become public knowledge. At the same time, by reflecting and reinforcing the consensus view of expert financial sources, the financial media can become complicit with the tendency for self-reinforcing feedback loops to drive cycles of periodic bubbles and crises. Financial reporting practices can therefore be legitimately criticized for their reluctance to critically interrogate the assertions of expert sources, and their default tendency to frame financial events in terms of the knowledge frameworks underpinning the prevailing consensus of the investment community. However, the contention that if only the financial media provided more accurate and timely information then perhaps crises like the 2008 credit crunch might be averted is not sustainable. The financial system's tendency towards crisis stems not from a lack of information/transparency, but from its self-generating tendency to respond reflexively to signals its own processes generate. The financial media's shortcomings need to be understood in the context of reflexive information flows and the structural factors that make it difficult for journalists to identify asset value inflation as an indicator of increasing systemic fragility when the collective market consensus frames this as evidence of continuing growth. The problem is therefore not a failure of professional journalistic values per se, but the structural relations between the financial news media and the market-based sources who act as primary definers of financial events. Overcoming these limitations requires the financial media to re-evaluate their relation to financial market actors and develop greater sensitivity to the processes of informational reflexivity to which they inadvertently contribute.

Notes

1 The author gratefully acknowledges the invaluable contributions of the research partici-
    pants, especially Deutsche Bank, ANZ, and the Reserve Bank of New Zealand. He
    would also like to thank Cathy Greenfield, Graham Murdock, and Dwayne Winseck
    for their advice and encouragement, and the editors for their interest and patience.
2 The author's doctoral research included 39 semi-structured interviews with NZ-based
    investment professionals and periods of trading-floor non-participant observation. The
    data was collected between 2004 and 2005. Where cited/quoted, source and institu-
    tional anonymity is maintained throughout.
3 Minsky's use of the term 'Ponzi state' is analogous to the more familiar Ponzi or
    unsustainable pyramid-style investment scheme wherein constant injections of new
    investment money are needed to maintain the inflation of asset prices and attract new
    investment money that provides the revenue to repay previous creditors. In other
    words, asset values require propping up by more and more borrowing to cover the
    debts incurred in purchasing them.
4 Keynes drew a (now politically incorrect) analogy between financial investment and a
    newspaper competition inviting readers to guess the winner of a beauty contest from a
    set of contestant photographs. Readers' votes would determine the winner, but guessing
    'correctly' depended not on any objective set of criteria for beauty, but on second-guessing
    which contestant the majority of readers would pick.
5 The notion of 'consensus' here does not imply investors all share the same view of the
    market. There will always be a range of perspectives underpinned by the prevailing
    knowledge frameworks that performatively define market reality. These serve to indi-
    cate the parameters of the current orthodoxy and the benchmarks for interpreting dif-
    ferent market views. Divergent views may attract critical scrutiny, but if they are
    accompanied by a persuasive 'story' or 'frame' that suggests the prevailing consensus is
    mistaken or that some new variable needs to be considered, then there may be the
    potential to trigger buying/selling and move the market.

References

Arnoldi, J. (2006) 'Frames and Screens: The Reduction of Uncertainty in Electronic
    Derivatives Trading', *Economy and Society*, 35 (3), pp. 381–99.
Beunza, D. and Garud, R. (2005) 'Securities Analysts as Frame-Makers'. Paper presented to
    American Sociological Association 2005 Annual meeting, Philadelphia, 12 August.
Bryan, D. (2001) 'Reporting the "Asian Financial Crisis": Australian Financial Journalists'
    Construction of a National Threat', *Southern Review: Communication, Politics and Culture*,
    34 (2), pp. 14–25.
Bryan, D. and Rafferty, M. (2013) 'Fundamental Value: A Category in Transformation',
    Economy and Society, 42 (1), pp. 130–53.

Burrough, B. (2008) 'Bringing Down Bear Stearns', *Vanity Fair*, August. Available at: www.vanityfair.com/politics/features/2008/08/bear_stearns200808 [Accessed 12 September 2012].

Busse, J.A. and Green, T.C. (2002) 'Market Efficiency in Real Time', *Journal of Financial Economics*, 65, pp. 415–37.

Cohan, W.D. (2009) *House of Cards: A Tale of Hubris and Wretched Excess on Wall Street*, New York: Anchor Books.

Davis, A. (2005) 'Media Effects and the Active Elite Audience: A Study of Communications in the London Stock Exchange', *European Journal of Communication*, 20 (3), pp. 303–26.

——(2006) 'The Limits of Metrological Performativity: Valuing Equities in the London Stock Exchange', *Competition and Change*, 10 (1), pp. 3–21.

——(2007) 'The Economic Inefficiencies of Market Liberalization', *Global Media and Communication*, 3 (2), pp. 157–78.

Doyle, G. (2006) 'Financial News Journalism: A Post-Enron Analysis of Approaches Towards Economic and Financial News Production in the UK', *Journalism*, 7 (4), pp. 433–52.

Fama, E. (1970) 'Efficient Capital Markets: A Review of Theory and Empirical Work', *Journal of Finance*, 25 (2), pp. 383–417.

Golding, T. (2003) *The City: Inside the Great Expectation Machine: Myth and Reality in Institutional Investment and the Stock Market*, London: FT Prentice Hall.

Hudson, M. (2007) 'Debt Bomb – Lending a Hand: How Wall Street Stoked the Mortgage Meltdown', *Wall Street Journal*, 27 June, p. A1.

Keynes, J.M. (1936) *The General Theory of Employment, Interest and Money*, London: MacMillan & Co.

Kindleberger, C.P. (1996) *Manias, Panics, and Crashes: A History of Financial Crises*, 3rd edition, Basingstoke: MacMillan.

Kunczik, M. (2002) 'Globalisation: News Media, Images of Nations and the Flow of International Capital With Special Reference to the Role of the Rating Agencies', *Journal of International Communication*, 8 (1), pp. 39–79.

Kurtz, H. (2000) *The Fortune Tellers: Inside Wall Street's Game of Money, Media, and Manipulation*, New York: The Free Press.

Lee, I.H. (1998) 'Market Crashes and Informational Avalanches', *Review of Economic Studies*, 65 (4), pp. 741–59.

MacKenzie, D. (2004) 'The Big, Bad Wolf and the Rational Market: Portfolio Insurance, the 1987 Crash and the Performativity of Economics', *Economy and Society*, 33 (3), pp. 303–34.

——(2012) 'Knowledge Production in Financial Markets: Credit Default Swaps, the ABX and the Subprime Crisis', *Economy and Society*, 41 (3), pp. 335–59.

MacKenzie, D. and Millo, Y. (2003) 'Constructing a Market, Performing Theory: The Historical Sociology of a Financial Derivatives Exchange', *American Journal of Sociology*, 109 (1), pp. 107–45.

Manning, P. (2012) 'Financial Journalism, News Sources and the Banking Crisis', *Journalism*, 14 (2), pp. 173–89.

Minsky, H.P. (1977) 'A Theory of Systemic Fragility', in Altman, E. and Sametz, A. (eds.), *Financial Crises: Institutions and Markets in a Fragile Environment*, New York: John Wiley, pp. 138–52.

——(1982) *Can 'It' Happen Again? Essays on Instability and Finance*, Armonk, NY: M.E. Sharpe.

Parsons, W. (1989) *The Power of the Financial Press: Journalism and Economic Opinion in Britain and America*, Aldershot: Edward Elgar.

Pryke, M. and Allen, J. (2000) 'Monetized Time-Space: Derivatives – Money's "New Imaginary"?' *Economy and Society*, 29 (2), pp. 264–84.

Rothkopf, D. (1999) 'The Disinformation Age', *Foreign Policy*, 114, pp. 83–97.

Sant, R. and Zaman, M.A. (1996) 'Market Reaction to *Businessweek* "Inside Wall Street" Column: A Self-Fulfilling Prophecy', *Journal of Banking and Finance*, 20, pp. 617–43.

Sherman, B.D. (2011) 'Verdict? Vanity Not Fair', *Wall Street Law Blog*, 22 September. Available at: http://wallstreetlaw.typepad.com/sherman/2011/09/conspiracy-not-so-fast-bryan-burrbringing-down-bear-stearns-bad-journalism.html [Accessed 24 September 2012].

Sherman, S. (2002) 'Enron: Uncovering the Uncovered Story', *Columbia Journalism Review*, 40 (6), pp. 22–8.

Soros, G. (1994) *The Alchemy of Finance: Reading the Mind of the Market*, New York: John Wiley.

Starkman, D. (2008) 'Boiler Room: The Business Press Is Missing the Crooked Heart of the Credit Crisis', *Columbia Journalism Review*, September/October, pp. 48–53. Available at: www.cjr.org/essay/boiler_room.php?page=all [Accessed 25 August 2012].

——(2009) 'Power Problem: The Business Press Did Everything But Take on the Institutions That Brought Down the Financial System', *Columbia Journalism Review*, May/June. Available at: www.cjr.org/cover_story/power_problem.php?page=all [Accessed 12 October 2012].

Tambini, D. (2010) 'What Are Financial Journalists for?' *Journalism Studies*, 11 (2), pp. 158–74.

Tett, G. (2007) 'The Unease Bubbling in Today's Brave New Financial World', *Financial Times*, 19 January. Available at: www.ft.com/intl/cms/s/0/92f7ee6a-a765-11db-83e4-0000779e2340.html#axzz2DNMRGHw8 [Accessed 24 September 2012].

——(2009) *Fool's Gold: How Unrestrained Greed Corrupted a Dream, Shattered Global Markets and Unleashed a Catastrophe*, London: Little Brown Book Group.

Thompson, P.A. (2003) 'Making the World Go Round? Communication, Information and Global Trajectories of Finance Capital', *Southern Review: Communication, Politics and Culture*, 36 (3), pp. 20–43.

——(2009) 'Market Manipulation? Applying the Propaganda Model to Financial Media Reporting', *Westminster Papers in Communication and Culture*, 6 (2), pp. 73–96. Available at: www.wmin.ac.uk/mad/pdf/WPCC-Vol6-No2-Peter_A_Thompson.pdf [Accessed 4 March 2013].

——(2010a) 'Convenient Fictions? A Critical Communicative Perspective on Financial Accumulation, Autopoiesis and Crisis in the Wake of the Credit Crunch'. Paper presented to the Political Economy Section, IAMCR Conference 2010, Communication and Citizenship – Rethinking Crisis and Change, 18–22 May 2010, Braga, Portugal. Available at: http://unitec.researchbank.ac.nz/handle/10652/1557 [Accessed 4 October 2013].

——(2010b) *Worlds Apart? The Political Economy of Communication, Information and Institutional Investor Media Usage in Global Financial Markets*, RMIT University PhD thesis, Melbourne.

——(2013) 'Invested Interests? Reflexivity, Representation and Reporting in Financial Markets', *Journalism*, 14 (2), pp. 208–27.

Vickers, M. and Weiss, G. (2000) 'Wall Street's Hype Machine', *Businessweek*, issue 3675, 4 March [Accessed online 31 July 2003 at Academic Search Premier].

Winseck, D. (2010) 'Double-Edged Swords: Communications Media and the Global Financial Crisis of 1873'. Paper presented to the History Section, IAMCR Conference 2010, Communication and Citizenship – Rethinking Crisis and Change, 18–22 May 2010, Braga, Portugal.

13

PAYING FOR CRISIS NEWS

The dilemmas of news organizations

Gerben Bakker

Today just a few news agencies, such as Reuters, the Associated Press, and AFP, dominate the international supply of raw news.[1] They make money from news even though it is protected rather imperfectly by intellectual property rights, even though it can be endlessly copied, and even though news gets old quickly. Despite these challenges, these news agencies have dominated the international news trade since the mid-nineteenth century. They survived the rise of mass-circulation newspapers that had their own correspondents, as well as the advent of radio, television, and the Internet.

This paper examines how this handful of firms came to dominate the international raw news supply, how these agencies have been able to make money from raw news, and what business models they developed to this end. We examine how these business models interacted with market structure, and how they held their ground during crises.

To answer these questions we will examine especially the period in which these business models emerged, and we will look at theory that can explain how news traders operated. Our method is historical, analytic, and economic. We restrict ourselves here to international news agencies that aim to offer their customers global coverage.[2]

The changing market structure of news

Since the Middle Ages news has been traded in many different ways. As a reciprocal custom, diplomats and merchants wrote the latest news and prices at the bottom of letters. Some news brokers sold hand-copied newsletters to which customers could subscribe, and many cities had a news caller who verbally told the latest news for a fee. Some business organizations, such as the Fuggers from Augsburg, had their own internal news service. In the sixteenth century trading exchanges started to issue newsletters, and more than a century later the predecessors to modern newspapers were founded.[3]

During the 1840s and 1850s many of the modern news agencies emerged, such as Havas in France, which acquired a number of older news agencies, Reuters in Britain, Wolff-Continental in Germany, and the New York Associated Press in New York. Making use where they could of the new electric telegraph, these agencies set up worldwide networks of correspondents and had as their main customers newspapers, governments, merchants, banks, insurance companies, and other businesses.

Four tendencies are visible in the evolution of most media industries. Interacting with history, they led to particular historical expressions (Table 13.1).[4] In the case of news, sunk costs led to a quality race, leading to a handful of news agencies dominating the international news trade after the 1850s; the fact that marginal revenues equalled marginal profits stimulated vertical integration, as for example expressed in the many news cooperatives across the world and the Press Association's acquisition of Reuters;[5] the toll-good character of news led to business models focused on ways to exclude customers so a fee could be asked. And the project-based character of newsgathering led often to agglomeration and co-location of news traders with other media industries.

TABLE 13.1 Major economic characteristics of the news trade and their implications for the business of gathering and selling news

Economic characteristic	Dynamic implication	Historical expression
Sunk costs	Quality race	Emergence and rise to dominance of a handful of agencies during the 1850s
Marginal revenue = marginal profits	Vertical integration	News agencies often owned by cooperatives of newspapers
	Dual market structure	AP; merger of Reuters with the Press Association (1919); Australian news cooperative; Dutch news cooperative (1930s)
Toll-good character (non-diminishable but excludable)	Business models	Focus on sellable economic data since 16th century; Subscription models; copyright (since late 19th century)
Project-based character	Agglomeration	Most news agencies in metropolises, co-located with customers, other news companies, and other media industries

Source: Based on the framework introduced in Gerben Bakker, 'Sunk Costs, Dynamic Efficiency and the Structure of Creative Industries: A Very Long-Run Perspective', in Candace Jones, Mark Lorenzen, and Jonathan Sapsed (eds.) *Oxford Handbook of Creative Industries* (Oxford University Press, 2014, forthcoming).

Business models: the fundamental paradox

As the news agencies developed, they had to devise new ways of organizing and transacting to make the gathering and distribution of news profitable. The major challenge they faced was being able to trade information for money. According to the 'fundamental paradox in the determination of demand for information', put forward by the economist and Nobel laureate Kenneth J. Arrow, buyers cannot assess how much they would want to pay for information without knowing its content, but once they know its content, they no longer need to pay: 'its value for the purchaser is not known until he has the information, but then he has in effect acquired it without cost'.[6] This made selling news piece by piece rather problematic.

The diplomats and merchants of the Renaissance, who noted the latest news at the bottom of their letters, and later the exchanging newspapers in the United States and elsewhere used reciprocity as a mechanism to make the marginal price of the news zero, even though the marginal cost to the news supplier might have been higher than zero.

The early modern news traders suffered less from Arrow's paradox when they supplied trade information that consisted of the numerical value of a measurable property of an economic quality. Six main categories of values were traded (Table 13.2). First, a price was a measurable property of the economic quality 'scarcity' and was abundantly traded in letters and through price currents. Imported and exported quantities at specific ports, as tabulated in bills of entry, formed another measurable property of scarcity.[7] Second, exchange rates formed a measurable property of the general terms of trade between two areas. A third important category, which was more often dealt with in private correspondence and internal news services, such as that of the Fuggers, was the reputation of clients or trading partners.[8] The quality 'reputation' had the measurable property 'credit rating', which in theory could be 'creditworthy' or 'not creditworthy', or some steps on an ordinal scale in between. Money could be asked for by simply mentioning the quality (reputation or creditworthiness) and supplying qualitative information from which the buyer could distil a judgement, or, as would happen during the nineteenth century, a numerical value itself (the credit rating) could be sold. Morse would later mention inquiries about creditworthiness as an important potential application of the telegraph.[9]

A fourth category was formed by ship arrivals in harbours, as supplied in *Lloyd's List*, a measurable property of the quality 'existence of a ship', which was useful for insurers, large trading companies, and navies.[10] Later, share prices and interest rates would become two important new categories, measurable properties of the scarcity of a firm's total (tangible and intangible) assets and of the scarcity of the future, respectively. For each of these six economic qualities, the seller could advertise its measurable property, and only reveal its numerical value after being paid, thus resolving Arrow's paradox. It was still impossible to ask premiums for unexpected changes in numerical values, such as price implosions, exchange rate collapses, or the loss of an entire merchant convoy, such as the capture of the Spanish silver fleet by the Dutch Republic.

TABLE 13.2 Measurable properties of economic, political, and social qualities

Quality	Measurable property	Typical range of numerical values	Typical sources
Scarcity	Price	$\langle 0, \rightarrow \rangle$	Price currents
	Quantity	$[0, \rightarrow \rangle$	Imports/exports (bills of entry)
Terms of trade	Exchange rate	$\langle 0, \rightarrow \rangle$	Price currents
Reputation	Credit rating	$\{0, 1\}$	Letters; reports of credit agencies
Existence of a ship	Arrival in a harbour	$\{0, 1, \varnothing\}$	Lloyd's List
Scarcity of the future	Interest rate	$\langle 0, \rightarrow \rangle$	Price currents
Scarcity of a firm's total assets	Share price	$\langle 0, \rightarrow \rangle$	Price currents; newspapers
Change of executive and/or legislative branch of the state	Outcome of the election; detailed election results	$\{0, 1\};$ $[0, n]$	Newswires/ newspapers
Performance of armies in known military battle	Outcome of the battle; losses/casualties	$\{0, 1\};$ $[0, \rightarrow \rangle$	Newswires/ newspapers
Contestants' performance in sports match	Sports match outcome; contestants' score	$\{0, 1\};$ $[0, \rightarrow \rangle$	Newswires/ newspapers
Prevailing opinion in a population	Responses to survey	$[0, 100]$	Newswires/ newspapers

Note: Numerical values are expressed in standard mathematical domain ranges, where, for example, a square bracket includes a value, whereas a diagonal bracket excludes it. For example, $\langle 0, \rightarrow \rangle$ implies that the numerical values are above zero, $\{0, 1\}$ that a battle has been lost (0) or won (1) and $\{0, 1, \varnothing\}$ implies that a ship can be listed as lost (0), can be listed as arrived (1), or is not listed ($\varnothing$). $[0, n]$ refers to a definite range, where n depends on the size of the respective legislature.

Source: See the section 'Evolution of News Agencies' and its sources; Gerben Bakker, 'Trading Facts: Arrow's Fundamental Paradox and the Origins of Global News Networks', in Peter Putnis, Chandrika Kaul, and Jürgen Wilke (eds.) *International Communication and Global News Networks: Historical Perspectives* (Hampton Press / International Association of Media and Communication Research, 2011), pp. 9–54.

Some general news did have measurable properties that could be specified in advance without their numerical value being revealed. The main such categories were election results, sports results, and, to a lesser extent, the outcome of known military battles (Table 13.2). Contrary to the economic categories, these three categories involved irreversible win-or-lose outcomes, although the intermediate election results, losses, or match scores could be reported in instalments. As a rule of thumb, any information on which one could place a definite bet, and for which thus in theory a futures market was possible, was at least partially tradable and suffered less from Arrow's paradox (Table 13.2). Other news was largely unexpected in quality, almost by its nature, as that was its main selling point. The emergence of opinion polls can probably be explained by the desire of polling firms to first create measurable properties for some news events and then sell their numerical values. Polls also resulted in more frequent instalment reporting for events such as elections, as each poll could be read as an intermediate election result.

In the course of the nineteenth century, the emerging international news agencies introduced their own two 'solutions' to Arrow's paradox. First, they used subscriptions, by which customers paid an advance fee for all the news reports. The price was based on the agency's past reputation in delivering reports and the guarantee that the subscriber received all the news the agency gathered, and often also was based on the subscriber's ability to pay, which could be approximated by factors such as circulation, prices or estimated margins. In the United States, for example, newspapers generally paid according to a complex formula, and in Britain provincial newspapers paid far lower fees than the London papers.[11] When subscribers had to decide whether it was worth renewing, they only had to think of the value of the few news items that had made a difference in their business, and these items probably differed from subscriber to subscriber. The subscription system made the marginal price of a news item to the customer equal to zero, and thus solved Arrow's paradox.[12]

Second, agencies bundled news in packages containing boring and exciting, relevant and irrelevant news that could differ from customer to customer. This admixture was mainly a characteristic of subscriptions, but sometimes also was achieved in other ways. A specific historical circumstance that allowed bundling, for example, was the arrival of scheduled mail steamers, such as those from Europe in the United States. Entrepreneurs such as Daniel Craig sold the news arriving from Europe first to New York merchants and then to the newspapers.[13] Knowing that they would be first to have the latest European information was enough for buyers to pay. The content did not have to be revealed before payment was agreed. Also, part of this news consisted of the numerical values of measurable properties of economic qualities that merchants knew they could use whatever its content would turn out to be. Expected new developments of existing stories probably formed a somewhat similar category. Undoubtedly, entirely unexpected news was the most valuable, but could not be sold separately. With the laying of permanent transatlantic cables in the 1860s, European news started to come in piecemeal in small, continuously arriving chunks. The opportunity to sell prime European news in a bundle disappeared. A similar case of 'natural' packaging was Reuters' exclusive first-use contract with Austrian Lloyd's for news and market information arriving at Trieste by ship from the East, starting in 1852.[14]

A third, regulatory, solution to Arrow's paradox was the use of copyright to protect news. Reuters campaigned for a copyright in news throughout the British Empire, but only found success in South Africa, while the Associated Press lobbied for news copyright in the United States, obtaining a quasi-property right in news in 1918.[15]

Fourth, ancillary services or revenue streams that exploited the news agencies' assets, brand name, or reputation could be used to 'cross-subsidize' the supply of news. Havas and Reuters, for example, introduced advertising services. In the

1890s, Reuters even started to offer a range of business and financial services, such as private telegrams, wire remittances, and eventually a bank.[16] Although meant to cushion fluctuations in news revenue, the bank eventually brought Reuters to the brink of bankruptcy.[17]

Arrow's fundamental paradox also might explain why recipients of postal letters and telegrams often did not pay a price for receiving each individual item. They would only want to pay if they knew what the message was or from whom it came, and if they did know, they often would no longer need to pay; thus the marginal price of receiving was often, but not always, set at zero.[18]

The list of business models discussed above (see Table 13.3 for an overview) is not exhaustive. Other models were used as well. In France during the nineteenth and early twentieth centuries, for example, it was customary for companies and for domestic and foreign governments to pay newspapers for editorial coverage. This usually happened through various successive intermediaries. Often a firm paid an investment bank, which paid another intermediary to pay the newspaper.[19] The practice did lead to some scandals, such as the campaign to sell shares in a company to invest in the building of a Panama canal in the 1880s. At the time many commentators claimed that the payments resulted in serious media bias. Yet present-day research suggests, surprisingly, that little bias in reporting can be observed, despite the widespread payments.[20]

Another business model used widely in France by the customers of the news agencies, especially during the interwar period, was the buying of newspapers to influence the political and business climate to the advantage of the new owner, and therefore accepting lower commercial returns. Over time, as the quality of information declined, those newspapers would decline and sometimes disappear, but the cartel in the French newspaper market which hampered new entrants meant that these periods could be very long.[21] The major news agencies may not have been entirely immune to this business model.

Business models: news as a toll good

In addition to the fundamental paradox, the news agencies faced a second and related challenge – news was a quasi-public good: it was non-rivalrous but excludable (Table 13.1). In practice, rivalrousness and excludability are often a matter of degree, and quasi-public goods can be further divided into rivalrous but excludable goods, called *common pool resources*, such as fishing grounds or natural water systems, and non-rivalrous but excludable goods, called *toll goods*, such as private clubs, day-care centres, or theatres.[22]

The fact that most media products were toll goods led to the adoption of business models that focused on the point of exclusion (Table 13.3).[23] Theatres, for example, could prohibit entry and thus charge ticket prices, printed and recorded media could sell physical products protected by copyright, and the early broadcasters could exclude advertisers from the airwaves and thus get their

TABLE 13.3 Overview of business models used by raw news traders in Europe since the Renaissance

Period	Business model	Point of exclusion	Example cases	Effect
Since early Middle Ages	Reciprocity	'Tit for tat'; withholding of reciprocal news	News summary written under diplomatic letters	Effective
Since early Middle Ages	Bundling	Entire bundle or nothing	News summary under merchant's letters	Effective
Since early Middle Ages	Speed	Lateness/ perishability	Horse couriers	Effective
16th c. −	Selling value measurements	Revelation of actual measurement	Amsterdam, Antwerp, and Italian exchange price currents	Effective
16th c. −	Subscription	Entire annual output or nothing	Italian *avvisi*; A. Casteleyn, Netherlands	Effective
19th c. −	Payments for news coverage	Access to editorial content	French newspapers; Wolff-Continental	Limited
19th c. −	Owner pays for using medium for own benefit	Ownership of medium	French newspapers; Wolff-Continental	Limited
1840s −	Vertical integration with customer group	Membership/ ownership of news agency	AP cooperative; Reuters' merger with Press Ass.	Effective
1850s −	Entry deterrence/ first-mover advantage	Sunk committed capacity	Reuters, Havas, Wolff-Continental	Effective
1860s–1930s	Exclusive territorial contracts	News stream of entire territory/ nation state	The international news cartel	Effective
Late 19th c. −	Copyright	Legal protection	Reuters' campaign; South Africa; Australia	Limited
Late 19th c. −	Ancillary services	Access to other services	Reuters' advertising business & fin. services; Bloomberg	Limited

Notes: 'News stream of entire territory/nation state' means all the news originating in the territory and gathered by the relevant news agency. Havas could, for example, withhold all the news from France and refuse to sell it to Reuters, or the Australian Press Association, a news cooperative, could withhold all the news coming from Australia through their organization from a foreign contracting partner such as Reuters.

Sources: See text.

revenue from them. Stars also were able to extract rents, with superstars earning very high fees.[24]

From the 1850s to the 1930s, Reuters, Havas, and Wolff-Continental, with acquiescence from the New York Associated Press (NYAP) and its successor companies as well as several smaller players, operated an international cartel in which they divided the world into areas where each had exclusivity for newsgathering.[25]

Crises: the ups and downs of news provision

An important aspect of the news that news agencies traded was the random appearance of calamities such as earthquakes, floods, wars, and political, economic, and financial crises. Arrow's paradox discussed above implied that agencies could not easily ask a higher price at the moment a crisis appeared, even though their reporting costs were likely to go up.

The historical accounts of the Associated Press suggest that wars led to increased expenditure. The cost of its foreign service shot up in 1898 during the Spanish–American War from 9 per cent of all expenditure to 22 per cent, reflecting a tripling of the dollar amount spent on foreign news.[26] It happened again at the outbreak of World War I, when foreign service expenditure increased from 8 per cent in 1913 to 20 per cent in 1918.[27]

One way in which news agencies made sure they made enough money from crises to cover their costs was through subscriptions. The annual subscription fee could reflect the reputation of the news agency, and the expectation that when crises happened, raw news would be delivered fast and effectively to the customer. Reuters emphasized this insurance aspect of subscription and stated that boring years paid for exciting years.[28]

Another possibility was to charge a premium for crisis news – not for the first news of the impending crisis, but for the whole package of crisis news once it had started. This was difficult in practice, however, as customer contracts needed to be renegotiated then, and it could not always be foreseen when exactly a crisis would start and what could be defined as a crisis. In the British market, Reuters was able to levy a 50 per cent war surcharge on London newspapers' subscription fee from 1885.[29]

Increased expenditure on newsgathering did not generally lead to more potential news events happening, especially the 'hard' events such as murders or wars, although if increased reporting shortened the feedback cycle, it could lead to some more news per unit of time.[30] At the same time, more potential news events happening, especially the hard events, did lead to more expenditure.

Besides vertical integration with the customers, war surcharges, and a subscription fee high enough to cover unforeseen crisis reporting, there appear to have been few other means by which news agencies were able to recover higher reporting costs during crises.

All the business data discussed above and tabulated in Table 13.2 obtained extra relevance during crises. Present-day studies in finance generally find that news affects the movement of financial markets. The size of the effect that studies find differs substantially. It also remains a question to what extent media reporting produces feedback effects, or self-reinforcing herd behaviour. Some authors, such as Robert Shiller, argue that there is a substantial effect of the media in instigating bubbles, while other authors find the obverse.[31] Campbell, Turner, and Walker, for example, find that press coverage did not feed the British railway mania in the 1840s, and Bhattacharya et al. find that media reporting played only a very limited role in the Internet bubble of the 1990s.[32]

During financial crises, everyone wanted to know the latest information about goods prices, quantities, exchange rates, credit rating, interest rates, share prices, election results, and battle outcomes, and also the results of opinion surveys such as those on consumer and business confidence. Longitudinal studies for the twentieth century show that during crises, the financial markets were far more sensitive to media reports, both reports containing new information and more 'persuasive' reports that served only to increase exposure of a particular stock.[33] This suggests that customers, especially corporate customers, may have had a higher willingness to pay during crises.

Yet the news agencies had little ability to transform this willingness to pay into higher revenues. In theory, they could increase the subscription fee for corporate subscriptions during crises, but in practice this was often not feasible.

The raw material that the news agencies transformed into sellable news bulletins was not the news, but the entire universe of all events that happened at a given time. The news agencies *selected* the events they *judged* as news, and then they further added value by *writing accurate reports* about these events and *combining various disparate facts into one coherent report*.

During crises surprising events happened in rapid succession. After a financial crisis broke, the key thing people started to expect was the unexpected. They became habituated to surprising events that continued to happen and stopped trusting other expectations. Keynes had already noted this in his General Theory when he discussed animal spirits: once a crisis was in progress, businessmen expected so many surprises that they held back investments, and were not prepared to make the jump into uncertainty they normally made when they green-lighted new investments. The only thing they felt sure about was that surprising things would continue to happen.

Various types of crises existed (Table 13.4). Wars and natural disasters were probably the most costly to report, since reporters needed to be at faraway and often dangerous locations. Telegraph lines needed to be leased, travel tickets booked, and additional correspondents hired. The cases of Reuters and AP discussed above show that these cost increases were large and significant. Financial crises, on the contrary, happened usually in known places such as financial and political capitals, where reporters and a whole reporting infrastructure were already present, making these crises far easier and less costly to report. Business customers' willingness to pay might have been exceptionally high for financial news. What they actually needed to pay was probably exceptionally low in comparison.

TABLE 13.4 Informal overview of aspects of news reporting in several types of crisis situation

Reporting aspect	Natural disasters and accidents	Famines	Wars	Financial and economic crisis	Political crisis	Elections
Reporting costs	High	Intermediate	High	Low	Low	Intermediate
Feedback effects caused by news transmission	Low	Low	Low	High	High	High
Customers' average willingness-to-pay	Lower	Lower	Intermediate	High	High	Intermediate
Degree of surprise	High	Intermediate	Intermediate	High	Intermediate	Intermediate
Duration	Short	Longer	Long	Long	Long	Short
Value of speed	Intermediate	Low	High	High	High	Intermediate
Value of accuracy	Intermediate	Low	High	High	High	High
Consequences of reporting errors	Lower	Intermediate	High	High	Intermediate	High
Salaries of journalists	Intermediate	Intermediate	High	High	Intermediate	Intermediate

Source: Informal judgement based on the historical literature discussed in this chapter.

It appears that the willingness of customers to pay might also have been high in the case of political crises, partially because the outcome of political crises could have a big effect on the business and financial world. In terms of duration, financial crises lasted longer than many other crises.

The value of speed and accuracy was probably highest in wars, financial crises, and political crises (Table 13.4). The consequences of reporting errors were probably most serious in wars, financial crises, and in elections – the latter partially because of self-feedback mechanisms. In addition, salaries for war correspondents and financial journalists were probably among the highest for news journalists.

In the long run, news providers made money from crises, and from financial crises in particular, because the possibility of crises meant that in quiet times many customers kept subscribing to the service at substantial fees.

New business models

One way in which news providers were *not* able to capture the benefit or the rents of the services they provided was through the analysis of large databanks full of news articles by hedge funds and other financial firms. Academic studies abound about relations between news reporting and movements in the market, and undoubtedly many financial firms do their own research using large news databanks. They can test relations between news pieces and the movements of the financial market at macro, meso, and micro levels. Though news providers derive some money from the use of databanks, it remains a question whether they just get a very small part of the rents/profits that others generate from the large aggregate of information that they create.

The only chance of rent capture may be to charge special access fees for database access and limit it to per-calculation access, in which the customer does not get copies of the news stories database, but can only send in an algorithm that the news organization will run for them on the news database, which they keep in-house. Access fees for social scientists and governments could also be levied, and this is already happening to some extent. Yet, since those activities may not generate a lot of profit, there may not be a lot of rent to be captured here. What kind of business model the news agencies will come up with next is an inspiring question that makes one look full of wonder and excitement to the times that lie before us. The answer will define the role of news in the other twenty-first-century financial crises.

Conclusion

This paper examined the problem, implied by Arrow's fundamental paradox, of how to ask for money for news facts. To get good money for important news, news traders need to reveal to the potential buyer what that news is, yet once they have revealed it, the buyer no longer needs to pay. We have noted how historically this paradox made it difficult for news agencies to profit from important news during crises.

In their quest to be able to derive money from news facts, news agencies developed business models that made them less sensitive to crises. These models did not easily allow the selling of crisis news at higher prices – many crises, such as wars and natural disasters, actually cost them much more to report. Financial crises were less costly to report than most other crises.

News agencies may not have been able to make money from particular crises, but in the long run the crises justified the existence of the agencies to the customers. No crises, no news agencies. When frequent financial crises started to become a trademark for the emerging world economy, the news agencies helped to report them, and helped to link crises in particular countries to the rest of the world. In this way news agencies shaped the emergence of the modern world economy as we know it today.

Notes

1 The author would like to thank Paul Auerbach, Richard R. John, Mary Morgan, Oliver Volckart, Peter Putnis, Richard Roberts, Steve Schifferes, Peter Scott, Jonathan Silberstein-Loeb, Krim Talia, as well as Jeff Hulbert and John Hobart for steering the paper through the editorial process. Previous versions benefited from comments received at the workshop on the history of the business press, University of Uppsala, at the International Economic History Association Conference in Helsinki, at the British Academy of Management Conference in Belfast, and at the Journalism and the Global Financial Crisis Symposium, City University, London. The research for this chapter was partially funded by the Social and Economic Research Council (UK) and the Advanced Institute of Management Research under the ESRC/AIM Ghoshal Fellowship Scheme, grant number RES-331-25-3012. The author alone, of course, is responsible for the final text and any errors of fact or interpretation that may remain.
2 On the interaction between the development of new communication technologies and news agencies, see Gerben Bakker, 'Trading Facts: Arrow's Fundamental Paradox and

the Origins of Global News Networks', in Peter Putnis, Chandrika Kaul, and Jürgen Wilke (eds.) *International Communication and Global News Networks: Historical Perspectives* (Hampton Press / International Association of Media and Communication Research, 2011), pp. 9–54.

3 For a detailed historical overview, see Bakker, 'Trading Facts'.

4 This model for historical analysis of media industries is discussed in more detail in Gerben Bakker, 'Sunk Costs, Dynamic Efficiency and the Structure of Creative Industries: A Very Long-Run Perspective', in Candace Jones, Mark Lorenzen, and Jonathan Sapsed (eds.) *Oxford Handbook of Creative Industries* (Oxford University Press, 2014, forthcoming).

5 The importance of the capture of marginal revenues for media organizations is further explored in Gerben Bakker, 'The Making of a Music Multinational: Polygram's International Businesses, 1945–1998', *Business History Review*, 80 (2006), pp. 81–123. Oliver E. Williamson, The Economic Institutions of Capitalism: Firms, Markets, Relational Contracting (The Free Press, 1985), and John Roberts, *The Modern Firm: Organizational Design for Performance and Growth* (Oxford University Press, 2004) provide theories to explain why activities are done within or without an organization.

6 Kenneth J. Arrow, 'Economic Welfare and the Allocation of Resources for Invention', in Richard Nelson (ed.) *The Rate and Direction of Inventive Activity* (NBER / Princeton University Press, 1962), pp. 609–26; 615.

7 John J. McCusker, 'The Business Press in England Before 1775', in: *Essays in the Economic History of the Atlantic World* (Routledge, 1997), pp. 149–67.

8 On the importance of reputation, see, for example, Paul R. Milgrom, Douglass C. North, and Barry R. Weingast, 'The Role of Institutions in the Revival of Trade: The Law Merchant, Private Judges, and the Champagne Fairs', *Economics and Politics*, 2 (1990), pp. 1–23.

9 Menahem Blondheim, *News over the Wires: The Telegraph and the Flow of Public Information in America* (Harvard University Press, 1994).

10 For credit rating and ship arrivals, the information was binary (creditworthy or not creditworthy, ships on the list the buyer of the information had obtained have arrived or not).

11 High fixed costs made price discrimination important. With one price, total revenue may not be enough to cover fixed costs and the service would not be provided, even though aggregate willingness-to-pay (the consumer surplus) could be enough to cover fixed costs. By charging differential subscription fees the firm transforms more of the consumer surplus into revenue and so can incur the high fixed costs. Bakker, 'Sunk Costs'.

12 It may, however, not be optimal in efficiency terms, as the price signal cannot be used to reach the most efficient allocation, and because of this absence of the price signal for individual news items users have to 'overconsume' information to find the information that is most valuable for them. The present-day 'information overload' may be illustrative of this suboptimal allocation mechanism. Another solution to Arrow's fundamental paradox is to make the marginal price zero by bundling it with sponsored messages, which is often used in end (consumer) markets (e.g. television advertising).

13 For a detailed account of the races to get this information first and how and to whom it was sold, see Blondheim, *News*.

14 Donald Read, *The Power of News: The History of Reuters, 1849–1989* (Oxford University Press, 1992), p. 14.

15 Jonathan Silberstein-Loeb, 'The Structure of the News Market in Britain, 1870–1914', *Business History Review*, 83 (Winter 2009), pp. 759–88. The Supreme Court ruled that information contained in news was not copyrightable but that the Associated Press had a quasi-property right in 'hot' news. See, for example, Richard Epstein, 'International News Service v. Associated Press: Custom and Law as Sources of Property Rights in News', *Virginia Law Review*, 78 (1992), pp. 85–128.

16 Silberstein-Loeb, 'News Market', p. 777.

17 Ibid.

18 Exceptions are 'collect calls' in which the receiver agrees to pay on hearing who is calling. Historically, several postal systems also had a model by which the recipient of

the letter would pay, such as the US Post Office Department before 1855, when customers collected their letters at the post office: 'frequent correspondents often found themselves paying large sums for letters that they would never have bothered with had they known their contents in advance'. Richard R. John, *Spreading the News: The American Postal System from Franklin to Morse* (Harvard University Press, 1995), pp. 160–1.

19 Charles P. Kindleberger and Robert Z. Aliber, *Manias, Panics, and Crashes: A History of Financial Crises* (Palgrave Macmillan, 6th edn, 2011), pp. 145–6; Maurice Lévy-Leboyer, *Les banques Européennes et l'industrialisation internationale dans la première moitié du XIXe siècle* (Presses Universitaires de France, 1964), pp. 632–3.

20 Vincent Bignon and Antonio Miscio, 'Media Bias in Financial Newspapers: Evidence from Early Twentieth-Century France', *European Review of Economic History*, 14 (2010), pp. 383–432. See also Vincent Bignon and Marc Flandreau, 'The Economics of Bad-mouthing: Libel Law and the Underworld of the Financial Press in France Before World War I', *Journal of Economic History*, 71 (2011), pp. 616–53.

21 Vincent Bignon and Marc Flandreau, 'The Price of Media Capture and the Looting of Newspapers in Interwar France', *Graduate Institute of International and Development Studies Working Paper*, No. 09 (Geneva, 2012).

22 Elinor Ostrom, *Governing the Commons: The Evolution of Institutions for Collective Action* (Cambridge University Press, 1990); Elinor Ostrom, 'Beyond Markets and States: Polycentric Governance of Complex Economic Systems', *American Economic Review*, 100 (2010), pp. 641–72.

23 Stephen Shmanske, 'News As a Public Good: Cooperative Ownership, Price Commitments, and the Success of the Associated Press', *Business History Review*, 60 (1986), pp. 55–80.

24 Gerben Bakker, 'Stars and Stories: How Films Became Branded Products', *Enterprise and Society*, 2 (2001), pp. 461–502.

25 Jacques Wolff, 'Structure, fonctionnement et évolution du marché international des nouvelles: Les agences de presse de 1835 à 1934', *Revue Économique*, 42 (1991), pp. 575–601; Terhi Rantanen, 'Foreign Dependence and Domestic Monopoly: The European News Cartel and U.S. Associated Presses, 1861–1932', *Media History*, 12 (2006), pp. 19–35.

26 Richard Allen Schwarzlose, *The American Wire Services: A Study of Their Development as a Social Institution* (University of Illinois PhD, 1965, reprinted by Arno Press, 1979).

27 At the same time, real revenue decreased during the war, 20 per cent in total between 1914 and 1918, and most of it – 16 per cent – when the United States entered the war. Ibid., p. 251.

28 Silberstein-Loeb, 'News Market', p. 778.

29 Schwarzlose, *American Wire Services*, p. 251.

30 One could argue that a potential news event only became news once it was reported. See Robert E. Park, 'News As a Form of Knowledge: A Chapter in the Sociology of Knowledge', *American Journal of Sociology*, 45 (1940), pp. 669–86.

31 Robert J. Shiller, *Irrational Exuberance* (Broadway Books, rev. 2nd edn, 2009), pp. 85–105.

32 Gareth Campbell, John D. Turner, and Clive B. Walker, 'The Role of the Media in a Bubble', *Explorations in Economic History*, 49 (2012), pp. 461–81; Utpal Bhattacharya, Neal Galpin, Rina Ray, and Xiaoyun Yu, 'The Role of the Media in the Internet IPO Bubble', *Journal of Financial and Quantitative Analysis*, 44 (2009), pp. 657–82.

33 Paul C. Tetlock, 'Giving Content to Investor Sentiment: The Role of Media in the Stock Market', *Journal of Finance*, 62 (2007), pp. 1139–68; Diego García, 'Sentiment During Recessions', *Journal of Finance*, 68 (2013), pp. 1267–300. Joseph E. Engelberg and Christopher A. Parsons, 'The Causal Impact of Media in Financial Markets', *Journal of Finance*, 66 (2011), pp. 67–97, examining regional news, find also that stock price movements are very sensitive to the reporting and publishing of new information.

PART IV

The lessons of history

14

FINANCIAL CRISES AND THE BIRTH OF THE FINANCIAL PRESS, 1825–1880

James Taylor

Financial journalism in the UK is almost two hundred years old, first emerging in tandem with the expansion of capital markets in the early nineteenth century. However, historians have neglected financial journalism's origins, with most research focusing on the period from the 1880s, which saw the arrival of the financial dailies.[1] But understanding the earlier history is important because many issues that have emerged in the wake of the recent global financial crisis – the quality of financial reporting, the role of the press in hyping investment bubbles, the ethical standards of financial journalists, and ambiguity over which constituencies they aspire to serve – first rose to prominence during the first three quarters of that earlier turbulent century. Nineteenth-century crises – in particular those of 1825, 1845, and 1866 – presented challenges to the new profession of financial journalism, but also opportunities, and if the picture that emerges is not quite a heroic story of an idealistic press opening up the secretive City to the public gaze, nor is it the catalogue of shortcomings and failures suggested by some media scholars.[2] This chapter begins by exploring financial journalism in its earliest forms, emphasizing the crucial impact of the speculative boom of the early to mid 1820s. It goes on to chart the rising power and prestige of financial journalism, taking in the rise of the specialist press connected with the railway booms of the 1830s and 1840s. The third section moves on to the 1860s and 1870s, when crisis and scandal highlighted to the public the fallibilities of financial journalists. It explains how the financial press was able to retain its credibility, the chief factor being the various benefits it brought the investing public.

The birth of financial journalism

The spread of the newspaper press coincided with the development of capital markets after the 'Glorious Revolution' of 1688, and since their earliest days, newspapers have carried financial news alongside other types of news. During the first companies' boom, which took place in the 1690s, newspapers reported key events such as the formation of the Bank of England and company mergers. But such reports gave facts rather than analysis, were patchy and often unreliable, and were not always timely enough to be of much help to investors. Price lists, such as John Castaing's *The Course of the Exchange*, first published in 1697, gave investors another source of information, but print runs were generally small, and most lists were weekly rather than daily, limiting their usefulness.[3] Financial coverage developed through the eighteenth century, however, with specialist titles developing alongside the mainstream weeklies and dailies. By 1716, 'a London reader could spend more than £6 a year on subscriptions to seven different weekly or bi-weekly business newspapers'.[4] But this was not financial journalism in the modern sense, with content consisting chiefly of basic news items such as the arrival and departure of ships, supplemented with tables of imports and exports, and lists of stock prices.[5] With most papers at the time one-man operations, there were definite limits on the breadth of coverage they could contain.[6] Much of the most useful information came in the form of advertising: from an early stage companies used the press to communicate with their shareholders and the wider public, and reports of proceedings at general meetings often appeared as paid-for advertisements.[7] Into the early nineteenth century, then, newspapers were a hotchpotch of useful titbits of financial information, but coverage of the stock exchange was far from methodical and even when data was given, readers were denied much in the way of interpretation of events and price movements.

In the early 1820s, some weekly newspapers began to experiment with carrying more detailed market reporting. On 15 January 1821, *The Observer*, which until then had merely carried a concise table of the prices of the main public funds, carried a long paragraph headed 'The Funds' discussing the various factors depressing the price of securities, ranging from the recent publication of the manifesto of the Holy Alliance to the imminent resumption of parliament.[8] The experiment must have proven popular: although it did not immediately become a regular feature, the column reappeared sporadically through the year until in December it began appearing every week (though it did not enjoy a fixed place in the paper). Driving this increased coverage was an upswing in stock market activity, particularly in foreign loans – from late 1821, the column sometimes carried a separate section on 'Foreign Funds' with a table summarizing the most popular loans.[9] *The Observer*'s proprietor, William Innell Clement, purchased one of the leading London dailies, the *Morning Chronicle*, in 1821, and early the following year, it began publishing market information on most days.[10] Appearing under the heading 'City', followed by the previous day's date, these pieces were initially terse affairs, but they expanded through the course of 1822, soon regularly occupying half a column or more, and consisting of analysis and interpretation of current events as well of predictions of future trends.[11] That they were prepared by a regular member of staff rather than on a more casual basis by amateurs is suggested by frequent references in other parts of the paper to 'our City Correspondent'.[12] The innovation was imitated by some, though not across the board.[13] *The Times*, for example, though very occasionally reprinting market news from *The Englishman* (another Clement-owned publication), resisted carrying anything like a daily update.[14]

While foreign loans were the main focus of investors in the early 1820s, by 1824 attention was beginning to switch to joint-stock companies.[15] The more progressive newspapers responded by diversifying their coverage. Early in the year, the *Morning Chronicle* began appending a small number of Mexican mining companies to the foot of their daily table of securities.[16] By the end of the year, more companies were being listed, and now they were at the head of the table.[17] Early in 1825, presumably in concession to the priorities of their readers, the paper began carrying a separate listing for company shares, divided into categories including Assurance Companies, Mines, Iron Railways, and Gas Light Companies.[18] But it was by no means an uncritical commentator. In March it did not hide its scepticism about the latest promotions:

> Human ingenuity is not yet exhausted, for innumerable mining and other schemes are still in embryo, notwithstanding the inauspicious appearance of those already brought before the public; but it seems now necessary to resort to a little manoeuvring, in order to make them go down with the public.[19]

Other newspapers, by contrast, continued in their resistance to such detailed and systematic coverage. It was not until November 1825 that the *Morning Post* and *The Times* began carrying slightly more frequent City news under the heading 'Money Market', just as confidence was beginning to ebb.[20] What turned these hesitant forays into a regular fixture of the daily press was the commercial crisis which struck in December, marked by widespread bank failures and hundreds of bankruptcies.[21] As the crisis unfolded, it was charted in great detail by these new columns, responding to the anxious public's need for commercial news as it broke. The authors of these articles knew that many readers were hanging on their every word: on 17 December, the first line of *The Times*'s Money Market column displayed a knowing sense of drama: 'Every day of late has teemed with important events in the City, but those of yesterday exceeded in interest all that have preceded them.' The latest revelation was that the Bank of England's directors had authorized the issue of £1 and £2 notes in an attempt to stem the crisis.[22] A week later and the worst had passed, *The Times* noting a 'more tranquil' atmosphere at the Bank.[23] But though the crisis faded, the Money Market column remained as a – more or less – regular feature of the London dailies.

The financial journalist's trade

That it was the bust rather than the boom that had made the City article a standing feature in London's press is underlined by one of the earliest descriptions of financial journalism, given during a court case in 1828. John Lawson, the printer of *The Times*, was being sued by a merchant aggrieved at a claim published in the paper's Money Market column that he was involved in the importation of smuggled tea. During the trial, Lawson's defence lawyer, James Scarlett, noted that 'since the year 1825, when the dreadful panic existed in the money-market, every newspaper had got a City correspondent – some man who collected the rumours of the market, and condensed them into an article for the newspaper by which he was employed'. This was hardly a flattering portrayal, but Scarlett's aim was to show that the financial journalist was exposed to risk by the nature of his sources. He claimed that it 'did not follow that this person either invented falsehoods, or, if he accidently collected falsehoods, that he inserted them in his report maliciously'.[24] Though the case went against *The Times*, the author of the article – Thomas Alsager – continued in his role, rapidly attaining a far loftier reputation than that of a mere gossipmonger. By the mid 1830s, a mystique had built around the paper's City correspondent. Those who knew Alsager personally, such as Scottish journalist James Grant, credited him with 'a more thorough knowledge of our monetary system and financial regulations, than any man alive'.[25] His warnings, claimed another commentator, had saved the Bank of England from 'many a tremendous blunder', thus rendering 'important services to his country'.[26] His City article was read 'as a matter of duty by merchants, stockbrokers, and speculators of every shade. You will hardly get a decided answer from any one of them till he has seen the *Times*.'[27]

Alsager's deputy at *The Times* was David Morier Evans, and it is from him that we get the first detailed characterization of the trade of the financial journalist by an insider. In 1845 he published *The City; Or, the Physiology of London Business*, a few pages of which were devoted to explaining his daily labours. He spent the day on 'Change and in the nearby coffee houses, 'watching the fluctuation of the funds' and securing interviews with merchants and brokers: the good City journalist cultivated 'numerous sources of information which never fail to provide [him] with material to instruct or inform the public on some topic of interest'. But his work only began in earnest when the markets closed: then he could be found tucked away in the North and South American Coffee House laboriously writing up the closing stock prices and preparing the rest of his copy for dispatch to the printing office. Though at one stage he describes himself as 'the City article collater', there was much more to his job than this phrase suggested. 'The great thing' financial journalists had to guard against was 'the admission of spurious or exaggerated information, which some of the more daring and adventurous of the speculators will endeavour to palm upon them'. But journalistic experience and judgement meant that such attempts succeeded only in 'very few cases'.[28] Evans admitted that the City journalist was well paid, but he earned his pay because of the public benefits he delivered. Through the medium of the City article, 'the roguery and tricks of designing speculators were held up to public contempt'. Indeed, the 'fearless exposure of anything like fraud or foul dealing' was, for Evans, the chief qualification of the financial journalist. Thanks to these exposures, 'a new power had erected itself' in the form of the press, watching over the commerce of the country, and protecting the interests of shareholders.[29]

Evans was writing at a critical moment in the development of the financial markets. What contemporaries called 'the railway mania' – a period of frenetic speculation in railway companies – was gaining pace through 1844–5. Railways 'had captured the imagination of the English propertied classes like no industrial enterprise had ever done', and nearly 1,400 new schemes were registered in the first 10 months of 1845.[30] While many of the projects were valuable and well intentioned, the enthusiasm for everything on rails encouraged opportunists and fraudsters to promote their own schemes. All this posed a profound challenge to the new financial journalists. How were they going to keep track of so many new companies? How could they distinguish the honest schemes from the dishonest and warn their readers accordingly?

In fact, a specialist railway press had already established itself to provide such information. The first periodical dedicated to the new industry was the *Railway Magazine*, a monthly, in 1835, followed by the weekly *Railway Times* two years later. When the enthusiasm for railways intensified the following decade, coverage rapidly expanded, and by the autumn of 1845, new titles were being formed almost daily: the *Railway Courier and Stock-Exchange Price-Current* issued its first number on 8 October; the next day the first number of the *Railway King and Universal Advertiser* hit the news stands, while on the 11th two new titles appeared: the *Railway Critic and Shareholders' Adviser*, and the *Railway Standard*. Evans was quite positive about the benefits the new railway press brought, commenting that while dishonest railway promoters had preyed upon investors, 'the just animadversions passed upon such nefarious transactions by the railway press' significantly limited the damage they could do.[31]

Yet objectivity and public service were not among the priorities of these early railway titles. The *Railway Magazine* was founded by the financier George Walter, a director of the London and Greenwich Railway Company, after he had seen how favourable coverage of that concern in the *Mechanics' Magazine* had boosted its profile among the public. The *Railway Magazine* duly went on to give plenty of publicity not only to the London and Greenwich, but to other schemes in which Walter was interested, such as the Preston and Wyre Railway Company. Walter sold the paper in 1836 to the engineer John Herapath, who proceeded to use it to further his own interests. At every opportunity the paper attacked the Eastern Counties Railway Company (which had declined to make Herapath its engineering consultant), and it often singled out the company's secretary, Joseph Clinton Robertson, for particular abuse, following a violent quarrel between him and Herapath. Robertson retaliated by forming the *Railway Times*, which he used to defend the Eastern Counties, and himself, against Herapath's attacks.[32]

Railway papers were a useful means of pursuing personal vendettas; they were also lucrative revenue-raisers during the mania. Promoters knew that they had to advertise to make their schemes stand out from the crowd, and the railway press generated large sums in advertising revenues: up to £250 weekly for each of the leading titles according to one estimate.[33] This dependence on advertising income, according to some critics, compromised the editorial integrity of the railway papers: 'no one ever thinks of perusing an article in them in the idea of receiving a bold and independent opinion', claimed *The Era*.[34] Furthermore, the papers were happy to print advertising matter as news items; such 'puffs' were another rich source of income for the papers.[35] Investors therefore stood little chance of identifying safe outlets for their capital by reading the railway press, which, according to one historian, 'traded in breach of trust on a vast scale'.[36]

But the corruption thus encouraged by the mania was not necessarily a bad thing for the press as a whole. Although mainstream titles benefited as much as the specialist ones from mushrooming advertising revenues, some also ostentatiously criticized the mania through 1845, warning the public that share prices could not continue rising indefinitely. In August, Alsager warned his readers of 'the crisis which must shortly ensue, if this spirit of gambling, which has now infected the whole of the United Kingdom, is not checked'.[37] Indeed, contemporaries credited *The Times* with bursting the bubble when railway share prices plummeted at the end of the year.[38] As a result, the mania served to emphasize the distinction between the respectable and the unrespectable press. In the 1850s and 1860s, a new wave of specialist financial newspapers began to form, but published on a weekly or monthly basis, and prone to scandal as they were, they were unable to challenge the pre-eminence of the financial reporting in the leading London dailies.[39] One commentator praised the ability of these City editors, writers who 'would have commanded the respect of Adam Smith' himself.[40] Their reach extended far beyond London: one 1861 survey of Manchester ('the commercial town *par excellence*') observed that while there were 'not a few who love books and literature ... the prime literature is the City Article of the *Times*'.[41] Evans, who by this point had left *The Times* to become City editor at *The Standard*, was hailed as 'a high-priest of finance'.[42] However, events from 1866 were to put this enviable reputation to the test.

Living oracles?

A speculative boom, centred on finance companies, had been growing since 1863, but confidence began to wane early in 1866, leading to the dramatic stoppage of the country's leading discount house, Overend and Gurney, in May.[43] This failure prompted a general collapse of credit on what *The Times* dubbed 'Black Friday'.[44] Post-mortems published soon after the collapse focused on the role of 'bears' who were thought to have undermined investor confidence, and some presented the financial press as accomplices, witting or otherwise, of these market manipulators. Soon after the crash, Malcolm Meason, a journalist who specialized in fictionalized accounts of current financial events, published *The Profits of Panics*, which claimed to reveal how the recent 'financial storm' had come about. Written from the perspective of a member of a confederacy whose aim is to 'bear' a large joint-stock bank, the first chapter details how the group manipulated the press. This was not achieved through bribery – the narrator testifies to the honesty of the London press – but by exploiting the financial journalist's infinite appetite for information:

> The City editors of papers, as every one knows, are supposed to be living oracles on all financial questions. However, with the exception of two or

three, these gentlemen have generally to trust entirely to others for their information, and to pick up the City knowledge they impart to their respective papers as best they can, but chiefly from half idle friends who 'loaf' in and out of their offices during working hours.

A member of the confederacy cultivated the City editor of an evening paper, passing on generally reliable information so that, 'little by little, the money article of the paper became, quite unconsciously, the organ of our confederacy, and was worked to bring about the results we wished'.[45]

The same year also saw the publication of curate, lecturer, and numismatist Henry Noel-Fearn's *The Money Market*.[46] Echoing Meason, the chapter on panics bemoaned the ease with which the bears could shake the markets, and suggested that the press played a part in the dissemination of misinformation. However, unlike Meason, Noel-Fearn hinted that journalists might be willing accomplices:

> Certain of our own papers are *said*, it is to be hoped incorrectly, to have been among the chief '*operators for the fall*'; and the curious but incorrect reports which they occasionally circulate, make it necessary for men of business to be very cautious, and to make very close inquiries before they act upon them.[47]

Though he did not develop this point, or provide any evidence to support it, this was an early questioning of the integrity of the City column, a questioning which was to intensify in the 1870s.

Marmaduke Sampson, who had replaced Alsager as *The Times*'s City editor in 1846, had continued his predecessor's good work, warning investors against dubious schemes and maintaining the high reputation of the paper's financial reporting.[48] In 1872, he had seemingly performed a significant public service, using his column to discredit a US company attempting to interest British investors in Arizonan mines that had been 'salted' with rough diamonds and rubies purchased in London.[49] Sampson had pointed the finger at two men: the US speculator Asbury Harpending and the Englishman Alfred Rubery, but both insisted they were innocent dupes rather than conspirators, and Rubery took out a libel action to defend his name.[50] At the ensuing trial, Rubery's lawyers revealed the real reasons for Sampson's hostility to their client. Before the Arizonan venture, Rubery and Harpending had promoted a mining scheme with the disreputable financier Baron Albert Grant that had proved popular with the investing public: the shares were twice oversubscribed and £300,000 was raised. But the men had fallen out over the spoils and Grant warned the pair that if they tried floating another company on the London market he would use his influence to crush it.[51] Grant's influence extended to a special relationship with Sampson – he had boasted to the men that 'he possessed some kind of mysterious hold' on the journalist – and at the trial Rubery's lawyers produced photographs of cheques for thousands of pounds from Grant to Sampson.[52] Grant was pressed on the nature of these transactions, and he reluctantly explained that the sums were paid either as indemnity for losses incurred by Sampson from investing in companies recommended by Grant, or were profits deriving from allotments of stock in Grant's companies. Grant explained that it was common practice to allot shares to 'persons of influence' and 'Sampson was a person whose position both financially and socially entitled him to the consideration of any board of directors in allotting stock.' He denied exercising any influence over what Sampson wrote, yet the prosecution was able to produce *Times* articles talking up the prospects of two companies in connection with which Sampson had received payments from Grant.[53]

The exposure of a financial relationship between a respected City journalist and a notorious company promoter triggered a major scandal. *The Times* cut Sampson adrift, stating in an editorial that they had read the evidence 'with mingled astonishment and indignation', and the 'humiliation' they had suffered was 'hard to bear'.[54] But the damage was done. For radicals, the revelations proved that corruption was endemic in the nation's financial journalism. In an article entitled 'The Purchased Caresses of the Press', *Reynolds's Newspaper* claimed that what went on in the financial columns of *The Times* was common practice in the City: 'when we reach this branch of journalism we touch pitch; we descend to the prostitution of journalism'.[55] Such a conclusion seemed hard to resist following a second trial in 1876 during the course of which it was revealed that Evans, recently deceased, had also been in receipt of cheques from Baron Grant.[56] *Reynolds's Newspaper* felt that its previous verdict had been borne out: the 'much vaunted free, independent, and incorruptible press' had been exposed as 'venal and corrupt even in its highest branches'.[57]

These revelations were so damaging not only because they undermined financial journalists' claims to integrity; they also challenged their claims to expertise. In his writings, Evans had helped to build up the prestige of the City editor, but in court, Grant did his best to demolish this. He painted Evans as an absurd character: 'a stout man with a stick, who walked about always anxious to "serve a friend" … He would come in a hurry – he was always in a hurry – and would say "was not that a splendid article in *The Standard*?"' But his articles were cut-and-paste jobs from prospectuses, and Grant declared that he 'should have been an utter donkey to give Mr. Evans any money value for his articles. He was likely to do more harm than good if he attempted anything original … [he] could not write six lines.' Grant was therefore 'content that he should stick to his scissors and paste'.[58]

Corrupt, ridiculous, the City editor also seemed to be impotent. Rubery's legal action was a reminder that journalists risked a brush with the law of libel every time they criticized a businessman in print. 'City men', complained one commentator, were 'so protected by the loose character of the English law of libel that the press cannot – however much it would – say a tithe of what may often be necessary in preventing fraud.'[59] Indeed, in July 1876 when the publishers of three papers – *Vanity Fair*, *The World*, and *The Hour* – were all facing libel actions, the London correspondent of the *Liverpool Mercury* was moved to complain that 'if a journalist denounces what he believes to be a fraud he runs a very serious risk', a risk that many quite reasonably chose not to run.[60]

Nevertheless, financial journalists did manage to recover their standing. Though their fallibility was now recognized, the radical critique did not gain widespread acceptance. In part this was because of the public good they did, or tried to do. In times of speculative enthusiasm, they did not simply hype bubbles. As the popular mania for new promotions was getting under way in the early 1860s, *The Times* warned its readers not to fall for high premiums, because 'premiums of any magnitude' could be 'run up for any company' and were no guide to the actual prospects of the business.[61] Three years later, as the bust was fast approaching, the paper was exasperated by the behaviour of investors whose optimism had turned to panic: because the majority of them did not base their decisions on rational calculation or research, 'their sanguine delusions in times of buoyancy and their abject loss of courage when a reaction ensues are equally intense', plunging the market into chaos.[62] While such critiques could be seen as examples of traditional condemnations of the madness of crowds in circulation since the days of the South Sea Bubble, they were also born of a genuine desire to help readers avoid being fleeced.

Indeed, at a time when the stock market was attracting many new investors, journalists made real efforts to improve the financial literacy of their readers, transcending the confines of their daily or weekly columns to publish popular volumes on the stock market. The prolific Evans had led the way: as well as his book on the City, he published histories of the commercial crises of 1847–8 and 1857–8, together with *Facts, Failures, and Frauds* and *Speculative Notes and Notes on Speculation*. In these, the emphasis was on storytelling, and they often drew directly on his journalism. Others produced handbooks and manuals with more practical advice to would-be investors. In 1874 Arthur Crump, Sampson's successor at *The Times*, wrote *The Theory of Stock Exchange Speculation*, containing chapters detailing 'The right temperament for a professional speculator' and explaining when to follow 'tips'. Three years later Robert Giffen, the City editor of *The Economist*, published *Stock Exchange Securities: An Essay on the General Causes of Fluctuations in Their Price*. Though not as lively as Crump's volume, it aimed to elucidate a variety of stock market phenomena from syndicates, rigs, and corners to fictitious securities, price cycles, and panics. It was a form which was to prove durable, with Charles Duguid, City editor of the *Westminster Gazette* (and later of the *Daily Mail*), first publishing the enduringly popular *How to Read the Money Article* in 1901, and the *Financial News*'s W. Collin Brooks producing a host of guides through the interwar years, including *The Theory and Practice of Finance* (1929) and *Profits from Short-Term Investment and How to Make Them* (1935).

And the boldness of at least some journalists in the face of the harsh libel law further improved the profile of the financial press. One of the most daring was Henry Labouchere, a bohemian sometime MP and writer on financial topics for *The World*. In 1876 he founded *Truth*, a society paper which gained a reputation from the exposure of fraudulent companies and charities. Frequent libel actions did not deter Labouchere, partly due to the vast fortune he inherited from his uncle, Baron Taunton, which enabled him to bear occasional reverses in the courts.[63] But this kind of journalism was made a little easier for those without deep pockets by a reform to the libel law in 1881 designed to increase the number of cases which could be dealt with summarily by magistrates before they were committed for trial. Disputes could now be resolved more quickly and at less expense, which encouraged journalists at the new financial dailies established in the 1880s, most notably Harry Marks at the *Financial News*, to be bold in exposing swindles.[64]

Conclusion

The pioneers of the 'new financial journalism' of the late Victorian era, like Duguid and Marks, tended to be rather contemptuous of their predecessors, mocking their boring columns of City reportage which, 'with dull coldness, set forth mere price movements, without embellishment, hint, or explanation of any kind'.[65] But the earliest definition of the financial journalist – the man who collected and condensed 'the rumours of the market' – suggests that there was always something more interesting going on. Many of the issues preoccupying media scholars and practitioners today were just as relevant in the earliest years of the financial press. Who (and what) is financial journalism for? What responsibilities do financial journalists have to their readers? How does the law affect the quality of reporting? What ethical standards should be expected of journalists and how can these be enforced? Born out of the public's need for information in a crisis, the history of financial journalism is to some extent also the history of crisis. The reputation of the railway press suffered during the mania of the 1840s, while exposures of fallibility and corruption in the 1870s fundamentally threatened the credibility of the financial press as a whole. However, journalists were able both to retain public trust and to resist outside intervention in their trade, whether in the shape of parliamentary inquiries into standards, or reforms to outlaw the bribery of journalists. But the reputation of the financial journalist was to be plunged into crisis again in the closing years of the century when the hypocrisies and excesses of the new financial journalism were exposed to public view.

Notes

1 Dilwyn Porter pioneered research into the history of the financial press: Dilwyn Porter, '"A Trusted Guide of the Investing Public": Harry Marks and the *Financial News*, 1884–1916', *Business History*, 28 (1986), pp. 1–17; Dilwyn Porter, 'City Editors and the Modern Investing Public: Establishing the Integrity of the New Financial Journalism in Late Nineteenth-Century London', *Media History*, 4 (1998), pp. 49–60.

2 A 'pessimistic' view of the origins of financial journalism is very briefly outlined in Gary James Merrill, 'The Revolution Must Wait: Economic, Business and Financial Journalisms Beyond the 2008 Crisis', *Ethical Space*, 9 (2012), pp. 41–51, at p. 42.

3 Anne Murphy, *The Origins of English Financial Markets: Investment and Speculation Before the South Sea Bubble* (Cambridge University Press, 2009), ch. 4.

4 Natasha Glaisyer, *The Culture of Commerce in England, 1660–1720* (Boydell, 2006), p. 144; see also J.J. McCusker and C. Gravesteijn, *The Beginnings of Commercial and Financial Journalism* (Aksant Academic Publishers, 1991).

5 Glaisyer, *Culture of Commerce*, pp. 175–83.

6 Kevin Williams, *Read All About It! A History of the British Newspaper* (Routledge, 2010), p. 50.

7   James Taylor, 'Privacy, Publicity, and Reputation: How the Press Regulated the Market in Nineteenth-Century England', *Business History Review*, 87 (Winter 2013), pp. 679–701, at p. 684.

8   *The Observer*, 15 January 1821.

9   See, for example, *The Observer*, 30 December 1821. For more on the popularity of loans, see Frank Griffith Dawson, *The First Latin American Debt Crisis: The City of London and the 1822–25 Loan Bubble* (Yale University Press, 1990).

10   *Morning Chronicle*, 1 January 1822.

11   See, for example, *Morning Chronicle*, 11 September 1822.

12   See, for example, *Morning Chronicle*, 4 April, 18 June, 7 August 1822.

13   *The History of 'The Times'*, 5 vols (Kraus Reprints, 1935–84), p. ii, 542.

14   *The Times*, 17 January, 11 September 1820.

15   James Taylor, *Creating Capitalism: Joint-Stock Enterprise in British Politics and Culture, 1800–1870* (Boydell, 2006), pp. 106–8.

16   The Anglo-Mexican Mines and the United Mexican Mines were listed in February: *Morning Chronicle*, 17 February 1824.

17   Six company stocks were listed at the end of November: *Morning Chronicle*, 30 November 1824.

18   *Morning Chronicle*, 24 January 1825.

19   *Morning Chronicle*, 21 March 1825.

20   *Morning Post*, 3 November 1825; *The Times*, 12 November 1825.

21   For the commercial crash, see Boyd Hilton, *Corn, Cash, Commerce: The Economic Policies of the Tory Governments, 1815–1830* (Oxford University Press, 1977), ch. 7.

22   *The Times*, 17 December 1825.

23   *The Times*, 23 December 1825.

24   *Beit v. Lawson*, reported in *The Times*, 24 December 1828.

25   [James Grant], *The Great Metropolis*, 2 vols (Saunders and Otley, 1837), pp. ii, 24–5.

26   'Private History of the London Newspaper Press', *Tait's Edinburgh Magazine*, 1 (December 1834), pp. 788–92, at p. 790.

27   'The Morning and Evening Papers', *Fraser's Magazine*, 13 (May 1836), pp. 620–31, at pp. 620–1.

28   [David Morier Evans], *The City; Or, the Physiology of London Business; With Sketches on 'Change and at the Coffee Houses* (Baily Brothers, 1845), pp. 135, 129.

29   Evans, *The City*, p. 134.

30   R.W. Kostal, *Law and English Railway Capitalism, 1825–1875* (Oxford University Press, 1994), pp. 28–9.

31   Evans, *The City*, p. 96.

32   This tangled web is ably traced in John E.C. Palmer, 'Authority, Idiosyncrasy, and Corruption in the Early Railway Press, 1823–1844', *Journal of the Railway and Canal Historical Society*, 31 (July 1995), pp. 442–57.

33   Evans, *The City*, p. 95.

34   *The Era*, 15 December 1844.

35   Goulven Guilcher, 'The Press Mania During the Railway Mania, 1844–45', *Journal of the Railway and Canal Historical Society*, 35 (March 2005), pp. 26–33, at p. 30.

36   Guilcher, 'The Press Mania', p. 33.

37   *The Times*, 11 August 1845.

38   John Francis, *History of the Bank of England: Its Times and Traditions*, 2 vols (Willoughby and Co., 1847), pp. ii, 207–10.

39   The proprietor and one of the journalists of one new financial weekly, the *Joint-Stock Companies' Journal*, were imprisoned for libel in 1857 for false accusations against the Bank of London: Taylor, 'Privacy', p. 697.

40   'English Journalism', *Saturday Review*, 18 September 1858.

41   [John Morley], 'Manchester: Its Social Aspects', *Dublin University Magazine*, 57 (January 1861), pp. 76–85, at p. 77.

42 P, 'City Intelligence', *Temple Bar*, 11 (July 1864), pp. 491–500, at p. 500.

43 Taylor, *Creating Capitalism*, pp. 176–7.

44 *The Times*, 12 May 1866.

45 [Malcolm Meason], *The Profits of Panics: Showing How Financial Storms Arise, Who Make Money By Them, Who Are the Losers, and Other Revelations of a City Man* (Sampson Low, Son, and Marston, 1866), pp. 15–17.

46 H.J. Spencer, 'Christmas, Henry (1811–1868)', *Oxford Dictionary of National Biography*, (Oxford University Press, 2004) [www.oxforddnb.com/view/article/5372].

47 Henry Noel-Fearn, *The Money Market: What It Is, What It Does, and How It Is Managed* (Frederick Warne, 1866), pp. 157–8.

48 *The History of 'The Times'*, pp. ii, 595.

49 *The Times*, 27, 28, 29, 30 August 1872.

50 *The Times*, 18 November, 20, 21 December 1872.

51 J.H. Wilkins (ed.), *Asbury Harpending, The Great Diamond Hoax and Other Stirring Incidents in the Life of Asbury Harpending* (University of Oklahoma Press, 1958), pp. 183–8.

52 Wilkins, *Great Diamond Hoax*, pp. 193–5; *Daily News*, 22 December 1874.

53 *Rubery v. Grant and Sampson*, reported in *Daily News*, 22 December 1874, and 19 January 1875.

54 *The Times*, 19, 20 January 1875.

55 *Reynolds's Newspaper*, 24 January 1875.

56 *Twycross v. Grant*, reported in *Daily News*, 8, 13 July 1876.

57 *Reynolds's Newspaper*, 18 June 1876.

58 *Daily News*, 13 July 1876.

59 W, 'The Foreign Loans Committee', *Macmillan's Magazine*, 32 (May 1875), pp. 90–5, at p. 93.

60 *Liverpool Mercury*, 3 July 1876.

61 *The Times*, 28 January 1863.

62 *The Times*, 23 March 1866.

63 Herbert Sidebotham, 'Labouchere, Henry Du Pré (1831–1912)', rev. H.C.G. Matthew, *Oxford Dictionary of National Biography* (Oxford University Press, 2004); online edn, October 2009 [www.oxforddnb.com/view/article/34367].

64 Taylor, 'Privacy', p. 696.

65 Charles Duguid, *How to Read the Money Article* (Effingham Wilson, 1901), p. 102.

15

BOOM, CRISIS, BUST

Speculators, promoters, and City journalists, 1880–1914

James Nye

The years from 1880 to 1914 were the City of London's 'Golden Age'. They were also the heyday of the City company promoter, but many of their undertakings were distinctly fool's gold. The company promoter of the pre-Great War decades was an ancestor of the modern investment bank and also of the private equity business. He was the forerunner of the investment bank in the sense of being the nexus for the key elements in the appearance of a firm in the equity market – securing the services of the professionals needed (lawyers, accountants, brokers, printers – perhaps underwriters) and arranging the necessary publicity and marketing. He also anticipated the private equity model, through the operation of a sequential approach to the market, in which an initial 'syndicate' of investors, involving 'friends and family', allowed for an incubator or proof-of-concept stage, to be followed by later public flotation and the release of significant value to the early insiders. Put simply, before the Great War, firms were formed and floated by individual entrepreneurs and not by banks. There were hundreds, if not thousands, of such entrepreneur promoters, but their lasting reputation has largely been cemented by a handful of significant rogues who ended up in jail – characters whose column inches made them the Bernie Madoffs of their day.

Promoters and the press

A critically important factor in the development of such a poor reputation was the relationship between the promoter and the press. There was a significant symbiotic, incestuous, and Machiavellian relationship that developed between the two groups. A high point of this fell roughly in the period 1895–1900, coincident with a boom in the stock market, largely comprising a speculative bubble centred on South African gold-mining shares, and later Western Australian gold shares. The steep rise in the market is clearly visible in the graph shown in Figure 15.1.

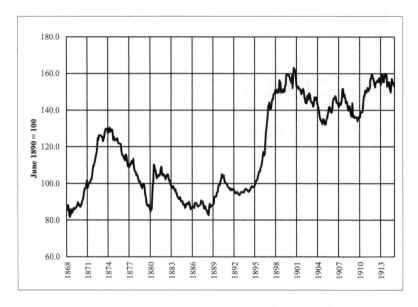

FIGURE 15.1 An equity index for the London stock market, 1868–1914

Source: Index recalculated from ~5,400 monthly prices for eleven industrial groups in K.C. Smith and G.F. Horne, 'An Index Number of Securities 1867–1914', Royal Economic Society Memorandum No. 47 (1934).

In the slightly wider context, the startling rise of the mid 1890s was prefigured by a mini-boom in the late 1880s. A feature of this was the run-up in romantic and exotic South African diamond stocks, which gave way to an early boom in South African gold shares, focused in Johannesburg but with a strong echo in London. However, things rapidly went horribly wrong for investors. It emerged that gold seams lay too deep to exploit with available technology and a collapse in shares in the extractive sector followed. This formed a prelude to another crisis, this time with its roots in Argentina. With a failed securities issue on its hands, Barings, long and wrong, nearly collapsed and had to be rescued in November 1890.

Did the press anticipate the Barings crash? By late 1890, the market had been talking about the huge problems of Argentina for months. Press comment suggests there was a widespread feeling that an unsustainable situation had emerged. The Argentinian government was greatly overextended with a debt burden it could not service. It appears that everyone could see this, yet the prevailing sentiment in the press was that more debt would be the answer, or at least a rearrangement of debt to manage maturities better. This was a common theme in the more recent financial crisis.

The finance minister of Argentina, Dr de la Plaza, was in London in the run-up to the Barings crisis. Everyone knew of his visit, and the press reported and speculated on his mission. It was well understood that he would be meeting Barings. But editorial comments seem to suggest that somehow the cracks would be papered over. Except perhaps in *The Standard*, where the paper had been talking down Argentina for weeks – 'If the financiers cannot themselves keep Argentine credit on its feet, it must tumble down, that is all' – failing, of course, to mention there might be wider consequences, close to home, in the City itself.[1] A fascinating research project, though perhaps difficult to undertake, would be to hunt for evidence of any prominent individual's personal dealings in Argentine securities in the days before the Barings crisis.

On Saturday, 8 November, when Lord Revelstoke, Barings' senior partner, finally faced up to facts and went to the Bank of England to confess all and to admit the dire straits in which Barings found itself, *The Economist* was still talking about the scope of Dr de la Plaza's plans for rearranging Argentina's finances, so an allied and intriguing question for future research would be to determine how much leakage there was and when – how much inside information there was flowing around in the few weeks prior to 15 November, when the rescue package was revealed. There is room to suspect a certain amount. *The Times* on Saturday, 15 November, reported: 'It is certain that all members of the "House" have been doing their best for some time so as to be prepared for any possible emergency'.[2]

On one view, this might be a hint that insider dealing had been going on all week – possibly longer. But while there may have been trading in the City designed to mitigate or even profit from whatever disaster the parlous state of Argentine finances might induce, press coverage by and large seems to have imagined that salvation was a question of keeping calm and carrying on, or at least muddling through.

Companies and IPOs

Although such stories are fascinating, in this chapter I want to turn the spotlight away from the world of fixed income *haute finance*, and towards the murkier world of equities. From the Barings crisis onwards, the press had to endure a lean few years in covering financial markets. Prior to explosive rises in the stock market from late 1894, the period 1890 to late 1894 was moribund, as can be seen in Figure 15.1. Interest rates were falling. Bank deposits and savings in general were on the increase. Confidence in Latin America had been dented significantly, South African gold stocks had collapsed, and there were foreign banking crises, such as in Australia. All of this contributed to mean that substantial liquidity was chasing a small universe of investments – a familiar pattern. It was a regular comment in the *Investor's Monthly Manual* during the period that there was nothing in which to invest. With investment horizons limited in both geography and period, overall confidence was low. This was reflected in more than a lacklustre stock market – it was visible in the slackening off in the number of UK company formations, shown in Figure 15.2.

Over the long term, and certainly if the graph in Figure 15.2 is extended well into the twentieth century, there is a clearly visible general rise in the annual rate of company formation. But the early 1890s stand out as a quiet period – indeed a downturn. This is echoed in another observation of market activity – the number of initial public offerings and other equity placements involving the public, shown in Figure 15.3.

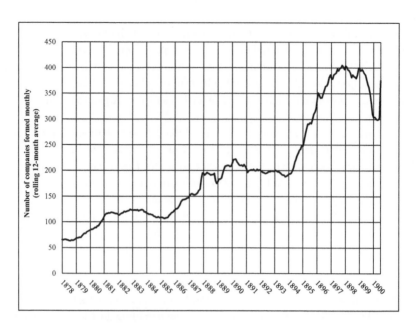

FIGURE 15.2 Number of companies formed in England and Wales, 1878–1900
Source: Returns Relating to Joint Stock Companies.

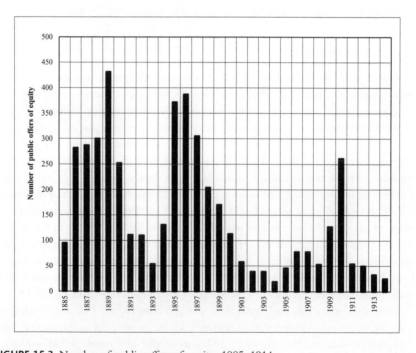

FIGURE 15.3 Number of public offers of equity, 1885–1914
Source: Annual statistics published by Spackman & Sons, stockbrokers, in *The Times* (1885–93, 1895), and *The Times*'s own statistical surveys in all other years. The data was derived by cross-referencing records of public issues of equity with records of company formations in the corresponding year.

In the City, this lack of equity new issuance and company formation activity was not good for the professions, and it was not good for the press. Newspapers benefited in many ways from new issuance activity. Advertising revenues naturally swing with confidence levels and underlying activity, while in terms of simple sales it is harder to raise revenues for a newspaper in quiet periods and hard to sell as many copies.

Two major newspapers that had started in the 1880s and that had to weather the moribund markets in the wake of the Barings crisis were the *Financial News* and the *Financial Times*. Each had strong characters at their helms. Harry Marks at the *Financial News* was a rogue, without doubt, and has been covered in detail by David Kynaston and Dilwyn Porter.[3] Douglas MacRae at the *Financial Times* is intriguing because part of his story is told through the pen of Henry Osborne O'Hagan, a larger-than-life character – actually a very large character altogether – generally judged on the strength of his two-volume autobiography to have been a reasonably good egg, or, put another way, among promoters he is seen as being at the least bad end of the scale. He reports keeping MacRae afloat with funds during the doldrums of the early 1890s, as well as sorting out journalistic spats with Marks at the *Financial News*.[4]

However, having spent some time shining a little light into a few dark corners of O'Hagan's life, I see his relationship with MacRae and Marks as significantly less philanthropic than O'Hagan paints it.[5] With the Leveson Inquiry we encountered the unusual phenomenon of Steve Coogan's publicist, who is apparently paid not for securing publicity, but instead for preventing it. The gist of Coogan's evidence to the Inquiry on this point was that he would prefer to stay out of the press altogether, on the basis that it is arguably better to avoid negative stories surfacing, even if this means forgoing positive ones appearing. O'Hagan would have been sympathetic. He much preferred not to appear, and he had some clear enemies in the press – Frank Harris at the *Saturday Review* and William Thomas Stead (the controversial editor of the *Pall Mall Gazette*) to name just two. Thus we can see O'Hagan's long-term support for MacRae as being largely self-serving. He also managed to keep Marks on side, and therefore remained out of both the *Financial News* and *Financial Times*.

Press and promoter symbiosis

I made the claim at the outset that there was a symbiosis between the promoters and the journalists – that each needed the other. At the simplest level, the promoter would need to advertise in the newspapers, which provided some low-level remuneration for the newspaper – of the order of 1s 6d per line. But a promoter would ideally wish for positive press coverage of his issue in some editorial comment. This will have cost a lot more than 1s 6d per line, and in order to grease the wheels, promoters developed a range of techniques for compensating journalists. They might offer them cash of course, keeping things simple, but more often than not the promoter did not have any cash to use up front – everything was done on a shoestring, with treasure being stored up for heaven, or at least being released only at the conclusion of a transaction. A promoter might therefore typically offer a tame journalist shares in the enterprise to be floated. Or even options.

The particular journalists that specialized in this field – not the best exemplars of their trade – came to depend upon their promoters. Think of the tick-bird on the rhinoceros. Or better still think of the pilotfish that can swim around the mouth of the shark, cleaning its teeth for food. Sharks are a useful reminder of an excellent 1904 novel, of that title, by Guy Thorne, in which the invidious practices of the parasitical gutter financial press find full expression. The picture painted is all very Dickensian, at first glance. Consider the visit by Mr Grady of the *Investor's Ferret* to the office of Slygne the promoter:

> Strongly inclined to be friendly with Mr Slygne [Grady hopes for] a year's subscription amounting to, say, £500. [Should this not be forthcoming] the *Ferret* would be reluctantly compelled to withhold its friendship from Mr Slygne and Mr Slygne's companies.[6]

This is all very well, you may say – this is fiction. What of real life? Such fictional accounts have strong roots in fact. In 1899, one of the novels judged to be among the best of the year was *The Market-Place*, by Harold Frederic. A distinguished stringer for the *New York Times*, working from London and a friend of all the key financial journalists as well as being acquainted with some colourful promoters, Frederic paints what I believe to be an accurate picture of the sordid relationship between press and promoter, drawing together, perhaps best of all such books, the variety of elements of the relationship that can be gleaned from numerous real-life court hearings, bankruptcy procedures, press reports, and the like. Contemporary reviewers went overboard in describing how true to life Frederic's account was. His anti-hero describes dealing with the press:

> There was one editor I had to square personally – that is to say, £100 cash (it had to be in sovereigns, for notes could be traced) and a call of 2,000 shares at par ... and, of course, there were odd ten-pound notes here and there; but as a rule, I just opened the door and fired the blackmailers out.[7]

This last reference leads us to another larger-than-life figure, known to Frederic, in the person of Ernest Terah Hooley, who went spectacularly bankrupt in 1898 – the first of four bankruptcies – all recounted in the refreshingly disarming auto-biography published in the 1920s in which he admits to significant sharp practice. At the height of his powers in around 1896–7, he operated a suite of rooms at the Midland Grand Hotel from which he ran his business:

> There was a financial paper ... which printed articles concerning my numerous companies. They never saw the light of day, for the simple reason that one of the people connected with the paper would come along to the Midland Grand and get £500 for suppressing the article.[8]

Recall that £500 is roughly £40,000–50,000 in 2015 terms – rather than firing the blackmailers out, as Frederic's character claimed he did, Hooley chose to settle. The proceedings of his bankruptcy in 1898 are littered with significantly more detail of his corrupt relationship with the press. And it is clear that this was merely the tip of an iceberg – *così fan tutte*. If there was a regular market going on in which payments for suppressing articles occurred, or payments for puffing a stock occurred, so there was room for the inevitable further intermediary – this is the City after all – and thus we have the advertising agent.

> The moment a fellow came in, and handed me his card, and said he had proofs of two kinds of articles in his pocket – one praising me, one damning me – I told him to go and see my advertising agent.[9]

In Headon Hill's *Guilty Gold* we learn from Daniels, again the advertising agent, about the scheme operated by the editor of the *Financial Lynx* and the tariff involved in paying off the press:

> An order for one insertion only secures you from attack during the first three days, while two insertions secure you for a month. But if you want complete immunity he insists on a present of at least fifty vendor's shares, as well as having the advertisement in three issues of his paper.[10]

Earlier we commented on the 1s 6d to 2s it cost per line to advertise. A typical prospectus in the major broadsheet newspapers used about 300 lines so the total cost was between £20 and £30. But this was a mere bagatelle by contrast with the sums that could become involved in a large IPO. In 1899, one of the major flotations was for the Linotype company, with a value of approximately £1 million. Events surrounding the launch led to a court case, and among the evidence heard on that occasion some interesting facts emerged from the advertising agent:

> Mr Horncastle, advertising contractor, gave evidence to the effect that £11,000 had been paid through him for advertising the company. He had frequently joined syndicates for promoting companies on the understanding that the advertising went through his agency.[11]

Such a sum was colossal. It is not difficult to find further evidence that untraceable sums of money floated around in support of the advertisement of new issues. Witness Harry Marks's uncomfortable admissions when he took the witness stand in a libel trial, as the plaintiff, in 1890 – a story to which we will return:

> He had received money only as advertisements from promoters, but had never received any money directly from promoters. ('Oh, oh.') Mr Marks afterwards explained that sums of money from advertising agents would be

paid at the office of the *Financial News* without his knowledge. He had nothing to do with the business matters of the paper, as the money received would be paid to the cashier.[12]

Rise and demise of financial newspapers

We made mention earlier of the notion of symbiosis. There is another image that comes to mind, and that is of the 'feeding frenzy'. Hot markets attract attention. In tandem with this, the observation was made from early on, by commentators such as David Morier Evans, that the company promotion sector attracted a degree of City low life. In the press, well below the dignified keels of *The Times*, *Economist*, and the *Financial Times*, large numbers of bottom feeders emerged. The second-hand evidence of the ubiquity of tip sheets is that contemporary authors of City fiction introduced publications such as the *Investor's Ferret* and the *Financial Lynx* as stock items, aping the reality of well-known real-life examples such as Hess's *The Critic* or Hooley's *Rialto*, or even Bottomley's *Joint Stock Circular*. But to date there appears to have been no systematic survey of the tip sheets or financial rags to determine their numbers or lifetimes.

The catalogue of the British Library provides a proxy for such publications. There are significant flaws in the methodology, but given that I was looking at newspapers I was comforted by Kelvin MacKenzie's description of an editor – someone paid to separate the wheat from the chaff, and then to make sure the chaff is printed.

The goal was to determine if there was any obvious link between City activity and the emergence of financial newspapers. For example, did a rising stock market go hand in hand with more newspapers emerging? And, vice versa, were bear markets associated with a decline in financial titles? The British Library catalogue seemed to offer the most comprehensive and relevant possible collection. It will not contain everything, and for any given newspaper there may be gaps in its holdings, but it is reasonable to suppose that any gaps are broadly distributed across its holdings. To the extent the catalogue might reveal trends, these should be interesting indicators, without being definitive.

I searched the catalogue using a variety of standard terms, such as 'financial', 'stock', 'share*', 'city', and so forth. In a series of iterations, titles would in turn suggest new search terms, and new search terms would yield yet more titles. After a day's searching and reaching a distinct degree of diminishing returns, I had arrived at a list of 89 financial newspapers that were launched and published between 1879 and 1915 (36 years). Of these, just three (including the *Financial News*) were launched between 1879 and 1885. Some names were repeated within the overall list, since there were separate establishments and failures over time under the same banner. The complete list of titles I devised can be viewed at: http://synchronome.org.uk/boombust.pdf. The first and most simple question to address was whether any correlation could be seen between the market cycle and the establishment or failure of a new financial newspaper, or tip sheet, or rag, or organ of puffery.

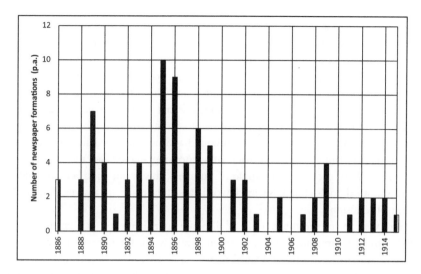

FIGURE 15.4 Number of financial newspapers launched, 1886–1915
Source: Survey of the British Library catalogue.

A simple observation is that new financial papers seem to have been formed more commonly when the market was hot. But how long were their publishing runs? Figure 15.5 uses the date runs for each title, drawn from the catalogue, to graph the lives of the same group of newspapers.

In this we can see that the raw catalogue data for publishing runs suggests that 43 per cent failed in the first year. A further 24 per cent did not make it beyond two

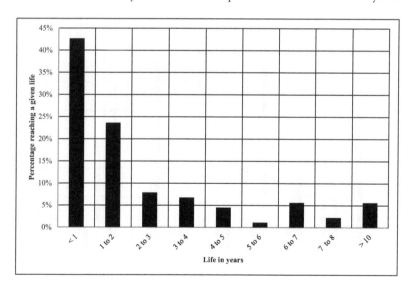

FIGURE 15.5 Lifetimes of financial newspapers launched, 1886–1915
Source: Survey of the British Library catalogue. For ease of calculation, there is a degree of rounding in the underlying data, to the nearest year.

years, and thus in aggregate 67 per cent of all the new financial newspapers in this study did not last more than two years. The failure rate then tails off, but clearly the majority of new financial papers in the period were not long-lived. Just five newspapers survived more than 10 years. Apart from the most obvious two, the other distance runners were *Financial Truth* and the *City Leader and Shareholders' Guardian* (~15 years) and the *Investors' Chronicle and Journal of Finance* (~25 years).

This first analysis led to a consideration of whether there might be any correlation between when a newspaper was founded and how long it lasted. For example, did the papers launched on the back of a booming market last the least time, or vice versa? With such a small sample of numbers, this is not the place for sophisticated statistical tools, but it seemed worth an attempt at an answer. Figure 15.6 offers some insight.

Here we can see the median life of all newspapers launched in a given year. For 1894, this was surprisingly long, at seven years, while for papers launched in the financial doldrums immediately before this, and then also during the enormous boom of 1895–9, the prognosis was much less favourable, with a median life of just one or two years. The year 1903 also stands out and invites further attention.

The survey described above and the graphic results drawn from it are necessarily crude. However, they show that there was likely a marked variation in the outcomes for newspapers launched at different times of the financial cycle, and indeed that the financial cycle itself might be an important component in the decision for a financial newspaper to be launched. Perhaps the data suggests a sufficiently interesting picture for someone to pick up the baton and to conduct a more rigorous survey, allied to more detailed analysis of individual newspapers, the editors,

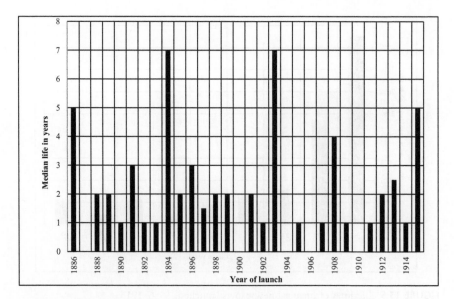

FIGURE 15.6 Median newspaper life by year of launch, 1886–1915
Source: British Library catalogue.

and the true backers – further teasing out and uncovering the tight bonds that appear to exist between the financiers and the journalists. It is also the case that I have ignored entirely issues such as circulation, how such newspapers were financed, and how and where they were sold, and these questions all merit further attention.

Each newspaper likely has some particular backstory of its own. In the list I compiled, there were several eye-catching titles, such as the *City Lantern*, or *Financial Truth*, which are clearly designed to convey an image of searching inquiry into the dark recesses of the markets, but one stood out – the *Financial Monitor and Lion's Mouth*. I had no previous knowledge of it and on a whim, to test the rather negative assessment of the genre I had formed, I decided to enquire more deeply. The results provide an amusing coda for this chapter.

I was attracted to the *Financial Monitor and Lion's Mouth* by its name alone – there was no other selection criterion. Its print run appears to have been from November 1889 to May 1890. Say five or so months. Its purpose and short life are bound up in the typical chicanery of promoter and pressman. Harry Marks of the *Financial News* was mentioned above as being something of a rogue. He suffered a lot of negative press coverage around 1889–90 for having been the hidden promoter behind a number of stock market flotations where investors lost their shirts, in particular in the Rae (Transvaal) Gold Mining Company – a few years later Henry Hess notably placed Marks in the pillory via a pamphlet entitled *Half-Forgotten Frauds*.[13] But of course Marks was usually on the giving not the receiving end of such attacks. He sold himself as the investors' guardian and was constantly exposing similar promotional frauds. One of his targets was Arthur Burr, a promoter and serial bankrupt (not an uncommon combination). Burr took great exception to his treatment by the *Financial News* in 1889 and summoned Marks for libel. The reporting of this case in September 1889 vindicates Steve Coogan's proposition that all publicity is to be avoided – *The Mercury* described Burr, despite being the plaintiff, as having 'elastic ideas of his obligations to investors', indeed

> he was obliged to admit that he might have been charged forty times with fraud, though of course the charges were always unfounded. He confessed to a number of transactions which the most amiable moralist would be forced to call 'shady' and whether he had committed fraud or not, he has had the misfortune to sow injurious suspicions in the minds of a good many people.[14]

A couple of months later, the *Financial Monitor and Lion's Mouth* was launched. From evidence given in a later libel trial, there is at least a suggestion it was a vehicle of Arthur Burr.[15] One might therefore expect it to carry puffery for his own promotions, but he also used it to take potshots at Harry Marks, raking up stories about Rae (Transvaal) Gold Mining Company, several years before Hess, and presumably in revenge for his recent embarrassments, both in the *Financial News* and in court. Thus we can see both Marks and Burr using their respective papers to promote their chosen new issues, but at the same time doing their utmost with knocking copy to destroy competition from the market. Like Holmes and

Moriarty, locked in combat, tumbling to their supposed doom at the Reichenbach Falls, Burr and Marks continually locked horns in the libel courts, seemingly indifferent to the harm it did each of their reputations as plaintiff to end up hearing the defendant plead justification with its attendant and highly detailed disclosure – disclosure usually accompanied by editorial insertions of ('laughter'). They failed to absorb a lesson that O'Hagan learned early in life through being caught up in a court case, that any sort of publicity can end up being a bad thing.

Such stories are not uncommon. They reveal a world in which an expected separation between the City and the press fades into grey – there is a close identity between the two. Editors are hidden promoters. Promoters become newspaper proprietors and form their own titles to further their financial goals. Wholesale bribery in one form or another is rife. The phenomenon of knocking copy allows for an arms race towards mutually assured destruction. Collectively the press/promoter combine did not talk itself up, it talked itself down, helping to cement a negative reputation, amply shored up by the headline-grabbing trials of the most egregious fraudsters – Bottomley, Wright, Hooley, and so on. An intriguing conclusion is that while we normally see a clear boundary between fiction and journalism, the new financial titles in the City of the 1890s suggest such a distinction could not so easily be drawn.

Notes

1 *The Standard* (6 November 1890), p. 6.
2 *The Times* (Saturday, 15 November 1890), p. 13.
3 David Kynaston, *The 'Financial Times': A Centenary History* (London: Viking, 1988), pp. 22–6, 28–30, 39; Dilwyn Porter, '"A Trusted Guide of the Investing Public": Harry Marks and the *Financial News* 1884–1916', in *Speculators and Patriots: Essays in Business Biography*, ed. R.P.T. Davenport-Hines (London: Frank Cass, 1986), pp. 1–17.
4 H. Osborne O'Hagan, *Leaves from My Life, Vol. I* (London: Bodley Head, 1929), pp. 103–11.
5 James Nye, 'The Company Promoter in London: 1877–1914' (unpublished PhD thesis, King's College London, 2011), pp. 307–63.
6 Guy Thorne, *Sharks* (London: Greening, 1904), p. 194. The suggested subscription would amount to £40,000–50,000 in 2010 terms, using an RPI adjustment.
7 Harold Frederic, *The Market-Place* (London: Heinemann, 1899), pp. 28–9.
8 Ernest Terah Hooley, *Hooley's Confessions* (London: Simpkin, Marshall, Hamilton, Kent, 1925), p. 161.
9 Frederic, *The Market-Place*, pp. 28–9.
10 Headon Hill, *Guilty Gold: A Romance of Financial Fraud and City Crime* (London: Pearson, 1896), p. 39.
11 *The Times* (23 August 1889), p. 11 for the report of the trial of Augustus Martin Moore, editor of *The Hawk*, in which he had made disobliging remarks about the promotion. See also *Financial Times* (23 August 1889), p. 2.
12 *The Echo* (15 December 1890), p. 3.
13 Henry Hess, *Half-Forgotten Frauds: Being the First Series of Some Articles Exposing the Promotion, Flotation, and Management of Twelve Fraudulent Joint-Stock Companies* (London: British & Colonial Publications, 1900). See also Porter, 'A Trusted Guide', p. 9.
14 *The Mercury* (14 September 1889), p. 3.
15 *The Times* (16 December 1890), p. 4. The same trial is covered in detail in *Old Bailey Proceedings Online*.

16

'RUN ON THE BANK'

Covering the 1914 financial crisis

Richard Roberts

In summer 1914, as it became clear that a European war was on the cards, London, the world's foremost international financial centre, experienced its most acute financial crisis.[1] Its financial markets suffered a comprehensive breakdown; the London Stock Exchange shut and stayed shut for five months. It was feared that a run on the banks had begun, threatening the country's payments and credit mechanisms – and all as Britain teetered on the verge of war, and then plunged into the Armageddon. But the crisis was successfully contained and the markets fitfully revived; in the process, the function of the City was transformed from the finance of global trade and development to the provision of Allied war finance. What roles did the financial press and financial journalists play in this extreme financial crisis?

Financial press in 1914

Readers seeking financial news were well served in 1914. The 'Finance and Investment' section of *May's British and Irish Press Guide* listed 109 titles: up from 19 in 1874, 32 in 1884, 50 in 1894, and 92 in 1904.[2] There were two 'great financial dailies', the *Financial Times* and the *Financial News*, as well as the *Financier and Bullionist*.[3] 'The average reader would be amazed to learn of the variety of expert knowledge represented by the staff of a financial daily,' stated Henry Simonis, newspaper director, columnist in *Newspaper World*, and author of *The Street of Ink* (1917), an account of Fleet Street.[4] The foremost financial and business weeklies were *The Economist* and *The Statist*.[5] There were 11 London-based nationally distributed morning newspapers, and eight national Sunday papers.[6] There were also six London evening papers.[7] These publications comprised 15 'serious' titles with combined circulations of 1 million; and 15 'popular' or illustrated titles with aggregate sales of 9.7 million (Table 16.1). All the serious titles contained significant financial

TABLE 16.1 The UK financial press in 1914

	Newspaper style	Circulation	Price (pence)	Politics	Editor‡/ City editor
Financial daily press					
Financial News	Serious	20,000	1	Con	Ellis T. Powell‡
Financial Times	Serious	15,000	1	Ind	C.H. Palmer‡
Financier and Bullionist	Serious	5,000★	1	?	?
Total circulation		40,000			
Financial weeklies					
The Economist	Serious	4,500	8	Lib	F.W. (Francis Wrigley) Hirst‡
The Statist	Serious	4,500	6	Lib	Sir George Paish‡
Total circulation		9,000			
London morning press					
The Times	Serious	150,000	1	Con	Hugh Chisholm
Daily Telegraph	Serious	190,000	1	Con	C.A.R. (Charles Arthur Reeve)
Morning Post	Serious	80,000	1	Con	E.H.Y. (Edward Hilton Young)
The Standard	Serious	80,000	1	Con	Arthur Kiddy
Daily Express	Popular	300,000	0.5	Con	?
Daily Mail	Popular	950,000	0.5	Con	Charles Duguid
Daily Chronicle	Popular	400,000	0.5	Lib	?
Daily News	Popular	550,000	0.5	Lib	?
Daily Graphic	Illustrated	60,000	1	?	?
Daily Mirror	Illustrated	1,000,000	0.5	Con	?
Daily Sketch	Illustrated	800,000	0.5	?	?
Total circulation		4,560,000			
London evening press					
Pall Mall Gazette	Serious	10,000	1	Con	?
The Globe	Serious	20,000	1	Con	Herbert H. Bassett
Westminster Gazette	Serious	20,000	1	Lib	?
Evening Standard	Popular	180,000	1	Con	?
Evening News	Popular	600,000	0.5	Con	?
The Star	Popular	500,000	0.5	Lib	?
Total circulation		1,330,000			
Sunday papers					
The Observer	Serious	175,000	1	Con	C.H.T. (Charles Herbert Thorpe)
Sunday Times	Serious	35,000	1	Con	Cornhill Magpie (Hermann Schmidt)
Daily Telegraph	Serious	190,000	1	Con	?
The People	Popular	550,000	1	Con	?
Weekly Dispatch	Popular	500,000	1	Con	?

TABLE 16.1 (continued)

	Newspaper style	Circulation	Price (pence)	Politics	Editor‡/ City editor
Lloyd's Weekly News	Popular	1,250,000	1	Lib	?
News of the World	Popular	1,500,000	1	Lib	?
Reynold's News	Popular	600,000	1	Lib	?
Total circulation		*4,800,000*			

Provincial newspapers with a City office
Daily Dispatch (Manchester)
Daily Sketch
Glasgow Herald
Yorkshire Post
* estimate;
? City editor unknown

Sources: McEwen (1982); individual newspaper histories; *Post Office London Directory 1914*; individual newspapers.

coverage, while the popular titles mostly featured a chatty daily 'money article'.[8] 'Somewhat to my surprise,' recalled T.P. O'Connor, founder editor of *The Star*, 'my City article was one of the most popular features of the paper.'[9] This London popular evening paper, started in 1888, was described by Simonis as 'the original home from which sprang the modern powerful daily Press'.[10]

Financial matters in the daily and Sunday press were covered by a specialist City editor often based at a separate City office near the Stock Exchange. Four provincial papers had City offices, while the London offices of most of the others were in nearby Fleet Street.[11] Investors were served by the weekly *Investors' Chronicle* and *Investors' Review*, as well as numerous less substantial titles; bankers were served by *Bankers' Magazine*; and various highbrow weeklies regularly featured financial articles, including *The Citizen*, *The Critic*, *The Nation*, *The Rialto*, *The Round Table*, *Truth*, and *The World*.

Charles Duguid, the doyen of popular City editors, started at *The Economist* and then became City editor of the *Pall Mall Gazette* (1893–7), *Westminster Gazette* (1897–1902), *Morning Post* (1902–6), and *Daily Mail* (1906–20). He was author of the bestselling *How to Read the Money Article* (1901) in which he related the development of financial journalism from its origin around 1825 (see Chapter 14). The 'older form' of money article comprised 'a mere statement of how prices had moved … the bare record, very seldom indulging in any outspoken comment or venturing any opinion'.[12] A 'new financial journalism', based on American practice, was introduced with the launch of the *Financial News* in 1884, and was subsequently imitated by other newspapers.[13] Simonis recounted that:

> Up to the time of the appearance of the *Financial News* the City articles in newspapers consisted in the main of dry and colourless reviews of price

movements. This newspaper sought to enliven the City article by a graceful literary touch, as well as by freedom of criticism and humour of treatment. It was, therefore, a novelty in more ways than one, and set a fashion which achieved popularity in the Press.[14]

'The modern financial journalism with its policy of brightness for the weary, and by way of enlightenment for the bewildered, has rapidly made progress against staid dull formalities,' observed Duguid in 1909; it 'calls to aid some literary style, some incisive criticism, the interview, the attractive headline, even the quip and crank'.[15] In 1914 the *Financial News* was also published daily in Paris, in French, and had offices in New York, Brussels, and Mexico City. Simonis commented approvingly that the paper made a practice of giving 'the younger members of its staff a course in journalism in other centres of financial activity besides London'.[16]

The *Daily Chronicle*, an early adopter of the new financial journalism among the general press, made 'an obvious attempt to make its money article attractive as well as solid' and its reviews of company prospectuses 'by no means colourless'. Its City editor, A.J. Wilson, the 'leading financial journalist of the day' according to Duguid, pioneered the signed financial article. Lecturing at the Institute of Bankers in 1913 on 'The Daily Money Article', Duguid observed that: 'The growth of public interest in things financial was one of the features of the age. Finance had become democratic and the newspapers reflected the remarkable development.'[17] The new financial journalism met the requirements of the 'modern investing public' who, stated *The Economist* the same year, 'required of the financial newspaper something more than the market report' and 'cry out for criticism and advice, which only the expert skilled in finance and accounting methods can supply … But, unfortunately, advice often degenerates into tips, and the door is open to suspicious practices of all kinds.'[18]

'He began his career of editor at a time when financial journalism was growing in popularity, and old methods were giving way at the advent of a newer "snappier" school of writers,' stated an obituary in 1913 of Edward Johnstone, editor of *The Economist* from 1883 to 1907, the era of the advent of the new financial journalism and the heyday of the company promoter:

> The great development of the Stock Exchange and the enormous increase in the number of joint-stock companies led inevitably to the demand for other types of journalism; and there was a danger that the English press might become shallow and subservient to outside interests – the mouthpiece of financial interests and share-pushers, the enemy, instead of the friend, of the investing classes.
>
> To some extent journalism was contaminated by this touch of the company promoter, but as we look back over the history of the last 30 years we can fairly say (on comparing it with other systems) that the English financial Press might have fallen much further.
>
> We do not wish to overrate in this matter the power of one man, but those financial writers who knew him will, we think, agree that Mr Johnstone,

simply by the force of his example exercised a very wholesome and restraining influence on the development of this form of modern journalism ...

In the whole of his career he never criticized a venture without giving the ground of his objections, never gave a blind 'tip,' or permitted the insertion of a puff. Business could come and go – he never allowed considerations of additional income to sway the opinions of the paper. He stood, if we may say so, for the only sound type of financial journalism.[19]

Professionalism, integrity, and access

While the informed commentary of the new financial journalism was plainly superior to the 'staid dull formalities' of the traditional money article, the opportunity for abuse was a problem (see Chapter 15). Duguid's solution, argues Dilwyn Porter, was adherence by financial journalists to a professional code of practice.[20] He laid out his vision of professionalism and integrity in 'The City Editor', an article in the *Journal of Finance* in June 1897.[21] The ideal City editor was 'assiduous in collecting his financial facts. Level-headed in appraising them, precise in arraying them.'[22] He should express 'a definite opinion on his facts', which should be delivered with 'honesty and rectitude'. Duguid was praised by Henry Hess, a fellow City journalist, for having 'set before the brotherhood of which he is a leading member, a code of honour, a list of qualities, a set of ideals, to comprehend the whole of which would have been impossible under the old regime'.[23]

Duguid's manifesto marked publicly the beginning of a deliberate distancing of a set of leading financial journalists from the tipsters. He mentioned the recent quiet formation of an informal association of City editors who 'practise integrity in financial comment'.[24] An annual City Financial Writers' Dinner was inaugurated in April 1906 at Simpson's Restaurant in the Strand. A.J. Wilson was in the chair and guest of honour was Hartley Withers, City editor of *The Times* (1905–10), in recognition of his 'yeoman service' in securing earlier distribution to the press of the Stock Exchange Official List.[25] The following year some 40 financial writers marked Wilson's retirement from 'the arduous work of daily journalism' with Withers in the chair.[26] Other regular participants included Charles Duguid, Francis Hirst of *The Economist* (1907–16), Arthur Kiddy of *The Standard* (1900–15) who was also editor of the monthly *Bankers' Magazine* (for 50 years), Ellis Powell of the *Financial News* (1909–20), and Edward Hilton Young of the *Morning Post* (1910–14). It was Duguid's turn to be honoured at what proved to be the last City Financial Writers' Dinner in February 1914 with Wynnard Hooper, City editor of *The Times* (1910–14), proposing the toast. 'Financial journalism was never more respected than it is at the present time,' Duguid told the company. 'It was never more useful, it was never more pure. It was never more powerful.'[27] Simonis, writing in 1917, related that *Financial Times* editor C.H. Palmer had told him that 'some time ago an eminent judge was so impressed with the temptations to which financial writers were exposed that he expressed surprise that any of them should die poor. Those who did so, he said, deserved to have their names inscribed in letters of brass. It is to the honour of our financial journalism that those who do not qualify for the brass inscription are the exceptions from the rule.'[28]

The Financial Writers' Dinner set of City editors were the foremost financial and economic commentators of the day; some academic economists were influential, notably Keynes, but they were few in number and wrote only occasionally. A number of City editors moved between the press and the City, for instance Withers, who at the outbreak of the war was a partner in merchant bank Seligman Brothers, W.R. Lawson, editor of the *Financial Times* (1890–92),[29] who made a fortune as a stockbroker, and John Geard, City editor of *The Star* (1892–1909), who also joined the Stock Exchange. City editors were the foremost authors of books about finance for general and specialist readers, for instance Ellis Powell's *The Mechanism of the City* (1910) and Hilton Young's *The System of National Finance* (1915).[30] Withers and Lawson were prolific authors and both wrote vivid accounts of the 1914 financial crisis that were published in 1915.[31]

The professional standards of the upper echelon of financial journalists helped them achieve greater access to important City firms and the Bank of England. Sir Thomas Skinner, a veteran City editor, told the Financial Writers' Dinner of 1912 that early in his career only the City editor of *The Times* was 'recognised in high financial circles' and other City editors 'had to go to him to ascertain the gold movements in and out of the Bank of England and the result of the India Council Bill'.[32] Half a century later the Bank was still far from accommodating: 'We make it a serious rule here,' blustered Governor Walter Cunliffe (1913–18), 'never to either confirm or deny any of the very many reports that appear in the "Press" or elsewhere regarding the Bank of England.'[33] 'In getting news the City editor's chief difficulty,' wrote Withers reflectively in 1910:

> lies in the mystery with which most of the people who do the real work of the City like to veil their operations merely, I believe, because of the good old English prejudice in favour of privacy and the Englishman's love for putting up a big wall round himself, with 'Trespassers will be Prosecuted' writ large all over it. This prejudice the City journalist has to do his best to surmount in the interests of his work as a news-getter ...
>
> Still more delicate, in some respects, is the business of getting views, not only concerning the prospects of markets and the state of businesses, but at any time when some questions of policy in Threadneedle-street [Bank of England], or Lombard-street [discount market], or Capel-court [Stock Exchange] has to be discussed and made clear ...
>
> If his task of getting news and views is complicated by the personalities of those whom it is his daily business to see in search of them, this personal connection is, on the other hand, very pleasant ... and subjects him to a constant supply of good-natured criticism, which delights in detecting blunders, and keeps him up to his collar with most wholesome effect. More than any other kind of journalist, except, perhaps, the Parliamentary lobbyist, the

City editor lives in daily touch with an important part of his audience, and this is a most bracing attribute of his task.[34]

From 1909 Sir George Paish, editor of *The Statist* (1900–16), acted as outside economic adviser to the Chancellor, David Lloyd George. A prototypical special adviser, Paish was knighted for his services in 1912.[35] Guest of honour at the City Financial Writers' Dinner of March 1913, he was described by the chairman, Kiddy, as having worked his way up from the foot of the ladder to the highest distinction yet conferred on a financial journalist.[36] At the onset of the 1914 financial crisis, Paish was seconded to the Treasury as full-time adviser to the Chancellor. Fellow City editors were delighted. 'Financial journalism is honoured by his appointment,' wrote Kiddy in *The Standard*, while the *Financial Times* declared that:

> in selecting one of the editors of the 'Statist' for the important post of economic advisor the Treasury has conferred a signal honour upon the entire corps of financial journalists, and has recognized the ability and integrity with which this branch of a great profession is conducted.[37]

Financial crisis (1): breakdown

The financial markets were 'not ruffled' by the assassination of Austrian Archduke Franz Ferdinand in Sarajevo on 28 June.[38] After all there had been Balkan crises in each of the previous three summers and all had been defused. But market perceptions of the risk of war were transformed by Austria's 'stern' ultimatum to Serbia on the evening of Thursday, 23 July.[39] There was an international scramble for liquidity – meaning the dumping of assets and the withdrawal of credit. Continental bourses crashed and there were runs on savings banks that were reported in the British press. In London, the world's foremost financial centre, the foreign exchange and money markets broke down early in the week beginning Monday, 27 July, and stock prices slumped. Press reporting of these unprecedented developments was very numerical and very repetitive, and confined to the financial pages with plentiful mentions of depressed prices and dejected markets but no suggestion of a financial crisis. But depressed share prices were hardly front-page material in days when the European powers teetered on the brink of war.

'My own part in this story began on the last Wednesday of July [29th],' Paish related in his unpublished memoirs:

> As Editor of 'The Statist' part of my duties was to write an article each week on the London Money Market. This, of course, entailed visiting banks in the City, and accordingly, on the day in question, I went on my rounds, calling first on Mr Ruff, manager of Swiss Bankverein. He was a most friendly man as a rule, but it was not difficult to see that, on that day, he was desperately worried. He told me that the money market had broken down …

Consequently, he was in a position where if any of his clients needed £10,000 he would have to close down. It was grim news indeed, but what distressed me more than anything else was the dire plight of this charming man, and the fact that, on giving me this news, he broke down and cried.

Paish's next call was on merchant banker Frederick Huth Jackson, a senior City figure who was a director of the Bank of England. Evidently Paish had access to top City people:

> It was a moment for straight talk, and I opened the conversation with:-
> 'Well Mr Jackson, what has happened to the Money Market? They tell me that it has broken down.'
> 'It has,' he replied. 'We, the [merchant banks] … cannot get our remittances and eight of us are going to declare ourselves insolvent next week.'
> 'You can't do that,' I said …
> 'We can't help it,' said Mr Jackson with a shrug of his shoulders.
> At once I drove to Downing Street to see Mr Lloyd George. As briefly as possible I gave him my report, and at the end he said:
> 'Keep me posted. I will be available to you at any time, day or night.'[40]

Paish made another round of the City on Thursday, 30 July. He called on Henry Bell, chief executive of Lloyds Bank, Britain's biggest bank and number three worldwide. Bell told him that:

> 'There is a general run on all the banks. Customers are asking for gold, but we are paying out in notes and telling them to go to the Bank of England to change them.'
> I hurried round to the Bank of England and there found an immense queue waiting to cash their notes. They filled the Issue Department of the Bank and spilled out, four deep, through the courtyard, down Threadneedle Street and half way up Prince's Street. Hundreds and hundreds of people waiting as patiently as possible to see if their money was still safe!
> A taxi took me to Downing Street to see Mr Lloyd George. 'There is panic in the City,' I said, 'and something has to be done about it.'[41]

Over the three and a half days from Wednesday, 29 July, to noon Saturday, 1 August, the Bank's stock of gold sovereigns fell from £26 million to £14 million – a 46 per cent slump – as a result of withdrawals by banks and individuals. The queue at the Bank was 'soon bruited abroad as a novel spectacle', related Withers, and a crowd gathered on the steps of the adjacent Royal Exchange to watch.[42] Yet there was no reporting of the queues in the London evening papers on Wednesday or Thursday, suggesting significant restraint by City editors, doubtless for fear of making matters worse. However, Lord Rothschild, the City's elder statesman, and

Sir Felix Schuster, Governor of the Union of London and Smiths Bank, 'who under ordinary circumstances will never consent to be interviewed', spoke on the record, probably for the first time ever, to the City editor of *Pall Mall Gazette*, a clubland London evening paper owned by millionaire Waldorf Astor MP, and provided 'reassuring views'.[43] Astor also owned *The Observer*, which featured outstanding financial coverage by City editor Charles Thorpe.[44]

On the morning of Friday, 31 July, for the first time in its history, the London Stock Exchange closed its doors leaving brokers milling around in Throgmorton Street like 'swarming ants around the destroyed heap'.[45] Three London evening papers ran front-page articles that featured the closure of the Stock Exchange and the queues at the Bank – a financial crisis in all but name. Lord Rothschild gave a further on-the-record interview to *Pall Mall Gazette* applauding the decision to close the Stock Exchange as: 'Beneficial. It prevents panic.'[46] *The Globe*'s account of the 'extraordinary scenes' in Threadneedle Street was accompanied by an 'explanation' by City editor Herbert H. Bassett as to why what looked like a run on the central bank was really no such thing: 'the idea that there was anything in the shape of a "run" on the Bank of England was never entertained'.[47]

Aware of the queue at the Bank on Friday, *The Star*, a London evening paper, decided that 'in view of the delicate state of public affairs ... it was undesirable to increase public anxiety by giving publicity to the incident'. But on Saturday, observing that other papers were running the sensational story, it changed policy, explaining to readers that: 'there is therefore no longer any public interest to serve by silence in our columns. In fact, we think it may allay the natural uneasiness of the public if the real facts are explained.'[48] That day the morning papers reported the Stock Exchange closure and the queues at the Bank – the first intimations to most readers of a financial crisis. A vivid account in the *Financial Times* reported the appearance of a red-cloaked official who shouted: '"Silver! Anybody want silver? Plenty of silver going cheap." A dead silence followed ... No, cheap silver was not wanted and the outflow of the precious yellow metal continued.'[49] A *Financial News* reporter retailed his witnessing of an evening newspaper vendor shouting 'Run on the Bank. Run on the Bank' to the crowd in Threadneedle Street. He summoned a policeman who arrested the newsboy.[50] But readers of *The Statist*, which also appeared that day, remained blissfully ignorant of these developments. Paish's bland column made no mention of queues in Threadneedle Street, runs on banks, or the threat of mass insolvency among the merchant banks. Instead he drew attention to a reassuring statement by Lloyd George in which he said that he had consulted with the Governor and there was no need at present for exceptional steps. Plainly Paish was doing his bit to avert panic, which was not inappropriate since by the time *The Statist* appeared on news stands he was working for the Chancellor at the Treasury.

Financial crisis (2): containment

Saturday, 1 August, saw the start of the summer holiday weekend; Monday's bank holiday was extended by a further three days providing a breathing space for the formulation of crisis management measures. In the middle of the unprecedented four-day public holiday, at 11 p.m. on Tuesday, 4 August, Britain declared war. They were days of innumerable and interminable meetings in the City and the Treasury making preparations for the reopening of the banks and money market on Friday, 7 August. 'These are exciting if interesting times,' wrote the deputy chairman of Lloyds Bank. 'I never thought I should have so many Bank Holidays together or that there should be so much Bank about them and so little holiday! I have spent them from morning till late at night in meetings and conferences.'[51] The key meetings were at the Treasury with energetic impetus from the Chancellor and policy direction by the Permanent Secretary, Sir John Bradbury. The daily diary of Basil Blackett, one of Bradbury's key Treasury aides, makes no mention at all of contact with the financial press during the crisis. Security considerations and a tradition of secrecy were certainly factors, but also there simply was no time for press briefings. Many measures were implemented by Royal Proclamation without explanation and the press simply printed the official notice. Major decisions were reported by the Chancellor to the House of Commons and it was under the byline of the parliamentary editor rather than the City editor that they appeared in the press.

The principal crisis-containment measures, devised and introduced during the long bank holiday, were the issuance of Treasury currency notes and a general moratorium. The Treasury notes were small denomination notes that were paper substitutes for the sovereign (£1) and half-sovereign (50p) gold coins that were the principal circulating payment mediums of the day. The issuance of the small denomination Treasury currency notes as complements to the existing large denomination Bank of England notes, which principally served as bank reserves, was devised by Bradbury and solved several problems.[52] Bearing the signature of the Permanent Secretary, they became popularly known as 'Bradburys'. Commentators welcomed the notes as a sensible step that would discourage the hoarding of gold coins and relieve pressure on bank deposits. The general moratorium was a legalized suspension of contracts designed to protect debtors until commercial conditions calmed down, and also as a further device to safeguard the banks against a run on deposits. Such a measure was unknown in Britain and newspapers offered guidance to bewildered readers. *Punch* magazine expressed the public puzzlement with a satirical array of vox pop suggestions as to the meaning of the word: 'It's a big ship … one of the Cunaders'; 'Sister ship to the Lusitania'; and 'A place for burying people – a sort of big tomb where they put dead kings. There's one at Windsor.'[53]

Bankers and the Chancellor believed that a run on the banks had begun in the final days of the last week of July, which threatened the breakdown of the country's money transmission and credit mechanisms as the country went to war. In the run-up to the reopening of the banks on Friday, 7 August, ministers vociferously denounced withdrawal of deposits and especially the hoarding of gold in speeches in the House of Commons. Lloyd George enlisted the press to mount a public campaign against hoarding. 'We must get the assistance of the Press,' he told a strategy meeting at the Treasury on Tuesday, 4 August:

I propose to call a meeting of the Editors or the Financial Editors, or those responsible for instructing the public in financial matters ... and appeal to them to insert special articles in their papers appealing to the public to assist us at the present moment, and pointing out that the duties of patriotism are not confined to those who have to fight either at sea or on the battlefield (applause) ...

If an appeal of that kind is made by the Leaders of every section of the community, assisted by the Press, I think you will find on Friday morning that there will be no necessity for these emergency measures but you will find they will rather be a reserve for the creation of confidence, than something which has to be drawn upon very liberally.[54]

The press played its part with enthusiasm. 'The Folly of Hoarding' was the head-line to a thundering editorial in *The Times*.[55] 'Everyone should understand the simple position. All the gold should be in the banks and available for the state as a whole,' exhorted the *Evening News*. 'In the same way as people are sending their sons to fight in case it should be necessary, so they should pay their gold into the banks, in case the state should require it. Use the notes, which are just as good, and by all means make as many payments as possible by cheque.'[56] *The Globe* on Friday, 7 August featured a prominent display box captioned: 'The Duty of Every Good Britisher'. 'Today when the £1 notes are ready at the banks it is the duty of every good Britisher to take all the sovereigns that he or any of his family possess to the nearest bank and change them for £5 or £1 notes,' stated City editor Bassett. 'Do not let your friends alone do this, do it also yourself. It is a duty, a small one it is true, but in the aggregate the result will be helpful to the country, and your country must be your first care today. All the gold coin we possess is required for the use of our forces in the field and for the purchases required by the country abroad.'[57] The campaign was successful; not only was there no run, but gold coin was indeed paid into the banks in return for new Treasury notes.

Financial crisis (3): revival

With the banking system secured, the authorities turned their attention to the revival of the City's moribund financial markets. Paish and Alfred Cole, a former Governor of the Bank of England, were the architects of a scheme to resuscitate the money market and recapitalize the banks through the purchase by the Bank of pre-war bills of exchange that were believed to be clogging the market and preventing the provision of new credits. Introduced on 12 August, the scheme resulted in the Bank owning £133 million of the £350 million of outstanding bills, almost two fifths of the market. This was state intervention in the financial system on an unprecedented and breathtaking scale. Lloyd George's 'Cold Storage Scheme' for bills, as he called it, 'staggered' the City and was hailed 'almost ecstatically' by the press as a 'stroke of financial genius'.[58] 'Another masterful financial scheme,' declared the *Daily Mail*; 'Fairly taken away the breath of observers,' the *Evening*

Standard; 'Absolutely unique,' *The Statist*; 'Could not have been carried out we believe in any other country but the United Kingdom,' *The Times*, though it added 'except perhaps France'.[59] 'So novel that many Ministers would have shrunk from authorising it,' marvelled the *Financial News*:

> Happily, the Chancellor of the Exchequer is not deficient in courage, and want of precedent never daunts him. We rejoice to have restored to us the Mr. Lloyd George who was President of the Board of Trade a few years ago, and won golden opinions in that office, mainly because he showed himself exceptionally quick in taking up a point presented to him, and almost instantaneous in putting into practice newly-acquired knowledge.[60]

The boldness of the move was emphasized repeatedly, the London evening papers *The Star* and *The Globe* calling it, respectively, 'bold but necessary' and 'another bold move'.[61] The *Financial Times* applauded the Chancellor's 'wise statesmanship' while the *Evening Standard* called the measure 'most statesmanlike' and reported that its effect on the City 'has been magical'.[62] 'A dazzling example of how the solidarity of the government with finance, trade, and industry can be given practical expression in an emergency,' was the verdict of the *Financial News*, while the Chancellor, who earlier in his career as a radical had been the City's Bogeyman, was transformed into 'quite a national asset'.[63]

Yet there were a couple of dissenting voices. 'There is no doubt that the Chancellor of the Exchequer has become exceedingly popular in the City,' observed 'Cornhill Magpie', the independent-minded weekly column in the *Sunday Times* written by Hermann Schmidt, a partner in a City bank and the principal owner of the paper from 1905 to 1915. His City article was 'an authoritative exposition of the mysteries of "high finance"' and one of the paper's 'chief features'.[64] Schmidt cautioned presciently that 'it would be better to reserve extravagant praise until final success is assured'.[65] The potential burden for taxpayers was of serious concern to *The Economist*. Editor Francis Hirst warned that Lloyd George's 'extraordinary measure', taken in the interests of the banks 'in the hope of indirectly reviving trade and credit', might, he calculated, cost the public purse from £50 million to £200 million depending on the length of the war.[66] This was by no means the first time that *The Economist* was critical of the responses to the financial crisis, including, uniquely, the closure of the Stock Exchange, which it described as 'a most deplorable mistake'.[67] But Hirst's foremost departures from mainstream opinion were his opposition to Britain's participation in the war and his remorseless criticism of the government's conduct of the war. As the war dragged on, *The Economist*'s trustees became increasingly embarrassed by Hirst and in summer 1916 he was replaced by Hartley Withers.[68]

John Maynard Keynes, aged 31 but already a notable authority, used the letters page of *The Economist* on 29 August to begin his attack on the behaviour of the big joint-stock banks during the crisis.[69] Keynes was a friend of Blackett who invited him to contribute to crisis policy formulation at the Treasury in an unofficial capacity during the long bank holiday. Blackett, Bradbury, Cunliffe, and ministers were incensed by what they regarded as the self-serving conduct of bankers in the crisis but were unable to publicly vent their outrage. But Keynes, a Cambridge don, was at liberty to censure the banks, which he did in *The Economist*, in articles in other newspapers, notably the *Morning Post*, and in the *Economic Journal*, an academic publication that he edited. His criticisms of the banks received much notice and were credited to him personally, but what he said was no different from what Treasury officials said behind closed doors and thus his writings were also public expressions of the authorities' frustrations that could not be openly aired.

As the management of a war economy became more routine, Paish's role as the Chancellor's special adviser became less clear. According to Keynes:

> for about a day and a half in August 1914 he was very important at the Treasury. As usual, however, Mr. Lloyd George soon got bored with him and stopped reading his lengthy memoranda. He was, however, given a good salary and an exalted title ... and ... a room at a considerable distance, over at the Road Board in Caxton House.[70]

In early October Paish was sent to Washington, accompanied by Blackett to keep an eye on him, as Britain's envoy to the US government about the repayment of American debts and the disequilibrium of the sterling–dollar exchange rate.[71] They eventually struck an agreement, but before Lloyd George got round to ratification, much to Paish's disappointment, the exchange rate righted itself in late November. Keynes was recruited to the Treasury in January 1915. 'I was nominally appointed Paish's assistant,' he recalled:

> But I was given a seat in Blackett's room, as well as with Paish at the Road Board. After a few days I came to the conclusion that Paish was barely in his right mind and before long I ceased going over to the rooms at the Road Board. Not long afterwards he had a complete nervous breakdown.[72]

The closure of the Stock Exchange led to the mushrooming of alternative forums for private cash transactions. Foremost among them was the Daily Mail Exchange, which had been established in 1912 by the enterprising Charles Duguid as a cut-price dealing service matching buyers and sellers through small ads in the City pages. On Saturday, 1 August 1914, the day after closure, half-page advertisements appeared in the *Financial Times* and the *Financial News* announcing:

> With the Stock Exchange closed the facilities offered by the Daily Mail Exchange to readers are more valuable than ever. Sellers who desire money for securities they hold, and buyers who desire securities at the present low prices and are prepared to pay money, can use the Daily Mail Exchange. Write, stating name of stock or share, the amount and the price required, together with a postal order for 2/6d for each item.

The Daily Mail Exchange operated busily until August 1915 when business was suspended 'owing to the war conditions now prevailing, the stagnation in stock and share dealing, and the pressure of war news on our space'.[73] The Stock Exchange itself eventually reopened on 4 January 1915. 'In the financial history of the war a new period begins today,' declared *The Times* – the financial crisis was over.[74]

Roles of the press

Did the British financial press foresee and forewarn about a financial crisis ahead of Austria's ultimatum? Absolutely not; the editor of *Investors' Chronicle*, for instance, had just gone on holiday on the Continent and only managed to get back to England 'by the skin of his teeth'.[75] With the benefit of hindsight, given the Sarajevo murders a month earlier, the lack of anticipation is perhaps surprising, but journalists were in good company – the Bank of England, the Treasury, bankers, brokers, diplomats, and politicians were equally unprepared.

Was press reporting of the financial crisis constrained by official censorship? Since 1912 there had been a voluntary Joint Standing Committee between the Admiralty, War Office, and the Press Committee (representing the four newspaper proprietors' associations) to determine what military information should be withheld from publication.[76] This was activated on Monday, 27 July, recalled Lord Riddell, owner of the *News of the World*.[77] But the work of City editors was beyond its remit. During the breakdown in the last week of July and the long bank holiday in the first week of August, there was no central institutional mechanism for either state censorship or the supply of information to the press. Friday, 7 August saw not only the reopening of the banks but the creation of the Press Bureau whose function was 'to provide a steady stream of trustworthy information supplied by both the War Office and the Admiralty'.[78] While a key dimension of the government–press relationship during the war, the Press Bureau had no relevance for the flow of news to City editors. As regards censorship, the key measure was the Defence of the Realm Act, which forbade the publication of any military or naval information of use to the enemy on 12 August 1914, by coincidence the same day as the launch of Lloyd George's 'Cold Storage Scheme'.[79] By then the critical phase of the financial crisis had already passed and the measure had little obvious application to the money article. State censorship was not a constraint in the reporting of the financial crisis either before Britain's entry into the war or after.

'Voluntary censorship' was another matter. City editors must have been aware that the breakdown was far more fundamental than was reported on the financial pages. Thus reporting did not accurately reflect what was known to be going on, but the motive was to avoid fuelling panic and making matters worse. The yawning gap between what the editor of *The Statist* heard and saw and what appeared in his paper is striking, but its rival *The Economist* was no more forthright about the financial collapse. The pitfalls of self-censorship on the part of an individual editor were illustrated by *The Star*. Its self-censorship regarding the queues at the Bank of England, in what it believed to be the public interest, meant that it allowed competitors to steal a march. The inconsistent exercise of voluntary censorship by papers was a major issue during the war, with the Press Bureau being deluged by complaints.[80]

Did reporting exacerbate the crisis? Possibly, in so far as coverage of the closure of the Stock Exchange and the queue at the Bank of England contributed to the acceleration of the withdrawal of sovereigns on the Friday and the Saturday. But the fundamental factor was the banks' refusal to pay out sovereigns and their making payment instead in large denomination notes that obliged people to change them for sovereigns at the Bank. *The Globe* called the queue a 'miniature run' on the Bank of England.[81] But the critical moment was the anxiously awaited reopening of the banks on Friday, 7 August. It featured in a novel by H.G. Wells, *Mr Britling Sees It Through*: 'When the public went to the banks for the new paper money, the banks tendered gold – apologetically. The supply of new notes was very insufficient, and there was plenty of gold.'[82]

Was the press critical of the behaviour of the banks? Yes, like Keynes, some City editors accused them in mild terms of selfishly hoarding gold. Though such measured public criticism was as nothing compared to the fulminations of Treasury officials and the Governor behind the scenes. And as for criticism of the authorities, there was precious little, though Hirst's *Economist* took a contrarian line on occasion. Otherwise, as possibly in the case of the 'Enlarged Scheme' of 5 September, an addition to the 'Cold Storage Scheme', reservations were indicated by editorial silence.

And what of the contributions of the financial press and financial journalists to the war effort? 'During the war the *Financial Times*, among other journals,' wrote Simonis in 1917, 'has rendered yeoman service to the Government, and specially to the Treasury, by its careful and clear exposition of the many financial measures which the conduct of the great struggle has rendered necessary.'[83] As individuals, the most illustrious was probably Edward Hilton Young who resigned as City editor of the *Morning Post* on 20 August, joined the Navy, and became a war hero. Subsequently he became an MP, serving as Financial Secretary to the Treasury in the early 1920s, before returning to financial journalism as editor of the *Financial News*, and later being made Lord Kennet. Hartley Withers worked at the Treasury for two years before taking on the editorship of *The Economist* in summer 1916. Of course, the most notable contribution was that of Sir George Paish who was at the centre of policymaking at the height of the crisis and then served as Treasury emissary to America. The reward for his contributions was a nervous breakdown.

Notes

1 Roberts (2013).
2 Porter (1986), p. 1.
3 Duguid (1901), p. 64.
4 Simonis (1917), p. 116.
5 Dudley Edwards (1993), p. 279.
6 McEwen (1982), p. 468.

7 Symon (1914), pp. 140–54.

8 Porter (1998), p. 51.

9 O'Connor (1929), pp. 259–60; Simonis (1917), pp. 109–15.

10 Simonis (1917), p. 9.

11 *Post Office London Directory 1914*.

12 Duguid (1901), p. 63.

13 Duguid (1901), p. 64; Porter (1986), pp. 4–6.

14 Simonis (1917), p. 119.

15 'Financial Journalism', *Financial Times*, 24 April 1909.

16 Simonis (1917), p. 121.

17 'The City Page', *Daily Mail*, 14 November 1913.

18 'The New Financial Journalism – News and Advertisements', *The Economist*, 1 November 1913.

19 'Mr Edward Johnstone', *The Economist*, 13 December 1913.

20 Porter (1998), pp. 49–60. I am grateful to Dilwyn Porter for kindly allowing me to read a draft of an unpublished chapter on the financial press during the First World War.

21 Duguid (1897), pp. 159–68.

22 Duguid (1897), p. 166.

23 *African Critic*, 5 June 1897, quoted in Porter (1998), p. 54.

24 Duguid (1897), p. 161.

25 'Financial Writers' Dinner', *Financial Times*, 23 April 1906.

26 'Mr. A.J. Wilson's Retirement', *Financial Times*, 8 April 1907.

27 'City Financial Writers' Dinner', *The Times*, 23 February 1914.

28 Simonis (1917), pp. 118–19.

29 Kynaston (1988), p. 26.

30 Powell (1910); Young (1915).

31 Withers (1915); Lawson (1915).

32 'City Financial Writers' Dinner', *The Times*, 26 February 1912.

33 Sayers (1976), p. 374.

34 Withers (1910).

35 Middleton (2004); Offer (1983), pp. 124–7; Blick and Jones (2013).

36 'City Financial Writers' Dinner', *The Times*, 17 March 1913.

37 'Sir George Paish at the Treasury', *The Standard*, 14 August 1914; 'Sir George's Appointment', *Financial Times*, 14 August 1914.

38 'The Great Crisis', *Bankers' Magazine*, vol. xcviii (September 1914), p. 320.

39 'The Power Behind the Stern Note to Servia: The Austro-Hungarian Army', *Illustrated London News*, 1 August 1914.

40 LSE Archives: Sir George Paish, 'My Memoirs', c.1950.

41 Paish, 'My Memoirs'.

42 Withers (1915), p. 15.

43 'Interview with Lord Rothschild', *Pall Mall Gazette*, 29 July 1914; Simonis (1917), p. 107.

44 Simonis (1917), pp. 126–8.

45 'The Scenes in the City', *Manchester Guardian*, 1 August 1914.

46 '"Beneficial": Lord Rothschild's View', *Pall Mall Gazette*, 31 July 1914.

47 'Today's Scenes Explained', *The Globe*, 31 July 1914.

48 'Scenes in Threadneedle Street', *The Star*, 1 August 1914.

49 'Scenes at the Bank', *Financial Times*, 1 August 1914.

50 'All Quiet at the Banks', *Financial News*, 1 August 1914.

51 Sayers (1957), p. 215.

52 Roberts (2013), pp. 119–25.

53 'The Nature of a Moratorium', *Punch*, 19 August 1914.

54 The National Archives: T170/55. Chancellor of the Exchequer's Conference With Bankers and Traders, 4 August 1914.

55 'The Folly of Hoarding', *The Times*, 4 August 1914.
56 'Use of the New Notes', *Evening News*, 5 August 1914.
57 'The Duty of Every Good Britisher', *The Globe*, 7 August 1914.
58 'The Great Crisis', *Bankers' Magazine*, vol. xcviii (September 1914); Lawson (1915), p. 118; 'City Chatter', *Sunday Times*, 16 August 1914.
59 'Chat on 'Change', *Daily Mail*, 13 August 1914; 'Government Step to Improve Trade', *Evening Standard*, 13 August 1914; 'Money', *The Statist*, 15 August 1914; 'The Credit of London Guaranteed', *The Times*, 13 August 1914.
60 'The Government and Bills', *Financial News*, 14 August 1914.
61 'Bold Government Step', *The Star*, 13 August 1914; 'Bills of Exchange and Government Action', *The Globe*, 13 August 1914.
62 'Restarting the Credit Machine', *Financial Times*, 14 August 1914; 'Energetic Action', *Evening Standard*, 13 August 1914.
63 'Effect of Step Taken by Government to Enable Country to Carry on Its Business', *Financial News*, 14 August 1914.
64 Simonis (1917), p. 131.
65 'City Chatter', *Sunday Times*, 16 August 1914.
66 'The War, Trade and Finance', *The Economist*, 22 August 1914.
67 'The Financial Situation at Home and Abroad', *The Economist*, 1 August 1914.
68 Dudley Edwards (1993), pp. 541–2, 565–73.
69 Roberts (2013), pp. 63–5.
70 Parliamentary Archive. Bonar Law Papers. Ms. 107/2/67. J.M. Keynes to Andrew Bonar Law, 10 October 1922.
71 Roberts (2013), pp. 175–80.
72 Parliamentary Archive. Bonar Law Papers. Ms. 107/2/67. J.M. Keynes to Andrew Bonar Law, 10 October 1922.
73 British Library. Ms. 62202. Northcliffe Papers, vol. L. Lord Northcliffe to Charles Duguid, 24 August 1915.
74 'The Stock Exchange Reopens', *The Times*, 4 January 1915.
75 Anderson (1960).
76 Lovelace (1978), p. 309.
77 Riddell (1933), p. 1.
78 House of Commons Debate, cols 2153–6, 7 August 1914.
79 Lovelace (1978), p. 312.
80 Lovelace (1978), p. 316.
81 'The Banking Situation', *The Globe*, 3 August 1914.
82 Wells (1916), p. 208.
83 Simonis (1917), pp. 119, 333.

References

Anderson, Charles (1960) 'One Hundred Years: *Investors' Chronicle* Centenary Number', *Investors' Chronicle*, 10 June.

Blick, Andrew and Jones, George (2013) *At Power's Elbow: Aides to the Prime Minister from Robert Walpole to David Cameron*, London: Biteback.

Dudley Edwards, Ruth (1993) *The Pursuit of Reason: 'The Economist' 1843–1993*, London: Hamish Hamilton.

Duguid, Charles (1897) 'The City Editor', *Journal of Finance*, June, pp. 159–68.

——(1901) *How to Read the Money Article*, London: Pitman.

Kynaston, David (1988) *The Financial Times: A Centenary History*, London: Viking.

Lawson, W.R. (1915) *British War Finance 1914–1915*, London: Constable.

Lovelace, Colin (1978) 'British Press Censorship During the First World War', in Boyce, George, Curran, James, and Wingate, Pauline (eds.) *Newspaper History from the Seventeenth Century to the Present Day*, London: Constable, pp. 307–19.

McEwen, John M. (1982) 'The National Press During the First World War: Ownership and Circulation', *Journal of Contemporary History*, 17, pp. 459–86.

Middleton, Roger (2004) 'Paish, Sir George, Financial Journalist and Economist', *Oxford Dictionary of National Biography*, Oxford: Oxford University Press.

O'Connor, T.P. (1929) *Memoirs of an Old Parliamentarian*, 2 vols, London: Ernest Benn.

Offer, Avner (1983) 'Empire and Social Reform: British Overseas Investment and Domestic Politics, 1908–1914', *Historical Journal*, 26 (1), pp. 119–38.

Porter, Dilwyn (1986) '"A Trusted Guide of the Investing Public": Harry Marks and the *Financial News* 1884–1916', *Business History*, 28 (1), pp. 1–17.

——(1998) 'City Editors and the Modern Investing Public: Establishing the Integrity of the New Financial Journalism in Late Nineteenth-Century London', *Media History*, 4 (1), pp. 49–60.

Post Office London Directory 1914.

Powell, Ellis T. (1910) *The Mechanism of the City: An Analytical Survey of the Business Activities of the City of London*, London: King.

Riddell, Lord George (1933) *Lord Riddell's War Diary 1914–1918*, London: Ivor Nicholson and Watson.

Roberts, Richard (2013) *Saving the City: The Great Financial Crisis of 1914*, Oxford: Oxford University Press.

Sayers, R.S. (1957) *Lloyds Bank in the History of English Banking*, Oxford: Clarendon Press.

——(1976) *The Bank of England 1891–1944*, Cambridge: Cambridge University Press.

Simonis, H. (1917) *The Street of Ink: An Intimate History of Journalism*, London: Cassell.

Symon, J.D. (1914) *The Press and Its Story*, London: Seely, Service.

Wells, H.G. (1916) *Mr Britling Sees It Through*, London: Cassell.

Withers, Hartley (1910) 'Aspects of City-Editing', *Financial News*, 1 April.

——(1915) *War and Lombard Street*, London: Smith, Elder.

Young, Edward Hilton (1915) *The System of National Finance*, London: Smith, Elder.

17

THE POUND AND THE PRESS, 1919–1972

Richard Roberts

Britain experienced a series of currency crises from 1919 to 1972 during the eras of the gold standard and the Bretton Woods fixed exchange rate system. The period as a whole saw three major crises and devaluations – 1931, 1949, and 1967 – and numerous lesser sterling crises from the 1940s to the floating of the pound in June 1972. The sterling crises generated press headlines, with the balance of payments and the condition of the pound becoming national preoccupations in post-war decades. Coverage provided readers with news, explanation, and editorial commentary. Financial journalists were assisted in varying degrees by guidance from the Bank of England and the Treasury. Generally the authorities took the view that the less said about the pound the better, but if events required comment it should be supportive of official policy and the current exchange rate. Mostly the press was anxious not to undermine the pound and wary of provoking or exacerbating a sterling crisis, whatever journalists' private views of policy. But how were these imperatives to be reconciled with the press's role as a source of news and editorial freedom to comment?

Inter-war financial press

The financial press of the inter-war years comprised two specialist dailies, the *Financial News* and *Financial Times* (the latter having absorbed the *Financier and Bullionist* in 1920), and four leading financial weeklies, *The Economist*, *The Statist*, *Investors' Chronicle*, and *The Banker*.[1] Among these titles, the *Financial News* was Conservative-leaning, while *The Economist* was a standard-bearer for liberal internationalism. Financial matters in the non-specialist London daily press were mostly the preserve of the City editor, who often worked from a separate office near the stock exchange, with securities' prices and investments at the core of financial reporting in these decades. They received substantial coverage in the three 'more serious' London dailies, *The Times*, *Daily Telegraph*, and *Morning Post*, each of which had a series of eminent City editors who were leading economic commentators of the day.[2] The leading mass circulation dailies also had a City editor, notably the Conservative-oriented *Daily Express*, *Daily Mail*, and *Daily Mirror*, the Liberal-supporting *News Chronicle*, and the *Daily Herald*, a Labour mouthpiece. So did the London evening papers, the *Evening Standard* and *Evening News*, the two 'serious' Sunday papers, the *Sunday Times* and *Observer*, and, among the provincial press, the *Manchester Guardian*, a leading liberal publication, and *The Scotsman*. The liberal-left weeklies *The Nation and Athenaeum* and the *New Statesman* had a financial editor.

Traditionally the Bank of England, the pound's foremost guardian, was wedded to secrecy (see Chapter 16). However, during the war Governor Walter Cunliffe (1913–18) developed personal contacts with a number of leading City editors, notably Charles Reeve of the *Daily Telegraph* and Arthur Kiddy of the *Morning Post*; on Cunliffe's instruction the Bank changed its newspaper order from *The Times* to the *Morning Post*.[3] Upon Cunliffe's retirement Reeve wrote that 'the Press on their side will be sorry to part with the kindliest and most accessible Governor that they have come in contact with in the course of their duties for many years'. Governor Montagu Norman (1920–44) accepted communication with the press as a 'regrettable necessity', though initially access was restricted to Kiddy, Reeve, and Courtney Mills of *The Times*; Oscar Hobson of the *Manchester Guardian* was added to this 'select list' in the mid 1920s through the intercession of Bank director Sir Charles Addis, London chairman of Hongkong and Shanghai Bank.[4] The privilege was 'gradually and sparingly extended' to Edward Hilton Young of the *Financial News* and Sir Walter Layton of *The Economist*, and to Francis Williams of the *Daily Herald* at the end of the decade.[5]

In 1927 the Bank appointed the Press Association as its 'medium for circulating official information to the Press' as well as for generating 'inspired' profiles and paragraphs.[6] The procedure was for a notice to be sent from the Bank Secretary's office to the Press Association, which was forwarded to key City editors with specification of the earliest time for publication. The City editors of *The Times* and *Daily Telegraph* (which absorbed the *Morning Post* in 1937) also received individual briefings from an executive director. Care was taken to ensure that the BBC and the evening papers were not in a position to make the initial disclosure of Bank notices. The Bank's first press conference for British journalists was held in April 1930. Requests for access by provincial and foreign journalists were mostly turned down. The Treasury was officially even less obliging, with no pre-war press relations function at all. However, Treasury officials, judged by their files, certainly kept an eye on what leading financial journalists were writing.[7] Moreover, there was doubtless social contact at places such as the Reform Club and the Political Economy Club that had both senior officials and City editors as members.

Suspension and resumption of the gold standard, 1919–1925

During the First World War, Britain nominally maintained the convertibility of pound notes into gold though access was highly restricted. The sterling–dollar exchange rate was pegged at $4.76 (pre-war $4.86). But in March 1919, in response to post-war pressures, intervention in support of sterling was suspended and an embargo on gold export was imposed.[8] This interruption to gold payments and to the operation of London's free market in gold constituted the suspension of Britain's adherence to the gold standard. The value of the pound hit $3.20 in February 1920 – a 33 per cent devaluation that in other contexts might have been regarded as a currency crisis.[9] However, as the City editor of *The Times* observed, the embargo 'did not cause much surprise in the City, for the reason chiefly that exports of gold have virtually been prohibited for a long time past'.[10] Despite the significance of the step, reports of the suspension were confined to the financial pages, perhaps because of its technical nature but also because of the absence of official guidance. The point was made by the *Daily Mail's* City editor Charles Duguid:

> The present abnormal conditions necessitate, in the opinion of many, abnormal measures ... It would be less harmful to business if our officials would stoop to issue some kind of explanation with the orders they draft, instead of waiting until the explanation is dragged out of them.[11]

The 1919 suspension of the gold standard was a temporary expedient. Deflationary policies were then pursued to raise the pound to the pre-war exchange rate against the dollar to allow a resumption of the status quo.[12] The return to gold became increasingly topical in the press from autumn 1924 as sterling rose towards the pre-war parity, and with the gold export embargo scheduled to expire automatically at the end of 1925. An unexplained mission by Norman to New York in January 1925 was correctly interpreted by the British press to mean that the preparations for the return had reached a critical phase. 'Distinguished bankers are not likely to be taking an ocean trip amid winter gales for the sake of their health,' observed *The Economist*.[13] Norman's host, Governor Benjamin Strong of the Federal Reserve Bank of New York, repeatedly encouraged him to be more open with the press. 'Of course there is no doubt that the attitude towards publicity with us and with you is very different,' Norman wrote to Strong concerning arrangements for the announcement of Britain's return to gold. 'Your experience seems to lead you to make public statements in order to protect yourself against the Press, whereas ours leads us to refrain from such statements and to ignore the curiosity of the Press regarding the private affairs of the Bank!'[14]

City editors supported the re-establishment of a fixed exchange rate for sterling at the pre-war parity, as did newspaper editors and proprietors both Conservative and Liberal:[15]

> At present the exchange value of the £ is at the mercy of political and other uncertain factors. By anchoring it to gold these uncertainties would be removed ... The continued prestige of the £ depends on a return to gold payments,

stated the *Daily Mail*'s City editor, Edgar Kissan, in February 1925.[16] 'The business and financial community is, with comparatively few exceptions, agreed that the gold standard of currency, whatever its defects, is best suited to our present practical needs,' wrote Hobson in the *Manchester Guardian*. 'We believe that the moment has arrived, and that the pound can now be restored to and maintained at its old gold value without difficulty and without danger.'[17] 'The predominant opinion in the country,' declared *The Economist*, 'is that the restoration of the gold standard affords the surest and, indeed, the only practicable guarantee against renewed violence of exchange fluctuations.'[18] Nevertheless, there were a few dissenting voices, notably *The Nation*, owned by Maynard Keynes and other socially minded Liberals. Keynes vigorously denounced the deflation that stemmed from the pursuit of the monetary conditions for a return to gold.[19] His alternative policy was a 'managed currency' (continued floating), but other countries were returning to gold and other experts deemed this untried and impractical; the Cambridge don was 'a voice in the wilderness'.[20]

The return to the gold standard announced in the Budget on 28 April 1925 was applauded across the British press. 'A real stride towards world recovery,' declared the *Financial News*, while the *Financial Times* hailed the restoration of London's free market in gold as 'the best thing that could have happened in the interests of British credit and prestige'.[21] Budget coverage in the popular press focused on the reduction in income tax and new import duties rather than the gold standard. However, the *Daily Express*, and also the *Daily Mail*, warned about 'the position of dependence on the United States in which the restoration of the gold standard here will place us'.[22] But J.L. Garvin, veteran radical editor of *The Observer*, observed that: 'On the whole, we think it may work out as an asset.'[23] Keynes voiced his objections in a series of articles in the *Evening Standard* that were quickly republished as a book, *The Economic Consequences of Mr Churchill*.[24]

1931 crisis

Following the return to gold, the maintenance of the fixed exchange rate was the cornerstone of British economic policy. It was regarded as the key to domestic and international economic prosperity and stability, to which everything else should be adjusted. This was the view of the Conservative and Liberal press, as well as both the incumbent Conservative government and, from 1929, the Labour administration led by Prime Minister Ramsay MacDonald and Chancellor Philip Snowden. The principal dissenting voices were Keynes, through *The Nation* and writings in the mainstream press, the *New Statesman* (which merged with *The Nation* in 1931), and the socialist *Daily Herald*, which held the gold standard responsible for many of the problems of British industry and unemployment.[25]

In summer 1931, banking and currency crises in Austria and Germany led to withdrawals of funds from London that generated anxieties about devaluation among foreign holders of sterling. A financial-cum-political crisis developed in August, with the depletion of the reserves compounded by Cabinet disagreement about spending cuts proposed by the Prime Minister and Chancellor to reduce the Budget deficit and boost confidence in the pound. On 17 August *The Times*, a strong advocate of cuts, stated that 'unless immediate steps are taken to remedy the situation, the stability of the whole financial position of the country will be seriously imperilled', with 'depreciation of the currency and all the manifold evils which this would entail'.[26] The political crisis culminated on Sunday, 23 August, with the disintegration of the Labour administration followed by an invitation to Mac-Donald by the King to lead a 'National Government', which would include Conservatives and Liberals, to address the national emergency. Up till then the press, either through patriotism or ignorance, had made no mention of the pressure on the pound; Beatrice Webb, whose husband was a Labour minister, recorded in her diary that day that 'the run on the banks by foreign financiers … has not been reported in the press'.[27] But Monday's edition of *The Times* had a sensational leaked revelation – Britain's reserves were 'approaching exhaustion'.[28] The formation of an all-party government later that day was not a moment too soon for the pound.

The new administration was welcomed by the press. 'Yesterday – at last – the announcement was made that we are to have a National Government, composed of leading representatives of the three political parties,' stated the *Daily Mirror*. 'We can say at once that this is a wise decision. This alone can rescue the country from a financial peril that threatens it in the eyes of a watching world.'[29] The *Manchester Guardian* evoked the wartime coalition, stating that: 'There is today an emergency of peace which is comparable to that of war. It demands a comparable effort in the form of national unity.'[30] In acknowledgement of the significance of the occasion, the *Financial News* devoted its front page to the news instead of stock prices.[31] But the *Financial Times*, which proclaimed political neutrality, maintained its customary layout, with the political earthquake relegated to inside pages. The *Daily Herald* accused MacDonald and Snowden of surrendering to the City and selling out; an 'indignant' denunciation by Francis Williams, financial editor, was headlined 'Bankers' Ramp' – and thus was launched 'one of the most famous phrases in modern politics'.[32]

The fundamental mission of the new government was to keep the pound on the gold standard. 'Nothing but a severe and courageous national effort can save us from disaster,' thundered *The Times*. 'The abandonment of the gold standard, with its corollary, inflation, which must be the inevitable and automatic consequence of a failure to make that effort, is no remedy for our troubles. It is merely an insidious palliative, a dangerous intoxicant, which can only lead to the general impoverishment of our economic system and a cruel and unnecessary diminution of the standard of living of the poorer classes of the community.'[33] 'Any depreciation of the pound, however moderate, would be deplorable enough,' stated *The Economist*, 'and the deliberate adoption of such a policy a counsel of despair.'[34]

Spending cuts were the key. 'A few days ago the nation found itself looking over a precipice. Strong and courageous hands have pulled it back,' declared *The Economist*. 'A National Government has been formed to meet a national emergency arising out of an unexampled international situation … It will balance the Budget; it will curtail the national expenditure within its means.'[35] An emergency Budget slashed unemployment benefits and public sector pay by 10 per cent. The cuts provoked disturbances and a protest by 12,000 sailors at the Invergordon naval base. 'This is a time when the welfare of the country mainly depends upon keeping up British credit abroad,' responded the *Daily Mail*. 'Nothing is more likely to undermine that credit than symptoms of disaffection in the Royal Navy, which is the special glory of the British Empire.'[36] But the very reporting of the 'Invergordon mutiny' intensified the selling of sterling.

In mid September, as the sterling crisis mounted, City editors, including Francis Williams, and Cecil Sprigge of the *Manchester Guardian*, were invited to the Treasury for a briefing, on the measures – mostly further cuts – proposed to check the run. Williams, 'being young and iconoclastic', questioned whether Britain could or should remain on gold. His challenge was echoed by Sprigge, but:

> On the rest of the men around the table it produced an effect of frozen horror ... Sir Warren Fisher, Permanent Secretary to the Treasury and Head of the Civil Service, was particularly shaken. He found it impossible to remain seated.
>
> 'To suggest we should leave the gold standard,' he declared rising magisterially to his feet and pacing heavily backward and forwards across the room, 'is an affront not only to the national honour but to the personal honour of every man and woman in the country.'
>
> There was nothing for Sprigge and me to do but to slink away.[37]

The financial crisis climaxed on Sunday, 20 September. The government resignedly accepted that Britain's reserves were so depleted and the run on the pound so relentless that there was no prospect of sterling staying on the gold standard. Williams further recalled that City editors were summoned to Hoare's Bank in Fleet Street, where they were told by a 'solemn but basically cheerful group of bankers' that later that evening an announcement would be made that the gold standard was to be suspended and that banks and the stock exchange would be closed the following day:

> 'What,' I asked, 'do you expect the result of this to be?'
>
> 'I am sure,' replied the bankers' spokesman, 'it will mean an immediate improvement in our affairs and I am confident the whole country will welcome it.'
>
> 'And you do not expect any suicides?' asked Sprigge. 'Not even at the Treasury?'
>
> 'No, of course not,' said the banker. 'Why ever should there be? This is excellent news.'[38]

At the *New Statesman* on 21 September, the regular Monday editorial lunch was in full flow when:

> Maynard Keynes arrived late from the Treasury rubbing his hands and chuckling like a boy who has just exploded a firework underneath someone

he doesn't like. There were a dozen of us there ... We all said: 'What's the matter? What's happened?' And Keynes said: 'At one stroke Britain has resumed the financial hegemony of the world.'[39]

The mainstream press that just days before had been patriotically backing Britain's adherence to the gold standard welcomed departure. Under the headline 'Load Off Our Backs', the *Daily Mail* congratulated the Prime Minister 'on the strong line which he has taken ... We are being greatly led.'[40] 'Let us look facts straight in the face and realise that the retreat from the gold standard is not a catastrophe but an opportunity,' stated the *Daily Express*, Britain's biggest-selling daily. 'It was the Gold Standard which tied the millstone about our necks.'[41] 'The news that the Government has decided to suspend the gold standard need not cause any alarm,' counselled the *Daily Mirror*. 'While this is a dramatic step, and one taken reluctantly, it is realised that only in this way can the panic withdrawals of gold on the part of foreign holders be checked ... it is merely an emergency act of financial protection.'[42] 'It is safe to predict that Monday, 21 September 1931, will become an historic date,' declared *The Economist*. 'The suspension of the gold standard in Great Britain on that day, after the six years of painful effort which followed this country's return to gold in 1925, marks the definite end of an epoch in the world's financial and economic development ... the decision which the Government reached last Saturday represented not a deliberate act of policy, but the acceptance of the inevitable.'[43] For the press the political and financial convulsions had an unlooked-for silver lining – circulations soared. But the boom was soon overwhelmed by the adverse impact of the depression on sales and advertising revenues and the 1930s saw closures and amalgamations.[44]

Post-war financial press

There were fewer financial titles and City editors in the post-war era, though amalgamation boosted the circulation of some papers. The *Financial Times* merged with the *Financial News* in 1945; circulation of the combined paper rose from 62,000, to 167,000 in 1967, and to 253,000 in 1986.[45] *The Economist* went from strength to strength, circulation advancing from 18,000 in 1945 to 69,000 in 1963, and to 530,000 in 1993; but *The Statist* shut in 1967.[46] Among the London daily titles, which numbered 24 in 1947, the most important as regards financial affairs were *The Times* (circulation 270,000 in 1947), *Daily Telegraph* (1 million), and *Daily Mail* (3.6 million), with the *Sunday Times* (550,000), *Observer* (360,000), *Evening News* (1.6 million), *Evening Standard* (770,000), and *Guardian* (140,000) also influential.[47] Radio and television were increasingly important sources of news and views, though financial coverage was sparse except for crises. The broadcast media's coverage of economic affairs was influenced by print journalism, newspaper cuttings being the TV researcher's prime source.[48]

Kenneth Fleet, City editor of the *Daily Telegraph* (1966–77), observed that during the Second World War and until the recovery of the markets in the 1950s, finance and investment 'virtually disappeared from newspapers'.[49] Moreover, in wartime the press became more dependent on government as a source of economic news, as noted *The Economist*:

> Financial markets became tightly regulated. Instead of the daily round of banks, brokers and bond dealers, journalists began to call on government departments to ask how the civil servants expected to keep the economy going and raise money to pay for the war.
>
> The habit of looking largely to government for material survived the war: to be on speaking terms with the chancellor was an asset worth striving for.[50]

The Bank of England effectively appointed its first press relations officer in 1941 to deal with inquiries arising from wartime financial arrangements.[51] Norman, however, recalled Hobson, 'would affect not to know of their existence or else pretend that their work was something quite different from what it was'.[52] Even in the mid 1950s there was officially no such position; the role has been characterized as 'to keep the Bank out of the press and the press out of the Bank'.[53] Public information about the Bank increased with the production of an *Annual Report* after nationalization in 1946, but more notably with the commencement of publication in December 1960 of the *Bank of England Quarterly Bulletin,* which contained articles by Bank officials and monetary statistics. Nonetheless, press liaison remained low-key, with the Bank reacting to events rather than actively providing expert guidance and leading opinion formation. At the Treasury, an Economic Information Unit was established in 1947, renamed the Information Division in the early 1950s, to deal with publicity matters.[54] Press liaison was revamped in the late 1950s with the creation of the post of Chief Press Officer, and the 1960s saw much increased attention to public opinion and press relations. Nevertheless, a Bank of England internal report in 1977 criticized the infrequency of press conferences and expert briefings, and the scarcity of Bank spokesmen on radio and television.[55] And that was in spite of three decades of post-war sterling crises.

The post-war financial press paid less attention to the City and the stock market and more to the economy as a whole. This was the outcome of several distinct, but interconnected, developments: the rise of a managerial class in both the private and public sectors; the spread of Keynesian macroeconomic analysis, and focus on national economic events and government policies; the expansion of economic information and reports; and an increase in economic literacy and growing numbers of university graduates. Thus the role of the post-war financial press evolved to encompass 'teaching as well as tipping'.[56] The focus on the macroeconomy and the evaluation of government performance led to the emergence of a 'new breed' – the 'economic journalist'. 'Twenty years ago there were scarcely any ... ten years ago the subject was still being pioneered by Andrew Shonfield [*Observer*] and Samuel Brittan [*Financial Times*], who remain to this day the only two really successful economic journalists Fleet Street has discovered,' wrote Peter Jay, the first 'economics editor' of *The Times*, in *The Listener* in August 1972, soon after the floating of the pound:

> By 'economic journalism' I mean regular journalism which seeks to apply some knowledge of economics to the broad development of such things as prices, output, employment, balance of payments, the world economic environment, monetary conditions ...
>
> ... which excludes both academic and business economists who occasionally write in the newspapers, or occasionally broadcast, and the much larger tribes of City, financial, industrial and labour journalists.
>
> ... a different kind of journalist: one who would specialise by subject rather than by source of information or type of article. This sort of person would, it was hoped, bring some specialist knowledge with him to the reporting, interpretation and comment on an unbroken chain of connected events.[57]

1949 crisis

After the war, the pound joined the new Bretton Woods system of fixed exchange rates pegged to the dollar at $4.03. There were some dozen sterling crises of varying severity between 1947 and the floating of the pound in June 1972, with the devaluations of 1949 and 1967 the most acute. The September 1949 devaluation was prefigured by dwindling reserves, secret Cabinet meetings, and a fever of rumours in Washington. 'The clues were becoming increasingly easy to find,' charged a case study of the press and the crisis. 'Washington was buzzing. The British press was, largely, deaf.'[58] British newspapers made no mention of the rumours and took ministerial denials at face value. The press generally 'had no idea, beyond the managed trickle of news from lobby briefings, what the real position was or what the options were' and accepted 'the most crass and non-inquisitorial explanation', observed journalist Peter Hennessey. 'The main channels of communication between government and the governed offered at best fragmentary, and at worst misleading, coverage.'[59] The *Financial Times* was something of an exception; an editorial on 5 July 1949 referred to 'what is beginning to look suspiciously like a loss of confidence in the present sterling rate, all over the world'.[60] Next day, against the background of an official statement of reserve losses, it criticized government secrecy over the pound: 'The British people ... are entitled to an outline of the immediate steps the Government proposes.'[61] But on 15 July, taking its cue from the Chancellor, Sir Stafford Cripps, it informed readers that: 'Sterling devaluation is as far from the Government's mind as ever.'[62]

Devaluation was announced on 18 September at the annual meeting of the IMF in Washington. The shock cut from $4.03 to $2.80 – 30 per cent – made nonsense of the public denials up to the last minute by Cripps. The *Financial Times* criticized the government for having 'dithered so long on the devaluation brink' squandering reserves, and wondered 'why it ever doubted the value of devaluation at all'.[63] *The Times* welcomed the realism – 'Facts have had the last word; the old rate was becoming too hard to uphold' – and recognized Cripps's courage in making the move.[64] Similarly *The Economist*: 'Devaluation should have been undertaken months ago ... But now that the decision has been taken ... the Chancellor deserves support.'[65] But the Tory press let rip. 'The Government's devaluation announcement begins to look like a pretty cynical confidence trick on the British public,' protested the *Daily Mail*. 'It is the desperate act of a desperate Government whose recklessness and extravagances have helped to push the nation to the edge of disaster – as they did in 1931. They hope by depreciating the £ to tide themselves over at least to the next election.'[66] 'Down goes the £. After months of official denials that devaluation was contemplated ... a reduction in the value of the currency against the dollar that exceeds the wildest forecasts,' declared the *Daily Express*.[67] By contrast the *Manchester Guardian* noted sympathetically: 'That [the Chancellor's] decision is right, in the circumstances as they have become, there can be no serious doubt ... The long game of speculation, bluff and double-bluff is over.'[68] But not for long, with further major sterling crises in 1956, triggered by the Suez crisis, and 1961.

1967 crisis

The first decision of the new Labour administration of 1964 was that there would be no devaluation of the pound; Prime Minister Harold Wilson even forbade ministers and civil servants from discussing devaluation, which became known as the 'unmentionable'. Faced by a run on the pound that had been gathering under the previous administration, the government, instead of the usual defensive package of overseas borrowing plus higher interest rates, which would have raised British unemployment, introduced a unilateral 'temporary import surcharge' to defend the pound.[69] This tariff by another name flagrantly violated Britain's international commitments and outraged trading partners who threatened reprisals. The row heightened mistrust of the administration's competence and good faith and intensified the run on sterling. 'The Government's handling of its import surcharge has almost passed belief,' exclaimed a *Times* leader following a furious meeting of European ministers and a government climbdown.[70] Further sterling crises erupted in 1965 and 1966; indeed the years from 1964 to devaluation in 1967 can be regarded as one long sterling crisis. A Bank of England internal report noted that talk of devaluation began to be heard and that 'the press was beginning to ignore patriotic-type appeals to remain quiet on the subject: *The Observer* [Andrew Shonfield] saying, "The sooner sterling topples the better."'[71]

'There are two ways in which economic journalists can influence economic policy,' wrote William Keegan and Rupert Pennant-Rea, who covered the travails of the pound in the 1960s for, respectively, the *Financial Times* and *The Economist*: 'by what they discuss and what they do not discuss':

> The biggest blot on the reputation of the financial press in economic matters, and still haunts all who lived through it, was the conspiracy of silence over the devaluation issue in 1964–7.

The establishment managed to persuade the serious press that mere discussion of the issue would be harmful to the national interest, one argument being that, through the effect on the financial markets, ventilating the subject would force the issue.

It is difficult to believe the devaluation decision would have been delayed quite so long if the press had not acquiesced in the conspiracy.[72]

Peter Browning, Treasury Chief Press Officer, who saw the relationship from the other side, observed that 'even had some mole of the day popped a perfectly sensible [government] discussion paper on devaluation into the offices of the *Financial Times* newspaper it is doubtful whether it would have been printed, so thoroughly had the media been indoctrinated with their patriotic duty'.[73] And this was despite the conversion from the mid 1960s of many academic economists and economic journalists to floating exchange rates.[74] Such views were expounded in academic journals and books, such as *The Pound Sterling: A Polemic*, by Fred Hirsch, financial editor of *The Economist*, but not in his or other newspapers; post-devaluation *The Economist* confessed that it had 'often visibly pulled its punches when discussing Britain's obviously crumbling exchange rate'.[75]

A new run on the pound got underway in autumn 1967, triggered by dock strikes plus a threatened railway stoppage. Whether restrained by 'patriotic duty' or disengaged from official policy, it was only in the final week before devaluation that financial journalists sounded the alarm.[76] By Thursday, 16 November, when the Chancellor, James Callaghan, was questioned in Parliament, the situation had got out of hand. Possibly mindful of the way that Cripps had been savaged for denying devaluation shortly before it occurred, Callaghan failed to make a forthright denial. This was interpreted as a signal that the decision had been taken – as was the case – and the press felt licensed to comment freely. Commenting next day on the Chancellor's equivocal response, *The Times* edged towards advocating the unmentionable: 'Nothing ... could be less useful than further borrowing in support of a policy which could not be shown to be realistic.'[77] On Saturday, 18 November, it explicitly endorsed devaluation as the best available option.[78] That weekend the value of sterling was reduced from $2.80 to $2.40, a 14.3 per cent devaluation.

Press reaction was scathing. 'The ball is over,' declared the *Financial Times*. 'Maintenance of the sterling exchange rate has been the overriding aim of the Labour Government's economic policy since it took office in 1964. Devaluation is an open and humiliating admission that the policy has failed.'[79] 'The first point to grasp about the tragic and unnecessary devaluation is that few people will trust the pound again,' stated the *Daily Mail*. 'They will not have faith in our money while we have Ministers whose obstinacy and bungling in three years transformed bearable economic troubles into major sterling crises.'[80] 'For *The Economist* this has been a beastly three to four years,' observed *The Economist*. 'Whenever we have pointed out this central fact about the British economy [sterling's overvaluation], we have been told that we were bearing the national currency, and that the speculative drain of blank million dollars from the reserves in such and such a week was all this newspaper's fault ... The same sad lot has befallen anybody writing on economic affairs in Britain between 1964 and 1967.'[81]

The press and the pound

The story of the pound since the First World War is a story of decline in its international role and value, mirroring the relative decline of the British economy. Successive British governments resisted sterling's devaluation, both because of its symbolism and because it impoverished consumers, who had to pay more for imports, and threatened inflation. Governmental priorities in this important dimension of economic policy were widely backed by the press, as in 1925. Moreover, during the crises of 1931 and 1949 the press was publicly supportive of ministers' denials about devaluation, as well as mostly sympathetic regarding the subsequent policy reversals.

For many years, significant relations between financial journalists and the authorities were largely personal and informal, doubtless contributing to an alignment of outlooks. It was not until the 1950s, but more so the 1960s, that relations became professionalized, with the appointment of press officers at the Treasury and the Bank, and the proliferation of official publications, press conferences, and briefings. These endeavours to enhance media information and guidance were part of a broader public relations drive by governments, though there were few other matters with the critical urgency of the pound in a crisis.

The expansion of the authorities' press relations activities paralleled, and to some extent was a response to, a generally diminishing deference on the part of the press and the rise of the economic journalist. The divergence of view about sterling policy between the government and prominent journalists, such as Fred Hirsch, Samuel Brittan, Peter Jay, William Keegan, and others, was a new phenomenon. During the crises of 1964–7, although they stayed silent about the big-picture issues of devaluation or floating, they were notably more harshly critical of crisis management blunders. Unlike 1931 and 1949, the defence of the parity received little engagement while the reception of the policy reversal was starkly harsher. 'Devaluation – who was to blame?' asked Peter Jay in *The Times* on Wednesday, 23 November, four days after the debacle. He fingered two culprits: Harold Macmillan, Prime Minister in the period 'in which the economic seed corn stemming from the 1949 devaluation was frittered away'; and Harold Wilson, 'for refusing to admit the basic facts of the economic situation and then pursuing policies that made devaluation inevitable'. Wilson's role was 'beyond belief' since not only was he 'the leading protagonist of orthodoxy' but 'having taken such an adamant stand against devaluation, he showed complete disregard for official advice on the ways and means to maintain it'. The signed article created 'quite a sensation' since the writer was both the son of a Cabinet minister who had recently been dropped by Wilson, and Callaghan's son-in-law.[82] The row contributed to the discrediting of the economic competence of Wilson and his administration, and thus ultimately to Labour's defeat in 1970.

The new Conservative administration led by Edward Heath conducted a review of arrangements between the Treasury and the press in late 1971 and early 1972 that may have been helpful when a further run on sterling developed in the summer.[83] This time the administration promptly capitulated. 'It is right to float the pound,' declared *The Times*.[84] 'For once a British Government has acted sooner rather than later,' stated the 'delighted' *Daily Mail*. 'We have campaigned for the £ to float permanently … He [the Chancellor] has removed the threat of panic and crisis. He has brought Whitehall one step nearer reality.'[85] 'It is the chief merit of the decision to float that it was taken so promptly,' agreed the *Financial Times*, observing that it was likely the prelude to another devaluation of sterling, as proved to be the case.[86] Though floating was notionally a temporary expedient, the breakdown of the Bretton Woods system in 1973 ensured that it continued. But it was not quite the end of sterling crises, with two further spectaculars to come: in 1976 (see Chapter 18), and in 1992 when the pound dramatically exited the European Exchange Rate Mechanism, with the media playing challenging and significant parts in both episodes.[87]

Notes

1 Anderson (1960).
2 Camrose (1947), p. 12.
3 Bank of England Archive: ADM 10/18. 'Part I: The Bank, the Press and the Public, 1890–1932/3', p. 4.
4 Hobson (1957).
5 BoE, 'I: Bank', p. 23; Bank of England Archive: ADM 10/18. 'Part II: The Bank, the Press and the Public, 1933-1941', p. 39; Sayers (1976), p. 377; Williams (1970), pp. 95–100.
6 BoE, 'I: Bank', pp. 13–14; Sayers (1976), p. 376.
7 Peden (2000), p. 25.
8 Mayhew (1999), p. 207.
9 Sayers (1976), pp. 116–17.
10 'City Notes: Gold Export Embargo', *The Times*, 31 March 1919.
11 'Locking Up the Gold', *Daily Mail*, 31 March 1919.
12 'Currency Problem', *The Times*, 9 November 1921; Feavearyear (1963), pp. 358–9.
13 'Some Tasks for the Coming Year', *The Economist*, 3 January 1925.
14 BoE, 'I: Bank', p. 22.
15 Boyce (1988), pp. 185–7.
16 'Battle of the Gold Standard. What It Is All About', *Daily Mail*, 16 February 1925.
17 'The Return to Gold', *Manchester Guardian*, 5 January 1925.
18 'Some Tasks for the Coming Year', *The Economist*, 3 January 1925.
19 Davenport (1974), pp. 25–8.
20 Harrod (1951), p. 357; Moggridge (1972), pp. 37–97.
21 Kynaston (1988), p. 93.
22 'A Pawn in Policy', *Daily Express*, 30 April 1925; 'A Very Ambitious Budget', *Daily Mail*, 29 April 1925.
23 'The Budget and the Future', *The Observer*, 3 May 1925.
24 Keynes (1925).
25 Hyams (1963), pp. 118–23.
26 'Mr. MacDonald's Task', *The Times*, 17 August 1931.
27 London School of Economics Digital Library. Diary of Virginia Webb Typescript, 23 August 1931; Bassett (1958), p. 114; Hodson (1938), p. 76.

28 'Still Waiting', *The Times*, 24 August 1931; Sayers (1976), p. 399; Moggridge (1972), p. 194.
29 'The Task Before a National Government', *Daily Mirror*, 25 August 1931.
30 'A National Government', *Manchester Guardian*, 25 August 1925.
31 Koss (1984), p. 515.
32 Williams (1970), p. 101.
33 'The National Task', *The Times*, 4 September 1931.
34 'Restoring the Balance', *The Economist*, 19 September 1931.
35 'The First Lap', *The Economist*, 21 September 1931.
36 '"England Expects-!"' *Daily Mail*, 17 September 1931.
37 Williams (1965), pp. 111–12.
38 Williams (1970), p. 105.
39 Rolph (1973), p. 164.
40 'Load Off Our Backs', *Daily Mail*, 21 September 1931.
41 'These Are the Facts', *Daily Express*, 21 September 1931.
42 'Britain's Policy of Self-Defence', *Daily Mirror*, 21 September 1931.
43 'The End of An Epoch', *The Economist*, 26 September 1931.
44 Koss (1984), pp. 512–13.
45 'Sixty Years of Financial Journalism', *Financial Times*, 10 October 1945; Kynaston (1988), p. 524.
46 Dudley Edwards (1993), pp. 875, 951.
47 Camrose (1947), p. 13; Ayerst (1971), p. 593.
48 Keegan and Pennant-Rea (1979), p. 137.
49 Fleet (1983).
50 'When Money Makes News and News Makes Money', *The Economist*, 26 December 1987.
51 BoE, 'II: Bank', p. 37.
52 Hobson (1957).
53 BoE, 'II: Bank', pp. 38–9; Capie (2010), p. 50.
54 The National Archives. T245/1–61. Treasury: Information Division Files, 1947–1973.
55 Capie (2010), pp. 776–7.
56 Parsons (1989), p. 92.
57 Jay (1972).
58 Cockerell, Hennessy, and Walker (1984), pp. 96–7.
59 Hennessy (1985), p. 96.
60 'Commonwealth Help?' *Financial Times*, 5 July 1949.
61 'Background to Cripps', *Financial Times*, 6 July 1949.
62 'Latest and Last', *Financial Times*, 15 July 1949.
63 'Chancellor's Chickens', *Financial Times*, 20 September 1949; 'Currency Realignment', *Financial Times*, 22 September 1949.
64 'Dearer Dollars', *The Times*, 19 September 1949; McDonald (1984), p. 188.
65 'Defeat or Opportunity?' *The Economist*, 24 September 1949.
66 'Humbug', *Daily Mail*, 20 September 1949.
67 'Opinion', *Daily Express*, 19 September 1949.
68 'The Pound', *Manchester Guardian*, 19 September 1949.
69 Roberts (2013), pp. 209–29.
70 'Mishandled', *The Times*, 21 November 1964.
71 Capie (2010), p. 223.
72 Keegan and Pennant-Rea (1979), p. 139.
73 Browning (1986), p. 6.
74 Leeson (2003), pp. 47–9.
75 Hirsch (1965); 'Life Begins at $2.40?' *The Economist*, 25 November 1967.
76 Grigg (1995), p. 67.
77 'Mr. Callaghan's Reply', *The Times*, 17 November 1967.
78 'Right Rate for Europe', *The Times*, 18 November 1967.

79 'After the Ball Was Over', *Financial Times*, 20 November 1967.
80 'Who'll Trust the £ Again?' *Daily Mail*, 20 November 1967.
81 'Life Begins at $2.40?' *The Economist*, 25 November 1967.
82 Grigg (1976), p. 71.
83 The National Archives. PREM 15/1146. Relations Between HM Treasury and Press, December 1971–March 1972.
84 'It Is Right to Float the Pound', *The Times*, 24 June 1972.
85 'Take the Plunge the Water's Lovely', *Daily Mail*, 24 June 1972.
86 'Swift Progress Needed', *Financial Times*, 26 June 1972.
87 Stephens (1996).

References

Anderson, Charles (1960) 'One Hundred Years: *Investors' Chronicle* Centenary Number', *Investors' Chronicle*, 10 June.

Ayerst, David (1971) *'Guardian': Biography of a Newspaper*, London: Collins.

Bassett, R. (1958) *1931 Political Crisis*, London: Macmillan.

Boyce, R.W.D. (1988) 'Creating the Myth of Consensus: Public Opinion and Britain's Return to the Gold Standard in 1925', in Cottrell, P.L. and Moggridge, D.E. (eds.) *Money and Power: Essays in Honour of L. S. Pressnell*, London: Macmillan, pp. 173–97.

Browning, Peter (1986) *The Treasury & Economic Policy 1964–1985*, London: Longman.

Camrose, Viscount (1947) *British Newspapers and Their Controllers*, London: Cassell.

Capie, Forrest (2010) *The Bank of England: 1950s to 1979*, Cambridge: Cambridge University Press.

Cockerell, Michael, Hennessey, Peter, and Walker, David (1984) *Sources Close to the Prime Minister: Inside the Hidden World of the News Manipulators*, London: Macmillan.

Davenport, Nicholas (1974) *Memoirs of a City Radical*, London: Weidenfeld & Nicolson.

Dudley Edwards, Ruth (1993) *The Pursuit of Reason: 'The Economist' 1843–1993*, London: Hamish Hamilton.

Feavearyear, Sir Albert (1963) *The Pound Sterling*, Oxford: Clarendon Press.

Fleet, Kenneth (1983) *The Influence of the Financial Press*, London: Worshipful Company of Stationers and Newspaper Makers.

Grigg, John (1995) *The History of 'The Times', Vol. VI: The Thomson Years, 1966–1981*, London: Harper Collins.

Harrod, R.F. (1951) *The Life of John Maynard Keynes*, London: Macmillan.

Hennessy, Peter (1985) *What the Papers Never Said*, London: Portcullis Press.

Hirsch, Fred (1965) *The Pound Sterling: A Polemic*, London: Victor Gollancz.

Hobson, Oscar (1957) 'As I See It … ', *The Banker*, June.

Hodson, H.V. (1938) *Slump and Recovery 1929–1937*, Oxford: Oxford University Press.

Hyams, Edward (1963) *The 'New Statesman': The History of the First Fifty Years 1913–1963*, London: Longman.

Jay, Peter (1972) 'On Being An Economic Journalist', *The Listener*, 24 August.

Keegan, William and Pennant-Rea, R. (1979) *Who Runs the Economy? Control and Influence in British Economic Policy*, London: Temple Smith.

Keynes, J.M. (1925) *The Economic Consequences of Mr Churchill*, London: Hogarth Press.

Koss, Stephen (1984) *The Rise and Fall of the Political Press in Britain, Vol. 2: The Twentieth Century*, London: Hamish Hamilton.

Kynaston, David (1988) *The 'Financial Times': A Centenary History*, London: Viking.

Leeson, Robert (2003) *Ideology and the International Economy: The Decline and Fall of Bretton Woods*, London: Palgrave.

McDonald, Iverach (1984) *The History of 'The Times', Vol. V: Struggles in War and Peace 1939–1966*, London: Times Books.

Mayhew, Nicholas (1999) *Sterling: The Rise and Fall of a Currency*, London: Allen Lane.

Moggridge, D.E. (1972) *British Monetary Policy 1924–1931: The Norman Conquest of $4.86*, Cambridge: Cambridge University Press.

Parsons, Wayne (1989) *The Power of the Financial Press: Journalism and Economic Opinion in Britain and America*, Cheltenham: Edward Elgar.

Peden, George (2000) *The Treasury and British Public Policy 1906–1959*, Oxford: Oxford University Press.

Roberts, Richard (2013) '"Unwept, Unhonoured and Unsung": Britain's Import Surcharge, 1964–1966, and Currency Crisis Management', *Financial History Review*, 20, August, pp. 209–29.

Rolph, C.H. (1973) *Kingsley: The Life, Letters and Diaries of Kingsley Martin*, London: Victor Gollancz.

Sayers, R.S. (1976) *The Bank of England 1891–1944*, Cambridge: Cambridge University Press.

Stephens, Philip (1996) *Politics and the Pound: The Conservatives' Struggle With Sterling*, London: Macmillan.

Williams, Francis (1965) *A Pattern of Rulers*, London: Longman.

——(1970) *Nothing So Strange: An Autobiography*, London: Cassell.

18

'GOODBYE, GREAT BRITAIN'?

The press, the Treasury, and the 1976 IMF crisis

Duncan Needham

Introduction

On 28 September 1976, hearing that sterling had fallen to a new low, the Chancellor of the Exchequer, Denis Healey, turned back from Heathrow Airport, returned to the Treasury, and announced that Britain was applying to the International Monetary Fund (IMF) for its largest ever loan.[1] Thus began the denouement of a crisis that had been playing for six months, ever since a botched devaluation in early March had taken the pound below $2 for the first time.[2] In certain respects, 1976 was just another in the long series of sterling crises that punctuates post-war British economic history (see Chapter 17). With a chronic shortage of foreign currency holdings, sterling was prone to speculative attack, and Healey's announcement came shortly after the Bank of England experienced its largest ever loss of reserves.[3] Nor was there anything new about turning to the IMF for assistance. Britain drew from the Fund on 10 separate occasions between 1947 and 1976.[4] But while the crisis may have started with 'the familiar tolling of the sterling bells', 1976 was different.[5] When Healey turned back, sterling was under attack because the British government had reached the limits of its credit, both at home and abroad. The crisis was resolved, not by further devaluing the pound, as in the past, but by providing Britain's creditors with the reassurance that, under the IMF's supervision, the government would finally get its borrowing under control. In modern parlance, 1976 was a sovereign debt crisis.

The 1976 crisis was also different because, to an unprecedented degree, it played out in and through the British press.[6] The broadsheets provided the forum for an academic debate that helped to bring a reluctant Cabinet to a realistic negotiating position with the IMF by undermining the alternative strategy of widespread import controls. The press also helped to usher the negotiations to a practical conclusion that ensured the government's survival by providing the outlet for extensive high-level leaking and briefing. The IMF mission flew back to Washington in December 1976, having extracted far less than it had expected in return for a $3.9 billion loan and its 'good housekeeping seal of approval'. This owed much to the role of the British press over three climactic months in 1976.

Prologue

While the origins of the 1976 crisis lie buried in decades of British relative economic underperformance, two decisions taken in the last weeks of the Heath government stand out. The first was an agreement to link wages to the Retail Price Index from November 1973. Having presided over the monetary explosion of 1972–73, Heath thus 'hardwired' inflation into the UK economy just before OPEC quadrupled the price of oil. The second was the decision to 'tunnel through' the oil shock to North Sea oil revenues with increased government borrowing. Financing the increased deficit rather than deflating enjoyed cross-party support, as well as the approval of the IMF.[7] Indeed, Edmund Dell, Secretary of State for Trade at the time, believes that by encouraging oil importers to finance their enlarged current account deficits with borrowing, the IMF provided the government with an alibi for not deflating.[8] But not every industrial nation could count on becoming an oil exporter within six years. As the former Permanent Secretary to the Treasury Sir Douglas Wass explains: 'the borrowing programme the Bank and Treasury ... embarked upon in 1974 was strictly for long-term credit intended to take care of the financing needs until North Sea Oil revenues began to flow and the current balance of trade improved'.[9]

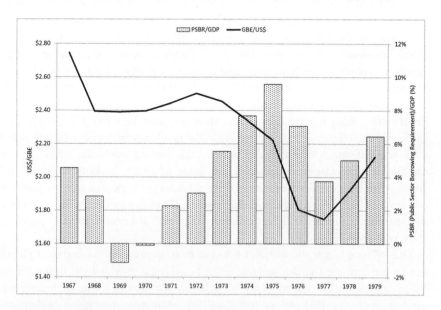

FIGURE 18.1 Sterling/dollar exchange rate and PSBR as a percentage of GDP, 1967–1979
Sources: Bank of England Quarterly Bulletin and N.H. Dimsdale, 'British Monetary Policy Since 1945', in N.F.R. Crafts and N.W.C. Woodward (eds.), *The British Economy Since 1945* (Oxford, 1991).

'Tunnelling through' also involved borrowing dollars.[10] In December 1975, Healey arranged to borrow a total of $2.3 billion from the Fund.[11] By then, the Public Sector Borrowing Requirement (PSBR) estimate had risen to £11.8 billion (11 per cent of GDP), with a further £12.4 billion anticipated in 1976/77.[12] The Fund's Managing Director told the Chancellor it was now 'essential to secure cuts in public expenditure which would produce substantial reductions in the PSBR over the next few years'.[13] However, the 1975 loan facilities came with low conditionality, and Healey was able to borrow against a vague promise to limit the PSBR to £12 billion in 1976/77.[14] Nonetheless, IMF officials had clearly signalled that further borrowing would be conditional upon a lower PSBR, something they confirmed five months later during the routine annual consultation.[15] Summing up the May 1976 consultations, Wass concludes: 'there could have been little doubt in the minds of UK policy makers that if recourse had to be made to the IMF for help later in the year the terms would involve a big fiscal policy change'.[16]

'Tunnelling through' rather than deflating contributed to UK inflation of nearly 25 per cent in 1975. While this exceeded the OECD average, the pound remained remarkably stable, propped up, in part, by the reflux of sterling from those newly enriched oil producers with historical ties to the UK.[17] While increased sterling balances were welcomed as a short-term expedient, they created problems elsewhere. Higher UK inflation meant domestic costs outstripped global costs. British manufacturers needed a weaker pound if they were to produce the desired export-led recovery. Exchange rate policy in 1975 was therefore, opportunistically and discreetly, to depreciate sterling to maintain 'constant competitiveness', while 'creaming off' foreign currency whenever the pound was strong, i.e. selling on a rising market. As the IMF's European Director explained: 'the Chancellor has also to consider the effects of depreciation on the large holders of sterling. In this area, the tactics are to avoid the appearance of seeking a depreciation but rather to accept depreciation, after the expenditure of some reserves, whenever market pressures are strong.'[18] If the international holders of sterling realized what was afoot they could, in theory, demand repayment in dollars at a moment's notice. With the reserves standing at a fraction of the sterling balances, the Bank did not have the money to repay.[19]

In 1968, the previous Labour government had persuaded the official holders to keep a portion of their reserves in sterling by writing dollar-price guarantees. The need for continued financing after the oil shock saw the guarantees extended beyond their scheduled expiry in December 1973. This came at a cost that the Treasury was unwilling to bear indefinitely. And, as Samuel Brittan pointed out in the *Financial Times*, the Treasury was 'more concerned for our competitive position than with allaying the nerves of foreign holders of sterling'.[20] With the guarantees finally expiring in December 1974, the sterling balance holders had to rely on the willingness and ability of the British monetary authorities to maintain the value of the pound. In 1975, they gave fair warning that they would run down their balances if sterling weakened.[21] The fulfilment of this warning after March 1976 helped to transform a sterling crisis into a sovereign debt crisis.

The botched devaluation

On 1 March 1976, with sterling still stubbornly high, the Chancellor and the Governor of the Bank of England decided to force the pace, albeit they had yet to agree the modalities of how the pound might be lowered without dislodging the sterling balances.[22] Two days later, Bank and Treasury officials met to discuss tactics.[23] A step change was ruled out as too risky.[24] Officials preferred the subterfuge of an 'induced slide'. This might be achieved through more aggressive creaming-off, and/or by lowering the interest-rate differential against the dollar. The key was 'to avoid exposing that the government was directly responsible'.[25]

Somewhat unexpectedly, 'D-Day' arrived the next day.[26] On 4 March, Bank dealers complied with Treasury instructions 'to resist robustly any further appreciation whatsoever' by aggressively creaming off $282 million.[27] As the Bank's chief foreign exchange dealer explained: 'in order to counter the Treasury's near pathological fear of a narrowing effective depreciation, we came back as sellers of sterling at lower levels on a number of occasions'.[28] This was interpreted by currency dealers as the Bank selling on a falling market, something it was pledged never to do. When sentiment turned against sterling in the afternoon, Bank dealers withdrew until the last hour of trading:

> In normal circumstances, with such a swift reversal, we should have begun to buy a little sterling almost immediately. Had we done so immediately however and been successful, those elements in the Treasury anxious for further depreciation could well have accused us of trying to stabilise the effective depreciation at 30.1% [below the 1971 value].[29]

The next day, the Bank followed through with a planned 25 basis point reduction in Minimum Lending Rate. After aggressively creaming off on 4 March, this was the second phase of the strategy to lower the pound by narrowing the interest rate differential with the dollar. The market was in no doubt that there had been a change in tactics and took sterling below $2 for the first time. As the *Financial Times* pointed out: 'the fall was in line with the Government's known long-term policy of allowing sterling to fall to reflect the difference between inflation rates in the UK and other countries in order to maintain the competitive position of UK exporters'.[30] Over the next fortnight, the Bank spent almost 20 per cent of its precious reserves stabilizing the rate around $1.92.[31] With a continued balance of payments deficit to finance and the falling pound triggering the predicted withdrawals of the sterling balances, each dollar spent made another approach to the IMF more likely. Commenting on the pound's weakness, the *Daily Telegraph* warned:

> Only painful cuts in public expenditure will convince the world that we mean to live within our real income. Probably we shall have to wait until the Government is forced to seek a major loan from the IMF. Then there may well be stringent terms on public spending.[32]

Ironically, as a direct result of botching the devaluation in March 1976, Britain was thrown one last lifeline before the increasingly likely session with the Fund. The Europeans were annoyed at the British for instigating the exchange rate volatility that saw the French franc ejected from the European monetary 'snake' on 15 March.[33] Britain had reneged on an agreement, signed at Rambouillet the previous November, that the leading central banks would cooperate to 'counter disorderly market conditions or erratic fluctuations in exchange rates'.[34] When sterling reached a new low in early June, the leading industrial nations invoked 'the spirit of Rambouillet' to assemble a $5.3 billion credit facility for Britain.[35] However, the loan came with conditions. There was a presumption on the part of the creditors that the government would use the breathing space to cut the PSBR.[36] If not, Healey would be forced to repay any amounts outstanding after six months with a high conditionality loan from the IMF. Fay and Young, in a series of *Sunday Times* articles from 1978, make great play of this 'IMF take-out' (replacement loan), suggesting that the Under-Secretary of the US Treasury, Ed Yeo, dispelled the euphoria that greeted the credit facility in London by imposing the take-out on a reluctant Prime Minister and Chancellor.[37] However, IMF take-outs were a long-standing feature of multilateral credit arrangements.[38] The clause was no surprise to the Governor, Gordon Richardson, who reassured his Federal Reserve counterpart, Arthur Burns, from the outset that any drawings would be 'fully covered by our undrawn tranches at the IMF'.[39] American officials had been telling the British for months that drawings would require an IMF take-out and, in case Healey had forgotten, Johannes Witteveen, Managing Director of the Fund, reminded him during a telephone conversation on 3 June.[40] Healey's claim that the $5.3 billion facility came 'with no strings attached' was disingenuous.[41] It was precisely the 'strings' that marked the transformation from a sterling crisis into a sovereign debt crisis that would be resolved only by reducing the PSBR.

The reactions of the different financial markets to the loan facility were revealing. With the Bank able to call upon an additional $5.3 billion, the sterling market entered a period of relative calm. The gilt market went on a buyers' strike. As *The Times* pointed out, all Healey had done was 'borrow' another six months in which to reduce the PSBR before cuts were imposed by the IMF.[42] This he set about doing, extracting £1 billion of cuts after an 'appallingly difficult' round of Cabinet meetings.[43] Combined with a £1 billion rise in National Insurance contributions sprung upon ministers at the eleventh hour, this reduced the PSBR estimate for 1977/78 to £9 billion. Despite heavy briefing of the press before the announcement, the package was poorly received. There was a sense that Healey had fluffed his last opportunity to cut spending unilaterally and the markets resumed their slide. On 9 September, following the publication of a £905 million drop in the sterling balances, and with no prospect of repaying what had already been drawn on the loan facility, the Bank was instructed to 'let the rate go'.[44] The next day, the Permanent Secretary informed Healey that another visit to the Fund was inevitable.[45]

The battle of the PSBR

There are several accounts of the often fraught negotiations that preceded the IMF's $3.9 billion loan in December 1976, with Sir Douglas Wass providing the most detailed.[46] There were three core issues: the 'correct' level for sterling, acceptable monetary targets, and an appropriate level for the PSBR in 1977/78.[47] Since all involved in the negotiations believed that export-led growth would require a 'competitive' pound and Healey had already announced a monetary target in July, the PSBR was the most contentious issue.[48] The Prime Minister, James Callaghan, claims that his fallback position was always the £9 billion figure agreed by Cabinet in July.[49] Healey's position changed over the course of the negotiations, reflecting the split within the Treasury between the Home Finance Department, in favour of minimal cuts, and the Overseas Finance Department, more in tune with international opinion, which argued for cuts of up to £3 billion. The IMF's initial negotiating position had emerged during preliminary discussions in July.[50] Fund economists were concerned that a PSBR above £6.5 billion might 'crowd out' the private sector borrowing required to finance export-led growth, and this was the figure communicated to the Treasury.[51] Arcane negotiations about the correct level of the PSBR were usually conducted behind closed doors and reported, if at all, in the specialized financial press. However, such was the sense of crisis in the autumn of 1976, with the survival of the government in real doubt, that a public debate erupted within the broadsheets. It is worth, therefore, briefly sketching the positions taken by the quality press on the PSBR. *The Times* wanted £5 billion of cuts in 1977/78, with further reductions leading to a Budget in 'near balance' by 1979/80.[52] The *Daily Telegraph* and *The Economist* took broadly similar positions.[53] The *Financial Times* argued for a minimum of £2 billion, while *The Guardian* was closest to the final outcome with its call for just £1 billion of cuts.[54] By the time the package emerged, after several weeks of tense negotiations in Whitehall, most of these positions had shifted, partly as a result of a lively academic debate that took place within the letters page of *The Times*.

The academic debate

On 2 December *The Times* political columnist, Ronald Butt, wrote:

> The most amazing feature of the debate on the economy and the IMF loan which has preceded the assembly of the package on public spending and taxation now put by Mr Healey in front of the Cabinet is the extent to which the argument has been carried on, in, and (which is not quite the same thing) through the press.[55]

The debate 'in' the press involved a theoretical battle between several of Britain's leading economists. The catalyst was a *Times* editorial, 'Programme for Economic Stability', published on 20 September.[56] As well as an immediate £5 billion cut in public expenditure, the newspaper called for a series of declining money supply targets, a 'cleanly' floating pound, and indirect tax rises. The Cambridge economist and former Treasury adviser Wynne Godley responded a week later, calling the article 'a useful stimulus to the public discussion, which has so far been curiously impoverished'.[57] Godley was a founder of the New Cambridge School, which, disillusioned with the practical results of devaluation, was then advocating a 1930s-style General Tariff behind which British industry could be nursed back to health. He believed *The Times* programme to be 'dangerously mistaken', with politically unacceptable consequences for unemployment. Only 'large scale nonselective industrial protection' would solve Britain's endemic balance of payments problem. This drew out the monetarists. Brian Griffiths of the London School of Economics (LSE) and Geoffrey Wood of City University argued, from a largely theoretical standpoint, that protection would simply divert resources to unproductive sectors of the economy and raise the exchange rate.[58] This would have negative consequences for export volumes and unemployment. On 11 October the former IMF economist John Williamson joined the fray, labelling protection 'the latest, and silliest, example of the tendency to search for simple answers to complex problems that has left such unhappy scars on British economic policy'.[59] This prompted a withering response from the Cambridge economist (and former Treasury adviser) Lord Kaldor, for whom Williamson argued 'as if Sir Roy Harrod, Lord Keynes and other distinguished economists of the twentieth century had never existed'.[60]

The debate centred on the merits of protection versus devaluation, particularly on the contribution of the 1967 devaluation to the eventual improvement in the current account in 1969. Godley and Kaldor believed it had contributed little. Rather, it was tight fiscal and monetary policy that had generated the surplus by restraining domestic demand. The Oxford economists John Flemming and Maurice Scott disagreed. Devaluation had failed because of supply-side constraints. Remove these, they argued, and devaluation would work.[61] They were supported by another former Chief Economic Adviser, Sir Alec Cairncross, also by then at Oxford, who was convinced that devaluation would work 'in the end'.[62]

With views sufficiently entrenched to rule out a consensus, the debate shifted to the PSBR. The public sector deficit might be the proximate cause of the balance of payments deficit, as the New Cambridge economists argued, or it may work through the private sector, by generating a higher private sector surplus, as the 'international monetarists' of the London Business School (LBS) believed.[63] Either way, all were agreed that the PSBR was too high. The question was how far and how fast it should be reduced. In his 21 October Mansion House speech, Healey argued that cuts on the scale proposed by *The Times* would reduce the standard of living by at least 10 per cent, lower output by 5 per cent, and add a million to the ranks of the unemployed.[64] *The Times* reaffirmed its position, prompting an intervention from another former Treasury adviser, Michael Posner, recently enough departed to represent the 'Treasury view'.[65] While 'the public must by now be a little fed up with economists' theoretical posturings', Posner nonetheless felt *The Times* programme merited a considered response.[66] An immediate cut of £5 billion was 'merely the Treasury doctrine of 1925'.[67] It would take years rather than months for the private sector to fill the gap in demand. In any event, the newspaper had given little indication of where the axe would fall, something *The Times* rectified on 15 November with a detailed programme of cuts.[68]

By the middle of November, negotiations in Whitehall between the Treasury and the IMF were deadlocked. This provided the context for a detailed intervention from seven economists (the 'seven'), led by Wilfred Beckerman of Balliol College, Oxford, who sought to chart a course between the deflationists and the protectionists.[69] As the *Financial Times* pointed out, the group boasted impressive establishment connections and, together, comprised 'an almost archetypal [Treasury] Economic Adviser'.[70] Their powerful case against rapid deficit reduction and protection in favour of further devaluation provided 'the warmest endorsement the Chancellor has received for a very long time'.[71] While the 'seven' originally set out to refute the New Cambridge case for protection, they succeeded in establishing some common ground. All were agreed that Britain needed an export-led recovery. The Cambridge economists thought British industry was in such poor shape that this could only happen behind a tariff wall; the 'seven' believed that with the right supply-side reforms, devaluation could be made to work. Both groups agreed that to slash the PSBR along the lines suggested by *The Times*, the LBS, or the monetarists of the LSE and City University would be hugely and unnecessarily damaging.

On 25 November, having opened the two-month-long debate, Godley drew it to a close.[72] He still differed with the 'seven' on the merits of protection, but he hoped they were right that the pound had already dropped far enough to generate a balance of payments surplus. Summarizing the debate in *The Guardian*, Peter Jenkins wrote:

> it was in the columns of the newspapers, notably in the columns of the Times – under the very eye of the enemy, so to speak – that the intellectual dispute took place ... The rallying of the neo-Keynesians (with honours especially to Wilfred Beckerman, Michael Posner and Wynne Godley, in spite of the last-named's protectionist heresies) caused the monetarists at least to shift their ground. Extreme talk of reductions in the PSBR of as much as £5 billions in a single year (by the editor of the Times, for example) was exposed as the dangerous nonsense it had always been.[73]

While Jenkins was careful to point out that there were few theoretical monetarists within either the Treasury or the Bank, and none within Cabinet, monetarist arguments *had* been used to justify large spending cuts. The conclusion of the academic debate in favour of a small reduction in the PSBR and against tariffs helped Callaghan and Healey to overturn an initial Cabinet majority against the deal then being negotiated with the IMF. On 27 November, on the eve of the crucial series of Cabinet meetings, the *Evening Standard* reported: 'What is now discernible is a movement among both economists and politicians towards a common view that really savage cuts in public spending at this juncture would do more harm than good.'[74] The IMF's official historian is, naturally, more circumspect: 'the policies of Prime Minister Callaghan were shaped amid the domestic political debate within the United Kingdom'.[75] The theoretical part of that debate took place in the press, primarily in the letters page of *The Times*. The debate was also carried out 'through' the press. We therefore turn to the dark arts of leaking and briefing.

Leaking and briefing

The IMF was paranoid about leaks. After checking into their Mayfair hotel on 1 November under assumed names, officials were warned by a Bank contact that their rooms were bugged.[76] Their paranoia was justified since, despite a prohibition on mentioning specific targets for the pound, the *Sunday Times* a week earlier had reported that 'The Fund thinks that sterling should be let down to about $1.50 to the £ (against today's $1.64).'[77] The next day, the pound suffered its biggest ever single-day fall outside of a formal devaluation.[78] Healey was forced to issue a statement that, while falling short of an explicit denial, described the article as 'irresponsible'.[79] The Acting Managing Director of the Fund said there was 'absolutely no basis in fact' to a story which the US Treasury Secretary called 'irresponsible and patently untrue'.[80] The journalist responsible, Malcolm Crawford, was accused in Parliament of being 'thoroughly unpatriotic' and the *Sunday Times* was reported to the Press Council.[81] In the event, the Council ruled in favour of the newspaper on the grounds that it had taken 'reasonable steps' to check its story.[82] Not only was the story true, Crawford's source was impeccable – the UK's own IMF Director, Bill Ryrie.[83] Shortly afterwards, the IMF's European head, Alan Whittome, informed his Managing Director that 'all those nearest the calculations and almost all the economists believe that a rate at around $1.50 to $1.60 per £1 sterling is probably "right" at the present time', and that 'a further depreciation of the rate is unavoidable'.[84]

For the first two weeks of November, Treasury officials were prohibited from discussing policy changes with the IMF. They were less taciturn with British journalists. Just before the Malcolm Crawford story broke, Frances Cairncross wrote in *The Guardian*: 'The Treasury and the Bank of England, tired of being told by people like us that they have been doing their job badly, have started to ring up and remonstrate sadly with critical financial journalists.'[85] While officials were remonstrating, their ministers were briefing. On 6 November, the *Financial Times* carried the scoop that the latest Treasury forecasts had the PSBR for 1977/78 overshooting the £9 billion figure agreed in Cabinet in July by £2 billion.[86] The article reported the 'growing fear' that savage cuts in the PSBR 'could further deflate the economy at the worst possible time, adding to unemployment and damaging what is a very weak economic recovery'.[87] Whittome had conceded that if the forecasts 'showed both a continued high level of unemployment and a somewhat better balance of payments picture, he would be more sympathetic to a larger PSBR than otherwise'.[88] A higher unemployment estimate duly helped the Treasury 'massage' the PSBR estimate up to £11 billion.[89] The Fund was immediately dubious. The Managing Director 'expressed a strong suspicion that the figure for £11 billion for the PSBR in 1977/78 was "a trick", so that the British could make "cuts" of £2 billion and thus keep to their chosen figure of £9 billion'.[90] Even the Prime Minister doubted the forecast. On 10 November the Fund's Managing Director was told that Callaghan had asked 'for an assessment of the estimates from ourselves, whom he deemed a trustworthy independent group'.[91] Former Treasury official Andrew Britton has since revealed:

> The IMF were very keen to give us targets that we could meet. That was their main priority and therefore if it appeared that we were over-forecasting Domestic Credit Expansion (DCE) or the PSBR, that was actually helpful in a sense because it meant that in the event it was going to be easier to get them to the numbers we'd agreed. Remember, as well as agreeing the size of the cuts we also had to agree what the target numbers were to be and it was very important to them, as it was to us, that the targets should in fact be achieved.[92]

Two days after the PSBR leak, *The Times* carried a front-page story under the byline 'Our Economics Staff' which, in contrast to its own editorial stance, reported: 'the general feeling, with which the IMF is expected to concur, is that the Treasury's new "bearish" forecasts for the level of economic activity make it less rather than more desirable to change the strategy to a smaller target deficit for the Budget next year'.[93] Former Treasury press officer Peter Browning calls this 'a most curious piece' which 'read like a Ministerial lecture to the IMF: perhaps that is what it was'.[94] If this first article read like a lecture, a subsequent article (also by 'Our Economics Staff') was a rebuke: 'it is not the function of middle-ranking IMF civil servants to treat with national governments on questions of policy'.[95] Indeed, 'there is no question of the IMF visitors making demands or laying down terms for the British drawing, although there has been some convergence of official Treasury and IMF opinion about the likely course of credit creation in Britain and the budget deficit next year'.[96] Conservative Party strategists compared this series of articles to the Kremlin's official pronouncements through the pages of the Soviet newspaper *Pravda*.[97] The briefing was certainly effective. While the academic debate was still raging in *The Times* letters page, ministerial briefing was changing the terms of the public debate in the opinion pages. The *Financial Times*, which had been calling for £2–£2.5 billion of cuts, scaled back to £1.5 billion.[98] The *Economist* now considered that £5 billion might be too much.[99] Even the hostile *Wall Street Journal* now argued that 'the last thing Great Britain needs is more austerity'.[100]

The Prime Minister opened the first of the crucial Cabinet meetings to discuss the package by stressing the need for absolute secrecy, since 'any leaks of views expressed in Cabinet could only be harmful to the country and the Government'.[101] The well-informed reporting of these Cabinet meetings in the press shows how little heed was paid to this warning. Indeed, there were so many leaks that Granada TV was able to reconstruct the Cabinet meetings in a documentary where senior ministers were played by journalists.[102] Did all this leaking and briefing make any difference to the final outcome? *The Guardian* certainly thought so:

> Seldom can the visit of an IMF mission to a country in difficulties have been accompanied by such an intense and open public debate. There is not much doubt that without the debate the Cabinet would have followed the Treasury in conceding to the IMF harsher terms than will now be agreed.[103]

The Cabinet finally agreed to cut public expenditure in 1977/78 by £1 billion, which, combined with the sale of £500 million of the Bank's holding in British Petroleum, reduced the PSBR forecast to £8.7 billion, with a further £1.5 billion of cuts in 1978/79 conditional upon the economy growing by 3.5 per cent. As such, the final outcome was remarkably close to Callaghan's opening position.[104] It could in no way be described as a victory for the IMF, as the US Senate Foreign Relations Committee recognized at the time: 'Callaghan apparently succeeded in convincing the IMF that there would be dire consequences if the British Government were pushed to the wall and forced to accept a tough deflationary package as a condition for the loan.'[105] The report suggested that the issues at stake were so 'basic to the fabric of British society that they required the broadest debate and consensus within the full spectrum of the Labour Party'.[106] The British press played a vital role in forging that consensus. Nonetheless, having shifted their own positions during the course of the negotiations, the newspapers reacted grudgingly to the 15 December package. The *Financial Times* felt that the measures were 'the very least that the IMF would accept' while the *Daily Telegraph* saw 'no cure' in a package described by *The Times* as a 'hotch-potch of wild guesses and pious hopes'.[107] *The Guardian*'s reaction was the most surprising:

> The Government has failed. It has produced a package which satisfies no-one, convinces no-one and in which nobody believes – least of all the people who put it together. The only thing which the package has achieved is to persuade the IMF to agree to recommend the loan. The cynical may say that this is all it was ever meant to achieve. But from the grudging way in which the Fund is parting with its money, even the IMF would appear to regard the package as only just good enough.[108]

The market's initial reaction was to agree, with sterling, equities, and gilts all losing ground. And yet, within a fortnight, the pound was 15 cents off its October lows and the Bank was intervening to stop it rising too far above the $1.60–$1.65 range agreed with the Fund.[109] By October 1977, the authorities had added more than $15 billion of reserves, lowered interest rates by 10 percentage points, and were enjoying export-led growth. Even the PSBR was undershooting the IMF ceiling, with an out-turn in 1977/78 of just £5.6 billion. This led Healey to lament that if the true facts had been known at the time, Britain might have avoided the whole painful experience.[110]

Conclusions

It would be absurd to claim that the 1976 crisis was resolved entirely, or even largely, by the UK press. After intense negotiations between the Treasury and the IMF, the crucial decisions were made in a series of Cabinet meetings which represent, for Bernard Donoughue, 'the high point of old style Cabinet government'.[111] Indeed, as Peter Jay points out, Callaghan was partly using the IMF as a weapon to impose economic discipline on his Cabinet colleagues.[112] And we must not forget that the IMF was undergoing its own existential crisis as it sought to carve out a role for itself in a new world of floating exchange rates.[113] But it was a close-run thing. Without the academic debate in the letters page of *The Times* concluding in favour of the Treasury's position, and extensive ministerial leaking and briefing, it would have been even harder for Callaghan and Healey to overturn an initial Cabinet majority against the final package. And, as the US Senate Foreign Relations Committee recognized, the consensus had to include the full spectrum of the Labour Party. With a Parliamentary majority of just one in December 1976, it was by no means certain that Healey's December mini-Budget would pass through the floor of the House. That it did owed a great deal to the role played by the UK press.

Notes

1 I am grateful to Sir Samuel Brittan, Sir Alan Budd, Frances Cairncross, Peter Jay, William Keegan, Adam Raphael, Richard Roberts, Hugh Stephenson, the participants of the 'Soothsayers of Doom' symposium held at City University on 12 December 2011, and the members of the Cambridge Social and Economic History seminar for their comments on earlier versions of this chapter. In this chapter, 1972/73 means the fiscal year ending April 1973. '1972–73' means the two calendar years 1972 and 1973.

Having received Cabinet Committee approval to approach the IMF, Healey was en route to the IMF's annual conference to open negotiations.

2 While the pound had been floating since June 1972, the Bank was operating a managed float.
3 'Big Capital Outflow Swells UK Deficit', *The Times*, 8 September 1976.
4 Britain drew upon IMF resources in 1948, 1956, 1961, 1964, 1965, 1968, 1969, 1972, and twice in early 1976.
5 The phrase comes from B. Donoughue, *Prime Minister: The Conduct of Policy Under Harold Wilson and James Callaghan* (London, 1987), p. 67.
6 K.M. Burk and A.K. Cairncross, *Goodbye, Great Britain: The 1976 IMF Crisis* (London, 1992), p. xi.
7 M.G. de Vries, *The International Monetary Fund, 1972–1978, Vol. I: Narrative and Analysis* (Washington DC, 1985), pp. 465–6.
8 E.E. Dell, *A Hard Pounding: Politics and Economic Crisis, 1974–1976* (Oxford, 1991), pp. 56–7.
9 The Treasury was careful to schedule debt maturities to coincide with peak oil production in the early 1980s, effectively mortgaging the North Sea; D.W.G. Wass, *Decline to Fall: The Making of British Macro-Economic Policy and the 1976 IMF Crisis* (Oxford, 2008), p. 197.
10 In 1974, the government borrowed $1.5 billion from a syndicate of commercial banks, guaranteed $2.6 billion of loans to the nationalized industries, and increased its swap line with the US Federal Reserve by $1 billion.

11 Healey drew down what remained of the UK's gold tranche after the Heath government's 1972 drawing (SDR 304 million, $356 million), applied for the first credit tranche (SDR 700 million, $819 million), and also SDR 1 billion ($1,170 million) from the new facility set up to recycle the surpluses of the oil producers. IMF members were allocated a quota comprising four tranches. The first tranche (the gold tranche) represented the member's contribution of assets other than its own currency, originally gold. Members drawing on the successive 'credit tranches' above the gold tranche could expect increasingly harsh conditionality.

12 HM Treasury, 'Financial Forecast, 1975/76 and 1976/77', 29 October 1975, London, The National Archives (hereafter 'TNA'), T389/34.

13 Quoted in Wass, *Decline to Fall*, p. 158.

14 D.W. Healey, 'Letter of Intent', 18 December 1975, TNA, T364/50.

15 N.J. Monck, 'Note of a Meeting Held in the Chancellor of the Exchequer's Room', 25 May 1976, TNA, T364/50.

16 Wass, *Decline to Fall*, p. 192.

17 At the end of 1973, the Arab nations held about 20% of the sterling balances. Two years later, they held approximately 75%. 'Sterling Up Or Sterling Down', *The Economist*, 12 June 1976.

18 'L.A. Whittome and C.D. Finch to Managing Director', 3 November 1975, Washington DC, International Monetary Fund Archive (hereafter 'IMF'), EURAI country files, United Kingdom, 1975–9, Box 106, File 2.

19 At the end of March 1976, the sterling balances stood at £7,354 million, with £4,016 million in the hands of central banks and international monetary institutions. The Bank's 'official' reserves stood at just over £3 billion equivalent. Adjusted for overseas borrowing by the public sector and nationalized industries, the net reserves were *minus* £2.5 billion equivalent.

20 'The Benefits of a Little Economic Mismanagement', *Financial Times*, 11 March 1976.

21 Wass, *Decline to Fall*, p. 115.

22 Ibid., p. 178.

23 'M.E. Hedley-Miller to J.L. Sangster', 3 March 1976, London, Bank of England archive (hereafter 'BOE'), C43/779; M.E. Hedley-Miller and D.A. Walker, 'Modalities of Securing a Depreciation', 5 March 1976, BOE, C43/779.

24 In October 1975 the Treasury had ruled out an overt 'step change' in sterling as like 'going for a ride on a tiger'. 'Exchange Rate Policy', 22 October 1975, BOE, C43/779.

25 M.E. Hedley-Miller and D.A. Walker, 'Modalities of Securing a Depreciation', 4 March 1976, BOE, C43/779.

26 Referring to the events of 4/5 March, Wass writes, 'The Treasury could hardly believe its luck', Wass, *Decline to Fall*, p. 179.

27 J.L. Sangster, '4th March 1976', 9 August 1976, BOE, C43/780; J.L. Sangster, 'Sterling's Depreciation: 4th–16th March 1976', 7 April 1976, BOE, C43/779.

28 J.L. Sangster, 'Sterling's Depreciation: 4th–16th March 1976', 7 April 1976, BOE, C43/779.

29 Nonetheless, the Bank spent $50 million smoothing the market, J.L. Sangster, 'Events of the Afternoon of Thursday 4th March 1976', 5 March 1976, BOE, C43/779; N.J. Monck, 'Note of a Meeting Held in the Chancellor of the Exchequer's Office', 5 March 1976, BOE, C43/779.

30 'Sterling Goes Below the Two-Dollar Barrier', *Financial Times*, 6 March 1976.

31 W.J.H. Godley, 'Contributors to the Recent Pressure on Sterling and Reserve Loss', 7 May 1976, BOE, C43/780.

32 Quoted in P. Browning, *The Treasury and Economic Policy, 1964–1985* (London, 1986), p. 77.

33 The 'snake' was set up in 1972 to limit fluctuations of the major European currencies to within a 4.5% band linked to the US dollar. The Treasury estimated that the French

spent over \$4 billion defending the franc between January and March 1976. 'D.A. Walker to Mrs Hedley-Miller', 12 March 1976, BOE, C43/779; 'Mr Healey Rejects French Blame for Retreat of the Franc', *The Times*, 16 March 1976.

34 *The Rambouillet Summit Declaration*, Cmnd 6314 (London, 1975), p. 3.

35 The Prime Minister had instructed the Bank to stop supporting the pound on 21 May. F.H. Capie, *The Bank of England: 1950s to 1979* (New York, 2010), p. 747.

36 US Treasury Secretary Bill Simon told President Ford on 7 June that 'as a condition to our agreeing to provide financial support, the British Government has communicated to me their intention to take immediate steps to reduce the availability of domestic credit, followed by a series of steps over the next six months to tighten fiscal and monetary policy', quoted in M. Harmon, *The British Labour Government and the 1976 IMF Crisis* (Basingstoke, 1997), pp. 144–5. Simon apparently also told Callaghan that 'if tough steps haven't been taken to restore confidence in the pound, it's going to hit the fan after Labor Day', Burk and Cairncross, *Goodbye, Great Britain*, p. 46.

37 'How the Hard Money Men Took Over Britain', *Sunday Times*, 14 May 1978.

38 S. Strange, *International Monetary Relations* (Oxford, 1976), p. 127.

39 I. Plenderleith, 'Telephone Conversation with Dr Burns: 3 June 1976', BOE, 2A77/1.

40 N.J. Monck, 'Note for the Record', 3 June 1976, BOE, 2A77/1.

41 'Mr Healey: Borrowing Money to Buy Time', *The Times*, 10 June 1976.

42 Ibid.

43 D.W. Healey, *The Time of My Life* (London, 1989), p. 428.

44 The Bank drew just over \$1 billion from the facility in June 1976; Cabinet Office, 'Minutes of 13th Meeting on Ministerial Committee on Economic Strategy', 23 September 1976, TNA, CAB 134/4025; 'Big Capital Outflow Swells UK Deficit', *The Times*, 8 September 1976.

45 D.W.G. Wass, 'The Approach to the IMF', 10 September 1976, TNA, T381/15.

46 Wass, *Decline to Fall*.

47 The IMF's preferred monetary aggregate was Domestic Credit Expansion which, in the UK's case, adjusted the broad money supply for the balance of payments.

48 Healey announced on 22 July 1976 that 'for the financial year as a whole money supply growth should amount to about 12 per cent'. HC Deb., 22 July 1976, vol. 915, cc2018–19.

49 L.J. Callaghan, *Time and Chance* (London, 1987), p. 433.

50 L.A. Whittome, 'Conversation With Mr Ryrie', 9 July 1976, IMF, EURAI country files, United Kingdom – correspondence and memos, January–September 1976, Box 106, File 3.

51 'United Kingdom: PSBR in 1977/78 on the Basis of Illustrative Financial Programme', 5 August 1976, IMF, EURAI country files, United Kingdom – correspondence and memos, January–September 1976, Box 106, File 3.

52 'Programme for Economic Stability', *The Times*, 20 September 1976.

53 'An Outline for Healey's Finest', *Daily Telegraph*, 4 November 1976; 'Repainting the Titanic', *The Economist*, 2 October 1976.

54 'Dealing With Intangibles', *Financial Times*, 1 November 1976; 'The Package That Could Stop the Rot', *The Guardian*, 15 October 1976.

55 'Why Mr Healey's Measures Must Be More Than Simply Window Dressing', *The Times*, 2 December 1976.

56 'Programme for Economic Stability', *The Times*, 20 September 1976.

57 W.A.H. Godley, *The Times*, 27 September 1976.

58 B. Griffiths and G.E. Wood, *The Times*, 2 October 1976.

59 J. Williamson, *The Times*, 11 October 1976.

60 N. Kaldor, *The Times*, 12 October 1976.

61 J.S. Flemming and M.F.G. Scott, *The Times*, 16 October 1976.

62 A.K. Cairncross, *The Times*, 4 November 1976.

63 The New Cambridge analysis assumed the private sector remained in small surplus; R.J. Ball and T. Burns, *The Times*, 20 October 1976.

64 'Mr Healey Woos CBI in Partnership Plea', *The Times*, 22 October 1976.
65 Posner served as Deputy Chief Economic Adviser to the Treasury until September 1976.
66 M.V. Posner, *The Times*, 27 October 1976.
67 Ibid.
68 'How the Budget Deficit Can Be Cut By £5,000m Next Year', *The Times*, 11 November 1976.
69 W. Beckerman et al., 'A Protectionist Policy Is Not the Way to Set Britain on the Road to Recovery', *The Times*, 15 November 1976.
70 'Mr Healey's New Allies', *Financial Times*, 17 November 1976.
71 Ibid.
72 W.A.H. Godley, *The Times*, 25 November 1976.
73 'Milton's Paradise Lost … ', *The Guardian*, 10 December 1976.
74 Quoted in Browning, *The Treasury*, p. 92.
75 de Vries, *International Monetary Fund*, p. 469.
76 C.D. Finch, quoted in Capie, *Bank of England*, p. 753.
77 'The Price Britain Faces for IMF Aid', *Sunday Times*, 24 October 1976.
78 With the clocks going back over the weekend, the Bank had forgotten that the continental exchanges would be open an hour earlier. The lack of early intervention apparently contributed to the precipitate fall. 'Sterling Yesterday', A.N. Ridley to M. H. Thatcher, 26 October 1976, Cambridge, Churchill Archives Centre (hereafter 'Churchill'), THCR 2/12/2/1.
79 HC Deb., 25 October 1976, vol. 918, c30.
80 HC Deb., 25 October 1976, vol. 918, c29.
81 HC Deb., 25 October 1976, vol. 918, c35.
82 Browning, *The Treasury*, p. 85.
83 '30th Anniversary of the British IMF Negotiations', *Mile End Group*, 6 December 2006, see <www.mileendgroup.com/event/30th-anniversary-british-imf-negotiations/>, last accessed 5 December 2013.
84 Whittome later contradicted himself: 'we were not saying that $1.50 was right at all … I don't know if we were putting figures on it, but no one was talking about $1.50', quoted in Burk and Cairncross, *Goodbye, Great Britain*, p. 74; 'L.A. Whittome to the Managing Director', 27 November 1976, IMF, EURAI country files, United Kingdom – correspondence and memos, January–March 1977, Box 107, File 3.
85 'Teetering Upon the Turning Point', *The Guardian*, 19 October 1976.
86 'Public Borrowing Up By £2bn. Next Year', *Financial Times*, 6 November 1976.
87 Ibid.
88 W.S. Ryrie, 'Note for the Record', 4 October 1976, TNA, T381/16.
89 The Treasury Policy Co-ordinating Committee met on 2 November to discuss 'the handling of the forecasts with the IMF'. While there were arguments for showing a lower PSBR estimate (there would be fewer reasons for further deflation), the PCC decided to show the IMF a higher estimate to 'give them a clearer view of the political difficulties of reaching the target'. As well as more bearish assumptions on unemployment and tax revenue, the Treasury also eliminated the £1 billion 'shortfall' used in previous PSBR forecasts. HM Treasury, 'Policy Co-ordinating Committee', 2 November 1976, TNA, T277/3175; L. Pliatzky, *Getting and Spending: Public Expenditure, Employment and Inflation* (Oxford, 1982), p. 160; K. Bernstein, *The International Monetary Fund and Deficit Countries: The Case of Britain, 1974–77* (Ann Arbor, MI, University Microfilms International, 1983), p. 500.
90 'B. Rose to L.A. Whittome', 10 November 1976, IMF, EURAI country files, United Kingdom, 1975–9, Box 106, File 2. In the event, the forecast was scaled back to £10.5 billion after discussion with the Fund.
91 L.A. Whittome, 'Memorandum for Files', 11 November 1976, IMF, EURAI country files, United Kingdom, 1975–9, Box 106, File 2.

92 K.M. Burk et al., 'Symposium: The 1976 IMF Crisis', *Contemporary Record*, vol. 3, no. 2 (November, 1989), p. 45.

93 'Government Seeking IMF Advice on How to Boost the Economy', *The Times*, 8 November 1976.

94 Browning, *The Treasury*, p. 91.

95 'Cabinet Given First Glimpse of IMF Loan Measures', *The Times*, 24 November 1976.

96 Ibid.

97 A.N. Ridley, 'Latest News from *Pravda*', 25 November 1976, Churchill, THCR 2/12/2/1.

98 'A Change of Direction', *Financial Times*, 29 November 1976.

99 'Sheep Not Lambs', *The Economist*, 13 November 1976.

100 'Britain's IMF Loan', *Wall Street Journal*, 30 November 1976.

101 Cabinet Office, 'Conclusions of a Meeting of the Cabinet Held at 10 Downing Street on Tuesday 23 November' (Limited Circulation Annexe), CM (76) 33rd Conclusions, Minute 2, TNA, CAB 128/60.

102 'A Cabinet in Conflict: The Loan from the IMF', *Inside British Politics*, Granada TV (first broadcast 15 February 1977).

103 'Day of Decision', *The Guardian*, 1 December 1976.

104 Burk notes that 'the scale of the cuts seemed to have little independent meaning: it was all symbolic ... not only were the actual cuts not very big, they were apparently all quietly restored over the subsequent year', Burk et al., *The 1976 Crisis*, p. 40.

105 'US Foreign Economic Policy Issues: The United Kingdom, France, and West Germany', *Staff Report of the Subcommittee on Foreign Economic Policy of the Committee on Foreign Relations*, United States Senate (Washington DC, 1977), p. 9.

106 Ibid., p. 11.

107 'Another Bite at the Cherry', *Financial Times*, 16 December 1976; 'Mr Healey Tries Again', *Daily Telegraph*, 16 December 1976; 'DCE Rules, OK?' *The Times*, 16 December 1976.

108 'Reflections of Dither', *The Guardian*, 17 December 1976.

109 N.J. Monck, 'Note of a Meeting Held in the Chancellor's room at H.M. Treasury at 10:45 A.M. on Friday 10 December 1976', TNA, T364/52.

110 Healey, *Time of My Life*, pp. 432–3.

111 '30th Anniversary of the British IMF Negotiations', *Mile End Group*, 6 December 2006.

112 Callaghan's personal emissary to the IMF, Harold Lever, notes 'the idea was that the IMF would bring the Cabinet to order', Burk et al., *The 1976 Crisis*, p. 45; private correspondence with Peter Jay, 1 February 2013.

113 Hugh Stephenson points out that Harold Lever 'understood, as a card player, that the IMF did not really have all that strong a hand, as it could scarcely destabilise one of its key members', private correspondence with Hugh Stephenson, 6 February 2013.

PART V

Media messengers under interrogation

19

UK FINANCIAL JOURNALISTS QUIZZED BY MPS

Edited by *Jeff Hulbert*

Introduction

It was inevitable that the banking crisis would come under the British parliamentary spotlight. The task of detailed examination fell to the House of Commons Treasury Committee. Its usual remit is to keep a watchful eye on key economic institutions of government – the Treasury and revenue-collecting departments – but also over associated public bodies, including the Bank of England and statutory financial watchdogs. As a select committee it conducts inquiries into key issues, holds public hearings, and makes recommendations to parliament, which may or may not be acted upon.

Its credit-crisis terms of reference included 'to investigate: "the role of the media in financial stability and whether financial journalists should operate under any form of reporting restrictions during banking crises".'[1] In February 2009 it invited five of journalism's 'big hitters' from print and broadcast media to give oral evidence: the BBC's Business Editor Robert Peston, whom the Committee described as 'the key commentator on the banking crisis'; *Financial Times* Editor Lionel Barber; *Daily Mail* City Editor Alex Brummer; Jeff Randall, a commentator for the *Daily Telegraph* and Sky News; and Simon Jenkins, the *Guardian* columnist and a former editor of *The Times*.

The Committee began work on this aspect of the crisis in late 2008 and published its report on 15 May 2009. Its chair was the former Labour whip and junior minister John (now Lord) McFall MP. The other Committee members who quizzed the journalists were: Nick Ainger MP, Graham Brady MP, Colin Breed MP, Jim Cousins MP, Michael Fallon MP, Sally Keeble MP, Andrew Love MP, John Mann MP, George Mudie MP, John Thurso MP, Mark Todd MP, and Sir Peter Viggers MP.

In what proved to be a unique testimony – nowhere else were journalists questioned like this – the Committee probed how they handled the crisis, what difficulties they faced, and whether they shared any of the blame. This edited extract reveals what they told MPs.

Testimony to the House of Commons Treasury Committee by leading financial journalists, 4 February 2009[2]

The run on the Rock

In autumn 2007 British bank Northern Rock got into difficulty. It had grown rapidly in previous years by large-scale short-term borrowing in the wholesale money market, which it then used to offer customers highly competitive long-term mortgage loans. When its funding sources began to evaporate its viability was quickly thrown into doubt. On 13 September the BBC's Robert Peston revealed that Northern Rock was about to be rescued by the Bank of England, causing the first run on a British bank in 150 years.

The Committee's chair began by asking whether there was ever 'a case for journalists to exercise self-restraint and temporarily delay publication of a story' especially if there was a risk of sparking off market instability or even an institution's collapse.

ROBERT PESTON: [I]t seems to me there is a public interest in letting millions of people know what is going on with their banks and what is going on with the economy, and if their banks are weaker than they think to be the case then there is a public interest in telling them such, and telling them the more general problems we have been experiencing with the economy. I can only speak for the BBC but we do not broadcast, publish on the blog, stuff without giving it huge amounts of thought, obviously going through a massive detailed verification procedure, and I will talk to senior editors about what we do, but at the moment where I feel that the story is being nailed down and the wider social public interest is served by publication of course we just publish … If we had delayed in any of the cases which have caused a bit of frisson, what would the benefit actually have been? I would argue very strongly, that where they are today is precisely where they would have been whether we had or had not shared that information with the general public.

JEFF RANDALL: In the case of Northern Rock … it was a deeply flawed bank with a broken business model, it did not collapse because Robert very cleverly revealed it had asked for help, it collapsed because it was a bust business. Had Robert delayed it for a couple of days, would it have made any difference, would it today be a solvent bank? Absolutely not. I think he was perfectly justified in putting out the story when he did.

LIONEL BARBER: There is a difference … between restraint and self-censorship. The fact is … there were rumours going around for a long time, months, before about Northern Rock's financial health, its excessive reliance on wholesale funding and nobody wrote about it because at that stage they were rumours. There are also very clear rules, at least at the *Financial Times*, that before we publish stories we want two sources, we also do not publish stories which we know, we think, may have a big impact on the market, and if they are anonymous quotes we try and identify them as best we can. Overall, I think the conclusion is absolutely clear, Northern Rock was operating a flawed business model and they were caught out, so nothing the BBC [did] and the way it was reported would have affected the outcome.

The Chair said that the Chief Executive of the British Bankers' Association had complained about how damaging 'the procession of leaks' had been, singling out Robert Peston for particular criticism. Was there a different point of view?

SIMON JENKINS: I am not sure I can give a different point of view. Let's take a hypothetical. In this case, I think those people involved can legitimately say they were acting in a considered fashion. They were not going to be telling a lie. They were not intending to wreck an otherwise valid bank and they were acting in the public interest ... Presumably the reason why you are asking these questions is, you want to know if there is some new regulatory framework which ought to restrain journalists ... otherwise you are describing the world as it is ... the truth of the matter is that there is the old saying, 'I am a responsible journalist, you are an editor and he is a censor', we are all in this game and we are all trying to be responsible. I think one of the virtues of established news media organisations is they are to a certain extent trained to be responsible. I am much more worried about the bloggers sphere [*sic*] where anything can go out.

The Chair asked Alex Brummer about his criticism of Robert Peston's initial Northern Rock reports, which he had described as 'excitable'.

ALEX BRUMMER: Robert and I have discussed it on occasions. What I thought was that the tone of the report rather than the content of the report may have made people slightly unsure what was going on. I am still of that view. However, we have to bear in mind here that most of the response was really the result of the poor systems that Northern Rock had, that they had computers which broke down, they had very few branches so the queues built up very quickly. Indeed when I think back on the episode now, I actually think Robert did everyone a big favour ... by alerting small depositors, they were taking a perfectly rational decision to withdraw their money because what was going on behind the scenes, which none of us could see, was the big, wholesale depositors ... were moving their money out by the billions. So they had inside information, they knew what was going down, the small depositors did not, so he alerted them to that. Maybe if he had a more calm, traditional BBC voice it may have not quite seemed like it did, but I was not arguing with him doing the reporting, I was only arguing with the tone of the reporting. Also ... he did mention in that report that everybody had deposit insurance of up to £35,000 ... which was an important fact to get out there.

Colin Breed asked Robert Peston directly whether he was responsible for the run on Northern Rock.

ROBERT PESTON: I have obviously given a lot of thought to this and the answer is, no. Alex and I agree on most things; we do not agree on the tone of my broadcast that evening. I have obviously reviewed it a few times, and I do not think it was excitable … There were structural reasons why Northern Rock was more prone to a retail run than most banks … it had kept its number of branches to an absolute minimum; it was obsessed with controlling costs. It had 50 branches and it had something like 1.3 million savers. You are probably aware that YouGov did … a survey, of what people who banked with Northern Rock thought in the hours after we broadcast. Most of them thought: this is an interesting story, this is a big story … we want to find out more, and they went to the website and, because there was not sufficient server capacity, the website kept crashing, which caused them a degree of alarm, and then … many, many thousands went to the branches to, again, find out more about what was going on. When they got there they discovered they could not find out because there were these queues … savers became very anxious, simply because they could not find out from the institution what was going on. I think also Northern Rock made a bit of an error itself in the way that it disseminated the information. They put out an announcement to the Stock Exchange which was in language which most ordinary people found impenetrable, and the piece about the Bank of England was on page two and in very technical language.

Colin Breed asked whether showing images of queues outside Northern Rock's branches added to the sense of panic.

ROBERT PESTON: It was very difficult for broadcasters … not to show those queues. I think it is also unarguably the case that pictures of the queues did reinforce the concern – of course they did.

With the benefit of hindsight would Robert Peston have handled it differently, Colin Breed asked.

ROBERT PESTON: In my broadcast, for example, I not only referred to deposit protection, I also said the fact that the Bank of England was lending this money to Northern Rock meant that the immediate danger of a collapse … was gone. I said that I did not think this bank would now collapse … I think what was striking was the behaviour of Bradford and Bingley … when they were faced with a similar report in the newspapers about problems … they flooded their branches with staff, they made sure they had appropriate server capacity, they made sure that information was available.

The Chair wondered if a reporting delay would have given Northern Rock time to prepare for anticipated high customer demand.

ROBERT PESTON: I did not know that they did not have enough server capacity. How could I have known until it was tested, as it were … it maybe was a failing on my part but, of course, it was only after the event that I realised the weakness for Northern Rock of having so few branches relative to the number of their customers.

JEFF RANDALL: [T]he idea that somehow a delay would have given Northern Rock breathing space, the problem for Northern Rock was its management was in denial. I remember very well the day after Robert's report all hell had broken lose [sic]. Up on the website was a message, which was intended to be comforting, which said, 'Do not worry', the phrase was something like, 'this is a well run bank.' Well, clearly, by then it was an insult to the public's intelligence. So I do not think giving Northern Rock 24 hours or 48 hours would have saved it.

John Mann wondered if the panic was worse because the BBC broke the story.

ROBERT PESTON: I genuinely do not know. I think it is very unlikely.

Nick Ainger asked if Robert Peston was the only journalist to have written about Northern Rock's weaknesses before the crisis broke.

JEFF RANDALL: [I]n 2004 I was beginning to bore my colleagues: people thought that I was a doomster, I was dismissed as someone who had a grudge against the Government, someone who was talking Britain down.

LIONEL BARBER: [A]t least three years ago Gillian Tett, the capital markets editor, [was] specifically warning about the risks in credit derivatives. These are the sophisticated financial instruments which are in part to blame for the problem … the crucial point here is that editors are prepared to put warning signs on company coverage on the front page if they think that things are going wrong – they certainly open up their op-ed page – but if we were to put stories which were warning about worries or doubts about individual companies' business models, first of all, we would definitely have lawyers on our backs for irresponsible journalism … and, second, we have a job to report what the governments are saying, what the banks are saying about the state of health of the economy … in 2005/2006 everybody thought the City of London was top of the world and I seem to remember certain politicians talking about abolishing boom and bust. We put that on the front page too.

ALEX BRUMMER: I think that what my colleagues say is true, that there has been a lot of early reporting out there. In 2002 … I remember writing about Northern Rock and securitisation in a very sceptical way. For the privilege of doing that I almost got my head beaten up by Adam Applegarth … The other thing to remember is that business journalists are in a very unfair competition. We are individuals working against some of the richest organisations in the world with some of the most powerful communications experts working for them.

Sourcing, verification, and complexity

Michael Fallon asked Robert Peston about his 'closeness to the Treasury'.

ROBERT PESTON: Mr Fallon, I think you will not be surprised that the one area where I am uncomfortable talking in public is about sourcing, of any sort. Over the years, I have benefited from private conversations with members of this Committee and I think it would be very unlikely any of those members would wish me to divulge those sorts of chats … I have been a journalist for 25 years … I like to think I have decent contacts … When I do a story it is normally a process of putting together a jigsaw puzzle. It is very, very, very rarely in my line that somebody has rung up and said, 'I have a corker for you, here you go' and handed me something on a plate; it almost never happens … and in the summer of 2007 when markets closed down I concluded this was likely to be the biggest story of my career and I immersed myself in it and more or less everything I have done since then has been a process of talking to hundreds of people working out the trends and working out what the stories were … I am perfectly happy to say that I do not have a pass to the Treasury.

Michael Fallon asked whether Robert Peston got information from a senior Treasury official and former 'FT' colleague, 'the Second Permanent Secretary, John Kingman'. Had this placed him in a privileged position?

ROBERT PESTON: I am simply not going to get into who I talk to about any story. I know lots and lots of people, including you, and I talk to lots and lots and lots of people.

MICHAEL FALLON: '[T]he suggestion has been that you have had access, I understood in the Treasury or indeed through the banks, to preferential information and that might well have been in the interests of those giving you the information as much as yourself?'

ROBERT PESTON: I can say that I have never felt I was in receipt of preferential information from any source at all. What I do is I try and understand what is happening in the world, and then I talk to as many people as possible to work out whether my ideas about where stories might go turn out to be correct, and I have never felt I was getting special help from any source at all.

Graham Brady asked Robert Peston about story verification and whether he had ever decided that the 'wider interest' would be served by not publishing a story known to be true.

ROBERT PESTON: No. I, however, have delayed publication until I am absolutely certain of all the material information ... In 2003 I first identified Northern Rock as a bank whose business model I was a little bit concerned about, it seemed to me it was growing far too fast, I wrote about it in the *Sunday Telegraph* and for years I looked like a bit of a plonker because the share price went up and up and up and the fact I said I thought this may be heading towards some kind of an accident looked wrong; I looked like an idiot. However, when wholesale markets, the market for mortgage-backed securities, closed down in August 2007, because I was aware that much of their funding came from that source, this was a bank I kept a very close eye on. Because plainly unless those markets re-opened it would have a very big problem, it was a story I followed over a period of weeks ... on that particular day, which was 13 September, when I felt the pieces fitted together ... I telephoned ... Peter Horrocks ... the Head of Television News, and we talked about how we would get it out, and we broadcast it.

GRAHAM BRADY: So as long as it is true and you are confident it is true, you publish?

ROBERT PESTON: Multiple sources, absolutely.

Graham Brady asked Lionel Barber about Northern Rock's business model and whether it was material.

LIONEL BARBER: It was not a justification for publishing the story ... it was an explanation. Our job is to explain and I pointed ... to the fact they were shown to have pursued a flawed business model which was excessively reliant on wholesale markets, and when those froze over in the summer of 2007 they were in deep trouble.

Graham Brady asked again about withholding stories known to be true.

LIONEL BARBER: There are other factors in judging whether to publish a story rather than the judgment made by the *Financial Times* or the BBC about whether the business model is sustainable, and those would be the movement of the share price and what financial advisers ... and what analysts are saying.

During the crisis had any of the journalists been put under pressure from regulators, financial institutions, government, or others not to publish, or to delay publication, Graham Brady wondered.

ALEX BRUMMER: There was one occasion involving Northern Rock ... early into 2008, when we as a paper came across a document which could have been highly damaging ... to Northern Rock [and could have damaged the bank's sale] ... we were asked by people at the highest level if we would restrain ourselves from publication because it was felt we might cause a second run on the institution. At that point in time, everybody knew what the insurance situation was, that their deposits were safe and those who had wanted to get their deposits out had done so, but we still did not want to cause a problem which might prevent it from being rescued if there was a rescue in the process, so we did hold off on that story. We were asked at the highest level to do so, so we did show some self-restraint.

Nick Ainger asked whether financial journalists 'were guilty of accepting what the business community told them in a way that would not happen when reporting on other issues'.

SIMON JENKINS: I am a bit suspicious, when all the policemen and all the monitors have failed, that they turn round and blame the press for not helping them out. It just does not wash, I do not think. There are plenty of journalists who were saying something was going wrong here and they have been quite willing to come forward and say so ... I think there is extraordinary closeness between British business journalism in the City in the same way that there is extraordinary closeness between British political journalism in Westminster, and these are essentially unhealthy relationships which tend to lead to the sort of mishaps that you have described.

Sir Peter Viggers and Mark Todd asked about sources and referred to criticism voiced by Richard Lambert, the CBI Director General, that unsubstantiated rumours were passed on, and that 'editors should do more to kick the tyres on unsourced quotes'.

LIONEL BARBER: [T]he use of anonymous quotes, negative quotes, from analysts or bankers regarding companies ... can be very damaging and, therefore, we at the FT at least are very careful in how we use those quotes because we know they can affect share prices. They are a matter of opinion. We are not saying we would not use them, but we need to know who they are and why they are making those comments.

Sir Peter Viggers asked about pressure applied to sources to reveal their names and the use of unattributable sources.

JEFF RANDALL: I do not put any pressure on sources to give their names. It is up to them, but what I do is weigh up their credibility and their integrity ... there is no disclosure without motivation. So when people disclose something to me I try to work out what that motivation could be, and if they are happy [to] go on the record, then so be it, and if they are not I weigh up why they are not happy to go on the record.

ALEX BRUMMER: [E]veryone assumes that you are talking to junior officials, but you could be talking to the chief executive of some of the banks. When you say to them at the end of the conversation, 'Would you be willing to put that onto the record?', they always say, no.

Sir Peter Viggers asked if journalists ever printed 'undigested' handouts.

ALEX BRUMMER: I think a lot of the people who are working in financial offices at the moment have only seen boom times, and they took the press releases that they saw, they took the briefings they got, they went to the press conference and listened to the bullish talk. Right up to the very end some of the bankers were talking in the most bullish terms about recovery, about the famous ABN AMRO takeover by Royal Bank, which destroyed Royal Bank of Scotland. Even at the press conference in 2008 they were still boasting about how much income they would get out of that takeover. People just took it down and wrote it because the bankers were believed, and I think a lot more scepticism is required.

LIONEL BARBER: One of the very important aspects of this crisis involves the opaqueness of the banking system. We know [little] about the shadow banking system [and] off balance sheet vehicles. This was a very, very difficult aspect of the financial system for journalists to report on. There was very little information available. It was not even available in annual reports ... we tried to talk to people. None of them would talk. Eventually Gillian Tett ... had to publish information based on emails on the condition that those people were warning about the risks in structured investment vehicles, in credit derivatives that they would not be named or even have their firms or associations mentioned.

JEFF RANDALL: I think it is pretty clear that the sources of this credit crunch are twofold: too much debt and not enough information, and, frankly, Lionel is correct, the banks did not put out there the information that everybody needed, not just the financial press but their own investors, their own employees. They did not know what was going on and, I suspect, right up to the very top, people did not understand what was going on ... I do not think you realise how hard it is sometimes to nail down the truth, given that we have a huge industry out there which is generating huge numbers of fees to distort the truth ... Can I just tell you something? This is how tough it is. On 8 October [2008] the Daily Telegraph ran a front-page story saying that as part of the Royal Bank of Scotland rescue its Chief Executive, Fred Goodwin, would go, the Chairman, Tom McKillop, would go, they had been replaced by Stephen Hester and Philip Hampton. The day that that came out RBS issued an on-the-record denial, called the proprietors of the Daily Telegraph demanding an apology and Alistair Darling, in front of the cameras, also denied it. Five days later it was true, so when you say why do we not nail down the truth, sometimes we have to rely on people in positions of seniority to tell us the truth.

BBC reporting

John Mann asked what conclusions the BBC had drawn about the appropriateness of its rules for business reporting, given its 'special status as a public service broadcaster'.

ROBERT PESTON: I do think that the rules that we followed before and subsequently are pretty demanding actually. We did learn, obviously, the power of images on the public mood, and there was an example actually ... You were asking about pulling stories. There was an occasion with, in fact, Bradford and Bingley where a couple of our regional offices said that they had pictures of people queuing to get their money out ... and we did not run them because we checked with the institution ... whether this was genuinely evidence of a run or just not enough people turning up on the day.

SIMON JENKINS: Northern Rock ... was a dud bank and I think to tell newspapers not to say it is a dud bank [at] any stage would have been ridiculous. I personally think much more serious was the predicament that many financial journalists found themselves in over RBS, Barclays, Lloyd's, Bradford and Bingley, where it was fairly clear the Government, knowing it was about to acquire large chunks of these banks, were, I sense, using the press to force down the share price.

Royal Bank of Scotland (RBS) collapse

In October 2008 in what was to be one of the UK's largest nationalizations, the UK government announced that it would inject £37 billion into three UK banks – Royal Bank of Scotland (RBS), Lloyds TSB, and HBOS – to keep them viable as businesses. All were dangerously exposed to high levels of bad debt, particularly RBS, which had taken over the toxic assets of the Dutch bank ABN AMRO one year before.

John Thurso asked if there was any conspiracy to affect the share prices of RBS and HBOS, which ultimately collapsed.

ROBERT PESTON: Since it was, in the case of Royal Bank of Scotland and HBOS, my blog and my Radio Four broadcast that led to the dramatic falls in share prices, and I know the history of how I got that story, I absolutely do not believe, for what it is worth, that there was any conspiracy here and that I was, in a sense, an instrument of manipulation, but, again, it is also important to think about the economic substance. It was a fact that these banks needed capital and, therefore, the share price was wrong. When I put in the public domain that the banks needed capital, of course the share price fell. The notion that this was a false market is crazy. In fact, what then happened was the correct price was established because the information was then in the market place.

ALEX BRUMMER: I would say that almost the opposite is probably the case, because every time the share price fell it meant that the Government was going to have to put in more capital in some way or other, provide more support, so it had no interest in getting those share prices down. The moment that Lehman's failed it was absolutely clear ... to experts, the short sellers, the people who study the balance sheets of these banks, that these banks were in deep, deep trouble, that they had far too much toxic debt on their balance sheets and the markets had frozen over … It was not the Government creating that atmosphere, it was a reality check to what had been going on over the previous months.

Gloom and doom

Was there too much gloom and doom in the journalists' reports, John Thurso wondered.

LIONEL BARBER: I do not think if we put happy talk on the front page it is either going to be good commercially or editorially. This just does not make any sense. We have to tell it the way we see it using multiple sources … the *Financial Times* is not going to say everything is fine when it obviously is not.

JEFF RANDALL: It is not the job of broadcasters or newspapers … to jolly along the public. Our job is to tell them what is going on … In fact you can argue for too long … people were allowed to go along in this stupor believing that ever more debt would be okay, borrowing up to the gills would be all right; nobody rang the bells, or too few of us rang the bells.

The Committee's conclusions

In terms that could hardly be more stark the Treasury Committee said that before the crisis broke the financial environment had been 'rich in overconfidence' and this had led to a 'stifling of contrary opinions'. Its headline conclusions were that 'some of the banks have been the principal authors of their own demise', and that the 'culture within parts of British banking has increasingly been one of risk taking leading to the meltdown that we have witnessed'. Its uncompromising conclusion was that 'Bankers have made an astonishing mess of the financial system.'[3] The Committee could hardly have concluded otherwise.

Having heard the journalists' evidence, the Committee declared:

> Our evidence does not support the case for any further regulation of the media … A free and functioning press is a basic requirement of a democracy. Regulation of the media in the context of internet publication would be impractical as well as undesirable … The press has generally acted responsibly when asked to show restraint in particular areas.[4]

Clearly taking the journalists' point about access to information, the Committee ended by saying:

> It is crucial that the public are kept informed about institutions holding their money. If the public is to trust the banks in the future it needs to be confident it has sufficient information on how they are operating, and that such

information is not restricted to those on the inside ... Government may wish to look carefully about the disclosure obligations applying to banks and other financial institutions to see if further transparency would be beneficial.[5]

Notes

1 House of Commons Treasury Committee, 2008/09, *Banking Crisis: Reforming Corporate Governance and Pay in the City* (Ninth Report), HC 519, 15 May 2009, p. 97.
2 Oral evidence, Volume I, HC 144 [Ev 197–Ev 211], 1 April 2009.
3 House of Commons Treasury Committee, 2008/09, *Banking Crisis: Dealing With the Failure of the UK Banks* (Seventh Report), HC 416, 1 May 2009, p. 3.
4 HC 519, Op. Cit., p. 102.
5 Ibid.

INDEX